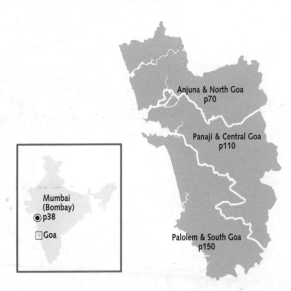

Anjuna & North Goa
p70

Panaji & Central Goa
p110

Palolem & South Goa
p150

Mumbai
(Bombay)
● p38

☐ Goa

Directory A-Z 220
Transport 232
Language 238
Glossary 243
Index 250
Map Legend 255

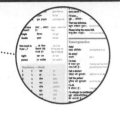

THIS EDITION WRITTEN AND RESEARCHED BY

Amelia Thomas

welcome to
Goa &
Mumbai

Marvellous Mumbai

More than just a gateway to Goa, Mumbai is a place that takes eating, drinking and making merry seriously. Luxuriate at a grand hotel, explore glorious Gothic architecture, munch on street eats galore and party hard in this sizzling-hot city beside the sea.

Beach Bounty

Goa's greatest drawcard is without doubt its legendary beaches. Strung in a shimmering gold strand from the tip to the toe of the state, they cater to every possible tropical whim: choose from happy, hippy Arambol or bolder, brasher Baga; from the lively sands of Palolem, or lovely, laid-back Mandrem; from expansive groomed sands of fancy five-stars or from hidden crescent coves, where the only footprints will be sea eagles' and your own.

Spiritual Sanctuary

For those keener to top up their Zen than their tan, Goa's crop of spiritual activities grows more bountiful each year: silent Vipassana retreats, sunrise t'ai chi sessions, reiki healing courses and just about every other form of spiritual exploration are readily available statewide. By far the most popular of myriad regimes on offer is ayurveda, the ancient science of plant-based medicine; second only to ayurveda comes yoga, whose dozen-or-more varieties make it easy to find the pose and poise that suit you best.

Colourful and colliding, spiritual and soothing, crammed with deserted beaches, yogic bliss and heady nightlife. Goa is many things to many people, but everyone agrees: there's nowhere on earth quite like it.

(left) A cow shares the beach near the flea market at Anjuna
(below) Luscious pomegranates for sale, Crawford Market, Mumbai

The Spice of Life

Throughout every waking hour, the scents and flavours of Goa's cuisine will rarely elude you. Prepare to be enchanted by many Portuguese-influenced dishes, from a *bhaji-pau* (bread roll dipped in curry) at breakfast time to a lip-smacking *vindahlo*, with its infusions of wine vinegar and garlic. South Indian treats abound in breakfast joints and streetside carts: fill up on dosas (paper-thin lentil-flour pancakes), *idlis* (spongy, round, fermented rice cakes), and *vadas* (doughnut-shaped, deep-fried savouries made from lentil flour), before enjoying the traditional lunchtime repast of zingy *fish-curry-rice*, all washed down with a cold Kingfisher beer.

Cultural Crockpot

Though Goa now receives some two million annual visitors, its longest-staying callers came a-knocking in 1510, when Portuguese conquerors arrived, lured by the promise of lucrative spice routes, not relinquishing their hold on Goa until 1961. Their indelible mark is still evident in the state's baroque architecture, crumbling forts, colourful Catholic ceremonies, mournful *fado* music and culinary quirkiness. Combine this heritage with a modern Hindu majority, migrant workers from as far afield as Nepal and Kashmir, and a whole calendar full of happy, heady festivals, and you have the ingredients that make Goa one truly mesmerising melting pot.

KARNATAKA

MAHARASHTRA

Mumbai
Eat, drink, shop and party (p38)

Arambol
Backpacker-friendly beach scene (p71)

Mandrem
Yogic beach bliss (p74)

Mapusa
Shop with locals at Mapusa market (p84)

Dr Salim Ali Bird Sanctuary
Boat out to avian action (p125)

Panaji
Wander the languid state capital (p111)

Old Goa
Former 'Rome of the East' (p126)

Ponda
Sweet-scented spices near Ponda (p135)

Backwoods Camp
Spot feathered friends galore (p142)

Anjuna
Happy, hippy Thursday market action (p87)

To Mumbai (580km)

To Savantvadi (32km)

To Londa (111km); Dharwar (146km); Belgaum (155km); Anegundi (280km); Hospet (280km)

To Londa Junction;

Fort Tiracol (Terekhol)

Querim

Terekhol River

Chapora River

Konkan Railway

Pernem Train Station

PERNEM

Mandrem

Arambol

Aswem

Morjim

Chopdem

Colvale

Siolim

Chapora

Vagator

Assagao

Thivim (Mapusa Rd) Train Station

Bicholim

Mandrem Beach

Aswem Beach

Morjim Beach

Chapora Fort

Vagator Beach

Anjuna Beach

Mapusa

Arpora

Baga

Baga Beach

Calangute

Calangute Beach

Candolim

Candolim Beach

Sinquerim Beach

Reis Magos Fort

Aguada Fort

Aguada Bay

Cabo Raj Bhavan

Dona Paula

BARDEZ

Anjuna

Pomburpa

Aldona

Torda

Saligao

Britona

Betim

Nerul (Coco) Beach

Miramar Beach

Miramar

Mormugao Bay

Vasco da Gama

17A

Mormugao

BICHOLIM

Corjuem Fort

Corjuem Island

Chorao Naroa Island

Shri Saptakoteshwara Temple

Mayem Lake

Ribandar

Divar Island

Dr Salim Ali Bird Sanctuary

Panaji (Panjim)

Goa Velha

Agassaim

Sancoale

Cortalim

TISWADI

Pilar

Karmali (Old Goa) Train Station

Old Goa

Carambolim

Talaulim

Shri Manguesh Temple

Shri Mahalsa Temple

Shri Shantadurga Temple

PONDA

Caves of Khandepar

Safa Shahouri Masjid

Shri Ramnath Temple

Ponda

Usgao

Khandepar

Usgao Tisk

Mandovi River

Bondla Wildlife Sanctuary

SATARI

Sanquelim

Savoi Verem

Onda

Valpoi

Anjunem

Gontel

Nanus Fort

Cotorem

Backwoods Camp

Bhagwan Mahavir Wildlife Sanctuary

Darbandor

Mhadei Protected Area

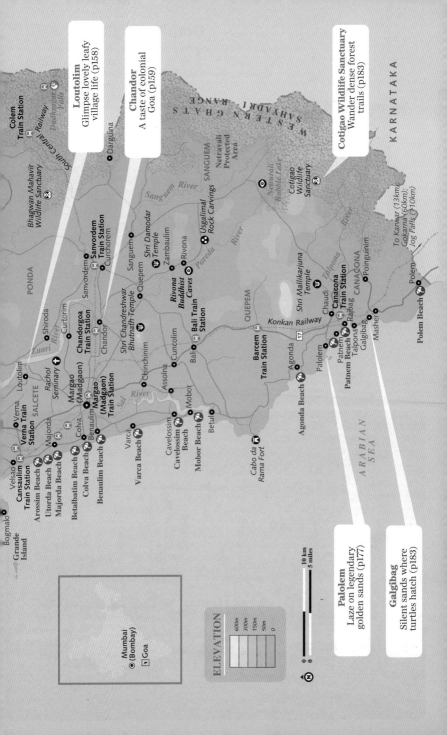

Loutolim
Glimpse lovely leafy village life (p158)

Chandor
A taste of colonial Goa (p159)

Cotigao Wildlife Sanctuary
Wander dense forest trails (p183)

Palolem
Laze on legendary golden sands (p177)

Galgibag
Silent sands where turtles hatch (p183)

ELEVATION

600m
300m
150m
50m
0

0   10 km
0   5 miles

Mumbai (Bombay)
Goa

WESTERN GHATS
SAHYADRI RANGE

KARNATAKA

PONDA

SALCETE

QUEPEM

SANGUEM

CANACONA

ARABIAN SEA

Bhagwan Mahavir Wildlife Sanctuary

Cotigao Wildlife Sanctuary

Netravali Protected Area

Colem Train Station

Dudhsagar Falls

South Central Railway

Darguina

Sanvordem Train Station

Sanvordem

Curchorem

Quepem

Zambaulim

Shri Damodar Temple

Sanguem

Rivona

Usgalimal Rock Carvings

Pareda

Rivona Buddhist Caves

Bali Train Station

Bali

Cuncolim

Assolna

Chandor

Chandorgoa Train Station

Curtorim

Shri Chandreshwar Bhutnath Temple

Chinchinim

Shiroda

Luari River

Loutolim

Verna

Verna Train Station

Velsao

Cansaulim Train Station

Arossim Beach

Utorda Beach

Majorda Beach

Betalbatim Beach

Colva Beach

Benaulim Beach

Colva

Benaulim

Margao (Madgaon)

Margao (Madgaon) Train Station

Rachol Seminary

Sal River

Varca

Varca Beach

Cavelossim

Cavelossim Beach

Mobor Beach

Mobor

Betul

Cabo da Rama Fort

Agonda Beach

Agonda

Palolem

Shri Mallikarjuna Temple

Chaudi

Netravali Bubble Lake

Cotigao Wildlife Sanctuary

Barcem Train Station

Konkan Railway

Patnem Beach

Patnem

Talpona

Galgibag

Masher

Rajbag

Canacona Train Station

Poinguinim

Polem

Polem Beach

To Karwar (13km); Gokarna (60km); Jog Falls (110km)

Talpona River

Bogmalo

Grande Island

10 TOP EXPERIENCES

Gothic Mumbai

1 Mumbai (p38) is not all eating, drinking and shopping. After you've had your fill of all three, take time to explore the city's Victorian colonial-era architecture, with a stroll past the Gateway of India, the 1848-built High Court, the splendid University of Mumbai and the extravaganza that is Chhatrapati Shivaji Terminus (Victoria Terminus) railway station. You can even take up residence in Gothic opulence at the heritage Taj Mahal Palace Hotel, Mumbai (p51), gazing over Mumbai's harbour, for that most Raj-era of city retreats. Chhatrapati Shivaji Terminus (Victoria Terminus; p47), Mumbai

Panaji (Panjim)

2 If only all India's state capitals were as languid as this. Slung along the banks of the broad Mandovi River, Panaji (p111) is an easy, breezy city with the delightful old Portuguese districts of Fontainhas and Sao Tomé just ripe for a lazy afternoon of wandering. Sip firewater *feni* (liquor distilled from coconut milk or cashews) with locals in a hole-in-the-wall bar, clamber up to the wedding-cake-white Church of Our Lady of the Immaculate Conception or poke about in boutiques and book shops, and you'll find you're not missing the beach one bit.

HUW JONES / LONELY PLANET IMAGES ©

Spice Farms

3 It might be more than a touch touristy, but touring one of Ponda's spice farms (p137) remains a worthwhile way to spend a Goan day. Try the Tropical Spice Farm for an illuminating look into how the spices in your curry are produced, along with a buffet lunch served up on a banana leaf, an array of sweet-scented gifts and an optional close encounter with the resident elephant. Alternatively, seek out the hidden Savoi Plantation, lower-key and pachyderm free, for a mellower, organic introduction to the fragrant world of spice production. Sahakari Spice Farm (p137)

To Market

4 Whether you're in the market for some serious souvenirs or simply looking for an injection of local life, Goa's manifold markets won't fail to please. Head to Mapusa for its mammoth Friday market day (p86), where you'll find fresh produce, spices and plenty of tacky plastic nonsense in tightly packed stalls thronging with locals. Alternatively kick back over a cold beer or a reviving chai at Anjuna market (p87) with its compelling mix of migrant workers, backpackers, package tourists and ancient hippies in residence. Local woman, Mapusa market

Mellow Mandrem

5 Downward-dog the days away in lovely, laid-back Mandrem (p74), where yoga retreats of all shapes and sizes are in no short supply. When you're done with stretching and toning, retreat to a calm stretch of golden sands to while the rest of the day away, emerging later for a massage, an organic shake and perhaps an evening motorbike ride to nearby Arambol (p71) to get a fix of the backpacker action. Ashiyana Retreat Centre (p74), Mandrem

Historic Goa

6 Millennia of visitors, invaders and assorted outside influences make Goa a fascinating place to soak up some history. Motorbike out to melancholy, crumbling Portuguese forts, glimpse the marvellous mansions of Chandor (p159) and Loutolim (p158), stroll the streets of old Panaji (p111), and explore the saintly relics of Old Goa (p126), once widely known as the 'Rome of the East'. Alternatively, rest up in one of the numerous boutique hotels, housed in exquisitely renovated mansions, that are scattered along the length of the state. Church of St Cajetan (p130), Old Goa

Palolem Beach

7 A blissful crescent of golden sand, bath-tub-balmy seas, gently swaying palm trees, good food, beach huts galore and a colourful backpacker-oriented beach bar scene makes Palolem (p177) a favourite with scores of travellers from across the globe. Though some say it's past its prime, there's little that can beat a day, or a week, spent watching the waves from the comfort of your beachside hammock before wandering down the sands to choose a seafood supper and a killer cocktail under a swath of starry sky.

Watch Wildlife

8 Whether you prefer to do it by boat or creeping through the forest canopy, avid naturalists will relish the chance to seek out Goa's wildlife of the skies, the seas or rustling somewhere in the bushes. Mingle with monkeys at Cotigao Wildlife Sanctuary (p183), spot a Ceylon frogmouth at the beautiful Dr Salim Ali Bird Sanctuary (p125), watch baby olive ridley turtles hatch beneath a full moon at Galgibag beach (p183) or hole up in the hinterland at bird-abundant Backwoods Camp (p142). Crocodile, Mandovi River

Biking the Byways

9 Hire a moped or roaring Royal Enfield motorbike (p157) at any one of Goa's beach resorts, and head out into the hinterland to experience a slower, pastoral pace of life in the green Goan countryside. South Goa is particularly rich in scenic byways: seek out the hidden Netravali 'bubble lake' (p182) or take to the village lanes on the way out to remote Usgalimal (p160) to see how rural Goans really live. Arambol (Harmal; p71)

By Train to Goa

10 Sure, there's never been an easier time to fly into Goa, with internal flights buzzing through the skies with the frequency of seagulls over a shoal of Arabian Sea fish. But there's something sublime about hopping aboard the Konkan Railway (p233) in Mumbai, then sitting back and letting western India ease by outside your window. It might take considerably longer than a 45-minute hop by air, but there's nothing like a trip on the 12-hour Konkan Kanya Express or nine-hour Jan Shatabdi Express to get you thoroughly immersed in the real India. Konkan Railway

need to know

Currency
» Indian Rupees (₹)

Language
» English, Konkani, Hindi and Portuguese

When to Go

• **Arambol**
GO Nov–Mar

Anjuna
• **GO** Nov–Mar

• **Panaji**
GO Nov–Mar

Tropical climate, wet dry seasons

Mumbai
• **GO** Nov–Mar

Goa

Palolem
• **GO** Nov–Mar

High Season
(Nov–Mar)

» Warm, sunny weather, with long, balmy evenings.

» Calm seas, perfect for diving, boat trips and swimming.

» Peak tourists and prices, especially over firework-laden Christmas and New Year.

Shoulder Season (Apr, Oct)

» Fantastically quiet beaches, but less restaurants and beach huts open for business.

» Seas sometimes too blustery for swimming or boat trips.

» April can be hot, hot, hot, with humidity on the rise.

Low Season
(May–Sep)

» Most tourist operations close.

» The monsoon brings rain, humidity, green countryside and local celebrations.

» Few tourists so the perfect time to experience 'real' Goan life.

Your Daily Budget

Budget less than
₹1500

» Stay in beach huts at backpacker-favoured beaches

» Eat at local joints and hole-in-the-wall eateries

» Look out for 'sunset specials' at beach bars

» Travel by local buses

Midrange
₹1500– 3500

» Combine traveller-oriented beach restaurants with local eateries

» Take an autorickshaw, or rent a moped

» Stay in higher-end beach huts with great views

Top End over
₹3500

» Stay in boutique heritage hotels

» Rent a car, or travel by taxi

» Dine opulently, but don't miss meals at local hang-outs

Money

» Towns have ATMs; larger beach resorts usually have at least one ATM, but it's wise to carry cash as back-up. Top-end hotels and stores often accept Mastercard and Visa.

Visas

» Most nationalities need pre-arranged tourist visas to enter India. Check with your local Indian consulate well before your planned departure.

Mobile Phones

» To avoid expensive roaming costs, get hooked up to the local mobile-phone network. Longer-stayers might want to invest in a local Goan mobile phone.

Transport

» Confident drivers with nerves of steel can hire mopeds, motorbikes, cars or jeeps. Otherwise local buses, taxis and autorickshaws abound.

Websites

» **Lonely Planet** (www.lonelyplanet. com/india/goa) A great first go-to for information.

» **Goa Tourism** (www. goa-tourism.com) Goa's state tourism body.

» **Time Out Mumbai** (www.timeoutmumbai. net) Daily listings and reviews.

» **Herald** (www. heraldgoa.in) Popular Goan newspaper.

» **Goacom** (www. goacom.com) Listings, information and recipes.

» **Goa World** (www. goa-world.com) Information and Konkani music.

Exchange Rates

Australia	A$1	₹53
Canada	C$1	₹51
Euro zone	€1	₹69
Japan	¥100	₹66
New Zealand	NZ$1	₹40
UK	UK£1	₹80
US	US$1	₹51

For current exchange rates see www.xe.com

Important Numbers

From outside India, dial the international access code (🗹00), India's country code (🗹91), then the number you want, minus the initial '0'.

Country code	🗹91
Police	🗹100
Fire	🗹101
Ambulance	🗹102
General emergencies	🗹108

Arriving in Goa

» **Dabolim Airport, Goa** Prepaid taxi booth to all Goan destinations Many hotels do pick up

» **Madgaon Railway Station, Margao** Stop on Konkan railway Prepaid taxi booth to all Goan destinations

» **Karmali Railway Station, Old Goa** Closest to Panaji Reservations at Panaji Kadamba Bus Stand

» **Kadamba Bus Stand, Panaji** Long-distance and local buses Private long-distance bus companies have ticket booths here, but depart from the interstate bus stand

Don't Leave Home Without...

» An Indian visa (p230) and travel insurance

» A reliable padlock, for securing belongings while staying in palm-thatched beach huts

» A torch to navigate poorly lit streets and negotiate frequent power cuts

» Sunscreen and insect repellent, plus wet wipes if you're travelling with children or messy companions

» Your driver's licence (and copies) for hiring a scooter, motorbike or car

» A copy of your passport, in case you want to buy a local mobile phone

» Your bank card for withdrawing cash: Goa's now fairly well equipped with ATMs state-wide

» Something long-sleeved to throw on when visiting churches, temples and mosques

if you like...

Good Food

No matter the culinary persuasion, you'll satisfy your cravings in Goa. From street vendors dishing up superb snacks to fine candlelit dining on the shores of the Arabian Sea, the crucial thing is to arrive hungry.

Mumbai A city of spectacular eateries, from the humblest *bhelpuri* street-stall to the fanciest Mughal feast, Mumbai will satiate the most demanding gourmand (p56)

Calangute and Baga Don your frock and eat upscale at one of Calangute and Baga's several swish bistros (p97)

Holiday on the Menu Learn how to whip up your own Goan creations with cooking courses in the village of Betim (p117)

Martin's Corner Sample a Goan *vindalho* (fiery curry in a marinade of vinegar and garlic) at this local institution, once a stop for hungry truckers and now a popular restaurant in little Betalbatim (p166)

Panaji Munch on tasty thalis, rich Portuguese-inflected curries, or simply take afternoon tea in the mellow state capital, Panaji (p120)

Pampering

Luxury of all sorts puts in an appearance in a state keen to get away from its grungy, hippy yesteryear. Boutique hotels abound, five-star hotels keep up appearances, and seasonal spas pop up with holistic treats.

Fort Tiracol (Terekhol) Unwind like Rapunzel's locks in your turret room at Fort Tiracol, a Portuguese fort turned boutique hotel tucked away in Goa's quiet northern reaches (p75)

Ayurveda Take time out for an ayurvedic massage at almost any Goan beach spot; ask around for recommendations, then let life's rigours disperse in a fragrant hour of ancient health regime (p28)

Vivenda dos Palhacos Linger awhile at this South Goan *palácio*, with its cute pool, fabulous bar and restful rooms (p165)

Park Hyatt Resort & Spa, Arossim Go five-star beside a great swath of empty beach at this swish escape. Float your cares away in the pool, then dine at the acclaimed Goan Casa Sarita restaurant (p164)

Shopping

Goa abounds with opportunities to blow your luggage allowance. Pick up bottles of *feni*, the local firewater distilled from coconut milk or cashews, for the folks back home, or decorative textiles, glass bangles and silver jewellery from stalls where haggling hard's a must.

Mumbai Whether it's antiques, clothes, handicrafts or meandering through markets that gets your retail juices flowing, Mumbai, probably India's best shopping spot, can't fail to please (p63)

Golden Heart Emporium, Margao Vending classics, new releases and harder-to-find Goan titles, this dusty, well-stocked delight of a book store is a treasure trove for bibliophiles (p156)

Mapusa Market Browse fresh produce, spices, clothes and knick-knacks with droves of locals, stopping off for tea and lunch at a hole-in-the-wall joint in its inner reaches (p86)

Anjuna Market Hang out with backpackers, hippies, and package tourists at this venerable old market institution, which has been banging out the tie-dye for decades (p87)

GRAHAM CROUCH / LONELY PLANET IMAGES ©

» Vegetarian thali, Colaba, Mumbai

Bars & Drinking

Unlike residents of other parts of India, many Goans enjoy a tipple or two upon occasion. A little local bar provides the perfect ice-breaker to strike up conversation with locals, while a cold sunset beer is almost obligatory along the state's sandy shores.

Mumbai Hip, minimalist clubs, grungy backstreet bars, cool jazz joints, '80s music-filled dives: you'll find them all in abundance in this hard-partying city (p60)

Local bars, Panaji No frills here, but decent drinks in down-to-earth surroundings make Panaji's teeny bars a great choice for whiling away an hour or two (p121)

Anjuna Take the edge off a hot market afternoon with a cold drink at Anjuna Market, while listening to an expat crooner murder yet another 'Hotel California' (p87)

Cafe Chocolatti, Candolim Sip a ginger-lime fizz or an old-fashioned English cuppa alongside a slice of chocolate cake in Chocolatti's shady, flowery garden (p105)

Architecture

Goa's heritage is probably most visible in its Portuguese-style mansions, many slowly crumbling away, others in glorious states of renovation. But there's other architecture, too, if you look carefully, allowing you to peel away the years and glimpse a much older Goa.

Braganza House, Chandor One of few *palácios* open to the public, the split-personality Braganza House is a fascinating insight into how the aristocratic Goan other half once lived (p159)

Palácio do Deão, Quepem A labour of love for its owners – you can take tea on the terrace of this stunning *palácio*, marvelling at the wealth of painstakingly renovated detail (p160)

Hampi Wander around stunning 15th- and 16th-century temples and palaces, at this World Heritage Site that time forgot (p143)

Goan forts The Goan coastline is dotted with the atmospheric remnants of a once mighty seafaring nation, all ripe for exploration (p175)

Religious Goa

If you're visiting at Christmas, don't be surprised to see Santas in saris and hear Christmas carols piped in Hindi. It's all part of the heady religious mix here, where Divali, Easter and even a 'fire-walking' goddess day all put in annual appearances.

Basilica of Bom Jesus, Old Goa Visit a saint's desiccated relics at this splendid basilica, just dripping with silver stars and ecclesiastical glory (p129)

Shigmotsav (Shigmo) Goa's version of the Hindu festival of Holi sees much flinging of coloured tikka powder in ebullient celebration of Spring (p16)

Christmas A highlight on the Goan calendar, Christmas involves nativity scenes beneath palm trees, twinkling lights and jiggle-hipped electronic Santas, making for a very merry vibe (p19)

Church of Our Lady of the Immaculate Conception, Panaji Clamber the steps to this wedding cake of a church, where sailors once stopped to thank the heavens for their safe arrival from Portugal (p113)

month by month

Top Events

1 **Shantadurga**, January

2 **Shigmotsav (Shigmo)**, February

3 **Ganesh Chaturthi**, September

4 **Diwali**, October

5 **Christmas**, December

January

The prime time for visiting Goa (book ahead!), January brings blue skies and warm weather, making it perfect for hitting the beach but not too hot for getting to grips with the state's cities.

Banganga Festival

A two-day classical-music festival held at the Banganga Tank (p49) in Mumbai (Bombay), in musical tribute to the Lord Ram, who, legend has it, once stopped over here and provided locals with water direct from the holy Ganges.

Reis Magos Festival

Held at Reis Magos, Chandor and Cansaulim on 6 January, this festival sees a re-enactment of the journey of the Three Wise Men to Bethlehem, with young boys playing the Magi and white horses providing their transport.

Shantadurga

Also known as the 'Procession of the Umbrellas', this is one of Goa's most attended festivals, wherein a solid silver statue of Hindu goddess Shantadurga is carried between the villages of Fatorpa and Cuncolim, fronted by 12 umbrella-carrying young men.

Festa das Bandeiras

Migrant working men return home to Divar Island (p133) in mid-January to celebrate their local saint's day by waving the flags of the countries in which they're currently working and, more bizarrely, firing dozens of peashooters at each other.

Republic Day

Though Goa only became part of India in 1961, India's celebration of the country's 1950 establishment as a republic is nevertheless celebrated here with gusto, or at least with office closures, every 26 January.

February

Another reliably warm and sunny month for lazing on the beach or seeing the sights, February sees fewer crowds (and lower prices) than January, making it a fabulous time to sojourn in Goa.

Elephanta Festival

Classical music and dance performances are held under starry night skies outside the Elephanta Caves on Elephanta Island (p68) on the outskirts of Mumbai, at this annual festival organised by the Maharashtra Tourism Development Corporation.

Kala Ghoda Festival

Growing bigger and more sophisticated each year, this two-week-long festival in Mumbai has a packed program of arts performances and exhibitions. Check www.kalaghodaassociation.com for more details.

Shigmotsav (Shigmo)

Goa's take on the Hindu festival of Holi marks the onset of spring over the full moon period with statewide parades, processions, and revellers flinging huge quantities of water and coloured tikka powder with wild abandon.

Carnival

Three days of mirth and mayhem characterise Panaji's annual Carnival, held on the three days prior to the onset of the Catholic calendar's Lent. Festivities come to a head on Sabado Gordo (Fat Saturday), when you'll see a procession of floats through the city's packed streets. See p118.

Hanuman Festival

Ten days in February see the Hindu monkey god Hanuman celebrated at Panaji's Maruti Temple (p116), with huge statues of the deity paraded about, and a street fair up and running throughout the surrounding neighbourhood.

Shivratri

To celebrate the traditional anniversary of the God Shiva's wedding day, large-scale religious celebrations are held at the many Shiva temples across Goa on the 14th (moonless) night of the new moon, in the Hindu month of Phalgun, which falls in either February or March.

March

Although things are starting to heat up considerably by now, it's still peak season in Goa. It might be a little too hot for much wildlife-watching, but beach lounging and swimming remain in their prime.

Procession of All Saints

Held in Goa Velha (p134) on the fifth Monday during Lent, this is the only procession of its sort outside Rome, where dozens of huge statues of the saints are paraded throughout the village, and people from all over Goa are drawn to the accompanying festivities.

Easter

Churches fill up statewide over the Christian festival of Easter, with plenty of solemn High Masses and family feasting (though fewer chocolate bunnies –they'd only melt) thrown in for good measure. The biggest church services are held in Panaji and Old Goa.

April

Most tourists have departed Goa, and temperatures begin rising in anticipation of the monsoon, still over a month away. If you can take the heat, it's quiet and calm, with great deals on accommodation.

Feast of Our Lady of Miracles

Held in Mapusa 16 days after Easter, this cheerful festival, also known as a *tamasha*, is famously celebrated by both Hindus and Christians at Mapusa's Church of Our Lady of Miracles (p85).

May

May is perhaps the most uncomfortable month in Goa, with heat, humidity, and everyone awaiting the coming of the rains. Most tourist facilities have closed for the season, and days slip by in a heat haze.

Igitun Chalne

One of Goa's most distinctive festivals, specific to the temple in Sirigao (near Corjuem Fort, p108). *Igitun chalne* means 'fire-walking', and the high point

comes when devotees of the goddess Lairaya traverse a pit of burning coals to prove their devotion.

June

It's here! The monsoon's arrival sparks a host of celebrations, and the land turns miraculously green overnight. Water buffalo bask, children dance in the showers, and frogs croak out elated choruses.

Feast of St Anthony

This feast on 13 June in honour of Portugal's patron saint takes on particular significance if the monsoon is late in appearing, whereupon each Goan family must lower a statue of the saint into its family well to hasten the onset of the rains and pray for bountiful crops.

Sanjuan

The Feast of St John (or *Sanjuan,* in the local Konkani dialect) on 24 June sees young men diving dangerously into wells to celebrate the monsoon's arrival, and torching straw dummies of the saint himself, to represent John's baptism and, consequently, the death of sin.

Sangodd

The annual Feast of St Peter and St Paul on 29 June marks another monsoonal celebration, and is particularly ebullient in Candolim, where boats are tied together to form floating stages and costumed actors play out *tiatrs* (Konkani dramas) to vast crowds.

Ramadan

Falling either at the end of June or early July, 30 days of dawn-to-dusk fasting mark the ninth month of the Islamic calendar. Muslims traditionally turn their attention to God, with a focus on prayer, purification and charitable giving.

August

Though the monsoon is slowly receding, the rains are still a-coming, making the countryside and jungle glisten. As the month progresses, fishermen await calmer waters and local life goes on, almost tourist-free.

Eid al-Fitr

Muslims celebrate the end of Ramadan with three days of festivities, beginning 30 days after the start of the fast. Prayers, shopping, gift-giving and, for women and girls, *mehndi* (henna designs) may all be part of the celebrations.

Nariyal Poornima

In both Goa and Mumbai, a coconut offering is made to Lord Varuna, god of the sea, to mark the start of the post-monsoon fishing season; fisherman pray for a bountiful harvest before hitting the first choppy waves of the August seas.

Independence Day

India's 1947 independence from Britain is celebrated with an annual public holiday on 15 August. Celebrations are a countryside expression of patriotism, with flag-hoisting ceremonies, parades and patriotic cultural programs.

Feast of the Chapel

Coastal Cabo Raj Bhavan (p124) draws scores of visitors each 15 August, on India's Independence Day, to a special church service in honour of its 500-year-old chapel's feast day, which long predates Independence Day.

Bonderam

Celebrated annually on the fourth Saturday in August on sleepy Divar Island (p133), in the middle of the wide Mandovi River. Locals take part in processions and mock battles to commemorate historical disputes that took place over island property.

September

The rains have all but subsided, leaving a scoured, green Goa just ripe for the upcoming tourist season. Local businesses begin building the season's first beach huts, and industriousness takes the place of monsoon rest.

Ganesh Chaturthi

Mumbai's biggest annual festival – a 10-day event in celebration of the elephant-headed Ganesh – sweeps up the whole city: the 10th day, which sees millions descend on Mumbai's Girguam Chowpatty (p48) to submerge the largest statues, is particularly ecstatic.

October

Though businesses aren't in full swing, October's warm days and deliciously cool breezes tempt a trickle of in-the-know travellers, who benefit from the widest choice in long-stay accommodation.

Feast of the Menino Jesus

On October's second Sunday, coastal Colva's village church sees its small and allegedly miracle-working statue of the Infant Jesus dressed up and paraded before scores of devoted pilgrims at this important village festival (p168).

Dusshera

This nine-day Hindu festival celebrates the god Rama's victory over Ravana in the Hindu epic Ramayana, and the goddess Durga's victory over Mahishasura. It's celebrated with bonfires – burning effigies of the baddies – and school-children's performances of scenes from the life of Rama.

Diwali

A five-day Hindu 'festival of lights', this beautifully illuminated festival celebrates the victory of good over evil with the lighting of oil and butter lamps around the home, lots of gentle familial celebration and loads of less peaceful firecrackers.

November

High season begins in earnest in November, when the countryside remains post-monsoon green, and Goans gear up for the tourist business. This, along with February, is perhaps the most perfect time to visit.

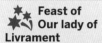

Feast of Our lady of Livrament

Each mid-November sees a cheerful saint's day street fair set up in Panaji (p111), outside the tiny Chapel of St Sebastian, in the Goan capital's atmospheric old Portuguese-infused Fontain-has district.

International Film Festival of India

This annual film festival (www.iffi.gov.in) – the country's largest – graces Panaji's big screens with a gaggle of Bollywood's finest glitterati jetting in for premieres, parties, ceremonies and screenings.

December

Packed with parties, December is an ebullient (if expensive) month to be in Goa. Spend Christmas Day swimming in clear seas, then spare the turkey by plumping for a Christmas dinner thali, to celebrate the season the Goan way.

Feast of St Francis Xavier

Thousands upon thousands of pilgrims file past the shrivelled old remains of St Francis Xavier in Old Goa (p129) every 3 December, kicking off a weeklong festival and fair, complete with large-scale open-air Masses.

Feast of Our Lady of the Immaculate Conception

Panaji's wedding-cake Church of the Immaculate Conception (p113) plays host to this feast and large, joyful fair on 8 December.

Liberation Day

This unusually sober celebration on 17 December marks Goa's 'liberation' from Portugal by India in 1961, with military parades.

Christmas

Midnight Masses abound in Goa on 24 December, traditionally known as *Misa de Galo* ('Cock's Crow') since they often stretch on far into the wee hours, while the following Christmas Day is celebrated with feasting, fireworks and festivities.

Sunburn Festival

In recent years, 'Asia's biggest music festival' has set up annually in Candolim (p99) over Christmas. Check locally for details; if it's running to form, you'll find a four-day dance-music extravaganza filled with international DJs.

Siolim Zagor

Siolim's multifaith Zagor (p79), which takes place on the first Sunday after Christmas, involves festivities, with a procession culminating in folk plays, music and celebrations.

itineraries

Whether you've got six days or 60, these itineraries provide a starting point for the trip of a lifetime. Want more inspiration? Head online to lonelyplanet.com/thorntree to chat with other travellers.

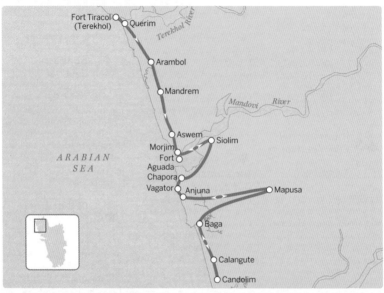

Two Weeks
Northern Nonpareil

The north encompasses a little of everything that's great about Goa. Start with a soothing stay at historic Portuguese **Tiracol (Terekhol) Fort**, and from here hop on a ferry for solitary sunbathing in **Querim**, then hit **Arambol** for beach huts and a permanent festival vibe. Continue south to mellow **Mandrem** for yogic serenity, **Aswem**, to dine at its renowned French-inspired beach shack, and **Morjim**, where rare turtles hatch and Russians rule, for a stroll along the estuary.

Next head inland via pretty **Siolim**, to **Chapora** and **Vagator** for the last dregs of the Goa trance scene. Kick back in **Anjuna**, visiting its legendary flea market to sniff out a bargain, then shop some more at workaday **Mapusa** with its immense local market.

Backtrack to **Baga** and **Calangute** to pick up the pace, hit the clubs, water-sport the days away and dine on fine foodstuffs, then finally head south to **Candolim** for a riverine wildlife-watching trip and a jaunt up to impressive **Fort Aguada**, ending your journey, as it began, in the shadow of Portugal's once-mighty colonial conquests.

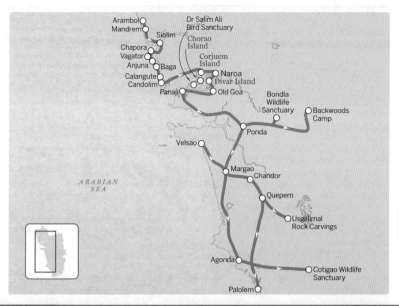

The Best of Goa

With a month to spare, you can truly get to the heart of the state. Start in the north, winding down for a few days in backpacker-central **Arambol**, and following up with some more quiet in **Mandrem**, with a yoga retreat or some solitude on its sands. Next head down through the pretty inland village of **Siolim**, to explore what's left of the trance scene at **Chapora** and **Vagator**, before moving on to hippyish **Anjuna** to hit the flea markets. Press on then to hard-partying and fine-dining in **Calangute** and **Baga** and then visit the hulking *River Princess* tanker at **Candolim**.

Meandering slowly south, stop off to explore the string of villages along the Mandovi River: drop in on **Corjuem Island** and **Naroa**, then hop a ferry to **Divar Island**, worth exploring for its slow, sleepy pace of life and crumbling old homes. Travel on, via **Old Goa**, once the fabled 'Rome of the East', to **Panaji** to eat well and soak up the easy city vibe. Once comfortably installed here, take a trip out to the lovely little riverine **Dr Salim Ali Bird Sanctuary** on **Chorao Island**. Striking out still further into the hinterland, now's the time to take a **spice plantation** tour near **Ponda**, and, if birdwatching is even faintly your thing, head out even further east to the **Bondla Wildlife Sanctuary** for a stay at the idyllic **Backwoods Camp**.

Backtracking to Ponda, head down south to **Margao**, the workaday gateway to the southern beaches, to install yourself in your beach hut or boutique hotel for at least a week, if not a fortnight, of seaside bliss. Go for **Agonda** if you're not one for crowds, or **Palolem**, if you're looking for a happy backpackery vibe. From here, rent a car or scooter to explore the stretch of coast between Agonda and **Velsao**, and delve into the hinterland to **Chandor**, **Cotigao Wildlife Sanctuary**, **Quepem**, and the **Usgalimal Rock Carvings**.

When you're finally ready to break your beach sojourn, consider a couple of nights away in glorious **Hampi** or pilgrim-heavy **Gokarna**, before returning to wash away the travails of the road with a last few days in your hammock beside the Arabian Sea.

» (above) Carved platform, Hampi (p143)
» (left) Querim beach (p75).

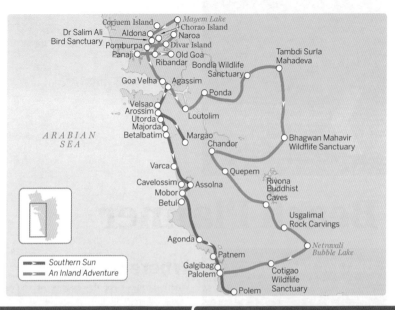

ARABIAN
SEA

Southern Sun
An Inland Adventure

Two Weeks
Southern Sun

Arriving at workaday **Margao**, hub of the south, cool down at old-fashioned Longhuino's, before heading northwest to begin a stay on the sands of **Velsao**. From Velsao, wind slowly down the coast, stopping off at the beaches of **Arossim**, **Utorda**, **Majorda** and **Betalbatim**, perhaps with a swanky night at the Park Hyatt or Vivenda dos Palhacos thrown in.

Continue on down along the lazy sands of **Varca** and stop for lunch in **Cavelossim**. Next detour to **Mobor** to get a feel for pristine estuarine life, then double back to Cavelossim to jump on a ferry to **Assolna**, and begin your exploration of Goa's southernmost stretch.

Follow the coastal road through bucolic **Betul** all the way to **Agonda** where you can relax in barefoot splendour, and get stuck into those books you've brought along for the ride. Next, hunker down in **Palolem** where the pace is less lazy, and track down one of its 'silent parties'. Base yourself here, or in nearby **Patnem**, to explore the south's beautiful beaches, or to take a day trip to **Galgibag** or **Polem**, two of the state's quietest beaches gracing the coast on the slow road down to Karnataka.

Ten Days
An Inland Adventure

Even in tiny Goa, it's possible to shrug off the crowds for a taste of the road less travelled. Begin in **Panaji**, the lovely, languid state capital, before heading to **Old Goa**, where the ghosts of Goan history await. Backtrack to pretty **Ribandar** to catch a ferry to **Chorao Island**, home of the **Dr Salim Ali Bird Sanctuary**, then ferry-hop to **Divar Island** for sleepy island life, and take a third ferry to **Naroa**, to the tiny, ancient Shri Saptakoteshwara Temple and quiet **Mayem Lake**.

Head west across to **Corjuem Island**, stopping in at **Aldona**, **Pomburpa**, and **Britona** on the Mandovi River. Turn south, skirting Panaji, via **Goa Velha** and **Agassim**, to historic **Loutolim**, before going east to the temples and spice farms of **Ponda**. Head further east to one of two wildlife sanctuaries: bird-filled **Bondla** or **Bhagwan Mahavir**, with its giddy waterfall. Detour to the ancient **Tambdi Surla Mahadeva temple**, then head south to **Chandor**. Here, explore one of Goa's grandest mansions, then visit busy little **Quepem** en route to the **Rivona Buddhist caves**, **Usgalimal rock carvings** and **Netravali Bubble Lake**. Stroll a trail in **Cotigao Wildlife Sanctuary** before ending on the picture-perfect sands of **Palolem**.

Beach Planner

Best for Partying
Calangute and Baga (p92)
Anjuna (p87)
Vagator (p79)
Candolim (p99)

Best for Families
Palolem (p177)
Mandrem (p74)
Patnem (p182)
Aswem (p76)

Best for Quiet
Agonda (p176)
Mandrem (p74)
Polem (p184)
Butterfly Beach (p177)
Querim (p75)

Best for Water Sports
Candolim and Sinquerim (p99)
Calangute and Baga (p92)
Colva and Benaulim (p166 and p169)
Arambol (p71)
Bogmalo (p163)

Where to Go

Whether time is of the essence or you've weeks (or even months) to spend in Goa, locating the perfect beach is the secret to making the best of your stay. Goa's beaches vary dramatically in character within short distances, and whether you're looking for backpacker-filled beach huts, silent sands or party people, you'll find what you're after... as long as you know where you're headed.

Safe Swimming

One of the greatest, most deceptive dangers in Goa is to be found just beyond your beautiful bit of beach. The Arabian Sea, with its strong currents and dangerous undertows, claims dozens of lives a year. Even the most tranquil beach can be a danger on a blustery day, or can prove safe at one end while treacherous at the other. Though most Goan beaches are now overseen by lifeguards during high season, you should heed local warnings, be vigilant with children, and don't venture into the water after drinking alcohol or taking drugs.

Beaches of North Goa

North Goa is home to the backpacker, party and package-tourist action, though you'll also find plenty of solitude between the sun-tanners.

» (above) A cow relaxes on Palolem Beach (p177)
» (left) Rock carving, Vagator (p79).

» **Arambol (Harmal) & Querim** Little Arambol (p71) is backpacker central, with simple huts scattered across a rocky headland. It's a popular choice for travellers and long-stayers, and makes a cheap and chilled spot to rest up, while the beach is generally safe for swimming. A little further north, Querim is a fishing village with a scattering of beach shacks, offering a quiet change of pace.

» **Mandrem** South from Arambol, Mandrem (p74) is a long ribbon of clean, uncluttered sand, and although it's certainly been discovered it still makes a great choice for getting away from it all (though this is becoming annually more of a challenge). The best digs here are in the midrange budget, many offering yoga courses, ayurvedic massage and other ways to help you rejuvenate.

» **Morjim & Aswem** Stretching down to the Chapora River, the long sandy stretches of Morjim (p78) and Aswem (p76) are calm and beautiful, though, especially in the case of Aswem, are becoming increasingly crowded, so go soon before the crowds truly descend. Morjim, popular with young Russians, has a somewhat desolate aura, and is a breeding site for endangered sea turtles.

» **Vagator & Chapora** Once the centre of Goa's trance party scene, things are quieter these days on Vagator's (p79) three covelike beaches, set around a rocky headland. Small Chapora (p79), just north and dominated by the hilltop remains of a Portuguese fort, has more puff than a magic dragon, and the scent of *charas* (cannabis or hashish) hangs thick in the village centre.

» **Anjuna** Famed for its weekly Wednesday flea market, scruffy Anjuna (p87) remains a firm backpacker favourite, with nice rocky beaches, good budget eating options, and a general sense of chilledness. It might not be as hip or hippy as in years past, but it still makes a terrific place to hang out into the wee hours with travellers and long-stayers from across the globe.

» **Calangute & Baga** If you're in Goa for the action, Calangute (p92) and Baga (p92) are the places for you. Here you'll find bars open until 4am, unbroken lines of beach shacks, international brand shops, water sports galore, and some classy dining and accommodation options. The beaches are busy (think sun-lounger central), but the bustle appeals to many who've been returning for decades.

» **Candolim & Sinquerim** Busy Candolim (p99) is a favourite with British package tourists, who set up here for their annual dose of sun 'n' fun. Sinquerim (p99), at its south end, is dominated by the Taj Group's two five-star hotels, and is a popular location for arranging water sports through ever-changing independent operators.

Beaches of South Goa

South Goa conceals some of the state's best beaches, great for picnicking and paddling.

» **Bogmalo** What was once a small but perfectly formed bay roared to life with the arrival of nearby Dabolim Airport. Nevertheless, if you've a night to kill before an early flight, Bogmalo (p163) makes an acceptable stop, and is best known for its highly respected diving operation.

» **Arossim & Velsao** Quiet and undeveloped, both Velsao (p164) and Arossim (p164) are perfect for a paddle with just seabirds and the occasional shack for company. The only blight on the horizon is the petrochemical plant to the north.

» **Utorda, Majorda & Betalbatim** Clean, quiet stretches of sand characterise these three villages (p165, p165 and p166), dotted with beach shacks and backed by Portuguese mansions.

» **Colva & Benaulim** Not the loveliest, nor the liveliest, of Goa's bigger resorts, Colva (p166) nevertheless bustles during the high-season. Benaulim (p169) next door is quieter and offers better options for the budget and midrange traveller. Both host a variety of water sports.

» **Varca, Cavelossim & Mobor** A string of luxury resorts, running south from Varca (p171) to the river mouth at Mobor (p174), lead onto empty beaches. Cavelossim (p172), while not a pretty development, sports a good range of eating and drinking options.

» **Palolem** Palolem's (p177) golden crescent of sand remains one of Goa's gems, despite unbridled beach-hut development along its entire length. The seas are shallow and swimmable, and the beach has an increasingly lively traveller scene.

» **Agonda** Agonda (p176), just north of Palolem, is expansive and idyllic, relatively undeveloped, and backed by a line of beach huts, but is frequently too rough for good swimming.

» **Patnem, Rajbag & Colomb** A quieter (if far smaller and less picturesque) alternative to Palolem, Patnem (p182) sports a nice sandy beach and good surf on windy days. Just south, small Rajbag Beach (p183) is dominated by the presence of a five-star, but makes a nice jaunt across the rocky headland. Colomb (p181), a tiny bay between Patnem and Palolem, offers relaxed beach-hut repose, though it's too rocky for good swimming.

» **Polem** Tucked away at the southern end of the state, Polem's (p184) empty little bay of golden sand, though notorious as a smugglers' den, makes for a fun day trip, by bus or scooter, from Palolem.

Yoga & Activities

Which Yoga Class?

Ashtanga Often referred to as 'power yoga', active and physically demanding, good for some serious toning.

Bikram Also known as 'hot yoga' and focusing on correct alignment, Bikram's 26 poses are performed at 105˚F (41˚C) and 40% humidity – not hard to achieve on a Goan April day.

Hatha Covers a whole gamut of styles, but generally refers to yoga focused on breath work (pranayama), and slow, gentle stretching, making it good for beginners.

Iyengar Slow and steady, often using 'props', in the form of blocks, balls and straps.

Kundalini Aims to free the base of the spine, to unleash energy hidden there, and usually involves lots of core, spine and sitting work.

Vinyasa An active, fluid series of changing poses characterises Vinyasa, sometimes called 'flow yoga'.

Yoga Central

From ashtanga through Zen, every imaginable form of yoga, along with ancient, ever-popular ayurveda, is practised, taught and relished in Goa.

But Goa's commitment to its visitors' well-being doesn't stop there. Take a Vipassana retreat (an intensive, silent, inward-looking form of meditation; see p76), lay your hands on a spot of reiki (healing through the laying-on of hands), or seek out t'ai chi, Buddhist meditation, belly dancing, sacred drumming circles, tarot, palmistry or healing colour therapies. It's all here in balmy – and sometimes barmy – Goa.

Where to Yoga

Palolem, Agonda and Patnem in the south of the state, and Arambol, Mandrem and Anjuna in the north, are particularly great places to take courses in manifold forms of yoga, and many also host retreat centres for longer yoga courses. But all beach centres offer courses and classes of various descriptions, and you'll find no shortage of sunrise yoga, sunset yoga, and pretty much everything in between.

Teachers and practitioners are largely an ever-changing parade of foreigners who set up shop in Goa as soon as the monsoon subsides, and offer their services to the scores who come seeking enlightenment, illumination or any spark of spiritual something. Check listings under individual destinations for permanent yoga and meditation retreats and operations, and peruse hotel, restaurant or café notice boards for current and upcoming courses.

Ayurveda

Goa offers plenty of opportunities to explore ayurvedic treatments. Briefly defined as an ancient science of plant-based medicine, ayurveda's Sanskrit name comes from a combination of *ayu* (life) and *veda* (knowledge); ancient ayurveda resources described 2000 species of plants, of which at least 550 are still in use today. Illness, in the doctrine of ayurveda, comes from a loss of internal balance, which can be restored through a regime of massage and *panchakarama* (internal purification).

The first part of this regime (and without doubt the most popular) comprises an hour-long massage with warm medicated oils, followed by a cleansing steam bath. This sort of massage is available almost anywhere in Goa, though it's best to go by local recommendation to seek out the very best ayurvedic hands on offer. For many people, this is as far as they delve into the ayurvedic world, and with good reason: a good ayurvedic massage, by itself, will leave you feeling thoroughly refreshed and rejuvenated.

The second part of the full regime, the internal purification, takes rather more than an hour, and most people opt for a fortnight's course of treatment in order to feel its full advantages. In this case, your cure will comprise a carefully tailored diet and exercise plan, along with a series of treatments to supplement your more frequent massages.

Ayurvedic clinics can be found at every beach destination, though again, it's best to ask around for personal recommendations. Meanwhile, if you're thinking of going upmarket, Goa's five-star palaces are the places to do it, where their swanky spas, with well-trained staff, give traditional practices a new, superluxurious spin.

Outdoor Activities

Goa has plenty to keep you active once you tire of the horizontal approach to its great outdoors. Increasingly, you'll find seasonal ecoslanted activities on offer: nature walks and day trips, and guided hikes through the state's national parks. As with most Goan activities, outfits change regularly and it's best to check noticeboards in hotels, restaurants and cafes for up-to-the-minute offerings.

Diving

Although Goa is not internationally renowned as a diving destination, its waters are regarded as the third-best spot for diving in India (after the Andaman and Lakshadweep Islands).

The shallow waters off the coast are ideal for less-experienced divers; typical dives are at depths of 10m to 12m, with abundant marine life to be seen. The only problem is that visibility is unpredictable; on some days it's 30m, on others it's closer to 2m, so it's best to check daily before deciding to go out. The dive season runs from November to April, and costs

---

GOA'S YOGA CENTRES

Scattered across Goa are a number of permanent, highly respected options for yoga classes, courses, retreats and teacher certification. Below are just some of them; see individual listings for more options.

Ayurvedic Natural Health Centre (p93) Drop-ins and courses are both available at this popular place, just 5km from the Calangute action.

Ashiyana Retreat Centre, Mandrem (p74) From drop-ins to full-blown retreats, yoga is on offer in lovely Mandrem, along with vegetarian food and beautiful accommodation.

Brahmani Yoga, Anjuna (p88) Daily drop-in classes: just bring your yoga mat.

Himalaya Yoga Valley, Mandrem (p74) Teacher training, along with lots of other options.

Himalayan Iyengar Yoga Centre, Arambol (p71) A variety of courses in Hatha yoga, running for five days and upwards from mid-November to mid-March.

ECOFRIENDLY DIVING

» Avoid touching or standing on living marine organisms or dragging equipment across the reef: polyps can be damaged by even the gentlest contact. If you must hold on to the reef, only touch exposed rock or dead coral.

» Be conscious of your fins. Even without contact, the surge from fin strokes near the reef can damage delicate organisms. Take care not to kick up clouds of sand, which can smother organisms.

» Practise and maintain proper buoyancy control. Major damage can be done by divers descending too fast and colliding with the reef.

» Spend as little time as possible inside underwater caves, as your air bubbles may be caught within the roof and thereby leave organisms high and dry.

» Resist the temptation to collect or buy corals or shells or to loot shipwrecks.

» Take home all your rubbish and any litter you may find as well. Plastics in particular are a serious threat to marine life.

» Don't feed fish, and *never* interact with turtles, should you be lucky enough to encounter them.

for an introductory dive plus four further guided excursions come in at around ₹14,000.

Marine life you're likely to encounter while deep beneath the sea includes angelfish, parrotfish, wrasses, lionfish, sharks (reef tip and shovel-nosed among others), stingrays, groupers, snapper, damselfish, barracuda, sea cucumbers and turtles.

The highlights of diving in Goa are the wreck dives – there are hundreds of wrecks along Goa's coastline, including Portuguese and Spanish galleons and more recent wrecks of merchant and naval ships. Goa's shipwreck history dates back to the 2nd century BC, though the wrecks you'll encounter beneath its waters are not quite so antique. It's said that vast quantities of treasure still lie on its ocean beds, remnants from the wrecks carrying wealthy Portuguese traders.

Popular dive sites include Grande Island and St George's Island, while south of Goa, Devbagh Island (near Karwar) and Pigeon Island off the Karnataka coast are also frequently used. Professional Association of Dive Instructors (PADI) accredited operations in Goa are the environmentally conscious **Barracuda Diving** (see p94), and the long-established **Goa Diving** (see p163).

Water Sports

Most water-sports outfits are run on a seasonal, itinerant basis, and it's enough to turn up at a beach and look around for a shack offering your activity of choice. There's an annually growing range of varieties on offer, the most popular being jet skiing, parasailing, kayaking and, on windier days, surfing. The beaches of Colva (p166), Benaulim (p169), Baga (p92), Sinquerim (p99) and Calangute (p92) are particularly heavy on all these options, and it's important to haggle for the best price among sometimes stiff competition. Palolem (p177) usually has a few kayaks on offer, too, while nearly all the five-star hotels offer a range of water sports, albeit at higher prices than their independent competitors.

Wildlife Watching

All creatures great and small are out in all their glory in Goa, from the blazing kingfishers that fleck the coastal strip's luminescent paddy fields, to the water buffalo that wander home come sunset after a hard day's wallowing.

There's little in life as restful as finding your deserted stretch of beach and then settling in to observe the crabs, gulls, sea eagles and the occasional cavorting dolphin that are so much part of Goa's seaside landscape, or watching the wary tree frog that appears croaking on your balcony each evening as the sun sets.

Goa's wilder expanses host little-seen wonders, such as gaurs (Indian bison), porcupines, wild boar and the occasional pangolin (scaly anteater) or leopard. A loud rustle in the leaves overhead often signals the arrival of a troop of mischievous langur monkeys, who appear in family groups to steal unattended food from backyards, and generally cause mirth and mayhem.

WHERE THE WILD THINGS ARE

It's worth noting that Goa's not the only place for wildlife watching; see p51 and p69 for what's on offer in Mumbai.

Best Bet for Birds

» Backwoods Camp, p142
» Dr Salim Ali Bird Sanctuary, p125
» Spice Plantations, p137

Best Bet for Beasts

» Cotigao Wildlife Sanctuary, p183
» Bondla Wildlife Sanctuary, p140
» Bhagwan Mahavir Wildlife Sanctuary, p141

Best Wildlife-Watching Trips

» John's Boat Tours, p102
» Betty's Place Boat Trips, p172
» Day Tripper, p94
» Canopy Ecotours, p155

Taking a riverine trip inland, you might be rewarded with a sighting of crocodiles, otters, and yet more birdlife, whose names alone make the trip worthwhile: just try spotting a Ceylon frogmouth or a fairy blue-bird without at least the hint of a satisfied smile.

Day Trips & Tours

A great way to see more of Goa, if you're on a tight time schedule, is to sign up for a day trip or two. Almost every beach resort has its own slew of tour operators, offering visits out to the hard-to-get-to sights that would otherwise be tricky without your own transport.

It's a good idea to look around a bit before plumping for the ideal tour – many of which can be undertaken on the water instead of on wheels, cruising Goa's coast or serene inland waterways. The state tourism group, the **GTDC** (see p230) offers a surprisingly good range of bus-based day trips, taking in an astonishing number of sights in just one day. Though it's not the most restful or thorough way to travel, the tours are good value for money, and the drivers are usually more careful than most.

Check individual chapter listings for particularly recommended day-tripping outfits, and don't forget about the local fishermen lingering around almost every beach, willing to take you out on the waves for a dolphin-watching expedition, or allowing you to accompany them on a fishing expedition, to see how a number of locals make their hard-earned living.

Mumbai, meanwhile, has its own huge range of innovative day trips on offer; choose from heritage walks and journeys through the city's slums, to a quick sail on the superluxurious Taj yacht. See p51 for more details.

Volunteering

More and more visitors to Goa are keen to put something back into this beautiful, alluring but sometimes vulnerable state. One great way to do this is to spend part of your stay volunteering: whether it's a few hours, days or weeks spent doing good for some of Goa's residents, you'll gain a unique and rewarding insight into your destination, and come away feeling that incredible high that can be obtained by helping others.

Planning

Many of Goa's volunteering options require a little advance planning, and it pays to be in touch with organisations well before you depart home, in order to make sure they know you're on your way. Moreover, working with children requires criminal record background checks, so takes a few months to organise. Some animal-related organisations, such as the Goa Animal Welfare Trust and International Animal Rescue, along with the **Goa SPCA** (www.goaspca.org), are happy to receive casual help: just turn up and they'll find you something useful to do.

Getting Involved

'Never work with children or animals', so the old thespian adage goes, but for those with the opportunity to volunteer some of their time while in the sunny state, many opportunities exist for helping small creatures with two or four – and sometimes even three – legs who need help most. Local charities include:

» **Children Walking Tall** (☏09822124802; www.childrenwalkingtall.com; 'The Mango House', near Vrundavan Hospital, Karaswada, Mapusa, Goa) Founded in 2004, this organisation helps Goa's street and slum children, with its daycare centre and medical, educational, nutritional and all sorts of other essential aid. Volunteers can fill a variety of roles, as teachers, childcare assistants and outreach workers, while there are also positions available for qualified doctors and nurses. Check Children Walking Tall's website for complete details.

» **El Shaddai** (☑6513286, 6513287; www. childrescue.net; El Shaddai House, Socol Vaddo, Assagao) A British-founded charity that aids impoverished and homeless children throughout Goa and beyond, running a number of day and night shelters, an open school and children's homes throughout the state. Volunteers (who undergo a rigorous vetting process) able to commit to more than four weeks' work with El Shaddai are encouraged to contact James the coordinator (james@childrescue.net). This is an undertaking to arrange in advance, since it can take up to six months to complete the vetting process; the application form is available online. You can also sponsor a child: check the website for details.

» **Goa Animal Welfare Trust** (GAWT; ☑ 2653677; www.gawt.org; Old Police Station, Curchorem) Based in South Goa and operates an animal shelter at Curchorem (situated in the Old Police Station on the main road), helping sick, stray and injured dogs, cats and even a calf or two, and is open daily from 9am to 5pm for visits. GAWT, like International Animal Rescue, undertakes extensive dog sterilisation projects throughout Goa, offers low-cost veterinary care, deals with animal cruelty cases and finds homes for stray puppies. Volunteers are welcome, if only for a few spare hours to walk or play with the dogs, and GAWT also operates a shop and information centre in Colva (see also p172).

» **International Animal Rescue** (IAR; ☑+441825767688; www.internationalanimalrescue. org; Animal Tracks, Mandungo Vaddo, Assagao) An internationally active charity, helping Goa's furry and feathery sick, unwanted and strays. It runs its Animal Tracks rescue facility in Assagao, near Mapusa, in North Goa. Visitors and volunteers (both short and long term) are always welcome, and IAR's website includes a 'Needs List' of things you might be able to fit into your backpack and bring from home, including antiseptic ointment, flea powder and puppy toys. You'll also find a downloadable PDF of info for willing volunteers.

PLAN YOUR TRIP YOGA & ACTIVITIES

Travel with Children

Beaches for Beach Babies

Palolem (p177) Shallow waters, soft sand and even a Baskin-Robbins for cool-off ice creams.

Patnem (p182) Paddling on calm days, a quiet, unhassled vibe and plenty of beach shacks.

Baga (p92) Lots of bucket-and-spade vendors and plenty of other children to make friends with.

Arambol (p71) Shallow seas popular with long-stayers, though hut accomodation may be too basic for some families.

Butterfly Beach (p177) A quick boat ride to a protected little cove, where little ones can splash about merrily.

Sand-Free Pastimes

Public Observatory, Panaji (p117)
Spice Farms, Ponda (p137)
'Crocodile Dundee' river trip, Candolim (p102)
INOX Cinema, Panaji (p121)

Child-friendly Boutique Hotels

Siolim House (p78)
Yab Yum, Mandrem (p74)
Sunbeam, Assagao (p84)
Vivenda dos Palhacos (p165)

Strolling Goa's sands today, you'll see more visiting children cavorting here than ever before. Goa's beaches are great for entertaining its younger travellers, with paddling opportunities and rock pools galore, while a host of inland activities await the intrepid young explorer.

Though India's sensory overload may at first prove overwhelming for younger kids, the colours, scents, sights and sounds of Goa more than compensate by setting young imaginations ablaze. Take a bath with an elephant at a spice farm near Ponda, ride a merry-go-round at a fair set up on a local cricket field, and dig your heels into white-sand beaches while your toddlers construct a sand-temple.

A Warm Welcome

Goa is probably the most family-friendly state in a family-friendly country. Hotels will almost always come up with an extra bed or two, restaurants with a familiar meal, and beach shacks might have borrowable buckets and spades. Bus conductors will produce boiled sweets and clucking old ladies will pinch rosy toddler cheeks.

But while all this is fabulous for outgoing children, it may prove tiring for those of a more retiring disposition. You might find that, while sitting on that glorious patch of sand, you're not only fending off trinket sellers, but also a constant stream of people wishing to photograph or interact with your increasingly reluctant children.

WHAT TO PACK

Items such as disposable nappies are available in almost every Goan town, but come at quite a premium and with the additional dilemma of how to dispose of them. Most contain so much plastic that they can produce a wicked heat rash. The enormous environmental damage caused by such waste leads some parents to do what the locals do: switch to cloth nappies, and have them washed by a local laundry service.

Wet wipes are also available, but are expensive in Goa: a small pack can cost between ₹100 and ₹200, so bring as much of this crucial product as you can from home.

Formula milk is available in both local and Nestlé brands, and is carried by most chemists and supermarkets, but if you require a specific brand, bring along enough for the whole trip. Jars of baby food are few and far between outside the foreigner-slanted supermarkets in Anjuna and Candolim.

For older and younger children alike, don't forget to bring swimming shoes, a hat and sunscreen, as well as mosquito repellent and a heat rash cream (natural Calendula cream works well for both heat and nappy rash). Travelling with a baby, it can make sense to pack the lightest possible travel cot you can find, since hotel cots may prove precarious.

The key, then, is to stay even more alert than usual to your children's needs, and to remain firm in fulfilling them. Don't be afraid to refuse those photo opportunities when they become a bit of a burden, or politely fend off unwanted attention. It's also worth remembering, even during your most stared-at moments, that the attention your children receive is almost always good natured; kids are the centre of life in many Indian households, and yours will be treated just the same.

Eating

Feeding even the fussiest children in Goa is easy as pie. With standard traveller menus available at almost every beach, you'll find toast, pancakes, pizzas, porridge, spaghetti and falafel, for when only the familiar will do.

Local foods, meanwhile, will appeal to the slightly more adventurous child: few can resist the finger-food fun of a vast South Indian dosa (a paper-thin lentil-flour pancake), while mango or banana lassis (yoghurt drinks) make for a good vitamin and calcium hit. At dinnertime, paneer (unfermented cheese) dishes, mild dhals (soupy lentil curries), buttered naans (tandoori breads), pilaus (rice dishes) and Tibetan *momos* (steamed or fried dumplings) are all firm favourites.

Most salads these days are washed in filtered or bottled water, but it pays to check, and avoid ice in drinks and shakes if in doubt.

While on the road, easy snacks include little 'cardamom' bananas, *puri* (puffy dough

pockets) and packaged biscuits (Parle G brand are a perennial hit). And for parents of vegetarian children, Goa is a breath of fresh air, with choices often more abundant than back home.

Health

Throughout Goa, it is almost always easy to track down a doctor at short notice (most hotels will be able to recommend one), and prescriptions are quickly and cheaply filled over the counter at numerous pharmacies.

Heat rash is common – if not inevitable – in Goa's warmer months, while conjunctivitis spreads like wildfire in October, and impetigo is rather rampant in April. All you can do is treat these things topically, and pop to a local doctor if you're concerned. Diarrhoea can be serious in young children; rehydration is essential, and seek medical help if persistent or accompanied by fever.

For more on general health, see p225.

Kindergartens

There are several kindergartens throughout Goa aimed at long-staying foreigners; some also accept children on a short-term basis. Most change with the seasons – check out noticeboards or ask other parents with children for leads – but two schools in south Goa have been reliably operating for some years: **Vrindhavan Kindergarten, Palolem** (www.vrindhavan-kindergarten.de) and **Vidya Aranya School, Palolem** (www.vidyaaranya.com).

regions at a glance

Though the state is small and distances aren't immense, Goa's regions are a world apart from each other.

North Goa's buzzing resorts offer plenty of night life, shopping and fine dining, while strips of silent sands lie undisturbed in between. The north also contains a couple of the state's most famous traveller enclaves – Anjuna and Arambol – perennially popular with long-staying visitors.

South Goa is more tranquil, with a largely laid-back traveller vibe and fewer activities on offer, though options grow annually in busy little Palolem.

Central Goa, meanwhile, is the place to glimpse history, architecture and authentic Goan life away from the chaos and charms of the coastal strip.

Mumbai (Bombay)

Food ✓✓✓
Architecture ✓✓✓
Shopping ✓✓✓

Food
Indulge all your foodie fantasies in this city of superlative cuisines from across India. Munch Mughlai kebabs and Punjabi banquets, but leave space for Mumbai's delectable street-food snacks.

Architecture
Mumbai's colonial-era architecture is some of the country's finest, with iconic sights such as the Gateway of India, High Court, Taj Mahal Palace Hotel, Mumbai and Chhatrapati Shivaji Terminus (Victoria Terminus) dominating the skyline.

Shopping
Teeming bazaars, high fashion from Indian designers, quality handicrafts, antiques and bric-a-brac in abundance make Mumbai a fabulous place to throw caution to your luggage allowance. Mutton St, is the place to discern a real antique from a fake, while Crawford Market is the spot to mingle with grocery-shopping Mumbaikers.

p38

Anjuna & North Goa

Entertainment ✓✓✓
Luxury ✓✓✓
Beaches ✓✓✓

Panaji & Central Goa

History ✓✓✓
Wildlife ✓✓
Temples ✓✓

Palolem & South Goa

Beaches ✓✓✓
Yoga ✓✓✓
Exploration ✓✓✓

Entertainment
North Goa is where it's at in terms of after-hours entertainment. Calangute, Baga, Anjuna and Candolim offer live-music joints, bars ranging from spit-and-sawdust to mixology central, and even the occasional nightclub.

Luxury
With a bumper crop of boutique hotels, North Goa offers the state's best luxury stays. Bed down in a converted fortress, a chic village bungalow or a minimalist beachside haven; many also offer spa services for additional pampering after a hard day's lounging.

Beaches
From the bustling beaches of Baga to the empty stretches at Mandrem, there's a beach to fit every inclination in North Goa. Arambol, Vagator and Anjuna's beaches are popular with backpackers; Calangute and Sinquerim are the places to head for water sports.

p70

History
Picturesque Portuguese-era bungalows abound in the historic villages of Central Goa, and in the slow-paced state capital, Panaji. Not far away, Old Goa's glorious cathedrals once earned it the moniker 'Rome of the East'.

Wildlife
Dr Salim Ali Bird Sanctuary, on lovely Chorao Island, makes for a leisurely spot of birdwatching beside the river. Further afield are Bondla and Bhagwan Mahavir Wildlife Sanctuaries, while Backwoods Camp is an ornithologist's dream.

Temples
Temples abound around Ponda, where the Shri Manguesh and Shri Laxmi Narasimha temples are especially worth a visit. Further east, Tambdi Surla is home to an interesting little 12th-century temple, which has survived centuries of conquerors and temple demolitions.

p110

Beaches
Excellent strips of quiet beach can be found throughout South Goa; Palolem's glorious crescent serves a lively traveller community, while a little further north, five-star hotels back onto beautiful undeveloped tracts of white, palm-fringed sands.

Yoga
Yoga, ayurveda and massage aplenty are on offer in Palolem, Patnem and Agonda, along with a whole host of other seasonally changing spiritual pursuits. Visitors should check local notice boards to find the yogi, guru or t'ai chi master of their choice.

Exploration
Getting off the beaten track is easy in South Goa, where tiny coastal villages invite exploration by scooter, motorbike or rental car. For adventurous souls, the trip out to the Usgalimal rock carvings makes for the ultimate Goan road less travelled.

p150

> **Every listing is recommended by our authors, and their favourite places are listed first**

> **Look out for these icons:**

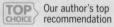 Our author's top recommendation

 A green or sustainable option

 No payment required

On the Road

MUMBAI (BOMBAY) . .38
GREATER MUMBAI. 68
Elephanta Island. 68

**ANJUNA &
NORTH GOA 70**
Arambol (Harmal) 71
Mandrem 74
Aswem 76
Morjim 78
Siolim 78
Vagator & Chapora 79
Mapusa 84
Anjuna 87
Calangute & Baga 92
Candolim, Sinquerim
& Fort Aguada. 99
Nerul (Coco) Beach 106
Along the Mandovi
River 106

**PANAJI &
CENTRAL GOA 110**
Panaji 111
West of Panaji. 124
Panaji to Old Goa 125
Old Goa 126
Divar Island. 133
Goa Velha. 134
Talaulim 135
Pilar 135
Ponda. 135
Around Ponda. 137
Bondla Wildlife
Sanctuary 140

Molem & Around 141
Tambdi Surla. 142
Further Afield 143
Hampi. 143
Around Hampi. 148
Hospet 149

**PALOLEM &
SOUTH GOA 150**
Margao. 151
Around Margao. 158
Vasco da Gama. 161
Around Vasco
da Gama 162
Bogmalo to
Betalbatim. 162
Colva. 166
Benaulim 169
Varca, Cavelossim &
Mobor. 171
Assolna to Agonda. 174
Chaudi 177
Palolem 177
Colomb. 181
Patnem. 182
Rajbag 183
Cotigao Wildlife
Sanctuary 183
Galgibag. 183
Polem 184
Further Afield 184
Gokarna 184
Jog Falls. 186

Mumbai (Bombay)

Includes »

Sights..............................40
Tours 51
Sleeping.........................51
Eating.............................56
Drinking 60
Entertainment 61
Shopping.........................63
Elephanta Island.............68

Best Places to Eat

» Samrat (p58)

» Peshawri (p59)

» Bademiya (p56)

» Trishna (p57)

» Culture Curry (p59)

Best Places to Stay

» Taj Mahal Palace, Mumbai (p51)

» Iskcon (p54)

» YWCA (p52)

» Hotel Moti (p52)

» Juhu Residency (p55)

Why Go?

Mumbai is a beautiful mess, full of dreamers and hard-labourers, actors and gangsters, stray dogs and exotic birds, artists and servants, fisherfolk and *crorepatis* (millionaires), and lots more. Its crumbling architecture in various states of technicolour dilapidation is a reminder that Mumbai once dreamt even bigger, leaving a bricks-and-mortar museum amid its chaotic streets.

Today Mumbai is home to a famously prolific film industry, one of Asia's biggest slums and the largest tropical forest in an urban zone. It's India's financial powerhouse, fashion epicentre and a pulse point of religious tension. Between the fine dining and frenetic streets, the urban grit and suburban glamour, the madness and the mayhem, there's a cinematic cityscape set to a playful and addictive raga – a complex soundtrack that dances to the beat of its own *desi* drum.

When to Go

Mumbai's most comfortable period is between November and March, when temperatures are manageable for outdoor sightseeing and balmy breezes blow in from the bay. By March, temperatures are rising, and by May, in anticipation of the monsoon, it's hot, hot, hot. From June onward, with the coming of the rains, accommodation prices drop, and in August to September, Mumbai experiences its biggest and most exciting festival, Ganesh Chaturthi; it's a great time to be in town, despite the downpours.

A Mouthful of Mumbai

Mumbai is a city shaped by flavours from all over India and the world. Throw yourself into the culinary kaleidoscope by sampling Parsi *dhansak* (meat with curried lentils and rice), Gujarati or Keralan thalis ('all you can eat' meals), Mughlai kebabs, Goan vindalho and Mangalorean seafood. And don't forget, if you see Bombay duck on a menu, it's actually *bombil* fish, dried in the sun and deep-fried.

Streetwise, don't miss Mumbai's famous beach *bhelpuri*, readily available at Girgaum Chowpatty, a flavour somersault of crisp-fried thin rounds of dough mixed with puffed rice, lentils, lemon juice, onions, herbs, chilli and tamarind chutney piled high on takeaway plates. Other street stalls offering rice plates, samosas, *pav bhaji* (spiced vegetables and bread) and *vada pav* (deep-fried spiced lentil-ball sandwich) do a brisk trade around the city.

DON'T MISS

For many, a visit to cosmopolitan Mumbai is all about dining, nightlife and shopping, but the city offers far more than nocturnal amusement and retail therapy. Nowhere is this more evident than in the spectacular maze of Gothic, Victorian, Indo-Saracenic and art deco architecture, remnants of the British colonial era and countless years of European influence. **Chhatrapati Shivaji Terminus (Victoria Terminus)**, **High Court**, **University of Mumbai**, **Taj Mahal Palace, Mumbai** and the **Gateway of India** are just the most prominent – little architectural jewels dot the urban quagmire throughout the metropolis and stumbling upon them is one of Mumbai's great joys.

Top Mumbai Festivals

» Elephanta Festival (February, Elephanta Island, p16) Classical music and dance on Elephanta Island

» Kala Ghoda Festival (February, citywide, p16) Two weeks of art performances and exhibitions

» Nariyal Poornima (August, Colaba, p18) Commemorates the beginning of the fishing season

» Ganesh Chaturthi (August/September, citywide, p18) Mumbai's biggest event celebrates all things Ganesh

MAIN POINTS OF ENTRY

Most travellers arrive at Mumbai's Chhatrapati Shivaji International Airport, Mumbai Central train station (BCT) or Chhatrapati Shivaji Terminus (CST; Victoria Terminus).

Fast Facts

» Population: 16.4 million
» Area: 444 sq km
» Area code: ✆022
» Languages: Marathi, Hindi, Gujarati, English
» Sleeping prices: **$** under ₹1000, **$$** ₹1000 to ₹4000, **$$$** above ₹4000

Top Tips

Many international flights arrive after midnight. Save yourself some moonlit hassle by carrying detailed landmark directions for your hotel – many airport taxi drivers don't speak English and can dwindle precious sleep time hunting it down.

Eicher City Map Mumbai (₹250) is an excellent street atlas, worth picking up if you'll be spending some time here.

Resources

» Maharashtra Tourism Development Corporation (www.maharashtratourism. gov.in) is the official tourism site.

History

In 1996, the city of Bombay officially became Mumbai. The original Marathi name is derived from the goddess Mumba, who was worshipped by the early Koli residents, whose fisherfolk have inhabited the seven islands that form Mumbai since the 2nd century BC. Amazingly, remnants of this culture remain huddled along the city shoreline today, particularly at the Sassoon Dock (see the box p45).

A succession of Hindu dynasties held sway over the islands from the 6th century AD until the Muslim Sultans of Gujarat annexed the area in the 14th century, eventually ceding it to Portugal in 1534. The only memorable contribution the Portuguese made to the area was christening it Bom Bahai, before throwing the islands in with the dowry of Catherine of Braganza when she married England's Charles II in 1661. The British government took possession of the islands in 1665, but three years later leased them to the East India Company for the grand annual sum of UK£10.

By then known as Bombay, the area flourished as a trading port. Its fort was completed in the 1720s, and a century later ambitious land reclamation projects joined the islands into today's single landmass. In 1864, massive building works transformed the city in grand colonial style, and when Bombay became the principal supplier of cotton to Britain during the American Civil War, the population soared, trade boomed, and money flooded in.

A major player in the Independence movement, Bombay hosted the first Indian National Congress in 1885, and the Quit India campaign was launched here in 1942 by Mahatma Gandhi. After Independence, the city became capital of the Bombay presidency, but in 1960 Maharashtra and Gujarat were divided along linguistic lines – and Bombay became the capital of Maharashtra.

The rise of the pro-Maratha regionalist movement, however, spearheaded by the Shiv Sena (Hindu Party; literally 'Shivaji's Army'), shattered the city's multicultural mien by actively discriminating against Muslims and non-Maharashtrians. The Shiv Sena won power in the city's municipal elections in 1985. Communalist tensions increased and the city took a battering when nearly 800 people died in riots in December 1992.

The riots were followed by a dozen bombings on 12 March 1993, which killed more than 300 people. The July 2006 train bombings, which killed more than 200 people, and November 2008's coordinated attacks on 10 of the city's landmarks, which lasted three days and killed 173 people, are reminders that tensions are never far from the surface.

India's '26/11' – as the 2008 attacks have come to be known – was a wake-up call for Mumbai. Security is now intense at prominent landmarks, hotels, and financial and government buildings. Some whole streets have been sealed off to traffic, providing impromptu cricket pitches for the city's youth. But Mumbai soldiers on, content to up the ante of inconvenience to maintain the Mumbaikar spirit, a defiant Marathi manner that still steadies India's commercial and financial powerhouse.

⊙ Sights

Mumbai, the capital of Maharashtra, is an island connected by bridges to the mainland. The city's (off-limits) naval docks dominate the island's eastern seaboard. Its commercial and cultural centre is at the southern, claw-shaped end of the island known as South Mumbai. The southernmost peninsula is Colaba, traditionally the travellers' nerve centre; directly north of Colaba is the busy commercial area known as Fort, where the old British fort once stood.

Though just as essential a part of the city as South Mumbai, the area north of here is collectively known as 'the suburbs'. The airport and many of Mumbai's best restaurants, shopping and nightspots are here, particularly in upmarket Bandra and Juhu.

The opening of the cable-stayed Bandra-Worli Sea Link in 2009 cut travel time between the two areas from one hour to just seven minutes, making these suburbs very easily accessible.

HAVE YOUR SAY

Found a fantastic restaurant that you're longing to share with the world? Disagree with our recommendations? Or just want to talk about your most recent trip?

Whatever your reason, head to lonelyplanet.com, where you can post a review, ask or answer a question on the Thorntree forum, comment on a blog, or share your photos and tips on Groups. Or you can simply spend time chatting with like-minded travellers. So go on, have your say.

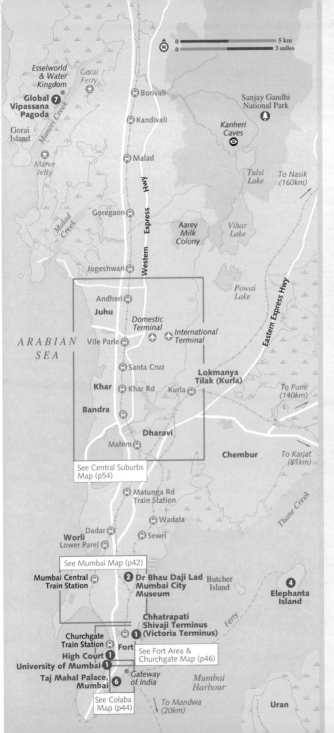

Mumbai Highlights

1 Marvel at the magnificence of Mumbai's colonial-era architecture: **Chhatrapati Shivaji Terminus** (p47), **University of Mumbai** (p48) and **High Court** (p47)

2 Ogle the Renaissance-revival interiors of the **Dr Bhau Daji Lad Mumbai City Museum** (p49)

3 Dine like a Maharaja at one of India's best **restaurants** (p56)

4 Behold the commanding triple-headed Shiva at **Elephanta Island** (p68)

5 Get lost amid the clutter in Mumbai's ancient **bazaars** (p63)

6 Sleep in one of the world's iconic hotels, the **Taj Mahal Palace, Mumbai** (p51)

7 Pay serene respects to an astonishing feat of spiritually fuelled engineering at the **Global Vipassana Pagoda** (p50)

Mumbai

0   1 km
0   0.5 miles

ARABIAN SEA

Haji Ali's Mosque

Mahalaxmi Temple

To Nehru Centre (200m);

Lala Lajpat Rai Rd

To Aer (700m); Four Seasons (700m); Bluefrog (1km); Zenzi Mills (1km)

Mahalaxmi Racecourse

Willingdon Sports Club Golf Course

Mahalaxmi Train Station

Mahalaxmi Dhobi Ghat

Dr Bhau Daji Lad Mumbai City Museum

Patanwala Marg

Victoria Gardens (Veermata Jijabai Bhonsle Udyan)

Reay Rd

Reay Rd Train Station

BYCULLA

Victoria Rd

S Belwant singh Rd

Jail Rd

Sandhurst Train Station

Byculla Train Station

J Jijibhoy Rd

Bapurao Jagtap Marg

Maulana Azad Rd

Clare Rd

Sir JJ Rd

Mutton St

Maulana Azad Rd

Dhabu St

17

12

Morland Rd

J Boman Betram Marg

Foras Rd

Grant Rd

Sardar V Patel Rd

26

28

Mumbai Central Train Station

Falkland Rd

Tardeo Rd

25

Dr D Bhadkamkar Rd (Lamington Rd)

OPERA HOUSE

Grant Rd Train Station

Vatsalabai Desai Chowk

4

22

10

8

G Deshmukh Rd (Peddar Rd)

23

16

14

21

A Kranti Marg

Augus Kranti Maidan

Labunum Rd

Sitaram Patkar Rd

1

Kemp's Corner

18

20

24

Tata Garden

Hanging Gardens

Priyadarshini Park

MUMBAI (BOMBAY)

Mumbai

◎ Top Sights

Dr Bhau Daji Lad Mumbai City
 Museum F1
Haji Ali's Mosque..B1
Kotachiwadi...D5
Mahalaxmi Dhobi Ghat............................E1

◎ Sights

1 Mani Bhavan...C4
2 St Teresa's Church................................D5

✕ Eating

3 Badshah Snacks & Drinks F6
Café Moshe..................................(see 14)
4 Cafe Noorani C2
5 Cream Centre...C5
6 New Kulfi Centre....................................C5
Olive Bar & Kitchen......................(see 8)
7 Rajdhani E6
8 Tote on the Turf D1

🍸 Drinking

9 First Floor...F6
10 Haji Ali Juice Centre C1

🛍 Shopping

11 Bhuleshwar Market E5
Biba..(see 14)
12 Chor Bazaar...E4
13 Crawford Market....................................F6
14 Crossword...B3
15 Mangaldas Market................................E6
16 Mélange..B3
17 Mini Market/Bollywood Bazaar.........E4
18 Shrujan...B2
19 Zaveri Bazaar E6

ℹ Information

20 Breach Candy Hospital B2
21 Italian Consulate B3
22 Japanese Consulate.............................C2
23 South African Consulate.....................B3
24 US Consulate..B3

ℹ Transport

25 Allibhai Premji Tyrewalla D4
26 Mumbai Central Bus Terminal...........D3
National CTC ....(see 26)
27 Private Bus Agents F6
28 Private Long-Distance Bus
 Stand & Ticket Agents D3

Colaba

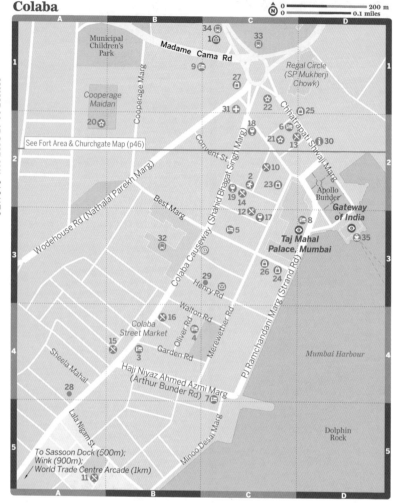

COLABA

Sprawling down the city's southernmost peninsula, Colaba is a bustling district of street stalls, markets, bars and budget to midrange lodgings. For mapped locations of the following sights, see Map p44.

TOP CHOICE **Taj Mahal Palace, Mumbai** LANDMARK
This iconic hotel is a fairy-tale blend of Islamic and Renaissance styles jostling for prime position among Mumbai's famous landmarks. Facing the harbour, it was built in 1903 by Parsi industrialist JN Tata, supposedly after he was refused entry to one of the European

hotels on account of being 'a native'. See p51, for information on bedding down here.

Gateway of India   MONUMENT
This bold basalt arch faces out to Mumbai Harbour from the tip of Apollo Bunder, an important embarkation pier in the 19th century. Derived from the Islamic styles of 16th-century Gujarat, it was built to commemorate the 1911 royal visit of King George V and was finally completed in 1924, long after he'd gone home. Britain then used it, just 24 years later, to parade off its last regiment as India marched towards Independence. These days,

Colaba

◎ Top Sights
Gateway of India D3
Taj Mahal Palace, Mumbai.................... D3

◎ Sights
1 National Gallery of Modern
Art.. C1

◎ Activities, Courses & Tours
2 Reality Tours & Travel............................ C2

◎ Sleeping
3 Ascot Hotel..B4
4 Bentley's Hotel..B4
5 Hotel Moti C3
6 Hotel Suba Palace C2
7 Sea Shore Hotel...................................... C4
8 Taj Mahal Palace, Mumbai.................... D3
9 YWCA B1

◎ Eating
10 Bademiya... C2
Cafe Moshe.................................... (see 13)
11 Colaba Market...A5
12 Indigo.. C3
13 Indigo Delicatessen C2
14 New Laxmi Villas..................................... C2
Saharkari Bhandar
Supermarket........................... (see 31)
15 Theobroma..B4
16 Wich Latte...B4

◎ Drinking
17 Busaba.. C3
18 Cafe Mondegar.. C2
19 Leopold Cafe.. C2

◎ Entertainment
20 Cooperage Football Ground A2
21 Polly Esther's.. C2
22 Regal C1

◎ Shopping
23 Antique & Curio Shops C2
24 Bombay Electric....................................... C3
25 Central Cottage Industries
Emporium... D1
26 Good Earth C3
27 Phillips.. C1

◎ Information
28 Akbar Travels...A4
29 Magnum International Travel &
Tours... C3
30 MTDC Booth D2
31 Sahakari Bhandar Chemist.................... C1
Thomas Cook................................(see 15)

◎ Transport
32 BEST Bus Depot.......................................B3
33 BEST Bus Stand C1
34 BEST Bus Stand C1
35 Launches to Elephanta Island
& Mandwa D3

MUMBAI (BOMBAY) SIGHTS

it's a favourite gathering spot for locals and a top location for people-watching. Boats depart from its wharfs for Elephanta Island (see Elephanta Island, p68).

KALA GHODA
Translated as 'Black Horse', the area between Colaba and Fort contains Mumbai's main galleries and museums alongside a wealth of colonial-era buildings.

TOP CHOICE **Chhatrapati Shivaji Maharaj Vastu Sangrahalaya (Prince of Wales Museum)** MUSEUM
(Map p46; www.themuseummumbai.com; K Dubash Marg; child/Indian/foreigner ₹5/30/300; ☉10.15am-6pm Tue-Sun) Mumbai's biggest and best museum, this domed behemoth displays a mix of dusty exhibits from all over India. Opened in 1923, its flamboyant Indo-Saracenic style was designed by

George Wittet – who also designed the Gateway of India. The museum recently underwent a ₹12 million renovation, which introduced a new miniature-painting gallery and another dedicated to Vishnu. Elsewhere, the vast collection includes Hindu and Buddhist sculpture, terracotta

DON'T MISS

SASSOON DOCK

Early risers should catch the intense and pungent activity at dawn (around 5am) when colourfully clad **Koli fisherfolk** sort the catch unloaded from fishing boats at the Sassoon Dock quay (off map p44). The fish drying in the sun are *bombil,* those used in the dish Bombay duck (which isn't a duck at all). Note that photography is forbidden.

Fort Area & Churchgate

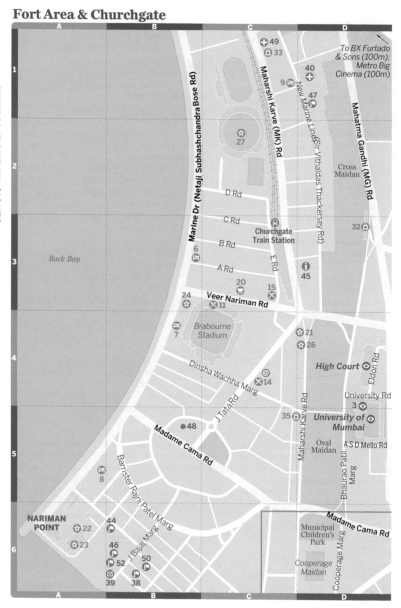

figurines from the Indus Valley, porcelain, and some particularly vicious weaponry.

Keneseth Eliyahoo Synagogue SYNAGOGUE
(Map p46; www.jacobsassoon.org; Dr VB Gandhi Marg; ☺9am-6pm) Built in 1884, this impossibly sky-blue synagogue still functions and is tenderly maintained by the city's dwindling Jewish community (and protected to Baghdad Green Zone levels by Mumbai's finest).

MUMBAI (BOMBAY) SIGHTS

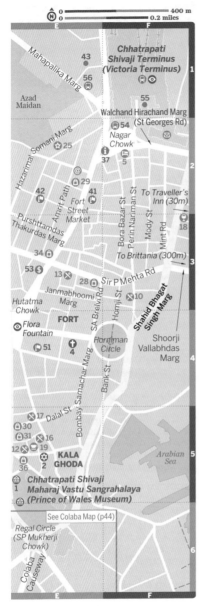

STREET SIGN DECIPHERING

Street numbers on buildings are almost nonexistent in Mumbai, and some street signs come in English, some in Hindi, some in both, and frequently not at all. Signs outside legitimate businesses, however, often include the street address; look for these to orientate yourself when street signs fail you.

FREE **Jehangir Art Gallery**   ART GALLERY
(Map p46; 161B MG Rd; ☉11am-7pm) Hosts interesting shows by local artists; most works are for sale. Rows of hopeful artists often display their work on the pavement outside.

FORT

Lined up and vying for your attention, many of Mumbai's majestic Victorian buildings pose on the edge of Oval Maidan. This land, and the Cross and Azad Maidans immediately to the north, was on the oceanfront in those days, and this series of grandiose structures faced west directly out to the Arabian Sea.

For mapped locations of the following sights, see Map p46.

TOP CHOICE **Chhatrapati Shivaji Terminus**
(Victoria Terminus)   HISTORICAL BUILDING
Imposing, exuberant and overflowing with people, this is the city's most extravagant Gothic building, the beating heart of its railway network, and an aphorism for colonial India. As historian Christopher London put it, 'the Victoria Terminus is to the British Raj what the Taj Mahal is to the Mughal empire'. It's a meringue of Victorian, Hindu and Islamic styles whipped into an imposing Dalíesque structure of buttresses, domes, turrets, spires and stained-glass windows. Today it's the busiest train station in Asia. Officially renamed Chhatrapati Shivaji Terminus (CST) in 1998, it's still better known locally as VT.

High Court   HISTORICAL BUILDING
(Eldon Rd) A hive of daily activity, packed with judges, barristers and other cogs in the Indian justice system, the High Court is an elegant 1848 neo-Gothic building. The design was inspired by a German castle and was intended to dispel any doubts about the authority of the justice dispensed inside, though local stone carvers presumably saw

National Gallery of Modern Art   ART GALLERY
(Map p44; MG Rd; Indian/foreigner ₹10/150; ☉11am-6pm Tue-Sun) Has a bright, and modern space showcasing changing exhibitions by Indian and international artists.

Fort Area & Churchgate

◎ **Top Sights**

Chhatrapati Shivaji Maharaj
Vastu Sangrahalaya
(Prince of Wales Museum)................E5
Chhatrapati Shivaji Terminus
(Victoria Terminus)............................F1
High Court...D4
University of Mumbai............................D5

◎ **Sights**

1 Jehangir Art Gallery...........................E5
2 Keneseth Eliyahoo Synagogue E5
3 Rajabai Clock Tower............................D4
4 St Thomas' Cathedral..........................E4

◎ **Sleeping**

5 Hotel City Palace.................................F2
6 InterContinental..................................B3
7 Sea Green Hotel...................................B4
Sea Green South Hotel ....(see 7)
8 Trident Nariman Point A5
9 West End Hotel....................................C1

◎ **Eating**

210°C..(see 14)

Café Moshe ....(see 31)
10 Five Spice F3
11 K Ruston C3
12 Khyber E5
Koh ....(see 6)
13 Mahesh Lunch Home............................E3
Relish...(see 14)
14 Samrat..C4
15 Suryodaya...C3
16 Trishna..E5
17 Wich Latte E5

◎ **Drinking**

18 Café Universal.....................................F3
Cha Bar.......................................(see 35)
Dome...(see 6)
19 Kala Ghoda Café..................................E5
20 Mocha Bar...C3
Samovar Café..............................(see 1)

◎ **Entertainment**

21 Eros D4
22 National Centre for the
Performing Arts (NCPA) A6
23 NCPA Box Office A6

things differently: they carved a one-eyed monkey fiddling with the scales of justice on one pillar. You are permitted (and it is highly recommended) to walk around inside the building and check out the pandemonium and pageantry of public cases that are in progress – just walk right in! You'll have to surrender your camera to the guards, then make your way through the maze-like building to the original building's courtyard opposite Court 6.

University of Mumbai (Bombay University) HISTORICAL BUILDING
Looking like a 15th-century French-Gothic masterpiece plopped incongruously among Mumbai's palm trees, this university on Bhaurao Patil Marg was designed by Gilbert Scott of London's St Pancras Station fame. There is an exquisite **University Library** and **Convocation Hall,** as well as an 80m-high **Rajabai Clock Tower,** decorated with detailed carvings, but since the 2008 terror attacks on Mumbai, the public is no longer allowed inside the grounds. The architecture is thus best admired by strolling along Bhaurao Patil Marg as trees obscure much of the splendour when viewed from the Oval Maidan.

St Thomas' Cathedral CHURCH
(Veer Nariman Rd; ◷6.30am-6pm) Recently restored to its former glory, this charming cathedral is the oldest English building standing in Mumbai (construction began in 1672, though it remained unfinished until 1718). The cathedral is a mixture of Byzantine and colonial-era architecture, and its airy, whitewashed interior is full of exhibitionist colonial memorials.

GIRGUAM CHOWPATTY AREA

For mapped locations of the following sights, see Map p42.

TOP CHOICE **Marine Drive & Girguam Chowpatty** BEACH
Built on land reclaimed from Back Bay in 1920, Marine Drive (Netaji Subhashchandra Bose Rd) arcs along the shore of the Arabian Sea from Nariman Point past Girguam Chowpatty (where it's known as Chowpatty Seaface) and continues to the foot of Malabar Hill. Lined with flaking art deco apartments, it's one of Mumbai's most popular promenades and sunset-watching spots. Its twinkling night-time lights earned it the nickname 'the Queen's Necklace'.

24 Not Just Jazz By The Bay B3
25 Sterling...E2
26 Valhalla.. D4
27 Wankhede Stadium............................... C2

⊗ **Shopping**
28 Bombay Store E3
29 Chimanlals...E2
30 Cotton Cottage E5
31 Fabindia...E5
32 Fashion Street Market D3
33 Kala Niketan C1
34 Khadi & Village Industries
     Emporium...E3
35 Oxford Bookstore C5
36 Rhythm House E5
   Standard Supply Co. ....(see 5)

ⓘ **Information**
37 Akbar Travels F2
38 Australian Consulate..............................B6
39 Blue Dart/DHL..B6
40 Bombay Hospital D1
41 Canadian Consulate E2
42 Dutch Consulate E2

43 Foreigners' Regional
     Registration Office (FRRO)................E1
44 French Consulate B6
   German Consulate ....(see 44)
45 Government of India Tourist
     Office...D3
46 Israel Consulate.....................................B6
47 Maldives Consulate................................D1
48 MTDC Reservation Office......................B5
49 Royal Chemists.......................................C1
50 Singaporean Consulate...........................B6
51 Sri Lankan Consulate..............................E4
   Swiss Consulate ....(see 50)
52 Thai Consulate.......................................B6
53 Thomas Cook..E3

ⓘ **Transport**
54 Bus Stand...F2
55 Central Railways Reservation
     Centre...F1
56 Chandni Travels/Private Buses
     to Goa E1
   Western Railways Reservation
     Centre.......................................(see 45)

Girguam Chowpatty (often referred to as 'Chowpatty Beach' in English, though this means 'Beach Beach' and often confuses locals) remains a favourite evening spot for courting couples, families, political rallies and anyone out to enjoy what passes for fresh air. Eating an evening-time *bhelpuri* at the throng of stalls found here is an essential part of the Mumbai experience. Forget about taking a dip: the water is toxic.

FREE **Mani Bhavan**   MUSEUM
(☎23805864; www.gandhi-manibhavan.org; 19 Laburnum Rd; ⊙9.30am-6pm) As poignant as it is tiny, this museum is housed in the building where Mahatma Gandhi stayed during visits to Bombay from 1917 to 1934. It showcases the room where the leader formulated his philosophy of satyagraha (nonviolent protest) and launched the 1932 Civil Disobedience campaign that led to the end of British rule. Exhibitions include a photographic record of his life, along with original documents, such as letters he wrote to Adolf Hitler and Franklin D Roosevelt. Nearby, August Kranti Maidan is where the campaign to persuade the British to 'Quit India' was launched in 1942.

MALABAR HILL
Mumbai's most exclusive neighbourhood of private palaces, Malabar Hill (Map p42) stands at the northern promontory of Back Bay and signifies the top rung for the city's social and economic climbers.

Surprisingly, one of Mumbai's most sacred and tranquil oases lies concealed among apartment blocks at its southern tip. Banganga Tank (off Map p42) is a precinct of serene temples, bathing pilgrims, meandering, traffic-free streets and picturesque old *dharamsalas* (pilgrims' rest houses). According to legend, the wooden pole at the centre of the tank is the actual centre of the earth, and Lord Ram created the tank by piercing the earth with his arrow. The tank hosts an annual music festival; see p16.

For great views of Girgaum Chowpatty and Marine Drive, visit little Kamala Nehru Park (Map p42).

BYCULLA
TOP Dr Bhau Daji Lad Mumbai City
CHOICE
Museum   MUSEUM
(Map p42; Dr Babasaheb Ambedkar Rd; Indian/foreigner ₹10/100; ⊙10am-5.30pm Thu-Tue) Jijamata Udyan – aka Veermata Jijabai

Bhonsle Udyan and formerly named Victoria Gardens – is a lush and sprawling 19th-century garden and zoo. It's home to this gorgeous museum, originally built in Renaissance revival style in 1872 as the Victoria & Albert Museum. Its 3500-plus objects centre on Mumbai's history, all set against simply stellar decor. The zoo, however, is far less charming, unless you've a penchant for iron bars.

MAHALAXMI TO WORLI

For mapped locations of the following sights, see Map p42.

TOP CHOICE Haji Ali's Mosque   MOSQUE

Floating like a mirage off the coast is this exquisite Indo-Islamic shrine. Built in the 19th century on the site of a 15th-century structure, it contains the tomb of the Muslim saint Haji; legend has it that Haji Ali died while on a pilgrimage to Mecca and his casket miraculously floated back to this spot. A long causeway reaches into the Arabian Sea, providing access to the mosque. Thousands of pilgrims, especially on Thursdays and Fridays, cross it to make their visit, many donating to the beggars who line the way. At high tide, water covers the causeway and the mosque becomes an island.

Mahalaxmi Dhobi Ghat   LANDMARK

If you've ever had your smalls laundered in Mumbai, chances are they have already made intimate acquaintance with this 140-year-old dhobi ghat (clothes-washing place). The whole hamlet is Mumbai's oldest and biggest human-powered washing machine: every day hundreds of people beat the dirt out of tonnes of soiled Mumbai clothes and sheets in 1026 open-air troughs. The best view is from the bridge across the railway tracks near Mahalaxmi train station.

GORAI ISLAND

FREE Global Vipassana Pagoda   LANDMARK

(www.globalpagoda.org; Near Esselworld, Gorai Creek; ⊙9am-6pm) Rising up from polluted Gorai Creek and the lush but noisy grounds of the Esselworld and Water Kingdom amusement parks, this breathtaking structure is a 96m-high stupa modelled after Myanmar's Shwedagon Pagoda. Its dome, which is designed to hold 8000 meditators and houses relics of Buddha, was built entirely without supports, using an ancient technique of interlocking stones, thus snatching the record away from Bijapur's Golgumbaz for being the world's largest unsupported dome. The pagoda also

BOLLYWOOD DREAMS

Mumbai is the epicentre of India's gargantuan Hindi-language film industry. From silent beginnings with a cast of all-male actors (some in drag) in the 1913 epic *Raja Harishchandra* and the first talkie, *Lama Ara* (1931), it now churns out over 1000 films a year – more than Hollywood.

These days, Hollywood-inspired thrillers and action extravaganzas vie for moviegoers' attention alongside the more family-oriented formulae, in which all-singing, all-dancing lovers conquer the forces keeping them apart. Bollywood stars can attain near godlike status in India and star-spotting is a favourite pastime in Mumbai's posher establishments.

Extra, Extra!

Studios sometimes want Westerners as extras to add a whiff of international flair (or provocative dress) to a film. It's become so common, in fact, that 100,000 junior actors nearly went on strike in 2008 to protest, among other things, losing jobs to foreigners, who work for less.

If you're game, hang around Colaba where studio scouts will find you. A day's work pays ₹500; you'll also get lunch and snacks. Transport is usually by 2nd-class train unless there are enough tourists to justify private transport. The day can be long and hot with loads of standing around the set; not everyone has a positive experience. Complaints range from lack of food and water to intimidation when extras don't 'comply' with the director's orders. Others describe the behind-the-scenes peek as a fascinating experience. Before agreeing to anything, always ask for the scout's identification and go with your instincts.

has a museum dedicated to the life of the Buddha and his teaching, and is affiliated with teacher SN Goenka; an on-site meditation centre offers 10-day Vipassana meditation courses (also see p76). To get here, take the train from Churchgate to Borivali, then an autorickshaw (₹28) to the ferry landing, where the Esselworld ferries (return ₹35) come and go every 30 minutes. The last ferry back is 5.25pm.

Tours

Fiona Fernandez's *Ten Heritage Walks of Mumbai* (₹395) contains excellent walking tours in the city, with fascinating historical background, and can be picked up at bookstores city-wide.

The Government of India tourist office (p66) can arrange multilingual guides (per half-/full day ₹600/750). Guides using a foreign language other than English will charge at least ₹225 extra.

Reality Tours & Travel WALKING
(Map p44; ☑9820822253; www.realitytoursandtravel.com; 1/26 Akbar House, Nawroji F Rd, Colaba; short/long tours ₹500/1000) Runs socially responsible tours of Dharavi (see boxed text p52). Photography is strictly forbidden and funds from the tour plus 80% of post-tax profits go to the agency's own NGO, Reality Gives (www.realitygives.org), which runs a kindergarten and community centre in Dharavi. Enter the office through SSS Corner store on Nawroji F Rd.

Bombay Heritage Walks WALKING
(☑23690992; www.bombayheritagewalks.com) Run by two enthusiastic architects, these are some of the best tours for getting beneath the city's skin. Private two-hour guided tours are ₹1500 for up to three people, ₹500 for each additional person.

MTDC CITY TOUR
(Maharashtra Tourism Development Corporation; Map p44; ☑22841877; Apollo Bunder; 1hr tour ₹120; ☺8.30am-4pm Tue-Sun & 5.30-8pm Sat & Sun) Runs open-deck bus tours of illuminated heritage buildings on weekends at 7pm and 8.15pm. They depart from, and can be booked at, the booth near Apollo Bunder.

Cruises CRUISE
(☑22026364; ☺9am-7pm) A ferry cruise on Mumbai Harbour is a good way to escape the city and a chance to see the Gateway of

BIRDWATCHING IN MUMBAI

Mumbai offers surprisingly good birdwatching opportunities. Sanjay Gandhi National Park is popular for woodland birds, while the marshlands of industrial Sewri (pronounced *shev*-ree) swarm with birds in winter. Contact the Bombay Natural History Society (BNHS; ☑22821811; www.bnhs.org) for information on upcoming trips.

India as it was intended to be seen. Ferry rides (₹60, 30 minutes) depart from the Gateway of India.

Taj Yacht CRUISE
(up to 10 people per 2hr ₹48,000) For a luxury gad about on the water, hire this yacht; contact the Taj Mahal Palace for details.

Sleeping

Recalibrate your budget here: Mumbai has the most expensive accommodation in India, and very little of it represents true value for money. If money's no obstacle, however, there is luxury in abundance; for the best rates, book online through the hotel's own website, where you'll often be quoted far less than standard rack rates and might get lucky with a 'three nights for the price of two' offer. For all accommodation types, book well ahead over Christmas and in Diwali season. Note that somewhere between a 4% tax (more common at the budget end) and a 10% tax should be added to all prices listed here unless otherwise stated; higher-end hotels may add additional taxes and charges of up to 20% on top of that.

COLABA
For mapped locations of the following options, see Map p44.

TOP CHOICE Taj Mahal Palace, Mumbai HERITAGE HOTEL $$$
(☑66653366; www.tajhotels.com; Apollo Bunder, Colaba; s/d tower from ₹21,500/23,000, palace from ₹25,250/26,750; ❄@☎☀) Wowee. The hotel formerly known as the Taj Mahal Palace & Tower debuted its new name and new spaces on Indian Independence Day 2010, the result of a meticulous restoration following the November 2008 terrorist attacks that nearly brought this 1903 Mumbai landmark to its

DHARAVI SLUM

Mumbaikars had mixed feelings about the stereotypes in 2008's runaway hit, *Slumdog Millionaire* (released in Hindi as *Slumdog Crorepati*). But slums are very much a part of – some would say the foundation of – Mumbai city life. An astonishing 55% of Mumbai's population lives in shantytowns and slums, and the largest slum in Mumbai (and Asia, for that matter) is Dharavi. Originally inhabited by fisherfolk when the area was still creeks, swamps and islands, it became attractive to migrant workers from South Mumbai and beyond, when the swamp began to fill in as a result of natural and artificial causes. It now incorporates 1.75 sq km sandwiched between Mumbai's two major railway lines and is home to more than one million people.

But the dusty alleys and sewer-lined streets of this city-within-a-city actually form a collection of abutting settlements. Some parts of Dharavi have mixed populations, but in others, inhabitants from specific parts of India, and with specific trades, have set up homes and tiny factories. Potters from Saurashtra live in one area, Muslim tanners in another. Embroidery workers from Uttar Pradesh work alongside metalsmiths. Other workers recycle plastics alongside women drying pappadams in the searing sun. Some of these thriving industries, around 10,000 in all, export their wares, and the annual turnover of business from Dharavi is thought to top a remarkable US$665 million.

Up close, life in the slums is strikingly normal. Residents pay rent, most houses have kitchens and electricity, and building materials range from flimsy corrugated-iron shacks to permanent multistorey concrete structures. Many families have been here for generations, and some of the younger Dharavi residents even work in white-collar jobs. They choose to stay, though, in the neighbourhood in which they grew up.

Slum tourism is a polarising subject, but if you opt to visit, Reality Tours & Travel (p51) runs a fascinating tour, and pours a percentage of profits back into Dharavi, setting up community centres and schools. Some tourists opt to visit on their own – just don't take photos. To get here, take the train from Churchgate station to Mahim (₹12), exit on the west side and cross the bridge into Dharavi.

knees. But, replete with sweeping arches, staircases and domes, it has risen again, defiantly opulent. Some of its 285 rooms have been lavishly restored in gorgeous, luxurious detail, and security is at Fort Knox level – guests of some parts of the hotel can only access their own floor via elevator keys and all luggage and hand baggage is x-rayed at the entrance. All the hotel bars – including the legendary **Harbour Bar**, Mumbai's first licensed bar – and restaurants have been redesigned, rounding out a triumphant return for one of Mumbai's most enduring symbols. Note that you'll likely find substantially cheaper room rates if you book online, well in advance, and that, though pricey, the heritage rooms represent by far the best value; some of the tower rooms could still do with a very thorough overhaul.

YWCA　　　　　　　　　　　GUESTHOUSE **$$**
(☏22025053; www.ywcaic.info; 18 Madame Cama Rd; s/d/t/q incl breakfast, dinner & taxes ₹2077/3077/4359/6154; ❈@☎) The YWCA presents a frustrating dilemma: it's immaculate and surprisingly good, considering it's a cool ₹1000 cheaper than most in its class. Rates include tax, breakfast, dinner, 'bed tea', free wi-fi...*and a newspaper,* so it's the best value (and location, for that matter) within miles. But there's a trade-off here with a series of unorthodox rules, including a stubborn policy of disallowing early check-in – even if your room is ready – unless you pay extra.

Hotel Moti　　　　　　　　GUESTHOUSE **$$**
(☏22025714; hotelmotiinternational@yahoo.co.in; 10 Best Marg; d incl tax from ₹1500-4000; ❈@) This traveller's haven occupies the ground floor of a gracefully crumbling, beautiful colonial-era building. Simple rooms have whispers of charm and some nice surprises, like ornate stucco ceilings and showers. Some are huge and all have fridges filled with soft drinks and bottled water, which is charged at cost – one of the many signs of the pragmatic and friendly management.

Hotel Suba Palace　　　　　HOTEL **$$$**
(☏22020636; www.hotelsubapalace.com; Battery St; s/d with AC incl breakfast ₹4700/5400; ❈@☎)

Teetering precariously on the brink of boutique hotel, the Suba Palace oozes soothing neutral tones, from the tiny taupe shower tiles in the contemporary bathrooms to the creamy crown moulding and beige quilted headboards in the tastefully remodelled rooms. Comfy, quiet and central.

Ascot Hotel
HOTEL $$$

(✆66385566; www.ascothotel.com; 38 Garden Rd; d with AC incl breakfast from ₹6000; ❄@🖵) Marble-meets-modern at this classy hotel with hardwood hallways leading to boutiquey rooms with big headboards, bathtubs, desks, new LCD TVs, and lots of natural light and tree views.

Bentley's Hotel
HOTEL $$

(✆22841474; www.bentleyshotel.com; 17 Oliver Rd; s/d incl breakfast & tax from ₹1590/2060; ❄) Colonial charm aplenty, with old-school floor tiles and wooden furniture, though its location spread out over several buildings on Oliver St and Henry Rd might give you a certain *The Shining*-like shiver, in view of its isolation.

Sea Shore Hotel
GUESTHOUSE $

(✆22874237; 4th fl, Kamal Mansion, Arthur Bunder Rd; s/d without bathroom ₹600/950) Though a recent renovation has much improved the Sea Shore's rooms, it's very much a hit-or-miss sort of place. Some travellers love the location and the budget (in Mumbai terms, at least) prices; others find the windowless rooms a bit claustrophobic, the staff unhelpful and the cold-water showers a mite too chilly.

FORT, CHURCHGATE & MARINE DRIVE

For mapped locations of the following venues, see Map p46.

Sea Green Hotels
HOTEL $$

(s/d ₹2950/3700; ❄🖵) Seagreen Hotel (✆663 36525; www.seagreenhotel.com; 145 Marine Dr); Sea Green South Hotel (✆22821613; www.seagreen south.com; 145A Marine Dr) These identical art deco hotels have spacious but spartan air-con rooms, originally built in the 1940s to house British soldiers. Snag a sea-view room – they're the same price as the others – and you've secured top value in this price range (even with the 10% service charge).

West End Hotel
HOTEL $$$

(✆22039121; www.westendhotelmumbai.com; 45 New Marine Lines; s/d with AC from ₹4800/5700;

❄🖵) This accidentally retro hotel boasts a nonchalant, funky vibe built around old-fashioned rooms that are spacious, with baths, shag-pile rugs and modish daybeds.

Trident Nariman Point
HOTEL $$$

(Oberoi Hotel; ✆66324343; www.tridenthotels.com; Marine Dr, Nariman Point; d from ₹14,000; ❄@🖵☃) The Trident is, along with the Oberoi, part of the highly luxe Oberoi Hotel complex, which frequently comes out Mumbai's number one in traveller polls. But the Trident wins out both on price and on the smart, streamlined design of its restaurants, bars and pool area. Check for special offers on the hotel website.

InterContinental
HOTEL $$$

(✆39879999; www.intercontinental.com; 135 Marine Dr, Churchgate; r incl breakfast from US$234; ❄@🖵☃) Very sleek, with its earth tones and Buddha chic, the spacious deluxe rooms are sizeable in their own right, while the half-moon corner suites mirror the curved elegance of Marine Drive's Queen's Necklace. The stunning **Dome** bar and restaurant stylishly graces the rooftop and overlooks the sea, while **Koh** turns Thai food on its head at the lobby level.

Traveller's Inn
GUESTHOUSE $$

(✆22644685; 26 Adi Marzban Rd, Ballard Estate; dm ₹580, d with/without AC ₹1650/1250; ❄@🖵) On a quiet, tree-lined street, the tiny Traveller's Inn underwent a spiffy renovation in 2010 and now boasts bigger rooms (and narrower hallways), and new air-con units, lockers and windows, making a good budget choice that much better.

Hotel City Palace
HOTEL $$

(✆22666666; www.hotelcitypalace.net; 121 City Tce, Walchand Hirachand Marg; d/t/q ₹3200/3900/4500; ❄) Organised and clean, and just across from CST. If you just got off an overnight train, the rooms are no bigger than a sleeper compartment, so you won't suffer any disorientation at wake-up.

THE SUBURBS

There are several midrange hotels on Nehru Rd Extension in Vile Parle East near the domestic airport, but rooms are overpriced and only useful for early or late flights. Juhu is convenient for Juhu Beach and for the restaurants, shops and clubs in Bandra.

For locations of the following venues, see Map p54, unless otherwise stated.

Central Suburbs

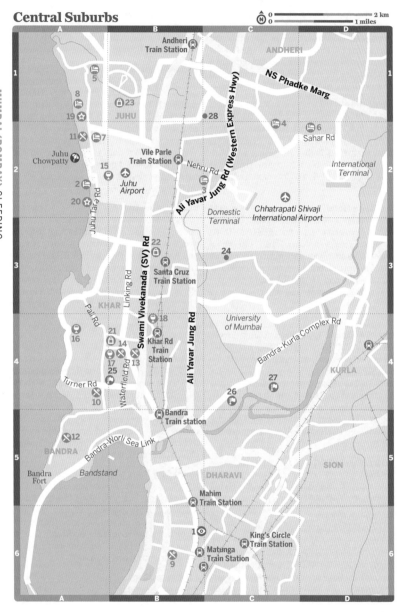

0 ——— 2 km
0 ——— 1 miles

ANDHERI

NS Phadke Marg

Andheri
Train Station

JUHU

Vile Parle
Train Station

Nehru Rd

Sahar Rd

Ali Yavar Jung Rd (Western Express Hwy)

Juhu
Chowpatty

Juhu Tara Rd

Juhu
Airport

International
Terminal

Domestic
Terminal

Chhatrapati Shivaji
International Airport

Swami Vivekanada (SV) Rd

Santa Cruz
Train Station

Linking Rd

Pali Rd

KHAR

University
of Mumbai

Ali Yavar Jung Rd

Khar Rd
Train
Station

Waterfield Rd

Turner Rd

Bandra-Kurla Complex Rd

KURLA

Bandra
Train station

BANDRA

Bandra-Worli Sea Link

Bandra
Fort

Bandstand

DHARAVI

SION

Mahim
Train Station

King's Circle
Train Station

Matunga
Train Station

TOP CHOICE Iskcon

GUESTHOUSE $$

(☎26206860; www.iskconmumbai.com/guest-house; Hare Krishna Land, Juhu; s/d incl tax ₹2595/2895, with AC incl tax ₹2995/3495; ✳@) If you are looking for an experience rather than simply shelter, this efficiently managed guesthouse, part of Juhu's lively Hare Krishna complex, is one of Mumbai's most interesting choices. The lobby looks out into the temple, while rooms in the two flamingo-pink towers have pretty *sankheda* (lacquered country wood) furniture from

Central Suburbs

◉ **Sights**
1 Wall Project................................B6

◕ **Sleeping**
2 Citizen Hotel............................A2
3 Hotel Columbus.......................C2
4 Hotel Suba International...........C2
5 Iskcon....................................A1
6 ITC Maratha............................D2
7 Juhu Residency........................A2
8 Sun-n-Sand..............................A1

✖ **Eating**
9 Culture Curry...........................B6
Five Spice.........................(see 17)
Goa Portuguesa................(see 9)
10 Lemongrass............................A4
11 Mahesh Lunch Home...............A2
Peshawri...........................(see 6)
Prithvi Cafe.....................(see 19)
12 Salt Water Cafe.......................A5
13 Sheesha.................................B4
14 Theobroma..............................B4

◉ **Drinking**
Elbo Room........................(see 14)

15 Mocha Bar..............................A2
16 Olive Bar & Kitchen.................A4
17 Toto's Garage.........................B4
18 WTF!.......................................B4

◉ **Entertainment**
Bonobo.............................(see 14)
19 Prithvi Theatre........................A1
20 Trilogy....................................A2

◉ **Shopping**
21 Azaadbazaar..........................B4
22 Fabindia..................................B3
23 Shrujan....................................B1

ℹ **Information**
24 Humsafar Trust.......................C3
25 Malaysian Consulate................B4
26 New Zealand Consulate...........C4
27 UK Consulate..........................C4

ℹ **Transport**
28 Qantas....................................C1

Gujarat and those in the original tower have semicircular balconies. The whole thing feels like you are in the thick of India, which is more than can be said for most of the resort or business-oriented hotels out this way. Don't miss the evening *aarti* (candle-lighting ritual).

Four Seasons Hotel HOTEL $$$
(off Map p42; ☎24818000; www.fourseasons.com; 114 Dr E Moses Rd, Worli; r from ₹15,200; ✻@🖥🏊) This modern Four Seasons is everything you expect it to be: exemplary service, psychic staff and everything classic yet slick as oil. Now with the addition of its fashionable rooftop lounge Aer (p61), it's hip as hopscotch, too.

Juhu Residency BOUTIQUE HOTEL $$$
(☎67834949; www.juhuresidency.com; 148B Juhu Tara Rd, Juhu; s/d with AC incl breakfast ₹5000/7500; ✻@🖥) A makeover two years ago turned this into a quasi-boutique hotel, with sleek marble floors, king-size beds (in the premium rooms), dark woods and artistic bedspreads imported from Singapore. There are three restaurants for 18 rooms, and one, the Melting Pot, garners accolades for its

Indian cuisine. A great choice if you're looking for something hip and intimate that won't cost you a fortune.

Hotel Suba International BOUTIQUE HOTEL $$$
(☎67076707; www.hotelsubainternational.com; Sahar Rd, Vile Parle East; r with AC incl breakfast from ₹5500; ✻🖥) Nearly new, this hi-tech boutique business hotel is just 1km from the international terminal, 3km from the domestic. It's laid out in slick blacks and glossy marble, with clean lines and lots of masculine hardwoods and design-forward touches. All the electronics in the rooms are controlled wirelessly by iPod Touch.

Sun-n-Sand HOTEL $$$
(☎66938888; www.sunnsandhotel.com; 39 Juhu Beach, Juhu; r with AC from ₹8650; ✻@🖥🏊) The good old Sun-n-Sand has been soldiering along, offering up beachfront hospitality for decades, in the face of ever-growing competition from glossy international five-stars. The newly renovated 4th floor offers shiny new hardwood floors and some bathtubs, but the best rooms remain the sea-facing ones (from ₹8500): lots of silk and the pleasant burnt-orange motif complement the

56

MUMBAI (BOMBAY) EATING

DON'T MISS

KOTACHIWADI

This storied *wadi* (hamlet) is a bastion clinging onto Mumbai life as it was before high-rises. A Christian enclave of elegant two-storey wooden mansions, it's 500m northeast of Girgaum Chowpatty (Map p42), lying amid Mumbai's predominantly Hindu and Muslim neighbourhoods. These winding laneways allow a wonderful glimpse into a quiet life free of rickshaws and taxis. It's not large by any means, but you can lose considerable moments wandering these fascinating alleyways – no doubt in shock that the hustle and bustle of the real Mumbai is but steps away.

To find it, aim for **St Teresa's Church** (Map p42) on the corner of Jagannath Shankarsheth Marg (JS Marg) and RR Roy Marg (Charni Rd), then head directly opposite the church on JS Marg and duck down the second and third lanes on your left.

pool, palm-tree and ocean views from the huge windows. It's off Juhu Rd, near the old Holiday Inn.

 ITC Maratha   HOTEL $$$
(☏28303030; www.itcwelcomgroup.in; Sahar Rd, Andheri East; r incl breakfast & tax from ₹12,065; ❄@⊛☎) The five-star with the most luxurious Indian character, from the Jaipur-style lattice windows around the atrium to the silk pillows on the beds, to Peshawri, one of the best restaurants in town. It's also now billing itself as 'responsible luxury', with carbon-offsetting schemes, its own corporate wind-farms, solar concentrators and waste-water filtration.

Hotel Columbus   HOTEL $$
(☏42144343; www.hotelcolumbus.in; 344 Nanda Patkar Rd, Vile Parle East; r with AC from ₹3000; ❄@☎) The best midrange in the domestic airport area, with gussied-up super-deluxe rooms (₹4000) with stylised wood-grain accents, flat-screen TVs and an aspiration to high design.

Citizen Hotel   HOTEL $$$
(☏66932525; www.citizenhotelmumbai.com; Juhu Tara Rd, Juhu; s/d with AC incl breakfast from ₹7000/7500; ❄@☎) The Citizen's location is what you're paying for here, but rooms are also well maintained, with marble floors and marble-top furniture, flat-screen TVs, wi-fi access, fridges and, of course, excellent beach views.

✖ Eating

In this gastro-epicentre, a cornucopia of flavours from all over India collides with international trends and tastebuds. Colaba is home to most of the cheap tourist haunts, while Fort and Churchgate skew upscale, a trend that continues as you head north to Mahalaxmi and the Central Suburbs, where you'll find Mumbai's most exciting, cutting-edge and expensive restaurants.

For self-caterers, the **Colaba market** (Map p44; Lala Nigam St) has fresh fruit and vegetables. **Saharkari Bhandar Supermarket** (Map p44; ☏22022248; cnr Colaba Causeway & Wodehouse Rd; ◷10am-8.30pm) and, even better, **Suryodaya** (Map p46; ☏22040979; Veer Nariman Rd; ◷7.30am-8.30pm) are well-stocked supermarkets.

COLABA

For mapped locations of the following venues, see Map p44.

TOP CHOICE **Bademiya**   INDIAN $
(Tulloch Rd; meals ₹50-100) If you can walk by this street-stall-on-steroids without coming away with some sort of tikka roll in hand, you are a better person than we are. This whole street buzzes nightly with punters from all walks of Mumbai life lining up for spicy, fresh-grilled treats, and vegetarians will especially delight in the whole stand devoted to flesh-free kebabs: try the aloo tikka or paneer tikka, spiked with fried onions: a perfect take-away supper if you're heading for a late train. If Mumbai street food scares the bejesus out of you, this is without doubt the spot to get over it.

Indigo   FUSION, EUROPEAN $$$
(4 Mandlik Marg; mains ₹525-945; ◷lunch & dinner) Over a decade in and still a star, Colaba's finest eating option is a gourmet haven serving innovative European cuisine, a long wine list, sleek ambience and a gorgeous roof deck lit with fairy lights. Favourites include excellent kiwi margaritas, tea-grilled quail (₹625), anise-rubbed white salmon (₹725) and inventive takes on traditional cuisine like juniper-berry-cured tandoori chicken (₹625). Its cool quotient has chilled a bit with the focus on the suburbs, but it remains a high-gastronomy favourite.

Indigo Delicatessen   CAFE $$$
(Pheroze Bldg, Chhatrapati Shivaji Marg; mains ₹245-495; ⊘9am-midnight) Indigo's casual and less expensive sister is just as big a draw as the original, with cool tunes, warm decor and massive wooden tables. It has breakfast all day (₹155 to ₹295), casual meals, French-press coffee, wines (₹300 to ₹690 per glass), and is also a bakery and deli.

Theobroma   CAFE $
(Colaba Causeway; confections ₹40-85) Theobroma calls its creations 'food of the gods' – and it's not lying. Dozens of perfectly executed cakes, tarts and chocolates, as well as sandwiches and breads, go well with the coffee here. The genius pistachio-and-green-cardamom truffle (₹30) or decadent chocolate overload brownie (₹65) should send you straight into a glorious sugar coma. A bigger location has opened in Bandra West (Map p54).

New Laxmi Vilas   SOUTH INDIAN $
(19A Ram Mansion, Nawroji F Rd; mains ₹23-85) A great budget pure-vegetarian eatery that serves delicious South India specialities, including a darn good *masala dosa* and a selection of good, filling thalis. It's clean and cheerful, and is just around the corner from the Taj Mahal Palace.

Wich Latte   CAFE $$
(Western Breeze Bldg, Colaba; sandwiches ₹120-175) Churning out excellent coffee but trumping both Coffee Day and Barista when it comes to food, Wich Latte bills itself as India's first sandwich cafe. For breakfast, the bagelwiches are an excellent homesickness remedy and throughout the day there are salads, sandwiches and pizza. There's also a convenient location in Kala Ghoda (Map p46), which opens from lunch onwards.

KALA GHODA & FORT

For locations of the following venues, see Map p46, unless otherwise stated.

TOP CHOICE Khyber   NORTH INDIAN $$$
(☑40396666; 145 MG Rd, Fort; mains ₹225-450; ⊘lunch & dinner) An iconic restaurant, the thought of which will spark Pavlovian drooling for years to come, with cavernous Afghan-inspired interiors, tasteful antique oil lanterns and urns, and railway-trestle ceilings. As mouth-watering Punjabi/North Indian kebabs, biryanis and curries saunter their way to a who's who of Mumbai's elite, your tastebuds will do a happy dance – before the disheartening realisation: too much food, too little space. Highlights of the meat-centric menu include the Reshmi Kebab Masala, a transcendent dish of cream and yoghurt-marinated chicken drowning in the restaurant's intricate red masala; and its pièce de résistance, *raan* (a whole leg of slow-cooked lamb). It's worth booking to secure a good table.

Five Spice   INDO-CHINESE $$
(296A Perin Nariman St, Sangli Bank Bldg, Fort; mains ₹220-275; ⊘lunch & dinner) A 30-minute wait is commonplace at this overheated, near-divey Indo-Chinese eatery that's so good, it'll make you downright angry you can't eat Chinese like this at home. The menu is packed with chicken, lamb, prawn and veg dishes, all tantalising, so choosing is an issue. Try chicken in burnt chilli sauce (₹235) on a bed of burnt chilli rice (₹185) – quite possibly the best thing since the fortune cookie. There's also one in Bandra (Map p54).

Trishna   SEAFOOD $$$
(☑22614991; Sai Baba Marg, Kala Ghoda; mains ₹170-575; ⊘lunch & dinner) An outstanding and intimate seafood restaurant focused on Mangalorean preparations. The crab with

DABBA-WALLAHS

A small miracle of logistics, Mumbai's 5000 *dabba*-wallahs (*dabba* means food container; they are also called tiffin-wallahs) work tirelessly to deliver hot lunches to office workers throughout the city.

Lunch boxes are picked up each day from restaurants and homes and carried on heads, bicycles and trains to a centralised sorting station. A sophisticated system of numbers and colours (many wallahs are illiterate) identifies the destination of each lunch. More than 200,000 meals are delivered daily, always on time, come (monsoon) rain or (searing) shine.

This system has been used for centuries and, on average, there's only about one mistake per six million deliveries. No wonder *dabba*-wallahs take immense pride in their work.

butter, black pepper and garlic and Hydera-badi fish tikka are house specialities that warrant the hype, while service is under-bearing, friendly and helpful. Reservations aren't neccessary before 8pm.

Brittania   PARSI $$
(off Map p46; Wakefield House, 11 Sprott Rd, Ballard Estate; mains ₹100-250; ⊙lunch Mon-Sat) The kind of place travellers' tales are made of – this Mumbai icon, and its endearing owner, has been going since 1923. The signature dish is the berry *pulao* (₹250) – spiced and boneless mutton or chicken buried in basmati rice and tart barberries, imported to the tune of 1000kg per year from Iran. The owner, Boman Kohinoor – born the year his father opened the place – will take your order and chat your ear off. Simple, and delicious.

Café Moshe   CAFE $$
(Fabindia, 1st fl, Jeroo Bldg, MG Rd, Kala Ghoda; light meals ₹120-270; ⊙lunch & dinner) After shopping downstairs, refuel with Moshe's excellent salads, sandwiches, baked goods, coffees and smoothies. There's also a Moshe's in Colaba (Map p44), where you'll find an extended menu, including the famed marinated garlic, mushroom, leek and capsi-cum open-faced sandwich with melted moz-zarella on brown bread.

Mahesh Lunch Home   SEAFOOD $$$
(☑22023965; 8B Cowasji Patel St, Fort; mains ₹150-600; ⊙lunch & dinner) A great place to try Mangalorean seafood in Mumbai. It's re-nowned for its ladyfish, pomfret, lobster and crabs; the *rawas tikka* (marinated white salmon) and tandoori pomfret are outstand-ing. There's also a branch on Juhu Tara Rd (Map p54).

Badshah Snacks & Drinks   INDIAN $
(Map p42; snacks ₹30-110) Opposite Crawford Market, Badshah's been serving snacks, fruit juices and its famous *falooda* (rose-flavoured drink made with milk, cream, nuts and vermicelli – like swallowing a bed of roses!) to hungry bargain-hunters for more than 100 years.

Rajdhani   INDIAN $$
(Map p42; 361 Sheikh Memon St, Kalbadevi; thali ₹249; ⊙lunch & dinner Mon-Sat, lunch Sun) Oppo-site Mangaldaas Market, Rajdhani is famous for its Gujarati and Rajasthani thalis. On Sundays, dinner isn't served and thali prices jump ₹50.

CHURCHGATE

For mapped locations of the following ven-ues, see Map p46.

TOP
CHOICE **Samrat**   SOUTH INDIAN $$
(Prem Ct, J Tata Rd; thalis ₹250; ⊙lunch & dinner) If this is your first thali, strap yourself in – the cavalcade of taste and texture will leave you wondering what just happened, and *then* they bring the rice. Samrat is the anchor be-hind a pure-veg empire in the same location, which includes **210°C**, an outdoor cafe and bakery, and **Relish**, a funky spot that's home to Asian-Mexican-Lebanese fusion.

Koh   THAI $$$
(InterContinental, Marine Dr; ☑39879999; mains ₹495-925; ⊙lunch & dinner) India's first sig-nature Thai restaurant is Mumbai's hot-test dining destination. Celebrity chef Ian Kittichai works his native cuisine into an international frenzy of flavour that starts with the 'liquid gastronomy', which might be a jasmine and honey martini or a Bloody Mary made with lemongrass-infused vodka and sriracha chilli; from there the envelope is further pushed into revelational dishes like the 12-hour lamb shank Massaman curry – pair it with hot-stone garlic rice – that throws preconceived notions about Thai food to the Mumbai curb.

K Rustom   SWEETS $
(87 Stadium House, Veer Nariman Rd; dessert ₹40; ⊙lunch & dinner) Nothing but a few metal freezers, but the delicious ice-cream sand-wich (₹40) has been pleasing Mumbaikar palettes since 1953.

GIRGAUM CHOWPATTY

For mapped locations of the following venues, see Map p42.

TOP
CHOICE **New Kulfi Centre**   SWEETS $
(cnr Chowpatty Seaface & Sardar V Patel Rd; kulfi per 100gm ₹20-40; ⊙9am-1.30am) Serves the best *kulfi* (firm-textured ice cream served in killer flavours like pistachio, rose and saf-fron) you'll have anywhere. When you order, the *kulfi* is placed on a betel-nut leaf and then weighed on an ancient scale – which makes it even better.

Cream Centre   CAFE $$
(Chowpatty Seaface; mains ₹100-249; ⊙lunch & dinner) This sleek and contemporary Indian diner is hugely popular for its pure-veg hodge-podge of Indian, Mexican and Lebanese

as well as its extensive menu of sizzling sundaes (₹195 to ₹220), which take 'hot fudge' up to boiling point.

MAHALAXMI TO WORLI

For the mapped locations of the following venues, see Map p42.

Tote on the Turf FUSION $$$
(☑61577777; near Gate No 5 & 6, Mahalaxmi Racecourse, Mahalaxmi; mains ₹485-985; ☺lunch & dinner) Funky, all-white tree-branch interiors and ridiculously beautiful crowds aside, this hip new restaurant from the folks who own Indigo dishes out Euro-fusion, divided into veg (like the yummy green garlic risotto with palm hearts, cherry tomatoes and chilli feta) and non-veg (grilled chicken with stuffed Bhavnagri chilli and mustard sauce).

Cafe Noorani NORTH INDIAN $$
(Tardeo Rd, Haji Ali Circle; mains ₹120-180; ☺lunch & dinner) This almost-retro diner is a requisite stop before or after visiting Haji Ali Mosque. On the menu is a gamut of Mughlai and Punjabi staples, all done well and cheaply.

THE SUBURBS

North Mumbai is home to the city's trendiest dining, centred on Bandra West and Juhu. For mapped locations of the following venues, see Map p54.

TOP CHOICE Peshawri NORTH INDIAN $$$
(☑28303030; ITC Maratha, Sahar Rd; mains ₹700-1675; ☺lunch & dinner) Make this Indian northwest frontier restaurant, just outside the international airport, your first or last stop in Mumbai. It's pricey, but you won't regret forking out the ₹2700 (feeds two easily) for the exquisite Sikandari *raan* (leg of spring lamb braised in malt vinegar, cinnamon and black cumin) – it will forever skew your standards. The buttery dhal Bukhara (a thick black dhal cooked for a day; ₹700) is also memorable.

Culture Curry SOUTH INDIAN $$$
(Kataria Rd, Matunga West; mains ₹209-459; ☺lunch & dinner) As the Culture Curry folks rightly point out, there's a lot more to South Indian food than *idli* (South Indian spongy, round, fermented rice cake) and dosas. Exquisite dishes from all over the south, ranging from Andhra and Coorg to Kerala, are the specialty here. Veggies are particularly well served: the Kooru Curry (kidney

and green beans in coconut gravy; ₹179) is extraordinary. The same owners run Goa Portuguesa (adjacent), specialising in fiery Goan dishes, where the 'Chicken Chilly Fry' is also a knockout (₹299). From Matunga station, it's about 750m west on Katinga Rd on the left.

Sheesha NORTH INDIAN $$
(☑66770555; 7th fl, Shoppers Stop, Linking Rd, Bandra West; mains ₹145-295; ☺lunch & dinner) With perhaps the most beautiful ambience in town, Sheesha's alfresco rooftop lair has glass lanterns hanging from wooden beams, comfy couches and coloured-glass lamps, high above the city and shopping madness below. You almost forget about the food, though you shouldn't – the countless kebabs and curries are outstanding. Otherwise, it's all hookah action (there's no alcohol here). Book ahead on weekends.

Lemongrass SOUTHEAST ASIAN $$$
(Carlton Ct, cnr of Turner & Pali Rds, Bandra West; mains ₹215-400; ☺lunch & dinner) A good spot for watching Bandra streetlife, Lemongrass serves up tasty southeast Asian fare from Myanmar (Burma) to Indonesia. The veg *khowsuey* (Burmese noodles with a coconut broth; ₹400) is superb, and the service is above and beyond for its price.

Salt Water Cafe FUSION $$$
(87 Chapel Rd, Bandra; mains ₹180-500) This foodie find offers one of Mumbai's most ambitious menus. It made a name for itself for marrying dramatically opposing flavours (for example, green peppercorn chicken with grape jus, cardamom and carrot mash), but most of the menu is just mouth-watering global fusion. The aesthetically cold design is as much of a contrast to India as some of the recipes, and service grinds to a crawl at lunchtime, but it's a lovely spot to twist up your tastebuds after a curry overdose.

Prithvi Cafe CAFE $
(Juhu Church Rd, Juhu; light meals ₹70-140) You'd never know it was there, but this bohemian cafe attached to the Prithvi Theatre is a cultural hub of intellectuals, artists and theatre types who tuck themselves away in the lush, bamboo-heavy spot for all-day breakfast, cheap kebab value meals, sandwiches and savoury croissants. The food might not be stellar, but the vibe, and the Irish coffee, more than make up for it.

MUMBAI (BOMBAY) EATING

🍷 Drinking

Mumbai's lax attitude to alcohol means that there are lots of places to drink – from hole-in-the-wall beer bars and chichi lounges to brash, multilevel superclubs – but the 25% liquor tax means bills can be swoonable. If it's the caffeine buzz you're after, Barista and Café Coffee Day cafes are ubiquitous in Mumbai.

🍴 Kala Ghoda Café   CAFE

(Map p46; 10 Ropewalk Ln, Fort) An artsy, modern and miniscule cafe that's a favourite among journalists and other creative types, who come for the organic Arabica and Robusta coffee sourced from sustainable plantations, organic teas, small bite sandwiches and salads, and charming breakfasts – and then fight for one of the few tables. Even the *jaggery* (hard, brown, sugarlike sweetner made from kitul palm sap) is organic.

Mocha Bar   CAFE

(⊙10am-1.30am); Churchgate (Map p46; 82 Veer Nariman Rd); Juhu (Map p54; 67 Juhu Tara Rd) This atmospheric Arabian-styled cafe is often filled to the brim with bohemians and students deep in esoteric conversation, Bollywood gossip, or just a hookah pipe. Cosy, low-cushioned seating (including some old cinema seats), exotic coffees, shakes and teas, and global comfort cuisine promote an intellectually relaxed vibe.

First Floor   CAFE

(Map p42; Sitaram Bldg, Dr Dadabhai Naoroji Rd; ⊙7pm-4am) This locals' secret is the comedown cafe of choice; there's no alcohol, but the party picks up here, anyway – especially on Wednesdays and Saturdays – when the cool kids pack the house from 1.30am to 4am to sop up the drunkenness over a Continental mix of burgers, Mexican, Italian and sheeshas. It's above Zaffran, a worthy Mughlai restaurant in its own right.

Haji Ali Juice Centre   JUICE BAR

(Map p42; Lala Lajpat Raj Rd, Haji Ali Circle; ⊙5am-1.30am Mon-Sat) An excellent juice megastand, strategically placed at the entrance to Haji Ali Mosque. A great cool off after the heat of the cross-water pilgrimage.

Samovar Café   CAFE

(Map p46; Jehangir Art Gallery, 161B MG Rd, Kala Ghoda; meals ₹60-90; ⊙closed Sun) This intimate place inside the art gallery overlooks the gardens of the Prince of Wales Museum.

Cha Bar   TEAHOUSE

(Map p46; Oxford Bookstore, Apeejay House, 3 Dinsha Wachha Marg, Churchgate; teas ₹30-80; ⊙10am-9.30pm) Thirteen pages of exotic teas, including organic and ayurvedic, and tasty snacks amid lots of books.

SOUTH MUMBAI

For the mapped locations of the following venues see Map p44, unless otherwise indicated.

Cafe Mondegar   BAR

(Metro House, 5A Shahid Bhagat Singh Marg, Colaba) Like Leopold's (p60), 'Mondys' draws a healthy foreign crowd, but with a better mix of friendly Indians, who all cosy up together in the much smaller space, bonding over the excellent jukebox, one of Mumbai's few. Good music, good people.

Busaba   BAR, LOUNGE

(☎22043779; 4 Mandlik Marg) Red walls and contemporary Buddha art give this loungey restaurant-bar a nouveau Tao. It's next to Indigo so gets the same trendy crowd but serves cheaper, more potent cocktails (₹330 to ₹480). There's a low-key DJ Wednesdays to Sundays from 8.30pm. The upstairs restaurant serves pan-Asian (mains ₹350 to ₹575); its back room feels like a posh treehouse. Reserve ahead if you want a table.

Leopold Cafe   BAR

(cnr Colaba Causeway & Nawroji F Rd) Love it or hate it, most tourists end up at this Mumbai travellers' institution at one time or another. Around since 1871, Leopold's has wobbly ceiling fans, open-plan seating and a rambunctious atmosphere conducive to swapping tales with random strangers. Although there's a huge menu, the lazy evening beers are the real draw.

Café Universal   BAR

(Map p46; 299 Shahid Bhagat Singh Marg; ⊙9am-11pm Mon-Sat, 4-11pm Sun) A little bit of France near CST. The Universal has an art nouveau look to it, with butterscotch-colour walls, a wood-beam ceiling and marble chandeliers, and is a cosy place for happy hour and Kingfisher drafts (₹100).

Dome   BAR

(Map p46; Hotel InterContinental, 135 Marine Dr, Churchgate) This white-on-white rooftop lounge has awesome views of Mumbai's curving seafront while cocktails beckon the hip young things of Mumbai nightly.

THE SUBURBS

For mapped locations of the following venues, see Map p54 unless otherwise stated.

TOP CHOICE Aer   BAR, LOUNGE

(off Map p42; Four Seasons Hotel, 33rd fl, 114 Dr E Moses Rd, Worli) With astounding city views on one side and equally impressive sea views on the other, we'll be damned if this isn't India's most impressive tipple. Aer is a slick, open-air rooftop lounge with its share of plush couches as well as weird, uncomfortable plastic 'lounge chairs' that cater more to form than function. You will need to re-mortgage your home for something shaken and stirred (₹600), but the ₹250 Kingfishers are a steal with these views. A DJ spins low-key house and techno nightly from 9pm, but who cares? It's all about the eye candy, both near and far.

Olive Bar & Kitchen   BAR

(☑26058228; Pali Hill Tourist Hotel, 14 Union Park, Khar West; ☉7.30pm-1.30am) Hip, gorgeous and snooty, this longtime Mediterranean-style restaurant and bar has light and delicious food (mains ₹525 to ₹950), soothing DJ sounds and pure Ibiza-meets-Mykonos decor (even the host is Greek). Thursday and weekends are packed (call to reserve); there's a second branch at Mahalaxmi Racecourse.

WTF!   BAR

(8 Vora Bldg, 3rd Khar Rd, Khar) Hilariously named and an equally good time, rambunctious WTF! (pronounced as letters) is a small venue divided into two rooms, one a lipstick-red den of pop culture kitsch and Formica, the other dumbed-down with the cricket likely to be on the big screen. The DJ spins right in your face beside the front door – a loud and brash wall of international pop trash.

Toto's Garage   BAR

(30 Lourdes Heaven, Pali Naka, Bandra West; ☉6pm-1am) Forget the beautiful people. Toto's is a down-to-earth local dive done up in a mechanic's theme where you can go in your dirty clothes, drink pitchers of beer and listen to music that gave us guilty pleasure with the back-to-back-to-back Savage Garden-Linkin Park-AC/DC set. Get there early or you won't get a seat.

Elbo Room   PUB

(St Teresa's Rd, Khar West) A genuine bar that approaches resto-lounge but thankfully falls short. Instead, it's a pub reminiscent of home and a good bet for wines by the glass (₹275 to ₹700) screening both English Premier League and Bundesliga football matches. The Italian-Indian menu is best enjoyed on the terrace while the serious drinkers – no shortage of expats among them – stay inside.

☆ Entertainment

The daily English-language tabloid *Mid-Day* incorporates a guide to Mumbai entertainment. Newspapers and *Time Out Mumbai* (www.timeoutmumbai.net) list events and film screenings, while www.nh7.in has live-music listings.

It would be a crime not to see a movie in India's film capital. Unfortunately, Hindi films aren't shown with English subtitles, though with usually simple plots, it doesn't take much effort to keep abreast of what's going on (for example, anyone laughing maniacally while stroking his curling moustache is likely to be a baddy). The cinemas we have listed all show movies in English, along with some Bollywood numbers.

Big club nights are (somewhat strangely) Wednesday, as well as the traditional Friday and Saturday; there's usually a cover charge. Dress codes generally apply, so don't rock up in shorts and sandals. The trend in Mumbai of late is towards resto-lounges as opposed to full-on nightclubs, perhaps down to serious tax implications on discos versus lounges and restaurants.

TOP CHOICE Bluefrog   LIVE MUSIC

(off Map p42; www.bluefrog.co.in; D/2 Mathuradas Mills Compound, NM Joshi Marg, Lower Parel; admission after 9pm Tue-Thu & Sun ₹300, Fri & Sat ₹500; ☉7pm-1am Tue-Sun) The most exciting thing to happen to Mumbai's music scene in a long time, Bluefrog is a concert space, production studio, restaurant and one of Mumbai's most happening spaces. It hosts exceptional local and international acts, and has space-age, orange-glowing 'pod' seating in the intimate main room.

Valhalla   RESTO-LOUNGE

(Map p46; ☑67353535; 1st fl, East Wing, Eros Theatre Bldg, Churchgate) This discrete resto-lounge caters to Mumbai's bold and beautiful, who turn up here amid aubergine walls and baroque aesthetics on Friday and Saturday club nights when everywhere else closes (it's unofficially open until 4am or so).

Getting in isn't easy – you need to call ahead and get on the list – but if you manage it, you'll rub elbows with a high-profile crowd.

Not Just Jazz By the Bay   LIVE MUSIC

(Map p46; 143 Marine Dr; admission weekdays/weekends ₹100/300; ☺noon-3.30am) This is the best, and frankly the only, jazz club in South Mumbai. True to its name, there are also live pop, blues and rock performers most nights from 10pm, but Sunday, Monday and Tuesday are reserved for karaoke. By day, there's a well done all-you-can-eat buffet (₹325).

Trilogy   NIGHTCLUB

(Map p54; Hotel Sea Princess, Juhu Tara Rd, Juhu; cover per couple after 11pm ₹1000; ☺closed Tue) One of Mumbai's newest clubs is all attitude –

rumour has it that staff size up potentials for looks and charge a varying admission accordingly. That bodes well for those who make it past face patrol. The tri-level space is gorgeous, highlighted by a black granite dance floor lit up by 1372 LED cube lights that go off like an epileptic Lite-Brite in an Indian power surge. The imported sound system favours house and hip-hop while the bartenders look imported from Ed Hardy's employee pool.

Polly Esther's   NIGHTCLUB

(Map p44; Gordon House Hotel, Battery St, Colaba; cover per couple Wed, Fri & Sat ₹800-1500) The city's *fashionistas* feel nauseous at its mere mention, but this mirror-plated, cheesy nightclub wallowing in retro gaudiness remains a fun choice to mingle with

---

LOCAL KNOWLEDGE

PRAMOD SIPPY: DJ PRAMZ

A Mumbai turntable veteran, DJ Pramz has spun the black circles in the city for over half his lifetime. Here are his top picks.

Cosiest Club

Bonobo (Map p54; Kenilworth, Phase 2, Off Linking Rd, Bandra West) is a home away from home. They don't impose a dress code, nor do they charge entry. It's a walk-in and offers some really good cocktails at very good prices. It doesn't take long for one to establish their comfort level. As a DJ, I love performing there because of the 'no mainstream music' policy and of course because the owners are very much on the same page as me. They are young entrepreneurs who understand the global trends and are ready to experiment and do things differently.

Most Stunning Club

Wink (off Map p44; Vivanta by Taj – President Hotel, 90 Cuffe Pde, Cuffe Parade) is a beautifully designed bar with a demarcated area for quick meals. The drinks and service are easily the best in town. Their Winktinis are world-renowned and the music is nothing short of spectacular. I love to perform here because they are open-minded and, in spite of being situated in a five-star [hotel], they don't entertain requests that fall outside the ambit of the DJ. It's frequented by a large expatriate crowd who are usually [hotel] guests. Although the space is bright and unlike a club, the pulsating music on weekends makes the vibe quite groovy.

Most Celebrated Club

Zenzi Mills (off Map p54; Mathuradas Mills Compound, Senapati Bapat Marg, Lower Parel; ☺closed Sun) is a paradise of sorts for all alternative music aficionados. It's basically an offshoot of the legendary Zenzi (Bandra), which essentially laid the foundation for alternative entertainment in the city. Zenzi widened its horizon by launching Mills, which had everything that the original Zenzi lacked – a state-of-the-art sound system, a beautiful set-up for visuals, a split-level space. It works for artists of all alternative genres as the club is open to experimentation. A lot of deep-rooted sentiments are attached to it and it has become immortal for many in their hearts, but word is out that it's undergoing an image makeover and will be seen in an all-new form and feel. What it's going to be like is yet a mystery, though.

THE GREAT WALL OF MUMBAI

An artistic initiative similar to Berlin's East Side Gallery, though without the 28 years of oppression and isolation, the **Wall Project** (Map p54; www.thewallproject.com) was started by a group of ex-art/design students who decided to paint their neighbours' walls with local themes and artsy graffiti. This soon spread into a public project that has splashed colourful murals on everything from houses to hospitals all over the suburb of Bandra. The idea quickly began spreading like kaleidoscopic Kudzu – a spray-painted virus that has turned crumbling structures and neglected walls into a living museum of contemporary urban culture. At the time of writing, hundreds of artists (and nonartists) have painted some 600 murals, the longest stretch of which starts at Mahim station (West) on Tulsi Pipe Rd (Senapati Bapat Marg) and runs along the Western Railway to Matunga Rd station – nicknamed the Great Wall of Mumbai.

Anyone can visit and paint the wall, as long as the art is not sexually explicit, political, religious or commercial. Would-be Banksys should bring some acrylic distemper paint – recommended due to harsh weather conditions – and get their art on.

middle-class Mumbai. The *Saturday Night Fever* illuminated dance floor stays packed with gossiping 20-somethings and ogling tourists. Wednesday is free for the gals and all but ₹200 is recoupable in drinks most nights.

Wankhede Stadium SPORT
(Mumbai Cricket Association; Map p46; ☑227 95500; www.mumbaicricket.com; D Rd, Churchgate) Test matches and One Day Internationals are played a few times a year in season (October to April). Contact the Cricket Association for ticket information; for a test match you'll probably have to pay for the full five days.

Cooperage Football Ground SPORT
(Map p44; ☑22024020; MK Rd, Colaba; tickets ₹20-25) Home to FC Air India, Mumbai FC and ONGC FC. Hosts national-league and local football (soccer) matches between October and February. Tickets are available at the gate.

National Centre for the Performing Arts THEATRE
(NCPA; Map p46; ☑66223737, box office 22824567; www.ncpamumbai.com; cnr Marine Dr & Sri V Saha Rd, Nariman Point; tickets ₹200-500; ☺box office 9am-7pm) Spanning 800 sq metres, this cultural centre is the hub of Mumbai's music, theatre and dance scene. In any given week, it might host Marathi theatre, poetry readings and art exhibitions, Bihari dance troupes, ensembles from Europe or Indian classical music. The Experimental Theatre occasionally has English-language plays.

Many performances are free. The box office is at the end of NCPA Marg.

Prithvi Theatre THEATRE
(Map p54; ☑26149546; www.prithvitheatre.org; Juhu Church Rd, Juhu) At Juhu Beach, this is a good place to see both Hindi and English-language theatre. It hosts an excellent annual international theatre festival and there's a charming cafe, too.

Regal CINEMA
(Map p44; ☑22021017; Opposite Regal Circle, Shahid Bhagat Singh Marg, Colaba; tickets ₹100-200) Check out the art deco architecture.

Eros CINEMA
(Map p46; ☑22822335; MK Rd, Churchgate; tickets ₹80-120)

Metro Big CINEMA
(off Map p46; ☑39894040; MG Rd, New Marine Lines, Fort; tickets ₹100-600) This grand dame of Bombay talkies was just renovated into a multiplex.

Sterling CINEMA
(Map p46; ☑66220016; Marzaban Rd, Fort; tickets ₹120-180)

Shopping

Mumbai is India's great marketplace, with some of the best shopping in the country.

You can buy just about anything in the dense bazaars north of CST (Map p42). The main areas are Crawford Market (fruit and veg), Mangaldas Market (silk and cloth), Zaveri Bazaar (jewellery), Bhuleshwar Market (fruit and veg) and Chor Bazaar (antiques and furniture). Dhabu St is lined with leather goods and Mutton St specialises in antiques and fine junk. Crawford Market (Mahatma Phule Market) is the last outpost of British Bombay before the tumult of the central bazaars begins. Bas-reliefs by Rudyard Kipling's father, Lockwood Kipling, adorn the Norman Gothic exterior.

Snap up a bargain backpacking wardrobe at Fashion Street, the strip of stalls lining MG Rd between Cross and Azad maidans (Map p46), or in Bandra's Linking Rd, near Waterfield Rd (Map p54) – hone your bargaining skills. Kemp's Corner has many good shops for designer threads.

Various state-government emporiums sell handicrafts in the World Trade Centre Arcade (off Map p44) near Cuffe Parade. Small antique and curio shops line Merewether Rd behind the Taj Mahal Palace (Map p44). They aren't cheap, but the quality is a step up from government emporiums. If you prefer Raj era bric-a-brac, head to Chor Bazaar (Map p42): the main area of activity is Mutton St, where you'll find a row of shops specialising in antiques (and many ingenious reproductions) and miscellaneous junk.

Fabindia
CLOTHING
(Map p46; Jeroo Bldg, 137 MG Rd, Kala Ghoda) Founded as a means to get traditional fabric artisans' wares to market, Fabindia has all the vibrant colours of the country in its trendy cotton and silk fashions, materials and homewares in a modern-meets-traditional Indian shop. If you are too cool for Indian-wear, try here. The Santa Cruz outpost (Map p54) is also good.

Bombay Electric
CLOTHES
(Map p44; www.bombayeletric.in; 1 Reay House, Best Marg, Colaba) High fashion is the calling at this chic unisex boutique next to the Taj Mahal Palace hotel. It sources fabrics (for its own hip brand, Gheebutter) and woven scarfs and jackets from NGOs in Madhya Pradesh and Gujarat, as well as select antiques, jewellery and handicrafts. It's a sharp spot to pick up *kurtas* (long shirts), dress shirts and T-shirts.

Phillips
ANTIQUES, CURIOS
(Map p44; www.phillipsantiques.com; Wodehouse Rd, Colaba) The 150-year-old Phillips has Nizam-era royal silver, wooden ceremonial masks, Victorian glass and various other gorgeous things you never knew you wanted. It also has high-quality reproductions of old photos, maps and paintings, and a warehouse shop of big antiques.

Shrujan
HANDICRAFTS
Breach Candy (Map p42; Sagar Villa, Warden Rd, opposite Navroze Apts; ⊙closed Sun); Juhu (Map p54; Hatkesh Society, 6th North South Rd, JVPD Scheme; ⊙closed Sun) Selling the intricate embroidery work of women in 114 villages in Kutch, Gujarat, the nonprofit Shrujan aims to help women earn a livelihood while preserving the spectacular embroidery traditions of the area. The sophisticated clothing, wall hangings and purses make great gifts.

Biba
CLOTHING
(Map p42; 1 Hughes Rd, Kemp's Corner; ⊙10.30am-9pm Mon-Sat) You'll be impossibly fashionable in LA or London in these sundresses.

Bombay Store
HANDICRAFTS
(Map p46; Western India House, Sir PM Rd, Fort; ⊙10.30am-8pm Mon-Sat, to 6.30pm Sun) A classy selection of rugs, clothing, teas, stationery, aromatherapy, brass sculptures and, perhaps most interestingly, biodegradable Ganesh idols for use in the Ganesh Chaturthi festival.

Good Earth
HANDICRAFTS
(Map p44; 2 Reay House, Colaba) This Delhi transplant hawks gorgeous, eco-leaning housewares, candles, cosmetics and glassware. Funky coasters, hand-decorated china, stylish coffee mugs – all higher end and artsy.

Oxford Bookstore
BOOKSTORE
(Map p46; www.oxfordbookstore.com; Apeejay House, 3 Dinsha Wachha Marg, Churchgate; ⊙8am-10pm) Mumbai's best book browsing, with a tea bar.

Crossword
BOOKSTORE
(Map p42; Mohammedbhai Mansion, NS Patkar Marg, Kemp's Corner) Enormous place for book-buying.

Khadi & Village Industries Emporium
CLOTHING
(Khadi Bhavan; Map p46; 286 Dr Dadabhai Naoroji Rd, Fort; ⊙10.30am-6.30pm Mon-Sat) Khadi Bhavan is a dusty, 1940s timewarp with ready-made traditional Indian clothing, material, shoes and handicrafts that are so old they're new again.

Cotton Cottage CLOTHING
(Map p46; Agra Bldg, 121 MG Rd, Kala Ghoda; ☺10am-9pm) Stock up on simple cotton *kurtas* and various pants – *salwars, churidars, patiala* – for the road.

Mini Market/Bollywood Bazaar ANTIQUES, CURIOS
(Map p42; 33/31 Mutton St; ☺11am-8pm Sat-Thu) Sells original vintage Bollywood posters and other movie ephemera as well as odd and interesting trinkets.

Kala Niketan CLOTHING
(Map p46; 95 MK Rd; ☺9.30am-7.30pm Mon-Sat) Sari madness on Queens Rd.

Mélange CLOTHING
(Map p42; 33 Altamount Rd, Kemp's Corner; ☺closed Sun) High-fashion ladies garments from over 100 Indian designers in a chic exposed-brick space.

Chimanlals HANDICRAFTS
(Map p46; 210 Dr Dadabhai Naoroji Rd, Fort; ☺9.30am-6pm Mon-Fri, to 5.30pm Sat) Beautiful writing materials made from traditional Indian paper. Enter from Wallace St.

Rhythm House MUSIC STORE
(Map p46; 40 K Dubash Marg, Fort; ☺10am-8.30pm Mon-Sat, 11am-8.30pm Sun) Non-pirated CDs; tickets to concerts, plays and festivals.

BX Furtado & Sons MUSIC STORE
(off Map p46; www.furtadosonline.com; Jer Mahal, Dhobitalao; ☺10am-8pm Mon-Sat) The best place in Mumbai for musical instruments – sitars, tablas, accordions, and local and imported guitars. The branch around the corner on Kalbadevi Rd is pianos and sheet music only.

Central Cottage Industries Emporium HANDICRAFTS, SOUVENIRS
(Map p44; Chhatrapati Shivaji Marg, Colaba; ☺closed Sun) Limited souvenir shopping at government-restricted prices.

Standard Supply Co PHOTOGRAPHY
(Map p46; Image House, Walchand Hirachand Marg, Fort; ☺10am-7pm Mon-Sat) Everything you could possibly need for digital and film photography.

❶ Information

Internet Access
It's easy to find wi-fi access in Mumbai: many hotels, restaurants and cafes have it on offer, the two latter generally free of charge. Internet cafes, too, are commonplace, though operations change frequently. Ask at your hotel or guesthouse reception for the closest to you; most come in at ₹40 to ₹50 per hour's browsing.

Media
To find out what's going on in Mumbai, check out the *Hindustan Times'* **Café** insert or **Time Out Mumbai** (www.timeoutmumbai.net; ₹50).

Medical Services
Bombay Hospital (Map p46; ☑22067676, ambulance ☑22067309; www.bombayhospital. com; 12 New Marine Lines)
Breach Candy Hospital (Map p42; ☑23672888; www.breachcandyhospital.org; 60 Bhulabhai Desai Rd, Breach Candy) The best in Mumbai, if not in India.
Royal Chemists (Map p46; ☑22004041-3; 89A Maharshi Karve Rd, Churchgate; ☺8.30am-8.30pm Mon-Sat)
Sahakari Bhandar Chemist (Map p44; ☑22022399; Colaba Causeway, Colaba; ☺10am-8.30pm)

Money
ATMs are everywhere and foreign-exchange offices changing cash and travellers cheques are also plentiful.
Akbar Travels Colaba (Map p44; ☑22823434; 30 Alipur Trust Bldg; ☺10am-7pm); Fort (Map p46; ☑22633434; Terminus View, 167/169 Dr Dadabhai Naoroji Rd; ☺10am-7pm Mon-Fri, to 6pm Sun)
Thomas Cook (☺9.30am-6pm Mon-Sat) Colaba (Map p44; ☑22882517-20; Colaba Causeway); Fort (Map p46; ☑61603333; 324 Dr Dadabhai Naoroji Rd)

Post
The **main post office** (Map p46; ☺10am-6pm Mon-Sat) is an imposing building behind Chhatrapati Shivaji Terminus (CST; Victoria Terminus). **Poste restante** (☺9am-8pm Mon-Sat) is at Counter 1. Letters should be addressed c/o Poste Restante, Mumbai GPO, Mumbai 400 001. Bring your passport to collect mail. The **EMS Speedpost parcel counter** (☺11.30am-7.30pm Mon-Fri) is across from the stamp counters. Opposite the post office, under the tree, are parcel-wallahs who will stitch up your parcel for ₹40.
Colaba post office (Map p44; Henry Rd) Convenient branch.
Blue Dart/DHL (Map p46; www.bluedart. com; Khetan Bhavan, J Tata Rd, Churchgate; ☺10am-8pm Mon-Sat); Private express-mail company.

Telephone

Justdial (☑69999999; www.justdial.com) and ☑197 provide directory enquiries.

Tourist Information

Government of India tourist office (Map p46; ☑22074333; www.incredibleindia.com; 123 Maharshi Karve Rd; ⊙8.30am-7pm Mon-Fri, to 2pm Sat) Provides information for the entire country.

Government of India tourist office airport booths domestic (☑26156920; ⊙7am-midnight); international (☑26813253; ⊙24hr)

Maharashtra Tourism Development Corporation booth (MTDC; Map p44; ☑22841877; Apollo Bunder; ⊙8.30am-4pm Tue-Sun, 5.30-8pm weekends) For city bus tours.

MTDC reservation office (Map p46; ☑22841877; www.maharashtratourism.gov.in; Madame Cama Rd, opposite LIC Bldg, Nariman Point; ⊙9.45am-5.30pm Mon-Sat) Information on Maharashtra and bookings for MTDC hotels and the *Deccan Odyssey* train package. This is also the only MTDC office that accepts credit cards.

Travel Agencies

Akbar Travels (Map p46; ☑22633434; www.akbartravelsonline.com; Terminus View, 167/169 Dr Dadabhai Naoroji Rd, Fort; ⊙10am-7pm Mon-Fri, to 6pm Sun)

Magnum International Travel & Tours (Map p44; ☑61559700; 10 Henry Rd, Colaba; ⊙10am-5.30pm Mon-Fri, to 4pm Sat)

Thomas Cook (Map p46; ☑22048556-8; 324 Dr Dadabhai Naoroji Rd, Fort; ⊙9.30am-6pm Mon-Sat)

Visa Extensions

Foreigners' Regional Registration Office (FRRO; Map p46; ☑22620446; Annexe Bldg No 2, CID, Badaruddin Tyabji Rd, near Special Branch) Does not officially issue extensions on tourist visas; even in emergencies it will direct you to its Delhi office. However, some travellers have managed to procure an emergency extension here after much waiting and persuasion.

ⓘ Getting There & Away

Air

Chhatrapati Shivaji International Airport (☑domestic 26264000, international 26813000; www.csia.in), is about 30km from the city centre. Both domestic and international terminals have ATMs, foreign exchange counters and tourist information booths. A free shuttle bus runs between the two every 30 minutes for ticket holders only.

See p232 for details of the plentiful daily domestic flights between Mumbai and Goa.

Bus

Numerous private operators and state governments run long-distance buses daily between Mumbai and Goa.

Long-distance government-run buses arrive and depart from **Mumbai Central bus terminal** (Map p42; ☑23074272/1524) by Mumbai Central train station.

Private buses, however, are usually more comfortable and simpler to book, but can cost significantly more than government buses. Most arrive and depart from Dr Anadrao Nair Rd near Mumbai Central train station (Map p42). Note that fares to Goa can be up to 75% higher during holiday periods such as Christmas and New Year. To check on departure times and current prices, try **National CTC** (Map p42; ☑23015652; Dr Anadrao Nair Rd; ⊙7am-10pm).

Even more convenient for Goa are the private buses run by **Chandni Travels** (Map p46; ☑22713901). They depart three times a day from in front of Azad Maidan (Map p46), just south of the Metro Big cinema. Ticket agents are also located near the bus departure point.

Train

The most atmospheric way to get to or from Mumbai is without doubt by train. There are a number of trains to and from Goa; book as far ahead as you can during peak season since they are very popular (and be sure to check for tourist quota tickets if the regular quota is full). The most popular services depart from the main Chhatrapari Shivaji Terminus (CST or Victoria Terminus); others, such as the daily Netravati Express and the daily Matsyagandha Express, depart from Lokmanya Tilak train station, which, it's crucial to note, is around 16km north of CST.

The reservations office is at CST on the 1st floor; the foreign tourist counter, for buying tourist quota tickets, is number 52, while the credit-card reservations counters are numbers 10 and 11.

ⓘ Getting Around

To/From the Airports

INTERNATIONAL AIRPORT The prepaid-taxi booths located at the international airport offer set fares for every neighbourhood in the city; Colaba, Fort and Marine Dr are AC/non-AC ₹495/395, Bandra West ₹310/260 and Juhu ₹235/190. The journey to Colaba takes about 45 minutes at night and 1½ to two hours during the day. Tips are not required.

Autorickshaws queue up at a little distance from arrivals, but don't try to take one to South Mumbai: they can only go as far as Mahim Creek. You can catch an autorickshaw (around ₹40) to

MAJOR TRAIN SERVICES BETWEEN MUMBAI CST & GOA

TRAIN NAME & NO	FREQUENCY	SAMPLE FARE	DEPART MUMBAI CST	ARRIVE MADGAON (GOA)
Konkan Kanya Express; 10111	daily	₹1832/1092/796	11.05pm	10.45am
Mandovi Express; 10103	daily	₹1832/1092/796	6.55am	6.45pm
Jan Shatabdi Express; 1251	daily	₹680/197	5.10am	2.10pm
Mangalore Express; 12133	daily	₹1103/812/308	10.15pm	7am

Prices refer to 1AC/2AC/3AC, except for the Jan Shatabdi Express, which refer to AC seat/second class seating, and the Mangalore Express, which refer to 2AC/3AC/sleeper.

Andheri train station and catch a suburban train (₹7, 45 minutes) to Churchgate or CST. Only attempt this if you arrive during the day outside of rush 'hour' (6am to 11am) and are not weighed down with luggage.

Minibuses outside the arrivals hall offer free shuttle services to the domestic airport and Juhu hotels.

A taxi from South Mumbai to the international airport should be between ₹350 and ₹400 by negotiating a fixed fare beforehand; official baggage charges are ₹10 per bag. Add 25% to the meter charge between midnight and 5am. We love the old-school black-and-yellows, but there are also AC, metered call taxis run by **Meru** (44224422; www.merucabs.com), charging ₹20 for the first kilometre and ₹14 per kilometre thereafter (25% more at night). Routes are tracked by GPS, so no rip-offs.

DOMESTIC AIRPORT Taxis and autorickshaws queue up outside both domestic terminals. The prepaid counter is outside arrivals. An AC/non-AC taxi to Colaba or Fort costs ₹400/350, day or night, plus ₹10 per bag. For Juhu, ₹200/150.

A cheaper alternative is to catch an autorick-shaw between the airport and Vile Parle train station (₹20 to ₹30), and a train between Vile Parle and Churchgate (₹7, 45 minutes). Don't attempt this during rush 'hour' (6am to 11am).

Bus

Mumbai's single- and double-decker buses are good for travelling short distances. Fares around South Mumbai cost ₹3 for a section; pay the conductor once you're aboard. The service is run by **BEST** (Map p44; www.bestundertaking. com), which has a depot in Colaba (the website has a useful search facility for bus routes across the city). Just jumping on a double-decker (such as bus 103) is an inexpensive way to see South Mumbai. Day passes are available for ₹25.

In the Mumbai Buses table are some useful routes; all of these buses depart from the bus stand at the southern end of Colaba Causeway and pass Flora Fountain.

Car

Cars are generally hired for an eight-hour day and an 80km maximum, with additional charges if you go over. For an AC car, the best going rate is about ₹1000.

Agents at the Apollo Bunder ticket booths near the Gateway of India can arrange a non-AC Maruti with driver for a half-day of sightseeing for ₹1000 (going as far as Mahalaxmi and Malabar Hill). Regular taxi drivers often accept a similar price.

Metro

Mumbai's US$8.17 billion metro project has broken ground. The Colaba-Bandra-Airport line will most benefit tourists, but is several years away from completion.

Motorcycle

Allibhai Premji Tyrewalla (Map p42; www. premjis.com; 205/207 Dr D Bhadkamkar Rd; 10am-7pm Mon-Sat), around for almost 100 years, sells new and used motorcycles with a guaranteed buy-back option. For two- to three-week 'rental' periods you'll still have to pay the full cost of the bike upfront. The company

MUMBAI BUSES

DESTINATION	BUS NO
Breach Candy	132, 133
CST & Crawford Market	1, 3, 21, 103, 124
Churchgate	70, 106, 123, 132
Girgaum Chowpatty	103, 106, 107, 123
Haji Ali	83, 124, 132, 133
Hanging Gardens	103, 106
Mani Bhavan	123
Mohammed Ali Rd	1, 3, 21
Mumbai Central train station	124, 125

TAXI TROUBLE

We won't name names, but Mumbaikar taxis and rickshaws *might* occasionally like to take advantage of foreign faces. If you find yourself in either with an old-fashioned meter (outside on the left-hand dash), you are vulnerable. Print out handy conversion charts from the Mumbai Traffic Police (www.traffic policemumbai.org/Tariffcard_Auto_taxi_form.htm) – end of discussion (until the next price hike).

prefers to deal with longer-term schemes of two months or more, which work out cheaper anyway. A used 150cc or 225cc Hero Honda Karizma costs ₹25,000 to ₹80,000, with a buy-back price of around 60% after three months (higher-cc Enfields are sometimes available). A smaller bike (100cc to 180cc) starts at ₹25,000. The company can also arrange shipment of bikes overseas (around ₹24,000 to the UK).

Taxi & Autorickshaw

Every second car on Mumbai's streets seems to be a black-and-yellow Premier taxi (India's version of a 1950s Fiat). They're the most convenient way to get around the city, and in South Mumbai drivers *almost* always use the meter without prompting. Autorickshaws are confined to the suburbs north of Mahim Creek.

Drivers don't always know the names of Mumbai's streets (especially new names) – the best way to find something is by using nearby landmarks. Taxi meters start at ₹16 during the day (₹20 after midnight) for the first 1.6km and ₹10 per kilometre after this (₹12 after midnight). If you get a taxi with an old-fashioned meter, the fare will be roughly 16 times the amount shown on it. The minimum autorickshaw fare is ₹11.

Train

Mumbai has an efficient but overcrowded suburban train network.

There are three main lines, making it easy to navigate. The most useful service operates from Churchgate heading north to stations such as Charni Rd (for Girgaum Chowpatty), Mumbai Central, Mahalaxmi (for the Dhobi Ghat; p50), Vile Parle (for the domestic airport), Andheri (for the international airport) and Borivali (for Sanjay Gandhi National Park). Other suburban lines operate from CST to Byculla (for Veermata Jijabai Bhonsle Udyan, formerly Victoria Gardens), Dadar and as far as Neral (for Matheran). Trains run from 4am till 1am. From Churchgate, 2nd-

/1st-class fares are ₹4/41 to Mumbai Central, ₹7/78 to Vile Parle or Andheri, and ₹9/104 to Borivali.

'Tourist tickets' permit unlimited travel in 2nd/1st class for one (₹50/170), three (₹90/330) or five (₹105/390) days.

Avoid rush hours when trains are jam-packed, even in 1st class; watch your valuables, and gals, stick to the ladies-only carriages.

GREATER MUMBAI

Elephanta Island

In the middle of Mumbai Harbour, 9km northeast of the Gateway of India, the rock-cut temples on Elephanta Island (http://asi.nic.in/; Indian/foreigner ₹10/250; ⊙caves 9am-5.30pm Tue-Sun) are a Unesco World Heritage Site and worth crossing the waters for. Home to a labyrinth of cave-temples carved into the basalt rock of the island, the artwork represents some of the most impressive temple carving in all of India. The main Shiva-dedicated temple is an intriguing latticework of courtyards, halls, pillars and shrines, with the magnum opus a 6m-tall statue of Sadhashiva – depicting a three-faced Shiva as the destroyer, creator and preserver of the universe. The enormous central bust of Shiva, its eyes closed in eternal contemplation, may be the most serene sight you witness in India.

The temples are thought to have been created between AD 450 and 750, when the island was known as Gharapuri (Place of Caves). The Portuguese renamed it Elephanta because of a large stone elephant near the shore, which collapsed in 1814 and was moved by the British to Mumbai's Jijamata Udyan.

The English-language guide service (free with deluxe boat tickets) is worthwhile; tours depart every hour on the half-hour from the ticket booth. Beware of touts that greet you at the jetty and try to convince you to employ their services – the included English guide will meet you at the entrance to the temples. Ask for government-issued ID if in doubt.

If you explore independently, pick up Pramod Chandra's *A Guide to the Elephanta Caves* from the stalls lining the stairway. There's also a small museum on-site, which

SANJAY GANDHI NATIONAL PARK

It's hard to believe that within 90 minutes of the teeming metropolis you can be surrounded by this 104-sq-km **protected tropical forest** (☑28866449; adult/child ₹30/15, 2-/4-wheeler vehicle ₹15/50; ☉7.30am-6pm). Here, bright flora, birds, butterflies and elusive wild leopards replace pollution and crowds, all surrounded by forested hills on the city's northern edge. Urban development and shantytowns try to muscle in on the fringes of this wild region, but its status as a national park has allowed it to stay green and calm.

In addition to well-worn trekking trails to Shilonda waterfall and Vihar and Tulsi lakes, there is a lion and tiger safari and Kanheri caves to occupy day-trippers escaping the Mumbai mayhem. Inside the main northern entrance is an information centre with a small exhibition on the park's wildlife. The best time to see birds is October to April and butterflies August to November.

has some informative pictorial panels on the origin of the caves.

❶ Getting There & Away

Launches (economy/deluxe ₹105/130) head to Elephanta Island from the Gateway of India every half-hour from 9am to 3.30pm Tuesday to Sunday. Buy tickets at the booths lining Apollo Bunder. The voyage takes just over an hour.

The ferries dock at the end of a concrete pier, from where you can walk (around three minutes) or take the **miniature train** (₹10) to the **stairway** (admission ₹5) leading up to the caves. It's lined with handicraft stalls and patrolled by pesky monkeys. Wear good shoes.

Anjuna & North Goa

Includes »

Arambol (Harmal)............71

Mandrem.........................74

Aswem............................76

Morjim............................78

Siolim.............................78

Vagator & Chapora.........79

Mapusa...........................84

Anjuna............................87

Calangute & Baga..........92

Candolim, Sinquerim
& Fort Aguada................99

Nerul (Coco) Beach.....106

Along the Mandovi
River.............................106

Best Places to Eat

» La Plage, Aswem (p77)

» Plantain Leaf, Calangute (p97)

» Villa Blanche Bistro (p84)

» Cafe Chocolatti, Candolim (p105)

Best Places to Stay

» Fort Tiracol Heritage Hotel (p75)

» Kaju Varo, Aswem (p77)

» Siolim House, Siolim (p78)

» Sunbeam, Assagao (p84)

Why Go?

Tucked between the Terekhol and Mandovi Rivers, North Goa encompasses the relentless action of Calangute and Baga, the happy hippieness of Arambol and Anjuna, the laid-back beaches of Aswem and Mandrem, and the luxury of boutique heritage hotels.

It was not, however, always this way. Until the 1960s Calangute was the sedate watering hole of the Portuguese elite, and the north coast was a simple string of fishing villages. Towards the end of the '60s came the heady days of naked revellers; next came the trance parties and, simultaneously, the package-holiday hordes.

Today, if you're here for spiritual bliss, don't go to Baga on a Friday night, it's more Ibiza than Inner Peace. Similarly, if you're looking to live it up, avoid Mandrem, whose liveliest moments are its ashtanga yoga sessions. Head inland, meanwhile, for enchanting villages, churches and temples. Choose carefully, then, and North Goa has delights aplenty, whatever your inclination.

When to Go

North Goa's party and holiday scene cranks up in November and lasts until March: the weather's picture-perfect, tourist facilities boom and beaches bustle. If something lower-key is what you're after, consider visiting in October or April; not everything will be open, but there are fewer crowds and lower prices.

From April to September, most tourist establishments close and resorts regain a local character: some long-stayers, especially in Arambol and Anjuna, swear this is the best time to be in Goa.

Arambol (Harmal)

📞 0832

Arambol (also known as Harmal) first emerged in the 1960s as a mellow paradise for long-haired long-stayers. Today, things are still decidedly cheap and cheerful, with much of the village's budget accommodation arranged in simple little huts along the cliff sides. It's a bit more mainstream festival in style than in days gone by, and it may be that many of today's 'hippies' shave off their fortnight's beards and take off their tie-dye once they're back to their nine-to-five lives.

The village's main covelike beach is gently curved and safe for swimming. Perhaps the reason why is that in recent years, Arambol has become popular among families with young children, who hang out happily with droves of uniformly dreadlocked, tattooed and creatively pierced individualists. Some people love Arambol for all this; others turn up their noses and move along, leaving today's long-stayers to enjoy the pretty beach and extensive 'alternative' shopping opportunities provided by nonstop stalls all the way down the beach road (known locally as 'Glastonbury St') and along round the cliff. If you're looking for a committed traveller vibe, this is the place to come. If you're seeking laid-back languidness, you might be better heading down the coast to Mandrem or Aswem instead.

🏃 Activities

Aside from yoga and beach lounging, the most popular pursuits in Arambol these days are paragliding and kite surfing. Several operators give lessons and rent equipment on the very south of Arambol beach; walk down there, or check out some noticeboards, to find out who's renting what this season.

Himalayan Iyengar Yoga Centre   YOGA
(www.hiyogacentre.com) Set amid the sand dunes of Arambol Beach is Himalayan Iyengar Yoga Centre, which runs five-day courses in hatha yoga from mid-November to mid-March. This is the winter centre of the Iyengar yoga school in Dharamkot, near Dharamsala in north India, and is run by the same teacher, Sharat Arora. Five-day courses for new and more-experienced students cost ₹3000, with additional days of instruction available at a reduced rate. Booking and reg-

istration must be done in person at the centre on Tuesdays at 2pm. Courses start on Fridays. There are also intensive two- to three-week courses for more experienced hatha yoga devotees and special short courses combining yoga with ayurvedic treatment. The centre also offers accommodation in the form of simple huts (₹300) for students. You'll find it a five-minute walk from the beach off the main road; look for the sign on the left-hand side as you head down to the beach road.

🛏 Sleeping

Accommodation in Arambol is plentiful, mainly of the budget variety, and it pays to trawl the cliffside to the north of Arambol's main beach for the best of numerous hut options. Here you can expect simple accommodation, mostly without private bathroom but with the benefit of incredible sea views (along with attendant breezes). Most cost around ₹500 to ₹700 in high season, and it's almost impossible to book in advance – simply turn up early in the day to check out who's checking out of your dream hut. The area around the Narayan Temple (take a left turn off the main road as you enter town) also has several guesthouses of similar quality.

Chilli's   HOTEL $
(📞9921882424; Glastonbury St; d ₹500) This clean and simple place is one of Arambol's best non-beachside bargains. Chilli's offers 10 decent, no-frills rooms on the road down to the beach, all with attached bathroom, fan and a hot-water shower. There's an honour system for buying self-service bottled water from the fridge on the landing.

Shree Sai Cottages   BEACH HUTS $$
(📞2362823, 9420767358; shreesai_cottages@ yahoo.com; huts without bathroom ₹400-500) A good example of what's on offer, Shree Sai has simple, cute, sea-facing huts a short walk north from the main Arambol Beach, with lovely views out over the water and a calm, easygoing vibe.

Om Ganesh   BEACH HUTS $
(📞9404436447; r & huts without bathroom ₹800) Popular huts, especially those on the seaside of the coastal path. The seaside Om Ganesh restaurant is also a great place for lunch or dinner, with almost everything you can think of on the menu (if you can manage to decode entries such as 'gokomadi' in

Anjuna & North Goa Highlights

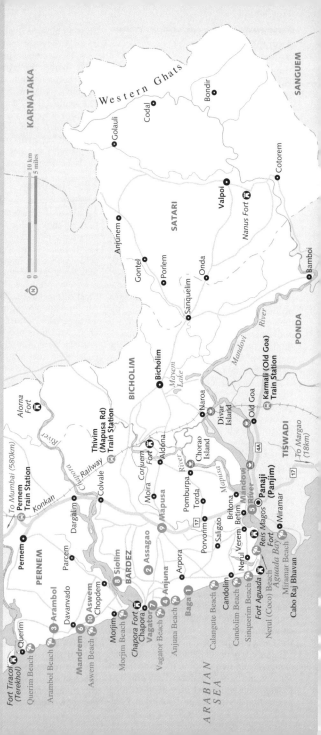

1 Live it up with the party people of **Baga** (p92)

2 Drive out to stroll the lanes of pretty little **Assagao** village (p84)

3 Settle in for the season with the long-stayers in traveller-central **Arambol** (p71)

4 Drive a hard bargain at tie-dyed, touristy but still charming **Anjuna Flea Market** (p87)

5 Get truly off the beaten track exploring the countryside along the **Mandovi River** (p106)

6 Bliss out with yoga and beach-time at **Mandrem** (p74)

7 Catch the tail end of the party scene in **Vagator** (p81)

8 Experience Goan village life in style with a stay at a heritage hotel in **Siolim** (p78)

9 Peruse the goods and tuck into a thali at **Mapusa's Friday market** (p84)

10 Take time over a lazy gourmet lunch at **La Plage** (p77) in Aswem

the Mexican section). Note that many people in the area will tell you their place is Om Ganesh (there are three on the coastal path next to each other); call ahead to avoid confusion.

Ludu Guest House   BEACH HUTS $

(☏2242734; r ₹700-1000) A cut above many other Arambol options, Ludu offers simply decorated, clean and bright cliffside rooms with attached cold-water showers. Hot water can be ordered by the bucketful.

Pitruchaya   BEACH HUTS $

(☏9881811098/9404454596; r/huts without bathroom ₹400/500) Very nice rooms facing the sea in this relatively spaciously situated little place, with a slightly Mediterranean feel. Six huts and eight rooms are available; the rooms are an especially good deal.

✖ Eating & Drinking

Plenty of cute, sparkly little places are dotted along the top part of the road curving down towards the beach. Many change annually, so stroll along and see what organic, glitter-ball and parachute-silk destination takes your fancy. Pizza places come and go, in case you're in need of a Margherita fix. For simpler fare, head up to the village, where chai shops and small local joints will whip you up a chai for ₹5 and a thali for ₹50.

Meanwhile, all along the beach you'll find the usual assortment of traveller-friendly menus, attempting (with wildly varying levels of success) everything from thick Tibetan *thukpa* (noodle soup) to crunchy Korean *kimchi* (pickled vegetable dish). Most drinking is undertaken in beach shacks, which often serve happy-hour cocktails alongside a dose of live music or a DVD film screening or two.

Shimon   MIDDLE EASTERN $

(light meals ₹60-120; ⊘9am-11pm) Understandably popular with Israeli backpackers, Shimon's, tucked into a lane on the right as you head down 'Glastonbury St' to the beach, is a good place to fill up on a tasty felafel (₹100) before hitting the beach. For something more unusual to try, go for *sabich* (₹110), crisp slices of eggplant stuffed into pita bread along with boiled egg, boiled potato, and salad. Or, in a crazy East-meets-Middle-East moment, try the thali (₹250), which comprises a little bit of almost everything on the menu. Pastry addicts should take note:

jachnun (a deliciously addictive Yemenite flaky boiled-dough breakfast) is served on Saturdays. Follow anything or everything that you eat with a nice strong Turkish coffee (₹40).

Fellini   ITALIAN $$

(mains ₹160-300; ⊘6.30pm-11pm) On the left-hand side just before the beach, this long-standing Italian joint is perfect for when you're craving a carbonara or calzone, delivering all your wood-fired pizza and fresh pasta requirements in the thick of the Arambol action. Choose from 46 different varieties of pizza, but save space for a very decent rendition of tiramisu (₹80).

Double Dutch   MULTICUISINE $$

(mains ₹110-190) An ever-popular option for its steaks, salads, Thai and Indonesian dishes and famous apple pies, all served up in a pretty garden setting on the road between the village and 'Glastonbury St', this is a great place to peruse the noticeboard for current Arambolic affairs, while munching on a plateful of cookies or a huge, tasty sandwich.

German Bakery   BAKERY, MULTICUISINE $

(Welcome Inn; cakes from ₹50; ⊘7am-late) This rather dim and dingy corner cafe is exceptionally popular, with good cakes including lemon cheese pie (₹60) and a scrummy chocolate biscuit cake (₹50). Consider washing it down with a pretty good espresso. Big breakfasts come in at around the ₹100 to ₹150 mark.

Blue Sea Horse   MULTICUISINE $

(mains from ₹70) Situated just where beach meets street, Blue Sea Horse serves a solid all-day menu with extensive seafood options when the catch comes in, but its popularity soars come sunset, with mean cocktails and a nightly movie (usually screened around 7pm) on offer.

Outback Bar   MULTICUISINE $

(mains from ₹80) Seafood is a speciality at this nice place, tucked away a little bit from the Arambol action, on the cliff path after Om Ganesh.

ℹ Information

It's important to note that there is no ATM in Arambol itself; the closest is at the northern entrance to the village, and if this isn't working, the next option is in Siolim, about 12km south. Everything else you'll need in the way

DON'T MISS

THE ROAD TO ARAMBOL

If you're coming to Arambol with your own transport from the south, the road from the NH17 highway to Arambol takes you through the pleasant, parochial town of Pernem. Take a right here when you reach the large temple complex, unmistakeable for its large elephant sculptures, and wind your way along a scenic high road beside the lazy, island-studded Terekhol River where fishermen in dugouts ply the waters. This trip alone makes a visit to Arambol worthwhile.

of services – dozens of internet outfits, travel agents, moneychangers and the like – you'll find in abundance on what's commonly known as 'Glastonbury St', the road leading down to Arambol's beach. Internet access here generally costs ₹40 to ₹60 per hour, and money-changing commission rates are all comparable. There are also several agencies towards the top of the road offering parcel services with Federal Express and DHL deliveries and by air and sea mail. Wi-fi is widespread, and mostly free, in beach huts and restaurants.

❶ Getting There & Away

Frequent buses to and from Mapusa (₹20, 1½ hours) stop on the main road at the 'backside' (as locals are fond of saying) of Arambol village, where there's a church, a school and a few local shops. Beware that from here, it's a 1.5km slog down through the village to the main beach drag, and 500m further to the beach itself. Alternatively hop into an autorickshaw or taxi for an extortionate ₹50.

Plenty of places in the village advertise scooters and motorbikes for hire for ₹200 and ₹300 respectively, per day; try Derrick's at Chilli's hotel, for a good rate.

A prepaid taxi to Arambol from Dabolim Airport costs ₹975; from Mapusa a taxi costs around ₹400.

Mandrem

Mellow Mandrem has in recent years become an in-the-know bolt-hole for those seeking respite from the relentless traveller scene of Arambol and Anjuna and, as such, is growing busier year by year. So far it has resisted large-scale expansion, with rare olive ridley marine turtles still turning up annually to lay their eggs in its soft sands – but go now, before it's completely consumed by rows of beach shacks fronted by rows of sun loungers, as has happened elsewhere on the north coast. The beach, right now, is still wide and beautiful, and there's little to do but laze on, and here's hoping it stays that way. Recent developments on the beach road, including plentiful bike hire places, and a spate of small supermarkets and souvenir stands, suggest the times may well finally be a-changin' in Mandrem.

Activities

Mandrem is something of a Spiritual Central, and there's plenty of yoga on offer here. Many classes and courses change with the season, but there are a few spiritually slanted places that reappear year after year. Ayurvedic massage, too, is widely available throughout the fledgling resort: ask around for recommendations, or try the long-standing listing below.

Amalia Camp   SPIRITUAL COURSES
(www.neeru.org) Its slogan – 'Meeting Yourself' – might give you a clue as to what's going on at Amalia Camp, where local guru Neeru hosts *satsangs* (devotional speech and chanting sessions) to help ease you towards everelusive enlightenment. Her own personal three-point plan invites you to join her in 'Step One: Realization of Truth; Step Two: Liberation of the Mind; Step Three: Integration Into Life'. Check her website for upcoming opportunities to do so.

Ashiyana Retreat Centre   YOGA
(www.ashiyana-yoga-goa.com) This 'tropical retreat centre' situated right on Mandrem Beach has a long list of classes and courses available from November to April, from retreats and yoga holidays to daily drop-in workshops, meditation and yoga sessions, along with a spa, massage and 'massage camp' for those wanting to learn the tricks of the tickly trade. Accommodation is in one of its gorgeous, heritage-styled rooms and huts; the super-cute Mango Tree House is especially lovely. The centre's largely organic, vegetarian restaurant dishes up tasty buffet brunches and dinners daily to guests and drop-in casuals alike. Costs start at ₹400 for a single drop-in yoga class; check the website for all-inclusive course packages and email all enquiries.

Ayurvedic Massage Centre

AYURVEDA, MASSAGE

(Massage from ₹900; ⊙9am-8pm) Ayurvedic massage is provided here by the delightful Shanti, whose former clients have included Dawn French. Try the rejuvenating 75-minute massage and facial package, or go for an unusual 'Poulti' massage, using a poulticelike cloth bundle containing 12 herbal powders, which is dipped in warm oil and comes especially recommended for treating back pain. You'll find her place on the right-hand side as you head down the beach road.

Himalaya Yoga Valley   YOGA

(☑9922719982; www.yogagoaindia.com) A popular choice, specialising in hatha and ashtanga teacher-training courses, Himalaya also has daily drop-in classes (1½ hour, 8am and 4pm daily).

🍴 Sleeping & Eating

There are lots of beach huts for ₹700 or thereabouts down on the beach. As with most destinations in Goa, the huts change appearance, owner and prices seasonally, so do a bit of trawling for the best before you take your pick. You'll also find plenty of

ANJUNA & NORTH GOA MANDREM

WORTH A TRIP

NORTH OF ARAMBOL: QUERIM & FORT TIRACOL (TEREKHOL)

Just a few kilometres north of Arambol, quiet Querim's beach is the place to come to while away the hours in peace, with only the occasional beach shack for company. Backed by a shady cover of fir and casuarina trees – though sadly this hinterland is becoming a little litter-blown – there's not much to do here but have a leisurely swim, settle back with a book, and revel in the tranquillity that descends so close, yet so far, from the Arambol action.

If you're keen to stay here, wander around the village set back from the beach. You'll find a scattering of 'rooms for rent' signs, and some entire village houses up for grabs.

To get to Terekhol (the most northerly point in Goa) and its fort, it's fun to hop on board Querim's **ferry** (pedestrians/motorbikes/cars free/₹4/₹10; ⊙7am-10pm, every 30 min) that chugs passengers and vehicles across the Terekhol River from the ferry landing at the very end of the village. If you find yourself stranded on the opposite side at low tide – when services are suspended for several hours – head downstream several kilometres, winding your way through a surreal amber landscape of iron-ore mines to a second ferry point.

Not far from the ferry landing, you'll find **Fort Tiracol (Terekhol)**, perched high above the banks of the river of the same name. Originally built by the Marathas in the early 17th century, the fort was captured by viceroy Dom Pedro de Almeida in 1746 and was rebuilt; the glum little Chapel of St Anthony, which takes up almost all of the available space within it, was added.

The fact that the fort falls on the 'wrong' side of Goa's natural northern border, the Terekhol River, led it to be involved in considerable controversy. In the late 18th century the British demanded that it be handed over to the Empire, and in 1825, when the first Goan-born governor, Dr Bernardo Peres da Silva, was ousted, his supporters took over the fort. His own forces mutinied at the last moment, and met their deaths at the hands of the Portuguese. Finally, in 1954 Goa's entire northern border came to be at the centre of anti-Portuguese demonstrations. Several pro-India supporters hoisted an Indian flag over the fort's ramparts, and two were killed as a result; a plaque here still attests to this today.

Today the fort is far more peaceable and better known as the **Fort Tiracol Heritage Hotel** (☑2366227631, 8326529653; www.forttiracol.com; d/ste ₹7600/9600). The hotel is a hit with travellers for its romantically decked-out rooms, impeccable service and stunning views out over Querim, the Terekhol River and the Arabian Sea. With only seven rooms, each one named after a day of the week, this is your chance to really get the feel for life in one of Portugal's maritime bastions, and perhaps live out all those fairytale fantasies. And even if you're not staying for the night, hop over for a peek at the fort and lunch at its lovely little restaurant.

VIPASSANA – THE ART OF SILENCE

Chances are that during your Goan sojourn you'll see Vipassana courses on offer, and wonder what exactly they involve. Vipassana, roughly meaning 'to see things for what they really are', is a meditation technique most often taught in Goa as a 10-day residential retreat, concentrating on 'self-trans-formation through self-observation'. In practice, this translates as 10 days of meditation, clear thought and near silence, abstaining from killing, stealing, lying, sexual activity and intoxicants, and concentrating at length on one's own breathing. Sounds like your cup of decaffeinated tea? Consult www. dhamma.org for more detailed informa-tion on the art of silence, or check the courses on offer at the Global Vipas-sana Pagoda in Mumbai (p50).

houses and rooms for rent throughout the village; just look for signs. Dining options are largely of the standard beach-shack va-riety, with most places dishing up a decent range of Indian and international cuisine.

Elsewhere   COTTAGES, TENTS **$$$**
(tents/rooms/houses per night from £122/250/
455; @) Though the exact location of this heavenly set of historic beachfront houses, and Otter Creek Tents (its canvas alter ego), is a quite closely guarded secret, it's safe to say that somewhere around Mandrem, on a secluded spit of land, lies Elsewhere. Choose from four beautiful beachfront houses, enticingly entitled the Piggery, Bak-ery, Priest's House and Captain's House, or from three luxury tents, each sleeping two (both houses and tents are only available for weeklong stays) and revel in the solitude that comes with a hefty price tag and a 60m walk across a bamboo bridge. Their website was not working at the time of research, but bookings can be made through i-escape (www.i-escape.com).

Dunes Holiday Village   BEACH HUTS **$$**
(☑2247219; www.dunesgoa.com; treehouse/r/hut ₹600/800/1400; @) Nice huts here are pep-pered around a palm-forest alley leading to the beach, and at night, globe lamps light up the place like a palm-tree dreamland.

Dune also has friendly, helpful staff, a good restaurant on the beach, and clean, cosy, muslin-lined huts with mosquito nets and balconies with comfy chairs or couches. It's a peaceful, feel-good kind of place, with yoga classes, yoga teachers-to-be hanging around drinking healthful juices, and a marked absence of trance.

Cuba Retreat   HOTEL **$$**
(☑2645775; www.cubagoa.com; d without/with AC ₹1250/1450; ✳@) Those enterprising folks from Cuba seem to get everywhere, includ-ing to this extremely spick and span set of suites just a few moments walk from the beach. The staff are friendly, there's a very nice bar-restaurant in the courtyard, and – unusually for Goa – you can actually book online.

Villa River Cat   GUESTHOUSE **$$$**
(☑2247928; www.villarivercat.com; d ₹1600-3300;✳@) This fabulously unusual circular guesthouse, filled with art, light, antiques, and an owner with a decidedly creative incli-nation, makes for an extremely popular stay. Hence, the management advises to book an astonishing eight months ahead for a stay during high season. Many travellers adore it, and some return visitors report that the service has picked up after a recent rocky patch.

ⓘ Information

Though most people head up to Arambol – or to little Madlamaz-Mandrem village at the top of the hill, set inland from the beach – for all their basic supplies and services, there are motorbike and scooter hire places, travel agents, and al-most everything else you'll need situated along the little road down to the beach.

ⓘ Getting There & Around

Getting to Mandrem and getting around by pub-lic transport isn't all that easy. Your very best bet is to hire a scooter (or a bicycle if you can handle the hilly coastal road) and trundle about at your own pace. Otherwise, hop in a taxi from Arambol (₹150).

Aswem
☑0832

A wide stretch of beach growing busier year by year (making it hard to know exactly where the beaches of neighbours Mandrem and Morjim begin and end), the lovely As-wem sands are, like Mandrem, growing in popularity annually, with an ever-increasing, ever-changing parade of beach-hut accommodation and beach-shack restaurants springing up each season. Though some stretches of the beach are becoming really quite busy, development here is nevertheless still generally low-key, swimming is usually safe, and the vibe remains reasonably mellow. Yoga and massage operations set up shop here each season; check notice boards or ask around for current classes and courses.

🛏 Sleeping

Aswem boasts a good and growing range of beach huts (operations change annually, but a basic hut should cost ₹700 and up, depending on the view, facilities and proximity to the beach). Stroll the sands and check out a good few before you make your decision. For something more luxurious, a number of stand-out higher-end choices are listed below.

🏄 Yab Yum   BEACH HUTS $$$
(www.yabyumresorts.com; domes from ₹2500; 🛜) A top-notch choice, whose unusual, stylish, dome-shaped huts are made of a combination of all-natural local materials, including mud, stone and mango wood. There are also cottages on offer, and a stellar 'suite pod' with two bedrooms and an amazing view out to sea. A whole host of yoga and massage options are also available, and parents will appreciate the paddling pools, babysitting, and kids' tepee, full of children's toys. Note that Yab Yum also maintains two other lovely properties in the nearby inland village of Dandos Wadda: the Artist's House, which sleeps eight people; and Jivana Plantation, which has a range of cottages to sleep between two and eight.

🏄 Kaju Varo   APARTMENTS $$$
(☏90110711911; www.shunyachi.com/villas-and-retreats-goa.html; apt from €130; ❄🛜🏊) Three stunning, minimalist loft suites (along with one intriguing modular house) set inside two converted old Goan homes, Kaju Varo is the place to stay if you're a fan of Scandinavian design and all things luxe. Splash about in the pool before hitting the beach, then consult with the in-house fusion chef about the evening's feast. Kaju Varo's sister concern is Noi Varo in Siolim; both aim to boost rural employment and develop sustainable building practices in Goa.

Amarya Shamiyana   TENTS $$$
(www.amaryagroup.com/amarya-shamiyana; tents from ₹7500; ❄🛜) Four huge, luxurious tents with all the modern trimmings (including wi-fi, room service and rain showers), located just off the beach behind the La Plage restaurant, makes this a highly tranquil spot to splurge.

The Meems' Beach Resort   BEACH HUTS $$
(☏3290703; www.meemsbeachresort.com; d/q huts ₹1500-5500; 🛜) A range of 10 good huts right on the beach, along with a new place offering 11 rooms and a cottage, Meems' is just across the road from the beach, with free wi-fi and an atmospheric restaurant. Accommodation options run from basic, atmospheric and cheerful through to a comfy, modern rooftop penthouse.

Leela Cottages   BEACH HUTS $$$
(☏22822874; www.leelacottage.com; ₹5000-8000; @) Ten cute little wooden cabins, falling somewhere between beach huts and cottages, are situated in a nice leafy garden, just steps from the beach, and not far from La Plage. Stand-out touches include antiquey bits and pieces in each cottage, individually named rooms (with some interesting name choices, like 'Magic Cappuccino' and 'Serene Cashew'), and lots of cute throw pillows.

🍴 Eating

Though you'll find no end of beach shacks offering the usual traveller-orientated menus, one place stands out head-and-shoulders above the rest.

🏆 La Plage   FRENCH $$
TOP CHOICE

(mains from ₹215; ⊙lunch & dinner) Oh me, oh my. Rightly renowned by those in the know, this beautiful, breezy beach restaurant has been dishing up sumptuous gourmet Mediterranean food since 2003, concocted by a genuine French chef. Its prices are astonishing: perfection for the price of a beach shack pizza, and on a recent visit, our lunchtime salad included, as a sweet aside, a surprisingly delicious black-olive ice cream. LA Plage offers great wines, fabulous desserts (try the chocolate thali) and even a truly unmissable gazpacho-style tomato juice, with exciting vegetarian options for those not convinced by the seafood and steaks.

Morjim

📞 0832

Greetings from Morjim, where the Arabian Sea meets the Baltic: for reasons perhaps known best to itself, the tiny village has become the destination of choice for young, long-staying Russians, along with big groups of domestic tourists, and receives only a (albeit slowly growing) trickle of visitors from other beaches. Situated at the mouth of the Chapora River, the south end of Morjim beach (also known locally as Temb) has lovely views down the headland to Chapora Fort, and makes for a pretty stroll down the estuary. This area is also where ever-decreasing numbers of olive ridley marine turtles come to lay their annual clutches of eggs. Drop into the Goa Forest Department's hut, set up to protect the eggs, to learn more.

Though it's a reasonably nice, quiet place to spend an afternoon on the sands (or to arrange a dolphin-watching trip, of which there are plenty on offer), and is certainly quite laid-back, the whole place gives off a distinct whiff of desolation (not helped by some decidedly lacklustre 'resorts'). There's very little bucolic charm in evidence, and the beach, in parts, is no longer pristine. Nevertheless, it could be a good place to look if you're seeking a full-season house rental; look for 'house to rent' signs around the village.

Siolim

📞 0832 / POP 12,000

The large village of Siolim, lying on the road north between the traveller epicentres of Anjuna and Arambol, is often overlooked by travellers, due to its riverside location some way from the nearest beach. But if you're looking for a change from sea and sand, it makes a pleasant place to stay, with lots of budget and midrange-priced houses for rent (just wander about a bit, and look out for handwritten signs) and a scattering of top-end heritage hotels.

Siolim is home to an atmospheric **daily market** near the ferry landing stage on the banks of the Chapora River, where you can watch women open mussel shells at a speed that will impress. On Wednesday mornings another small **market** (⊘7.30-10am), full of homegrown produce, sets up near central **St Anthony Church**, a building which dates back to the 16th century.

🛏 Sleeping

TOP
CHOICE **Siolim House**   HERITAGE HOTEL $$$
(📞 2272138; www.siolimhouse.com; ste from ₹6600; ✿) Comprising the seven-room Siolim House hotel and the smaller, three-bedroom Little Siolim, Siolim House is without doubt one of North Goa's boutique treats. Situated in an old *palácio* that was once home to the Governor of Macau, the hotel is elegant and carefully restored, and, though it has a pool, is devoid of many 'luxury' trappings. There's no air-con

---

THE TURTLE WIND

Each November, a strong breeze known as the 'turtle wind' heralds the arrival of olive ridley marine turtles to lay eggs on a clutch of Goan beaches. It's believed that these females – who live for over a century – return to the beach of their birth to lay eggs, courtesy of an incredible in-built 'homing device', often travelling thousands of kilometres to do so.

One such beach is Morjim, but turtle numbers over the last century have slowly dwindled to dangerous levels due to poaching. On investigation, it was found that locals were digging up the eggs and selling them as delicacies at the market, and any turtle found out of the water was generally killed for its meat and shell. Increased tourism to Goa has also taken its toll; eggs were, for years, trampled unwittingly at rave parties, while sea and light pollution continue to threaten the survival of those that manage, against the odds, to hatch.

In 1996 the Goa Foundation, on the urging of several concerned local residents, finally stepped in and enlisted the help of the Goa Forest Department to patrol the beach and instigate a turtle conservation program. Locals who once profited from selling the eggs are now paid to guard them at the several turtle protection sites (at Morjim, Agonda and Galgibag beaches) established for this very purpose. Drop into one of its information huts, or go to www.goaforest.com, to learn more.

SIOLIM ZAGOR FESTIVAL

Held annually on the first Sunday after Christmas, Siolim's Zagor Festival offers a happy glimpse into the peaceful coexistence of Goa's diverse religious communities.

Taking place on the Christian feast day of Nossa Senhora de Guia, the night-time festival blends both Hindu and Christian traditions, centring on a small Hindu shrine near the ferry dock, which is believed to house Zagoryo, the village deity. The guardian of the village *bunds* (the dams that keep the river from the rice fields), Zagoryo is offered thanks during the festival by every Siolim family. Hindu families offer the deity oil; Christians bring candles, and everyone also offers up *pohe* (small cakes of pressed rice).

Beginning with a candlelit procession, villagers file through the streets of Siolim bearing an effigy of Zagoryo, stopping at both roadside Hindu and Christian shrines for blessings along the way. Next comes a traditional dance drama, during which legends are re-enacted by members of two important Siolim families – the Catholic D'Souzas and Hindu Shirodkars – who've inherited the roles from their forebears.

At first light the next morning, Hindu and Christian blessings are chanted by village priests, and the deity is carried back to his shrine, amid a shower of further offerings. Once complete, the festivities are topped off with a Konkani *tiatr* (play) or two, a party and usually a performance by Siolim born-and-bred celebrity, Remo Fernandes (see p203). If you're in the area at the right time of year, don't miss a visit to the Zagor along with what is, at present, only a thin trickle of foreign tourists.

or vast plasma TV to be found in its antiquey rooms, and the dining, while delicious, is decidedly local. Siolim House also rents several other villas in Goa, including four located on a hilltop in Arpora, near Baga, and one in the village of Parra, near Mapusa. See its website for details.

Noi Varo   VILLA $$$
(☑9011071911; www.shunyachi.com; villa from ₹35,000, min 2 nights; ❄ 🛜 🐾) A spacious, stunning refurbished Portuguese mansion with three double bedrooms and a variety of extra sleeping spaces if your party requires it. You can kick back amid antiques, hang out in its river-view tree house, consult with its gourmet chef and float in a cool swimming pool. Note that artists, writers, musicians and the like should ask about special creative rates. A two-week minimum rental applies over Christmas and New Year.

Vagator & Chapora

🎵 0832

Dramatic red stone cliffs, dense green jungle and a crumbling 17th-century Portuguese fort provide Vagator and its diminutive village neighbour Chapora with one of the prettiest settings on the North Goan coast. Once known for their wild trance parties and heady, hippie lifestyles, things have slowed down considerably these days,

but Chapora – still reminiscent of the Mos Eisley Cantina *Star Wars* – remains a favourite for hippies and long-staying smokers, with the smell of *charas* (resin of the marijuana plant) clinging heavy to the light sea breeze.

Chapora is a working fishing harbour nestled at the mouth of the Chapora River, and hence is without much in the way of beach, whereas Vagator has three small, charismatic coves to choose from. The most northerly and largest is Vagator Beach, a beautiful stretch of sand, which only fills up for a few hours each afternoon when domestic coach tours unload their swift-clicking tourist hordes making the most of its good swimming. Avoid this time of day and you'll have plenty of room for lounging on its pretty, boulder-studded sands.

South from here, Vagator's two southerly coves are known as Little Vagator Beach and Ozran Beach; both are accessible by steep footpaths running down from near the Nine Bar. Both make upbeat, and sometimes cramped, places for a beach-shack lunch, a snooze on a sun lounge or a dip in the sea. With shacks dominating the sands, Goa trance heavy on the sound systems, and cows thronging among the people, there's a distinctly laid-back backpacker vibe, overseen at Ozran by the huge, happy carved Shiva face that gazes out serenely from the rocks.

Vagator & Chapora

ANJUNA & NORTH GOA VAGATOR & CHAPORA

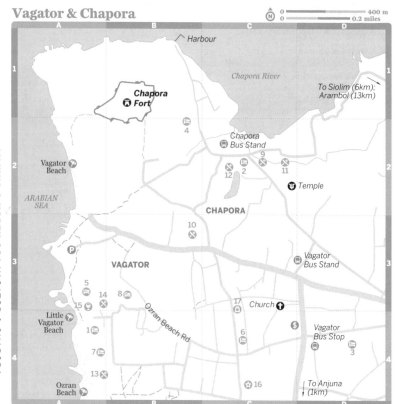

$\hat{N}$ 0 — 400 m
0 — 0.2 miles

- Harbour
- *Chapora River*
- To Siolim (6km); Arambol (13km)
- **Chapora** ⛫ **Fort**
- 4
- Chapora 🚌 Bus Stand
- *Vagator Beach* 🅿
- 9
- 12
- 2
- 11
- 🕌 Temple
- *ARABIAN SEA*
- **CHAPORA**
- 10
- 🅿
- **VAGATOR**
- Vagator 🚌 Bus Stand
- 5
- 14
- 8
- 17 Church ✝
- 15
- *Little Vagator Beach* 🅿
- 1
- 6
- Vagator Bus Stop
- 3
- 7
- *Ozran Beach Rd*
- 13
- 16
- *Ozran Beach* 🅿
- To Anjuna (1km)

⦿ Sights & Activities

Chapora Fort   FORT

Chapora's windswept old laterite fort, standing guard over the mouth of the Chapora River, was built by the Portuguese in 1617, to protect Bardez *taluka* (district), in Portuguese hands from 1543 onwards, from the threat of invaders. It was built over the remnants of an older Muslim structure, hence the name of the village itself, from 'Shahpura', meaning 'town of the Shah'.

Though heavily fortified, Chapora Fort was nevertheless captured several times by invaders: first by several groups of Hindu raiders, and next, in 1684, when it was reportedly conquered without a shot being fired. On this occasion the Portuguese captain of the fort decided to surrender to the Maratha forces of the chieftain Sambhaji, his decision perhaps stemming, if legend is to be believed, from the manner in which Sambhaji's forces managed to breach the fort's defences: it's said that they clung tight to tenacious 1.5m-long monitor lizards, who were able to scale the rocky walls with ease.

The Portuguese rebuilt the fort in 1717, adding features such as tunnels that led from the bastion down to the seashore and the river bank to enable resupply or escape in times of trouble, but Chapora fell again to the Marathas in 1739. Soon the northerly *taluka* of Pernem came into Portuguese hands, forming part of the Novas Conquistas (the 'New Conquests', the second wave of Portuguese conquests in Goa), and the significance of Chapora faded. The fort was finally abandoned to the ravages of the elements in 1892.

Today it is a crumble of picturesque ruins, though you can still pick out the mouths of two escape tunnels and a scattering of pre-Portuguese Muslim tombstones. The main reason to make the climb up the hill, though, is for the stunning views out along the coast, especially enticing at sunset.

Vagator & Chapora

⊙ Top Sights
Chapora Fort B1

⊕ Sleeping
1 Alcove Resort A4
2 Baba.. C2
3 Bean Me Up Soya Station D4
4 Casa de Olga..B2
5 Casa Vagator A3
6 Julie Jolly... C4
7 Paradise on the Earth...........................A4
8 Shalom B3

⊗ Eating
Bean Me Up Soya Station .... (see 3)

9 Jai Ganesh Fruit Juice Centre C2
10 Mango Tree Bar & Cafe B3
11 Scarlet Cold Drinks C2
12 Sunrise Restaurant C2
13 Thalassa A4
14 Yangkhor Moonlight..............................A3

⊙ Drinking
15 Nine Bar A3

⊗ Entertainment
16 Hilltop...C4

⊘ Shopping
17 Rainbow Bookshop C3

TOP CHOICE Chapora Harbour VILLAGE LIFE
The narrow road northwest of the village leads you past lots of village homes with rooms for rent, up to a small harbour where the day's catch is hauled in from colourful, bobbing fishing boats. Self-caterers with the desire for fresh fish can haggle for their supper directly with fishermen, while for most others, it makes for a scenic photo opportunity and provides an interesting window into traditional village life.

Yoga & Ayurveda YOGA, AYURVEDA
There's plenty of yoga and ayurveda on offer seasonally in both Vagator and Chapora; check the noticeboards at Bean Me Up Soya Station or Scarlet Cold Drinks for up-to-date details.

🛏 Sleeping

VAGATOR
Budget accommodation, much of it in private rooms, ranges along the Ozran Beach Rd in Vagator; you'll see lots of signs for 'rooms to let' on the side roads, too, in simple private homes and guest houses. Most charge around ₹600 per double.

TOP CHOICE Shalom GUESTHOUSE $
(☏2273166; www.shalomguesthousegoa.com; d with/without TV & fridge ₹1200/800, d with AC ₹1500, 2-bed apt ₹2000; ❄🛜) Arranged around a placid garden not far from the path down to Little Vagator beach, this place run by a friendly family (whose home is on-site) offers a variety of extremely well-kept rooms, and a two-bedroom apartment for long-stayers.

Casa Vagator HOTEL $$$
(☏2416738; www.casaboutiquehotels.com; d ₹8000-14,000; ❄@❄) A successfully rendered outfit in the deluxe Casa boutique mould, this is Vagator's most stylish accommodation option, with gorgeous rooms offering equally gorgeous views out to the wide blue horizon. The only downside is its proximity to techno-heavy Nine Bar, which pumps out Goa trance every night from 6pm until the 10pm shutdown – great, if you like that sort of thing, gruesome if you don't.

Bean Me Up Soya Station HOTEL $
(☏2273479; www.beanmeup.in; Ozran Beach Rd; d ₹350-550; 🛜) The rooms around a leafy, parachute-silky courtyard might look a bit cell-like from the outside, but step inside and you'll be pleased to find that the billowing silks and mellow, earthy shades follow you there. Bicycles, scooters and motorbikes are all available for hire, and there's a nice vegetarian restaurant (see p83).

Paradise on the Earth BEACH HUTS $
(☏2273591; www.moondance.co.nr; huts without bathroom from ₹400) Simple bamboo huts come with shared bathrooms, and cling to the cliff on the strip above Small Vagator beach. Paradise on Earth offers great value for the beachside location, though the name might be a little overkill.

Alcove Resort HOTEL $$$
(☏2274491; www.alcovegoa.com; standard without/with AC ₹3000/3500, cottages without/with AC ₹4000/4500, ste with/without AC ₹4000/4500; ❄@🛜❄) With attractively furnished rooms,

TRANCE PARTIES

Goa has a far longer and more vibrant history of hosting parties than most people realise. As far back as the 16th century, the Portuguese colony was notorious as an immoral outpost where drinking, debauching and dancing lasted till dawn, and, despite a more strait-laced interlude at the hands of the notorious Goan Inquisition, the tradition was finally resurrected full-force when the 'Goa Freaks' arrived on the state's northern beaches in the 1960s.

But the beach parties and full-moon raves of the 1970s and '80s came to seem like innocent affairs compared with the trance parties that replaced them in the '90s. At the peak of Goa's trance period, each high season saw thousands of revellers choosing synthetic substances such as ecstasy over marijuana and dancing to techno beats in Day-glo stupors, sometimes for days at a time.

In 2000 the country decided it was time to crack down, instigating a central government 'noise pollution' ban on loud music in open spaces between 10pm and 6am. This, combined with increasing crackdowns on drug possession, effectively put an end to the trance-party scene, with police teams swooping in to close down parties before they even began. This has largely been greeted with relief from locals, who were becoming increasingly worried at the peak of the trance-party phenomenon about the effects of drug dealing, alcohol and attendant promiscuity on Goa's own youth population.

With a tourist industry to nurture, the police still tend to turn a blind eye to a handful of parties during the peak Christmas–New Year period. Some monster mainstream clubs in Baga (p98) have managed to circumvent the ban, and pump on each weekend till 4am or later. Meanwhile in Vagator the once legendary Nine Bar (p84) still muddles along, but nowadays turns off the outdoor techno at 10pm sharp, at which point its partiers retreat indoors for more. Down south in Palolem, however, several people have found an ingenious way around the loud music restrictions: see the boxed text, p179 for more on Palolem's 'silent parties'.

If, though, you're determined to experience the remnants of Goa's true trance scene, hang around long enough in Vagator and you'll likely be handed a flyer for a party (many with international DJs), which can range from divine to dire. You may also catch wind of something going down in a hidden location – if you're lucky, it won't have been closed down by police by the time you arrive. In other words, keep your ear close to the ground, your fingers crossed and pray for a trance-music miracle.

---

slightly larger cottages and four suites within striking distance of Little Vagator beach, this place, which bills itself as three-star, is for those who want a touch of luxury at surprisingly reasonable prices. When you tire of the sands there's a cool central pool.

Julie Jolly   HOTEL **$$**
(☎2273620, 2274897; www.hoteljollygoa.com; d from ₹1290; ❄ @ ☎) Part of a local Vagator chain encompassing Julie Jolly, Jolly Jolly Lester and Jolly Jolly Roma (try saying that if you've just come back from Chapora). Receptionists are a little snooty at this comfortable place with a small pool and a wide variety of rooms and apartments, including some rooms with four beds. Still, despite a bit of a bleak location, the barber's-shop paint scheme is faultlessly jolly.

CHAPORA

Head down the road to the harbour and you'll find lots of rooms – and whole homes – for rent, far nicer than setting yourself up in the congested village centre; be sure to thoroughly trawl what's on offer before you land your catch.

Casa de Olga   GUESTHOUSE **$**
(☎2274355, 9822157145; d ₹1800, without bathroom ₹700) This exceedingly welcoming family-run choice, set around a nice garden, offers clean rooms of varying sizes. You'll pay more for the best of them, which come with hot showers, kitchenette and balcony. It also benefits from a pretty position, near the harbour.

Baba   GUESTHOUSE **$**
(☎2273339; babavilla11@yahoo.in; d with/without bathroom ₹450/200) The gaggle of men own-

ing this place, with 14 simple but serviceable rooms, seem a little like rulers of their own small empire. Nevertheless, they're a one-stop destination for most material needs, with their restaurant (serving the usual menu hodgepodge of Indian, Italian and just about everything else), internet cafe (₹50 per hour) and money-exchange service.

✖ Eating & Drinking

VAGATOR

There are a few eating options clustered around the entrance to Little Vagator beach, along with the usual range of much-of-a-muchness beach shacks down on the sands themselves.

TOP
CHOICE Thalassa   GREEK $$

(mains ₹180-440; ⊙4pm-midnight) Authentic and ridiculously good Greek food is served alfresco here on a breezy terrace to the sound of the sea just below. Veggie dishes also excel; the *spanakorizo* (spinach and rice cooked with Greek olive oil and herbs and topped with feta; ₹230) is hearty and deceptively simple; the fresh ingredients and expert preparation are what made us swoon. Reservations are essential; call in to make one. Thalassa also has **huts** (₹1000), which are almost as classy as the restaurant.

Yangkhor Moonlight   TIBETAN, MULTICUISINE $

(mains ₹70-220) Superfresh food is the key to the fabulous Tibetan and even Italian dishes here. Go for the veg *momo* (Tibetan dumpling) soup and a nice hot bowl of pasta, and you might just decide to stick around in Vagator an extra day or two, to do it all over again. The chairs and tablecloths are plastic and the walls are lime green, but – perhaps because of the friendly service and soft Chinese pop music – it's cosy to boot.

Bean Me Up Soya
Station   MULTICUISINE, VEGAN $$

(Ozran Beach Rd; mains from ₹150; ⊙8am-4pm & 6-11pm) A delicious, all-vegetarian restaurant at this popular place to stay, with lots of carefully washed salads and a wealth of tasty tofu, seitan and tempeh treats. Great for vegans, since you'll know for a fact there's no ghee lurking in that delightful dhal.

Mango Tree Bar & Cafe   MULTICUISINE $$

(mains ₹90-210; ⊙9am-4am) An ever-popular place for its big breakfasts, loud reggae, far-ranging menu and sometimes rambunctious bar scene (though not for its staff, who are largely disinterested), with films screened here most evenings around 7.30pm.

CHAPORA

Little Chapora doesn't have the breadth of eating choices of Vagator; here you'll find a cluster of simple joints, patronised by a cluster of people smoking the same. Comfort food in the form of omelettes, corn-on-the-cob, doughnuts and pizza are all available here for when the munchies strike.

Scarlet Cold Drinks   JUICE $

(drinks & desserts ₹30-80) Selling juice, lassis, fruit salads and muesli to travellers, a rickety table at Scarlet offers a perfect vantage point from which to observe Chapora's comings and goings; there's also an extremely useful noticeboard, bursting with news of the latest local yoga classes, reiki courses and the like. If you're hungry, try the fruit salad with a slab of butterscotch ice cream, but don't hold your breath: service can be slooooooow.

Jai Ganesh Fruit Juice Centre   JUICE $

(juices ₹30-70) Offering similar stuff to Scarlet, in equally close proximity to the thickest gusts of *charas* smoke, this diminutive juice centre is a great place for a vitamin fix and a fascinating spot for people-watching, with the added advantage of cold coffee and intriguing avocado lassis.

Sunrise Restaurant   MULTICUISINE $

(mains ₹70-150) Nothing special, but very decent food, with some good Goan specials and friendly staff, Sunrise is just opposite the Holy Cross Chapel, a tiny bit out of the centre of the Chapora action.

☆ Entertainment

Aside from secretive parties, there's not too much going on in Vagator and Chapora these days, though you might have more luck tracking down an event or two over the busy Christmas and New Year period. Beach shacks and the small local bars lining Chapora's main street make good choices for a cool evening Kingfisher. Nevertheless, a couple of die-hard places are still thumping on; and Russians, having taken the party crown away from the Israelis, seem to create their own nightlife at various spots around town.

ANJUNA & NORTH GOA VAGATOR & CHAPORA

WORTH A TRIP

ASSAGAO

On the road between Vagator and Mapusa, roughly equidistant from each, it's worth stopping off at Assagao, one of North Goa's prettiest villages. Pause here if only to take a peek at St Catejan's Church and seek out snacks at **Villa Blanche Bistro** (www.villablanche-goa.com; mains ₹160; ⏲9am-5.30pm Mon-Sat, 10am-3pm Sun), a lovely little place run by a German-Swiss couple, serving up cakes, salads, breakfasts and brunch on Sundays. Check its website for the exact location.

If you're planning on doing some volunteering work, you might find yourself in Assagao to make contact with **El Shaddai** (p30), a child protection charity with its base here. Alternatively, you may be here to check into **Purple Valley Yoga Retreat** (☎2268364; www.yogagoa.com; 142 Bairo Alto, Assagao), a popular upscale retreat set amid frangipani-scented tropical gardens, offering one- and two-week residential courses in ashtanga yoga. Rates begin at £500 for one week, and include accommodation and delicious all-vegetarian meals. A range of beauty therapies and ayurvedic treatments is also available on-site for course participants.

If, however, you're looking for something far less active, consider a stay at one of North Goa's most wonderful, idiosyncratic properties. **Sunbeam** (www.justjivi.com/goa.html; ste from ₹9000; ❄📶🏊) is a collection of just three incredible suites, owned and overseen by Jivi Sethi, a well-known and flamboyant Indian stylist. Think family heirlooms, high theatricality and lots and lots of luxury – as well as fabulous food, created by the talented Krishna.

Hilltop NIGHTCLUB
(⏲sunset-late) Deserted by day, this place comes alive after nightfall, its edge-of-town location allowing it on occasion to gleefully flout 10pm noise regulations to host concerts, parties and the occasional international DJ. Venture up to the site by day, and wander about until you find someone who'll tell you what's on and when.

Nine Bar NIGHTCLUB
(Sunset Point, Little Vagator Beach; ⏲6pm-4am) Once the hallowed epicentre of Goa's trance scene, custom has cooled at the open-air Nine Bar, though the trance still thumps away each evening until it's turned off promptly at 10pm outdoors, and the party moves inside. On a good night, a trace of parties past can still be found; on a bad night, its atmosphere is akin to a wedding reception, long after the bride and groom have gone home.

Shopping

Rainbow Bookshop BOOKSTORE
(☎2273613; ⏲10am-2pm & 3-7pm) This lovely little place, run by a charming elderly gentleman, stocks a good range of second-hand and new books, including this very guide.

Information

Vagator is equipped with an ATM at **Corporation Bank** on the road to Anjuna. You'll find that a number of shops and travel agencies also offer foreign exchange. The nearest alternate ATM facilities are in Mapusa.

Plenty of internet places are scattered along the road to Little Vagator Beach; most charge ₹40 per hour.

Getting There & Away

Fairly frequent buses run to both Chapora and Vagator from Mapusa (₹15) throughout the day, many via Anjuna. The bus stand is near the road junction in Chapora village. Many people hire a motorcycle to buzz back and forth; enquire wherever you see a man with a scooter. Prices tend to be around ₹200/400 per day for a scooter/motorbike.

Mapusa

☎0832 / POP 40,100

The market town of Mapusa (pronounced 'Mapsa') is the largest town in northern Goa, and is most often visited for its busy **Friday market**, which attracts scores of buyers and sellers from neighbouring towns and villages, and a healthy intake of tourists from the northern beaches. It's a good place to pick up the usual range of embroidered bed sheets and the like, at prices far lower than in the beach resorts. And even if you're not interested in the trappings of commerce, you'll likely pass through Mapusa in any case, since it's the major transport hub for northern Goa buses.

There's not a lot else to see here, though it's a pleasant, bustling and typically Indian town to wander for a while. Most amenities are arranged around the Municipal Gardens (the Kadamba bus station is just a short walk south on NH17), and around the market site, just to the south.

Both **International Animal Rescue** (see p30) and the environmental action group **Goa Foundation** (www.goafoundation.org) have their headquarters close by.

Sights & Activities

Church of Our Lady of Miracles   CHURCH
Founded in 1594 and rebuilt several times since, the Church of Our Lady of Miracles (also known as St Jerome's), around 600m east of the Municipal Gardens, is famous more for its annual festival than for its architecture. It was built by the Portuguese on the site of an old Hindu temple, and thus the Hindu community still holds the site as sacred. On the sixteenth day after Easter, the church's annual feast day is celebrated here by both Hindus and Christians – one of the best examples of the way in which Hinduism and Christianity often coexist merrily in Goa.

Maruti Temple   HINDU TEMPLE
In the centre of town, the small, pastel-coloured Maruti temple was built in the 1840s at a site where the monkey god Hanuman was covertly worshipped during more oppressive periods of Portuguese rule. After temples had been destroyed by the Portuguese, devotees placed a picture of Hanuman at the fireworks shop that stood here, and arrived cloaked in secrecy to perform their *pujas* (prayers). In April 1843 the picture was replaced by a silver idol and an increasing number of worshippers began to gather here. Eventually the business community of Mapusa gathered enough funds to acquire the shop, and the temple was built in its place. The intricate carvings at the doorway of the temple are the work of local artisans.

Sleeping

There's no particular or pressing reason to stay overnight in Mapusa, since the northern beaches are all so easily accessible from here. In case you have the need or inclination, however, Mapusa offers a couple of passable choices.

Hotel Satyaheera   HOTEL **$$**
(☏2262949; www.hotelsatyaheera.clammo.com; d with/without AC from ₹1150/850; ✸) Just next to the little Maruti temple beside the Municipal Gardens, this is widely considered Mapusa's best hotel – and don't they know it. Disinterested staff dole out comfy, yet dated, rooms, and the most thrilling thing about the entire experience is the forest-scene wallpaper in the elevator. Note the 9am checkout time and the stipulation that children up to age 12 will be charged ₹50 per day to share a room with their parents, though 'no extra linen will be provided'.

Mapusa Residency   HOTEL **$$**
(☏2262794, 2262694; d with/without AC ₹1155/870, ste ₹1550; ✸) Service is indifferent and the rooms are in the bland-but-functional mould you'd expect from GTDC accommodation, but if all else fails it's a clean place to spend the night, conveniently placed beside the bus stand for an easy getaway the next morning.

WORTH A TRIP

LUXURY IN COLVALE

If the thought of a night in one of Mapusa's hotels is just too much to bear, detour a measly 7km north up the NH17, to reach the small inland village of Colvale. Pretty and peaceful, it's the location of boutique hotel Casa Colvale (☏2416737; www.casaboutique hotels.com; d from ₹9000; ✸ @ ✸). With a stunning infinity pool, yoga and massage options, and just 12 river-view rooms, it's got all the luxe that Mapusa's accommodation options are lacking. If you really want to arrive in style, however, arrange to be picked up instead from Siolim (p78) by the hotel's speedboat and whisked off down the river just like Mr. Bond.

✗ Eating & Drinking

There are plenty of nice, old-fashioned cafes within the market area, serving simple Indian snacks, dishes and cold drinks to a local clientele. Thalis come in at the ₹50 mark, and chai at ₹5.

Hotel Vrundavan INDIAN, VEGETARIAN $
(dishes ₹8-50; ⊘7am-late) An all-veg place bordering the Municipal Gardens, this is a great place for a hot chai and a quick breakfast. Dip your *pau* (fluffy white bread roll) or *puri* (deep-fried, puffed-up bread) into a cashewnut *bhaji* (small curry) for just ₹10, or try the tomato version for a more modest ₹9.

Casa Bela BAR $
(⊘9.30am-3pm & 6-10.30pm) A windowless remnant of a more mahogany-clad era, the dingy Casa Bela is a good place to escape the Mapusa blather and sip silently on a cold Kingfisher (₹35). The service is surly, but this only enhances the slightly bizarre charm of this little scrap of days gone by. There's a simple menu to help wash down the drinks.

Ruchira Restaurant INDIAN, MULTICUISINE $
(mains ₹40-120; ⊘11am-11pm) On the top floor of Hotel Satyaheera (see p85), this place is very popular with tourists and is widely deemed one of Mapusa's best restaurants, serving Indian and Continental dishes. Though the views alone make a visit worthwhile, beware the occasional slightly bewildered, lacklustre service.

Pub MULTICUISINE $
(mains from ₹70; ⊘9am-10.30pm) Don't be put off by the dingy entrance or stairwell: this place opposite the market is great for watching the milling market crowds over a cold beer or long glass of *feni* (liquor distilled from coconut milk or cashews). Eclectic daily specials include roast beef and goulash with noodles.

Golden Oven BAKERY $
(pastries from ₹6; ⊘9am-6.30pm) For some clean and shiny comfort, duck into this bakery opposite the market, which is a civilised respite from the shopping chaos aross the street.

Ashok Snacks & Beverages INDIAN $
(thalis & mains ₹35-70; ⊘6am-10.30pm Mon-Sat, to 4pm Sun) There are excellent thalis at this place overlooking the market, and just next door to the Golden Oven, popular with local families and lunch-breaking workers.

🛍 Shopping

Though the market is Mapusa's main draw, if you're still not shopped-out, browse the handful of **antique and junk shops** that dot the Municipality Rd, to the north of the Municipal Gardens, or the couple of shops selling **chappals** (Indian leather sandals) in the same area, which have been dispensing their utilitarian wares for generations.

Mapusa Market MARKET
(⊘8am-6.30pm Mon-Sat) The Mapusa market goes about its business daily, except Sundays, but really gets going on Friday mornings. It's a raucous affair that attracts vendors and shoppers from all over Goa, with an entirely different vibe to the Anjuna market. Here you'll find locals haggling for clothing and produce, and you can also hunt out antiques, souvenirs and textiles. So significant is the market locally that the town's name is derived from the Konkani words *map* (meaning 'measure') and *sa* (meaning 'fill up'), in reference to the trade in spices, vegetables and fruit that's plied here daily.

TOP CHOICE ▷ **Other India Bookstore** BOOKSTORE
(☑2263306; www.otherindiabookstore.com; Mapusa Clinic Rd; ⊘9am-5pm Mon-Fri, to 1pm Sat) A little hard to find, but well worth the jaunt: go up the steps on the right as you walk down Mapusa Clinic Rd, north of the Municipal Gardens, and follow the signs. This friendly and rewarding little bookshop, specialising in 'dissenting wisdom', is at the end of an improbable, dingy corridor.

ℹ Information

There are plenty of ATMs scattered about town, and you won't have any trouble locating one. There's a bumper crop around the Municipal Gardens and the market area, where you'll also find a handful of tiny internet cafes.

Mapusa Clinic (☑2263343; ⊘consultations 10.30am-1.30pm Mon-Sat, 3.30-7pm Mon, Wed & Fri) A well-run medical clinic, with 24-hour emergency services. Be sure to go to the 'new' Mapusa Clinic, behind the 'old' one.

Pink Panther Travel Agency (☑2250352, 2263180; panther_goa@sancharnet.in; Coscar Corner; 10am-6pm Mon-Fri, to 1.30pm Sat) A very helpful agency, selling bus, train and air tickets (both international and domestic) as well as performing currency exchange and property consultancy services. It's situated just east of the Municipal Gardens.

🅐 Getting There & Away

If you're coming to Goa by bus from Mumbai, Mapusa's **Kadamba bus stand** is the jumping-off point for the northern beaches. Local bus services run every few minutes; just look for the correct destination on the sign in the bus windshield – and try to get an express. For buses to the southern beaches, take a bus to Panaji, then Margao, and change there.

Local services include:

Anjuna ₹15, 20 minutes
Arambol ₹25, 1 ½ hours
Calangute/Candolim ₹12/15, 20/35 minutes
Panaji ₹15, 25 minutes

Long-distance services are run by both government and private bus companies. Private operators' services are more comfortable, and hence more expensive, than government buses; they have their offices next to the bus stand. There's generally little difference in price, comfort or duration between them, but shop around for the best fare. **Mumbai tickets** come in at around ₹1700 for non-AC services, and ₹1800 to ₹2400 for AC services. The trip takes 14 hours.

There's a prepaid taxi stand outside the bus terminal; it has a handy signboard of prices. Cabs to Anjuna or Calangute cost ₹250; Arambol ₹400; and Margao ₹800. An autorickshaw to Anjuna or Calangute should cost ₹200.

Thivim, about 12km northeast of town, is the nearest train station on the Konkan Railway. Local buses to Mapusa meet trains (₹10); an autorickshaw to or from Thivim station costs around ₹150.

Anjuna
☑ 0832

Dear old Anjuna, that stalwart on India's hippy scene, still drags out the sarongs and sandalwood each Wednesday for its famous – and once infamous – flea market. Though it

continues to pull in droves of backpackers, midrange tourists are increasingly making their way here for a dose of hippie-chic without the beach-hut rusticity of Arambol further up the coast.

Meanwhile Anjuna remains filled with a weird and wonderful, if these days somewhat diminished, collection of defiant ex-hippies, overlanders, monks, gentle lunatics, artists, artisans, seers, searchers and itinerant expatriates who have wandered far from the organic confines of health-food emporia in San Francisco and London.

The village itself is certainly a bit ragged around the edges these days, but Anjuna remains a favourite of long-stayers and first-timers alike. It's spread out over a wide area, its most northerly point being the main Starco crossroads, where most buses stop and around which many eating options are dotted, and its southernmost point is the flea market site, about 2km to the south. Most accommodation and other useful services are sprinkled along the beach, or down shady inland lanes in between.

AUTHENTIC FLEA MARKETS: GOAN, GOAN, GONE?

Wednesday's weekly flea market at Anjuna is as much part of the Goan experience as a day on a deserted beach. More than two decades ago, it was still the sole preserve of hippies smoking jumbo joints and convening to compare experiences on the heady Indian circuit.

Nowadays things are far more staid and mainstream, with long-stayers complaining that package tourists seem to beat out independent travellers both in numbers and purchasing power. The market sprawls on...and on...and on, hawking stuff that is much of a muchness. A couple of hours here and you'll never want to see a mirrored bedspread, peacock-feather fan, or floaty Indian-cotton dress again in your life.

That said, though, it's still a great place for a spot of people-watching, and you can find some interesting one-off souvenirs and pieces of clothing in among the tourist tat if you trawl carefully. Remember to bargain hard and take along equal quantities of patience and stamina, applicable to dealing with local and expat vendors alike.

Anjuna

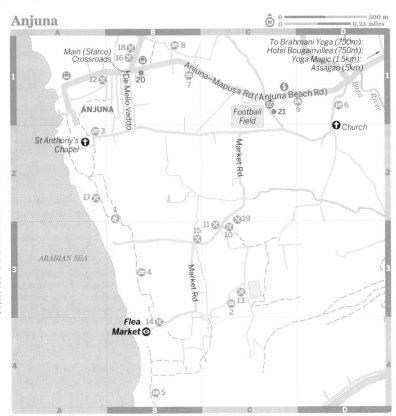

Map labels:
To Brahmani Yoga (750m);
Hotel Bougainvillea (750m);
Yoga Magic (1.5km);
Assagao (5km)

Main (Starco)
Crossroads

Anjuna–Mapusa Rd (Anjuna Beach Rd)

De Mello Vaddo

ANJUNA

St Anthony's
Chapel

Football
Field

Church

Market Rd

ARABIAN SEA

Market Rd

Flea
Market

🏃 Activities

If you're in the mood for a dip, Anjuna's charismatic, rocky beach runs for almost 2km from the northern village area right down to the flea market in the south. The northern end shrinks to almost nothing when the tide washes in. When the tide goes out, it becomes a lovely – and surprisingly quiet – stretch of sand, with lots of room to escape the presence of other people who are sunbathing. Stay away from the southern end of the beach, near the market site, which is sadly blighted with rubbish and engine oil.

There's lots of yoga, ayurveda and other alternative therapies and regimes on offer, seasonally, in town; look out for notices that are posted up at Cafe Diogo, Cafe Orange Boom and the German Bakery.

Paragliding   PARAGLIDING
For an adrenalin rush, paragliding usually takes place off the headland at the southern end of the beach on market days; tandem rides cost ₹1500.

Andy's Tattoo Studio   TATTOOS
(http://andys-tattoo-studio-anjuna-goa.com; ⏲11am-7pm Mon-Sat) If you're looking to embellish yourself while in town, try Andy's Tattoo Studio, attached to San Francisco Restaurant, where the Anjuna cliffside slides down to meet the beach. Drop in to make an appointment and receive a price quote for your permanent souvenir.

Brahmani Yoga   YOGA
(www.brahmaniyoga.com; classes ₹500, 10-class pass ₹3500) is a friendly drop-in centre, which opens its doors from November to April, and offers daily classes in ashtanga, vinyasa, hatha, dynamic, kundalini, restora-

Anjuna

◉ **Top Sights**
　Flea Market..B4

◉ **Activities, Courses & Tours**
　1　Andy's Tattoo Studio............................B2

◉ **Sleeping**
　2　Banyan Soul...C3
　3　Casa Anjuna..A2
　4　Florinda's Guest House.........................B3
　5　Hobbit...B4
　6　Palacete Rodrigues D1
　7　Paradise B1
　8　Peace Land B1
　9　Vilanova..D1

◉ **Eating**
　10　Cafe Diogo..C3
　11　Cafe Orange Boom.................................C3
　12　Dhum Biryani & Kebabs A1
　13　German Bakery.......................................C3
　14　Maria's Tea Stall....................................B4
　15　Martha's Breakfast Home.....................B3
　16　Munches..B1
　17　Om Made Cafe..A2
　18　Oxford Arcade..B1
　19　Whole Bean Tofu Shop &
　　　Vegetaria..C2

◉ **Information**
　20　MGM Travels...B1
　21　Speedy Travels C1

ANJUNA & NORTH GOA ANJUNA

tive and, intriguingly, 'superhero acro-flow' yoga, as well as pranayama meditation. There's no need to book: just turn up 15 minutes before the beginning of class, to secure space enough to spread your yoga mat.

Sleeping

Dozens of rooms of the largely concrete-cell variety are strung along Anjuna's increasingly dingy northern clifftop stretch; most come in at ₹500 to ₹700 per night. There are also plenty of small, family-run guesthouses tucked back from the main beach strip, offering nicer double rooms for a similar price; take your pick from the dozens of signs announcing 'rooms to let'. We've listed three exceptional choices for something a little bit different.

TOP CHOICE **Banyan Soul** HOTEL **$$**
(⌨9820707283; www.thebanyansoul.com; d ₹2000; ✳) A slinky 12-room option, tucked just behind Anjuna's scrummy German bakery, and lovingly conceived and run by Sumit, a young Mumbai escapee. Rooms are chic and well equipped, the decor is flawless, and there's a lovely library and shady seating area beneath a banyan tree. It's without doubt one of the best-value places in town, and the staff are extremely keen to please.

Yoga Magic GUESTHOUSE **$$$**
(⌨6523796; www.yogamagic.net; d ₹3500-4500) Solar lighting and compost toilets are just some of the worthy initiatives practised in this ultra-luxury bamboo hut-and-villa village,

where hand-printed textiles, locally made ironwork furniture and organic gourmet vegetarian food are the order of the day. Prices include breakfast and afternoon tea; daily yoga classes cost an extra ₹500 per session.

Hobbit VILLA **$$$**
(⌨9820055053; www.thehobbitgoa.com; house per night ₹14,400; ✳@) Bilbo himself would be proud of a hobbit hole like this, nestled away in the very southern part of Anjuna, known as St Michael's Waddo, with terrific views out to sea. This hidden gem of a three-bedroom house, with its own meditation room and cool, curvaceous spaces, is perfect for a big family or for a group of friends seeking respite from the Goan hustle.

Hotel Bougainvillea HERITAGE HOTEL **$$$**
(⌨2273270/71; www.granpasinn.com; d/ste from ₹2650/2950; ✳🛜🏊) An old-fashioned hotel housed in a pretty, yellow 200-year-old mansion, this place – also known as Granpa's Inn – offers charm with a touch of luxury with a lovely pool and well-decorated rooms. The grounds are lush, shady and make a cool respite after a stint at the calamitous market, though some travellers complain that the prices are too high and that the rooms could do with an overhaul.

Vilanova GUESTHOUSE **$**
(⌨64503889, 9225904244; mendonca90@rediff mail.com; d without/with AC ₹700/900; ✳) Big, clean rooms have a fridge, TV, 24-hour hot water and window screens and are set in three Portuguese-style bungalows in a cute

THE ALBUQUERQUE CURSE

Though two-and-more-storey buildings are slowly beginning to creep their way into Anjuna's periphery, every self-respecting Anjuna villager is aware of a local curse, which prophesies doom and gloom on anyone who dares build an upper level atop their ground-floor dwelling. Though no one knows quite where the curse originated, many locals tell the tale of Dr Manuel Albuquerque, physician to the Sultan of Zanzibar, who in 1920 built a two-storey replica of the Sultan's palace to serve as his retirement home. Soon beset with misfortunes, Albuquerque failed to produce an heir and fell into dire financial straits; his mansion – though still standing – remains a warning to Anjunans to keep their feet firmly on the ground.

little compound. There are good vibes and a comfortable family atmosphere, with friendly staff and a good restaurant. We almost hate to tell anyone about it!

Palacete Rodrigues HERITAGE HOTEL **$$$**
(☏273358, 2910086; www.palacetegoa.com; d ₹3000-5000; ❀) This lovely family-run mansion, filled with antiques and loaded with charm, is absolutely as quirky (perhaps too quirky for some) as you could hope for in Anjuna. Choose between the rather overgrandly named Palace or Emperor's Rooms.

Paradise GUESTHOUSE **$**
(☏9922541714; janet_965@hotmail.com; Anjuna-Mapusa Rd; d ₹1000-1200; ❀) This friendly place is fronted by an old Portuguese home and offers good, clean rooms with well-decorated options in the newer annexe. And owner Janet doesn't stop at accommodation: her enterprising family can service your every need, with its pharmacy, general store, restaurant, internet access (₹40 per hour), Connexions travel agency, money exchange, Western Union service and beauty parlour. You name it, Janet can probably arrange it for you.

Peace Land GUESTHOUSE **$**
(☏2273700; s/d ₹450/600; ☏) You can't get better on a budget than Peace Land, run by a friendly couple and arranged around

a tranquil courtyard garden. Rooms are small but spotlessly clean and comfortable, and their little restaurant cooks up some great Indian food. There's internet access for ₹40 per hour, and a small shop selling basic provisions.

Casa Anjuna HOTEL **$$$**
(☏2416737; www.casaboutiquehotels.com; d from ₹7000; ❀@☀) Yet another of the chain's decent top-end boutique hotels, this branch offers all the comfort you'd expect from a Casa, with a lovely pool and light, airy rooms.

Florinda's Guest House GUESTHOUSE **$**
(☏9890216520, 9762331032; r ₹600-1000) One of the better cheapies near the beach, Florinda's has clean rooms, with 24-hour hot water and window screens, set around a garden with the world's tiniest pool.

🍴 Eating & Drinking

Anjuna has a whole host of great eating options, with jostling cliffside cafes sporting the standard traveller-orientated menus, happy hours and stunning coastal views. The area around the Starco crossroads is also thick with dining options, as is Anjuna-Mapusa Rd (Anjuna Beach Rd).

Though Anjuna is no longer party central, and drinking is largely confined to hotel and clifftop bars, inside the flea market on market days you will also find a number of boozy bars, one with a stage that is manned by foreigners singing cover versions. Down on the beach, past the flea-market site, are some popular places for an evening drink, with an alternative crowd and the odd impromptu party.

Self-caterers will likely be excited to note that Anjuna is home to a great expat-slanted supermarket.

TOP
CHOICE **German Bakery** MULTICUISINE **$$**
(pastries ₹30-50, mains ₹70-290; ☏) Leafy and filled with prayer flags, frequent live music and jolly lights, this is the perfect place for a huge lunch chosen from an equally huge menu. Tofu balls in mustard sauce with parsley potatoes and salad is a piled-high winner at ₹190. As of late 2012, wi-fi will be available free of charge.

TOP
CHOICE **Om Made Cafe** MEDITERRANEAN **$$**
(dishes ₹90-190; ☏9am-sunset) A highlight on Anjuna's otherwise quite grim clifftop

strip, this cheery little place offers striped deckchairs from which to enjoy the views and the simple, sophisticated breakfasts, sandwiches and salads. Go for a raw papaya salad with ginger and lemongrass (₹180), accompanied by a vegetable smoothie (₹120) or a glass of 'perfumed water' (₹25). Om Made Cafe has two other locations in Goa: the first, just across the road from the back of La Plage in Aswem (p77); the second, next door to Le Poisson Rouge in Baga (p97).

Cafe Diogo
CAFE $
(Market Rd; dishes from ₹80; ⊙8am-5pm) Probably the best fruit salads in the world are sliced and diced at Cafe Diogo, a small locally run cafe on the way down to the market. Also worth a try are the generous toasted avocado, cheese and mushroom sandwiches, the jumbo fry-ups and the unusual gooseberry lassi.

Cafe Orange Boom
CAFE $
(Market Rd; dishes from ₹80; ⊙breakfast & lunch) Just past Cafe Diogo, on the opposite side of the road, this nice little place has the same good food and friendly service at equivalent prices, with a useful noticeboard for catching up on Anjunan goings-on.

Whole Bean Tofu Shop & Vegetaria
CAFE, VEGAN $$
(Market Rd; mains ₹80-170) This simple, tasty, tofu-filled health-food cafe – which proudly announces itself as 'Anjuna's premier soy destination' – focuses on all things created from that most versatile of beans.

Oxford Arcade
SUPERMARKET $
The massive Oxford Arcade, just next to the Starco crossroads, is a fully fledged supermarket, complete with shopping trolleys, ice-cold air-conditioning and checkout scanners. Hallowed ground for foreigners who pay dearly for little luxuries, it also sports a bakery, toiletries department, pet food, wine department and children's toys. Come Christmas, this is the place to buy your tinsel and baubles, fake tree and kids' gifts to stack beneath it.

Martha's Breakfast Home
CAFE $
(Market Rd; breakfasts from r₹80) As the name suggests, Martha's speciality is her all-day breakfasts, served up in a quiet garden on the way down to the flea-market site. The porridge and juice may be mighty tasty, but

the star of the breakfast parade is undoubtedly the piping-hot plates of waffles, just crying out to be smothered in real maple syrup.

Dhum Biryani & Kebabs
INDIAN $
(Biryani Palace, Anjuna-Mapusa Rd; mains ₹70-200) Loved by visitors and locals alike, call in for consistently good and fantastically tasty kebabs.

Maria's Tea Stall
CAFE $
(Flea Market; snacks from ₹12; ⊙market day) For a quick market shopping stop, look out for teensy Maria's Tea Stall, selling tasty chai and snacks made by colourful, elderly local Maria.

Munches
MULTICUISINE $
(dishes from ₹90; ⊙24hr) Near the Starco crossroads, this ever-popular place, serving up the full list of travellers' favourites, is a good choice for whenever any attack of the munchies demands you munch. Two doors down, Eatopia offers much the same sort of thing, with the added benefit of a nightly movie screening.

❶ Information

Anjuna has a whole host of ATMs, clustered together near Domino's pizza, on the opposite side of the road from the **Bank of Baroda** (Anjuna-Mapusa Rd; ⊙9.30am-2.30pm), which gives cash advances on Visa and MasterCard.

Internet joints in Anjuna – away from the mid-range hotels – open and close down regularly and some can be quite slow. Ask around for the best new option on the scene, or head to the German Bakery for reliable wireless access.

There are plenty of reliable travel agents in town. Try **Speedy Travels** (☎2273266; ⊙9am-6.30pm Mon-Sat, 10am-1pm Sun) near the post office, or the excellent **MGM Travels** (☎2274317; www.mgmtravels.com; Anjuna-Mapusa Rd; ⊙9.30am-6pm Mon-Sat).

❶ Getting There & Away

Buses to Mapusa (₹12) depart every half-hour or so from the main bus stand near the beach; some coming from Mapusa continue on to Vagator and Chapora.

Two daily buses to Calangute depart from the main Starco crossroads. Plenty of motorcycle taxis gather at the main crossroads and you can also easily hire scooters and motorcycles here. A prepaid taxi from Dabolim Airport to Anjuna costs ₹860.

ANJUNA & NORTH GOA ANJUNA

Calangute & Baga

☎0832 / POP 15,800

Depending on your definition of 'fun in the sun', the twin resorts of Calangute and Baga – once the habitat of naked, revelling hippies and nowadays package-holiday central – can prove holiday heaven or the Bosch-like depths of Hell.

Calangute was, long ago, the place to which well-heeled Goan townsfolk would retreat to escape the oppressive heat of the pre-monsoon hinterlands, and later became Goa's first heady '60s hippie-hangout hot spot. Meanwhile Baga, to the north, remained a sleepy fishing village until well into the 1980s, until it was seized by package-holiday developers. These days, though, Calangute and Baga's wide, continuous strip of sand sees relentless action. It's crowded with beach shacks, bars, water-sports operators, hawkers, sunbathers, and revellers of both the domestic and foreign varieties.

Calangute is divided into two basic areas, with very different characters. Its main northern beach area is very much bucket-and-spade territory, and the road leading to it is a tumult of tacky souvenirs, cheap eats, dingy local bars, soft-serve ice creams, and milling crowds of coach-tour visitors. Here you'll find touts vying for water-sports custom, and plenty of domestic-tourist-orientated seaside fun. Don't expect any kind of R&R but it's certainly an experience, if only for a pint-sized dose.

Rather more sophisticated, Calangute's southern beach is, in contrast, more relaxed and upscale. Its sands are quieter (though by no means deserted), its restaurants are fancier, and its pace altogether more relaxed. The south's the place for

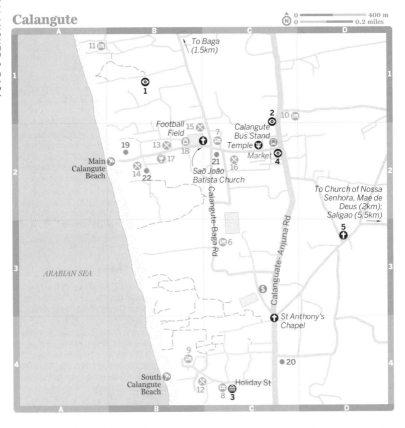

Calangute

sundowners, shopping and sumptuous dinners, away from the tourist tat a tad further north.

To the north, Baga is also not the ideal place to come for tropical tranquillity. Though wide and roomy, Baga's beach consists of jostling shacks, peppered with water sports and boat-trip touts, and row upon row of sun-beds. The crowd here is young and excitable, the music loud, and the atmosphere runs from cheerful to chaotic. This is the place for drinking and dancing, with clubs open until 4am – very unusual these days in Goa. Meanwhile, to escape the Baga beat, head north across the Baga river to some budget accommodation bargains clinging to the coast.

If you're coming to Goa seeking spiritual solitude and swathes of quiet tropical sand, you'll find quite the reverse here, with Calangute's main beach drag being India's modern 'Kiss Me Quick' capital, closer to Blackpool than Blissed-Out. But if you're looking for Ibiza-style action, dance-around-your-handbag clubbing, exquisite cuisine and nonstop shops (with the occasional holy cow or temple elephant thrown in to remind you where you really are) you simply couldn't hope for better.

🏃 Activities

Aside from frolicking in the waves with scores of other holidaymakers, there are plenty of activities on offer in both Calangute and Baga, including a highly respectable diving school.

Local fishermen congregate around the northern end of Baga Beach, offering dolphin-spotting trips (₹500 per person), boat trips to Anjuna Market (₹400 per person) and whole-day coastal excursions up to Arambol, Mandrem and back (₹1000 per person).

Yoga classes pop up all across Calangute and Baga each season, with foreigners flocking in both to run them and to unfurl their yoga mats and brush up on their asanas. Keep your eyes peeled for fliers posted on lamp posts and noticeboards, to get up-to-date with the season's latest yogic offerings. See also Pousada Tauma (p95), a lovely boutique hotel which offers extensive ayurvedic treatments.

CALANGUTE

Ayurvedic Natural Health Centre   AYURVEDA, YOGA
(☎2409275; www.healthandayurveda.com; Chogm Rd, Saligao; massages from ₹1200; ⊙7.30am-7.30pm) This highly respected centre, 5km inland in Saligao, offers a vast range of courses in reflexology, aromatherapy, acupressure, yoga and various other regimes. There's also a range of herbal medicines on offer and treatments available from an ayurvedic doctor, with treatments lasting from one hour to three weeks. Drop-in yoga classes (₹300) are also held daily. Some (but not all) buses

---

Calangute

⊙ Sights
1	Casa Braganza	B1
2	Casa dos Proença	C1
3	Kerkar Art Complex	C4
4	Old Customs Post	C2
5	St Alex's Church	D3

⊜ Sleeping
6	Casa de Goa	C3
7	Garden Court Resort	C2
8	Hotel Seagull	C4
9	Ospy's Shelter	B4
10	Pousada Tauma	C1
11	Vila Goesa	A1

⊗ Eating
12	A Reverie	B4
13	Casandré	B2

	Copper Bowl	(see 10)
14	Delhi Chaat	B2
15	Infantaria	B2
16	Plantain Leaf	C2

⊜ Drinking
17	Jerry John Jonesius	B2

⊜ Shopping
18	Book Palace	B2

ⓘ Information
19	Calangute Residency	B2
20	Day Tripper	C4
21	MGM International Travels	C2
22	Paulo Tours & Travels	B2

from Baga/Calangute to Mapusa stop in Saligao, just near the centre; check before boarding.

Kerkar Art Complex   ART GALLERY

(2276017; www.subodhkerkar.com; Holiday St, South Calangute; ⊙10am-11pm) This soothing art gallery showcases the colourful paintings, photographs and sculptures of local artist Dr Subodh Kerkar; it's worth a stop for a bite at its multicuisine **Waves Restaurant** (mains ₹300-500; ⊙11am-3pm & 7pm-2am). The complex also offers open-air dance recitals every Tuesday night; see p98.

BAGA

You'll find numerous jet-ski and parasailing operators on Baga Beach, and it pays to compare a few to find the most competitive rate. Parasailing usually costs around ₹1700 per ride; jet skis cost ₹1100 per 15 minutes, and waterskiing costs about ₹1200 per 10 minutes.

Barracuda Diving   DIVING

(2279409, 9822182402; www.barracudadiving. com; Sun Village Resort, Baga; courses from ₹4000) This long-standing diving school offers a vast range of classes, dives and courses, including a 'Bubblemakers' introduction to Scuba class of 1½ hours for children eight years and older (₹1000). It's also exceptional for its 'Project AWARE', which undertakes marine-conservation initiatives and annual underwater and beach clean-ups.

Jungle Guitars   MUSIC

(9823565117; www.jungleguitars.com; Baga) If you've always been one to strum to your own tune, Jungle Guitars might just be the place for you. Fifteen- to 20-day courses will allow you to build your very own steel string or classical guitar from scratch, overseen by resident master guitar-builder Chris. Courses cost ₹65,000, including all materials and a case for the finished product.

Tours

Day Tripper   TOURS

(2276726/2282857; www.daytrippergoa.com; Calangute-Anjuna Rd; ⊙9am-5.30pm Mon-Sat, Nov-Apr) Day Tripper, with its head office in south Calangute, is one of Goa's best tour agencies. It runs a wide variety of trips around Goa, including to Dudhsagar Falls (p142), and also interstate to Hampi (p143) and the Kali River (for rafting and birdwatching trips) in Karnataka.

Calangute Residency   TOURS

(2276024) GTDC tours (see p230) can be booked at the GTDC's somewhat dingy Calangute Residency hotel beside the beach; if you can't face entering, book online at www. goa-tourism.com.

DON'T MISS

ANOTHER SIDE TO CALANGUTE

It's undeniably hard to find traces of the old, gentile or 'authentic' Calangute among the 'fortnight-holiday' mayhem, but it's still there – if you just look hard enough. Little whitewashed chapels and old mansion houses still punctuate the rows of cell-like concrete hotels, and local markets exist among the malls, chains and souvenir shops.

Peek in, first, at **St Alex's Church**, with its magnificently golden and ornamented *reredos* (ornamental screen) and pulpit. Next, look out for the stately 18th-century **Casa Braganza** *palácio* (palace), and **Casa dos Proença**, a grand mansion built in the early 18th century by Calangute's then-wealthiest family. You'll notice the grand, tower-shaped verandah, screened off with oyster-shell windows, while the mansion's pitched roof was specially designed to create a sort of natural air-conditioning system, channelling in cool air from the building's doors and windows.

Another relic of Calangute's past can be found at the **old customs post**, now a barber's shop, at the market crossroads. Several of these posts were built during Portuguese rule to monitor the coming and going of goods, and deter smuggling, but this is one of the few that still survive. Nearby, the **covered market** makes for good local wandering, among a crush of Goans all here to buy fresh produce, spices, coffee, meat and fish. For those less in love with Calangute than others, the rapid journey from Ibiza back to India will likely come as a very welcome relief.

Baga

🔵 Activities, Courses & Tours
1 Barracuda Diving	B1
2 Jungle Guitars	A2

🛏 Sleeping
3 Casa Baga	B3
4 Cavala Seaside Resort	A2
5 Divine Guest House	A2
6 Indian Kitchen	B4
7 Nani's Bar & Rani's Restaurant	A2

✖ Eating
8 Britto's	A2
9 J&A's	A1
10 Le Poisson Rouge	A2
11 Lila Café	A1

🎭 Entertainment
12 Cafe Mambo	A3
13 Tito's	A3

🛍 Shopping
14 All About Eve	A2
15 Casa Goa	B4
16 Karma Collection	A2
17 Mackie's Saturday Nite Bazaar	B1
18 Star Magic Shop	A2

🛏 Sleeping

Calangute and Baga's sleeping options are broad and varied, though it's not a particularly budget-friendly destination and most decent options in the budget category are towards the top end of the range. Both destinations are heaving with concrete-block package-holiday hotels, which cater to planes full of British, Russian and Scandinavian tourists, and have little to offer independent travellers.

Generally, the quietest, most laid-back hotels lie in south Calangute, and across the bridge north of Baga. There are also dozens of simple, generic budget guesthouses set back in alleyways off Baga's Tito's Rd; double rooms go for around ₹1000, but shop around to secure yourself windows, a comfortable mattress and a bit of a breeze.

CALANGUTE

Pousada Tauma   BOUTIQUE HOTEL $$$

(☎2279061; www.pousada-tauma.com; ste from €260; ❄@✉) If you're looking for luxury with your ayurvedic regime, check right into this gorgeous little boutique hotel in Calangute. Costs for treatments range from €50 for a 1½ hour 'body and mind' treatment, up to €495 for a 14-day 'Pizhichil' course to treat complaints such as arthritis and sciatica. Its romantic little open-air Copper Bowl restaurant offers delicious coconut and spice-infused Goan cuisine served in the copper bowls after which it's named. Try the spicy *balchão* (seafood in spicy tomato sauce) or coconutty *xacuti,* and revel in the romance of the candle- and fairy-lit location.

Casa de Goa   HOTEL $$$

(☎2277777/9999; www.casadegoa.com; Tivai Waddo; d ₹5000; ❄@🛜✉) The pretty swish Casa de Goa is popular with Indian families and books up months in advance – for good reason. Portuguese-style yellow ochre buildings surround a pretty pool courtyard, decor is bright and fresh, and the big, clean rooms

WORTH A TRIP

CHURCH OF NOSSA SENHORA, MAE DE DEUS

As you explore the countryside, don't miss a peek into the **Church of Nossa Senhora, Mae de Deus** (Church of Our Lady, Mother of God). With its unusual neo-Gothic Christmas-cake style topped with a row of fanciful turrets, it's situated 2km from Calangute on the road towards the village of Saligao. Built in 1873, it houses a rather technicolour, and allegedly 'miraculous', statue of the Mother of God herself, rescued from the ruins of an old convent at Old Goa. The church is brightly lit every evening – making it a useful landmark for navigating the surrounding country lanes.

have safes, flat screen TVs and new fridges, with other high-end and thoughtful touches. Cottages are across the street from the main hotel and may not get wi-fi.

Ospy's Shelter GUESTHOUSE $
(✆2279505; Oscar_fernandes@sify.com; d ₹600-700) Tucked away in a quiet, lush little area full of palms and sandy paths between the beach and St Anthony's Chapel are a cluster of family-run guesthouses. Ospy's, just a two minute walk to the beach, is our favourite. Spotless upstairs rooms have fridges and balconies and look brand new even though they're not, and the whole place has a cosy family feel. Check out the gorgeous old floor tiles on the ground floor.

Hotel Seagull HOTEL $$
(✆2179969; www.villatheresagoa.com; Holiday St, Calangute; d ₹2070; ❈☒) Bright, friendly, welcoming, and renovated in the summer of 2011, the Seagull's rooms, set in a cheerful orange-painted house in quieter South Calangute, are light and airy, with antique bits and pieces of furniture to give them character. Downstairs there's a popular bar-restaurant with meals served all day. Note that the room price goes up by ₹230 per night over the weekend.

Vila Goesa HOTEL $$$
(✆2277535; www.vilagoesa.com; d from ₹4850; ❈☒) Nicely situated between south Baga and north Calangute and hidden in the palm thickets 200m back from the beach, this is a great place for lingering with a good book by the pool. Rooms are simple but pleasantly

furnished; the higher the tariff, the closer you get to the beach.

Nilaya Hermitage HOTEL $$$
(✆2276793/94; www.nilaya.com; Arpora; d incl breakfast, dinner & spa €300; ❈@☎☒) The ultimate in Goan luxury, set 3km inland from the beach at Arpora, a stay here will see you signing the guestbook with the likes of Giorgio Armani, Sean Connery and Kate Moss. Eleven beautiful red-stone rooms undulate around a swimming pool, alongside four stunning tents. The food is as dreamy as the surroundings, and the spa will see you spoiled rotten; the downside for pamper-hungry parents is that children under 12 aren't allowed.

Garden Court Resort GUESTHOUSE $
(✆2276054; luarba@dataone.in; r ₹700, with AC ₹1000, 1-/2-bedroom apts per month ₹18,000/25,000; ❈) Fronted by a Portuguese-style home, rooms here are set among pretty gardens and have balconies and big windows.

BAGA

TOP CHOICE **Indian Kitchen** GUESTHOUSE $
(✆2277555; ikitchen2602@yahoo.co.in; s/d/chalet ₹660/880/1100;@☎☒) If a colourful stay is what you're after, look no further than this family-run guest house, which offers basic, rather ramshackle rooms with much attempt at individual charm, set around a sparkly, spangly central courtyard. Each room has its own terrace or sit-out, but what really tips the budget scales in its favour is the small, sparklingly clean swimming pool out the back and the free wi-fi. Roomy air-conditioned apartments are also available for long-stayers, for ₹18,000 to ₹24,000 per month.

Cavala Seaside Resort HOTEL $$
(✆2276090; www.cavala.com; s/d/ste incl breakfast from ₹950/1700/2400; ❈☎☒) Idiosyncratic, ivy-clad Cavala has been charming Baga-bound travellers for over 25 years, and continues to deliver clean, simple, nicely furnished rooms, ranged about a large complex with two central swimming pools (₹200 for non-guests). The bar-restaurant cooks up a storm most evenings, with frequent live music.

Nani's Bar & Rani's Restaurant GUESTHOUSE $
(✆2276313; www.naniranigoa.com; d ₹1000; ❈@) Situated on the north side of the Baga River, just a short hop from the Baga beach action, Nani's is as charming as it is well situated, with comfortable rooms set around a garden

and a colonial bungalow that overlook the water.

Casa Baga
BOUTIQUE HOTEL **$$$**

(☑2253205; www.casaboutiquehotels.com; d ₹7000-8000; ✳@❄) Twenty Balinese-style rooms, some with huge four-poster beds, make for a classy and tranquil stay, with all the little stylish touches the Casa boutique team is so adept at providing.

Divine Guest House
GUESTHOUSE **$$**

(☑2279546, 9370273464; www.indivinehome.com; s/d from ₹900/1200; ✳@❄) You'll get the general vibe of this place as soon as you see the 'Praise the Lord' gatepost, and the gentle proselytising continues indoors with kitsch, quietly cheerful rooms embellished with the odd individual touch amid a quiet riverside location.

✗ Eating

Calangute and Baga boast probably the greatest concentration of dining options of anywhere in Goa, with everything on offer from the simplest kerbside *bhelpuri* (a Mumbai snack food, made with fried noodles, lime juice, onions and spices) to the finest Scottish smoked salmon.

For the best of the area's street food, try the main Calangute beach strip, which is thick with vendors grilling sweet corn, serving up *bhaji-pau* (bread roll dipped in curry), and spinning luminescent candy floss. Dining gets more sophisticated further towards both the north and south, with a number of Mediterranean stunners, while all along the beach you'll find the usual gamut of beach-shack cuisine. The market area, meanwhile, is filled with little local chai-and-thali joints, where an all-veg lunch costs a mere ₹40 or so.

CALANGUTE

TOP CHOICE Plantain Leaf
INDIAN **$**

(thali ₹70-90) In the heart of the market area, this clean, popular *udupi* (vegetarian restaurant serving South Indian dishes) dishes up South Indian breakfast classics – don't miss the *masala dosas* (curried vegetables inside a crisp pancake)– and abundant thalis to a constant stream of hungry locals.

Delhi Chaat
SNACKS **$**

(snacks from ₹20) In the thick of the seaside action, this highly popular takeaway joint dispenses all manner of spicy, savoury snacks to the milling masses, as well as delicious hot, sweet chai (₹10). A *bhaji-pau* comes in at ₹40; an *aloo fry masala chaat* (spicy fried potato) at ₹20.

Infantaria Pastry Shop
BAKERY, ITALIAN **$$**

(Calangute-Baga Rd; pastries ₹60-120, mains ₹150-300; ☺7.30am-midnight) Next to the Sao João Batista church is this scrummy bakery-turned-Italian-restaurant, loaded with home-made cakes, croissants, little flaky pastries, real coffee, Goan and Italian specialities, and lots of booze. The noticeboard here is a hotbed for all things current and countercurrent.

A Reverie
CONTINENTAL **$$$**

(Holiday St; mains from ₹350; ☺7pm-late) A gorgeous lounge bar, all armchairs, cool jazz and sparkling crystals, this is the place to spoil yourself, with the likes of Serrano ham, grilled asparagus, French wines and Italian cheeses. Try the delectable forest mushroom soup with truffle oil (₹275) or prop up the bar with a cocktail and a bowl of wasabi-flavoured guacamole (₹245).

Casandré
GOAN, MULTICUISINE **$$**

(mains from ₹120; ☺8.30am-3pm & 6pm-midnight) Housed in an old Portuguese bungalow, this dim and tranquil retreat seems mightily out of place amid the tourist tat of Calangute's main beach drag. With a long and old-fashioned menu encompassing everything from 'sizzlers' to Goan specialities, and a cocktail list featuring the good old gimlet, this is a loveable time-warp, with a pool table to boot.

BAGA

Le Poisson Rouge
FRENCH **$$$**

(mains from ₹330; ☺7pm-midnight) Baga manages to do fine dining with aplomb, and this French-slanted experience is one of the picks of the place. Simple local ingredients are combined into winning dishes such as beetroot carpaccio (₹200) and red snapper masala, and served up beneath the stars. You'll also find a branch of Om Made Cafe (see p90) just next door.

🌿 J&A's
ITALIAN **$$$**

(mains from ₹325) A pretty cafe set around a gorgeous small Portuguese villa, this little slice of Italy is a treat even before the sumptuous, if rather pricey, food arrives. Owned by a wonderful couple originally from Mumbai, the jazz-infused garden and twinkling evening lights makes for a place as drenched in romance as a tiramisu is in rum. Add to this triple-filtered water, the owners' electric car and composted leftovers, and you've got an experience almost as good for the world as it is for your tastebuds.

Lila Café   CAFE $$

(mains from ₹210; ☺8.30am-6pm Wed-Mon) This airy, white and enticing place located along the river is run by German long-term expats and serves up great home-baked breads and perfect frothy cappuccinos, as well as powerhouse mains like a very good goulash. The restful river view is somewhat obscured by the cafe's own guest parking places, but it still makes for a soothing place for a quiet cuppa.

Britto's   MULTICUISINE, BAR $$

(mains ₹130-350; ☺8.30am-late) Long-running, usually packed to the gills, and sometimes open as late as 3am, this Baga institution tumbles out onto the beach, serving up a mixture of Goan and Continental cuisines, cakes and desserts, with live music several nights a week.

🍷 Drinking & Entertainment

Boisterous, brash and booming, Baga's club scene somehow manages to bubble on long after the trance parties of further north have been locked down for good by late-night noise regulations. Just how this little strip of night-owls' nirvana has managed to escape the lockdown is anybody's guess, but escape it has, and if you're up for a night of decadent drinking or dancing on the tables, don your glad rags and hit the hot spots with the best of them.

If you're seeking something lower-key, go for the main Calangute beach access road, where simple bars are populated with a captivating mix of frazzled foreigners, heavy-drinking locals and tipsy out-of-towners.

CALANGUTE

Jerry John Jonesius   BAR

(JJJ; Calangute; ☺7am-10.30pm) Largely the preserve of locals, JJJ is a suitably dingy and atmospheric bar to down a few beers. Snacks and basic Indian meals (from ₹60) are also available, if you need to line your stomach with something more substantial than *feni* (liquor distilled from coconut milk or cashews).

Kerkar Art Complex   CULTURAL PROGRAMS

(per person ₹300; ☺6.45-8pm Tue & Thu) Held in the outdoor courtyard of the Kerkar Art Complex, these soothing recitals seem a world away from the brasher, bolder side of Calangute, and offer a little glimpse into local traditional music and dance forms.

BAGA

Tito's   NIGHTCLUB

(📞9822765002; www.titos.in; Tito's Rd, Baga; cover charge men/women from ₹350/free; ☺8pm-3am) Tito's, the titan on Goa's clubbing scene and the closest thing to Ibiza this side of the Arabian Sea, is trying its hardest to escape the locals-leering-at-Western-women image of yesteryear, though it's still hardly the place for a hassle-free girls' night out. Just in case you need them, Tito's has expanded into a range of other services, including tours, supermarkets, and, more mystifying, financial consultancy. Check the website for details.

Cafe Mambo   NIGHTCLUB

(📞9822765002; www.titos.in; Tito's Rd, Baga; cover charge before/after 10pm free/₹200; ☺10.30pm-late) Owned and managed by Tito's, this is a – very slightly – more sophisticated version of the same thing, with nightly DJs pumping out house, hip-hop and Latino tunes. Note that unaccompanied gents may not be allowed into either Mambo or Tito's.

🛍 Shopping

In line with its status as the tourist capital of Goa, Calangute has likewise grown to become the shopping capital. Flashy brand shops familiar to numerous international travellers (including a dedicated Crocs shop) have sprouted up along the main road to Candolim, just south of Calangute's market. Also here are upmarket gold and jewellery shops, boutique fashion stores and dozen upon dozen of arts-and-craft emporia.

However, it's probably the small-time stalls that will catch the eye of most foreign visitors. Calangute and Baga have been swamped by Kashmiri traders eager to cash in on the tourist boom. There is a fantastic range of things to buy – Kashmiri carpets, embroideries and papier-mâché boxes, as well as genuine and reproduction Tibetan and Rajasthani crafts, bronzes, carvings and miniature paintings. This is all the same sort of stuff, however, that you'll see in abundance at the Anjuna flea market (p87), so it might be worth comparing prices.

CALANGUTE

Book Palace   BOOKSTORE

(📞2281129; ☺9am-7pm) Next to the football field on the road to the beach, dusty old Book Palace has a good selection of reading material in all languages – including many titles on India and Goa – all sold by a man who loves his products.

A LITTLE LIGHT NIGHT MARKET

Both Mackie's **Saturday Nite Bazaar** (www.mackiesnitebazaar.com) in Baga, and the larger Ingo's **Saturday Nite Bazaar** (www.ingosbazaar.com) in Arpora, about 2km northeast of Baga, start around 6pm and are fun alternatives to Anjuna's Wednesday market. They were running at the time of research but have been cancelled from time to time in recent years due to bureaucratic troubles. Ask around before putting on your Saturday night shopping shoes, to check they're on.

BAGA

All About Eve   CLOTHING, ACCESSORIES
(☑2275687; ⊙10am-8pm) Just next door to Karma Collection, and owned and operated by the same proprietors, All About Eve stocks unusual clothes, bags and accessories, many designed by the owners themselves, and unlike any of the usual array you'll find on a beach-road stall.

Casa Goa   HOMEWARES
(☑2281048; ⊙10am-8pm) A lovely collection of furniture, textiles and home accessories housed in an old Portuguese mansion. Browse Casa Goa for a nice vase, a cute picture frame or even a four-poster bed.

Star Magic Shop   MAGIC
(⊙daily till late; sometimes closed Wed) While strolling Calangute, Baga and Anjuna markets, you're sure to spot Star's shop or one of its stalls, promising to teach you magic tricks in a startlingly brief two minutes. Stop off to purchase tricks and illusions to thrill your great aunties and uncles next Christmas, or simply to satisfy that inner thirst to be Thurston.

Karma Collection   SOUVENIRS
(☑2275687; www.karmacollectiongoa.com; ⊙9.30am-10.30pm) Beautiful home furnishings, textiles, ornaments, bags and other enticing stuff – some of it antique – has been sourced from across India, Pakistan and Afghanistan and gathered at Karma Collection, which makes for a mouth-watering browse. Fixed prices mean there's no need to bargain, a welcome relief after a stint amid the hard-haggling stalls.

❶ Information

Currency-exchange offices, ATMs, supermarkets and pharmacies cluster around Calangute's main market and bus stand, and continue north up to Baga, and south too along the main road leading to Candolim.

There are plenty of internet cafes (most charging ₹40 to ₹60 per hour) and prices tend to drop as you go further inland from the beach.

MGM International Travels (☑2276249; www.mgmtravels.com; ⊙9.30am-6.30pm Mon-Sat) A long-established and trusted travel agency near Calangute's central roundabout, MGM offers competitive prices on domestic and foreign air tickets.

❶ Getting There & Away

There are frequent buses to Panaji (₹15, 45 minutes) and Mapusa (₹12, 30 minutes) from both the Calangute and Baga bus stands, and a local bus runs between the Calangute and Baga stands every few minutes; catch it anywhere along the way.

A taxi from Calangute or Baga to Panaji costs around ₹350 and takes about 45 minutes. A prepaid taxi from Dabolim Airport to Calangute costs ₹645.

Paulo Tours & Travels (☑2281274) has a small office near the beach. It's the main, and one of the most dependable, operators for private buses to Hampi and Mumbai; pick-up is available in Calangute.

❶ Getting Around

Motorcycle and moped hire is easy to arrange in Calangute, and if you're here outside the peak season, you should be able to bargain a reasonable price. Try to pay around ₹120 a day for a Honda Kinetic if you hire it for a week or more. Expect to pay ₹250 a day around Christmas. You'll see plenty of signs on the main Calangute-Baga road.

Candolim, Sinquerim & Fort Aguada

☑0832 / POP 8600

Candolim's long, narrow, busy beach, which curves round to join smaller Sinquerim Beach to the south, is largely the preserve of slow-basting package tourists from the UK, Russia and Scandinavia, and is fringed with an unabating line of beach shacks, all offering sun beds and shade in exchange for your custom. There are some great independent budget hotels, which make for a decent stay in the area if you've got your own transport.

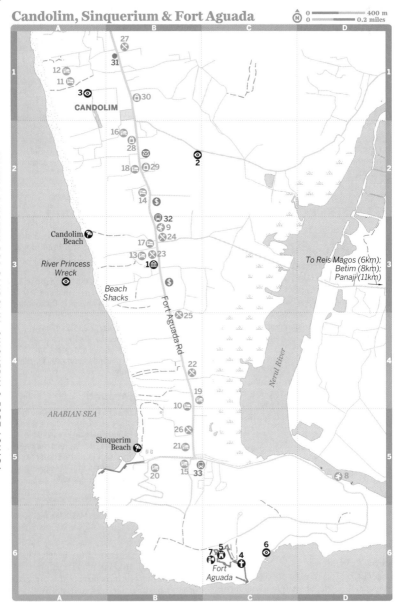

Though Candolim, for a beach resort, has its fair share of non-sand-based attractions, by far the most bewildering sight here was, until very recently, the hulking wreck of the massive *River Princess* tanker, which ran aground in the late 1990s and stayed put,

marooned just a few dozen metres offshore, for more than a decade, with tourists sunbathing in her sullen shadow.

Recently, however, after many years of campaigning on the part of locals, the tanker has undergone a laborious process of re-

Candolim, Sinquerium & Fort Aguada

⊙ Sights
1 Calizz B3
2 Casa dos Costa-Frias B2
3 Casa dos Monteiros................................A1
4 Church of St Lawrence C6
5 Fort Aguada C6
6 Fort Aguada Jail C6
7 New Lighthouse C6

⊙ Activities, Courses & Tours
8 Excursion Boat Jetty D5
9 John's Boat Tours..................................B3

⊜ Sleeping
10 Aashyana Lakhanpal.............................B4
11 D'Mello's Sea View Home......................A1
12 Dona Florina A1
13 Horizon Grill & Guesthouse...................B3
14 Lemon Tree Amarante Beach
     Resort..B2
15 Marbella Guest House...........................B5
16 Pretty Petals..B2
17 Ruffles Beach Resort.............................B3
18 Sea Shell Inn..B2
19 Villa Ludovici Tourist Home B4

20 Vivanta by Taj Fort Aguada...................B5
21 Vivanta by Taj Holiday Village...............B5

⊗ Eating
Banyan Tree..................................(see 21)
22 Bomra's B4
23 Cafe Chocolatti B3
24 L'Orange B3
Republic of Noodles.....................(see 14)
25 Stone House..B4
26 Tuscany Gardens B5
27 Viva Goa! B1

⊜ Shopping
28 Fabindia B2
29 Newton's...B2
30 Sotohaus B1

ℹ Information
31 Davidair..B1

ℹ Transport
32 Central Bus Stop B3
33 Fort Aguada Bus Stop B5

moval – piece by rusting piece. There's less than half of it left now, with boats continuing to appear daily to ship off the scrap. The beach, finally free from its industrial relic, is, however, revealed as rather characterless and, in some places, quite dirty.

Back from the beach, bustling Fort Aguada Rd is the best place to head for shops and services, and is home to dozens of restaurants that awaken each evening to provide cocktails, dinners of different culinary persuasions and the odd spot of live music. The beach, meanwhile, is Candolim's other option for nightlife, where the shacks host happy hours and jam sessions well beyond sunset.

⊙ Sights & Activities

Fort Aguada   FORT
Standing on the headland overlooking the mouth of the Mandovi River, Fort Aguada occupies a magnificent and successful position, confirmed by the fact that it was never taken by force. A highly popular spot to watch the sunset, with uninterrupted views both north and south, the fort was built in 1612, following the increasing threat to Goa's Portuguese overlords of attacks by the Dutch, among others.

The fort covers the entire headland, and the Mandovi River below was once connected with the coast at Sinquerim to form a moat, entirely cutting off the headland. One of the great advantages of the site was the abundance of water from natural springs on the hillside, making the fort an important first watering point for ships freshly arrived from Portugal; the spring also gave the fort its name, *agua* being Portuguese for 'water'. Like Reis Magos and Cabo Raj Bhavan, the British occupied the fort in 1799 to protect Goa from possible French invasion.

Today visitors flock to the **bastion** that stands on the hilltop, although, when compared with the overall area surrounded by defences, this is only a fraction of the original fort. Once protected by a battery of 200 cannons, steps in the main courtyard lead down to vast underground water tanks, able to hold 10 million litres of drinking water. These huge echoing chambers indicate just how seriously the architects of the fort took the threat of a prolonged period of siege.

The **old Portuguese lighthouse**, which stands in the middle of the fort, was built in 1864 and once housed the great bell from the Church of St Augustine in Old Goa

ANJUNA & NORTH GOA CANDOLIM, SINQUERIM & FORT AGUADA

before it was moved to the Church of Our Lady of the Immaculate Conception in Panaji. It's the oldest of its sort in Asia, and it is occasionally open to the public, allowing you to climb the spiral steps and enjoy the view from the top. Nearby, the **new lighthouse** (adult/child ₹5/3; ⊙4-5.30pm), built in 1976, can also usually be visited; cameras are not allowed inside.

To get to the hilltop fort, take the 4km winding road that heads east from Sinquerim Beach and loops up around the headland. Otherwise there's a steep 2km walking trail to the fort that starts just past Marbella Guest House (p104).

Church of St Lawrence
CHURCH

A short way to the east of the bastion is the pretty Church of St Lawrence, which also occupies a magnificent viewpoint. The church was built in 1643 to honour St Lawrence, the patron saint of sailors, whose image stands on the gilded *reredos* (ornamental screen), holding a model ship.

Fort Aguada Jail
OFFBEAT SIGHT

Down below the fort, gazing out melancholically to the broad Mandovi River is Fort Aguada jail, Goa's largest prison, whose cells stand on the site that once formed the square-shaped citadel of the hilltop Fort Aguada. Today the prison houses inmates mostly serving sentences for drug possession or smuggling, including a dozen or so long-staying foreigners. The road down to the jail's entrance – which is as far, thankfully, as most people ever get – passes a weird and wonderful compound known as **Jimmy's Palace**, home to reclusive tycoon Jimmy Gazdar. Designed by Goan architect Gerard de Cunha, it's a closely guarded froth of fountains, foliage and follies, of which you'll catch glimpses as you whiz past.

Calizz
MUSEUM

(☑3250000; www.calizz.com; ₹300; ⊙10am-9.30pm) Those with a thirst for Goan history and architecture shouldn't miss a visit to Candolim's Calizz (which means 'heart' in Konkani). An illuminating insight into Goan heritage, its roomy compound is filled with traditional, transplanted Goan houses, complete with authentic interiors. Tours last for 45 minutes and are conducted by local historians who bring the state's cultural history to life in a National Tourism Award–winning project.

Excursion Boat Jetty
BOAT TOUR

If you're looking to haggle for an on-the-spot dolphin-spotting trip, head up to the Excursion boat jetty on the banks of the Nerul River, where lots of independent local boatmen operate, selling their services to a domestic holidaying crowd. Prices vary (so bargain hard) but should be somewhere in the region of ₹200 for a dolphin-watching trip that passes Coco Beach, Fort Aguada Jail, the fort, and 'Johnny Millionaire's House'.

John's Boat Tours
BOAT TOUR

(☑6520190, 9822182814; www.johnboattours.com; Fort Aguada Rd) John's Boat Tours offers one of the most organised of Candolim's day-tripping options. John's has been offering a variety of boat and jeep excursions for years, as well as arranging fabulous river-based houseboat cruises. Choose from dolphin-watching trips, a return boat trip to the

---

THE PINTO REVOLT

In 1787 Candolim was the scene of the first serious local attempt to overthrow the Portuguese. The founders of the conspiracy were mostly churchmen, angry at the ingrained racial discrimination that meant they were not allowed to occupy the highest clerical positions. Two of them, Father Caetano Francisco Couto and Jose Antonio Gonsalves, travelled to Portugal to plead their case in the court at Lisbon. Unsuccessful in their attempts to remove the injustice, they returned to Goa and began plotting at the home of the Pinto family in Candolim. Gradually the number of conspirators grew, as army officers and others disaffected with their Portuguese overlords joined the cause.

The plans were so close to completion that a date had been fixed for the proposed coup, when the plot was discovered by the Portuguese authorities. A total of 47 conspirators, including 17 priests and seven army officers, were arrested. The lucky ones were sentenced to the galleys or deported to Portugal for a about a 20-year prison stint, while 15 of the lowlier and less fortunate were hanged, drawn and quartered in Panaji and their heads mounted on stakes as a deterrent to other would-be revolutionaries.

CANDOLIM'S MANSIONS

You'd be forgiven for thinking that architecture starts and ends with hotels and beach shacks in Candolim, but despite the wholesale development of this once-sleepy seaside village, some intriguing architectural remnants of a rather different past remain hidden in its quiet back lanes.

In the 17th and 18th centuries, Candolim saw the arrival of a number of wealthy Goan families, fleeing from the capital at Old Goa due to the ravages of typhoid, cholera and malaria epidemics. The homes they built were lavish and ornate, filled with oyster-shell windows, fine materials from Macau and China, and scrolling carved stonework.

Though it's not open to the public, seek out the beautiful Casa dos Costa-Frias, down a side road just opposite Candolim's football field, which belonged to relatives of the influential Pinto family (see the boxed text, the Pinto Revolt). It was built in the early 18th century, and stands behind a white, cross-topped gateway, with a family chapel tucked behind it. The recently renovated facade's architectural ornament gives a good indication of what Candolim's grand *palácios* (palaces) must have looked like in their heyday.

Nearer the beach, the Casa dos Monteiros is another tucked-away example of the peak of Candolim's architectural splendour, built by Goa's most powerful family, the Monteiros, with the pretty 1780 Nossa Senhora dos Remedios (Our Lady of Miracles) chapel standing opposite the entrance to the house. Still occupied by descendants of the Monteiros, the house is sadly not open to visitors, but is worth a look from the outside in any case.

Wednesday Anjuna market, or a 'Crocodile Dundee' river trip, to catch a glimpse of the Mandovi's crocodile 'muggers'. Call for prices and bookings.

Water Sports — WATER SPORTS
The southern stretch of Candolim Beach, and Sinquerim Beach beyond it, are home to plenty of independent water-sports operators, who offer jet skis, parasailing, waterskiing and the usual host of watery activities. Operations change seasonally; compare several to plump for the best rate.

🛏 Sleeping

Though Candolim is largely frequented by package tourists bussed straight in from Dabolim Airport, there's a great range of accommodation for the independent traveller, with the added bonus that many mid-range places include nice little swimming pools. Most of the best value budget choices are situated either in the northern part of Candolim or in the Sinquerim area further south; the little road up to Marbella Guest House has lots of private houses offering double rooms for around ₹500 per night.

Dona Florina — HOTEL $$
(☑2489051; www.donaflorina.co.in; Monteiro's Rd; s ₹800, d ₹1500-2000) It's hard to get better value in Candolim than friendly Dona Flo-

rina, just a quick walk from the sea and situated in the quiet northern part of the village. Front-facing rooms have spectacular sea views, there's daily yoga on the roof terrace, and the lack of vehicle access ensures a quiet night's repose.

Lemon Tree Amarante Beach Resort — HOTEL $$$
(☑3988188; www.lemontreehotels.com; r ₹5,400-15,500; ✵@☎☒) Squeezed in on the main strip, this boutiquey, luxey place conjures up a strange mixture of Thai-spa style and medieval motifs, intended to echo, apparently, 'the history and romance of 15th-century Portugal'. Whatever the mix, it works, with swish rooms equipped with wi-fi and DVD players, a luxurious spa and a roomy courtyard pool with swim-up bar.

Aashyana Lakhanpal — VILLA, COTTAGES $$$
(☑2489225; www.aashyanalakhanpal.com; main villa/Villa Venus/casinha per week ₹465,150/174,300/49,000; ✵@☒) A five-bedroom villa filled with art and three two-bedroom *casinhas* (little houses), set amid 1.6 hectares of lush, landscaped grounds spilling down to the beach, Aashyana makes the perfect retreat (especially grand for a family or large group of friends) from the brashness and bustle of Candolim. Featured in *Vanity Fair*, this is high-society luxe at its best, with

ANJUNA & NORTH GOA CANDOLIM, SINQUERIM & FORT AGUADA

a perfect pool, organic herbs and vegetables direct from the kitchen garden, and staff keen to cater to your every desire. There's also a new three-bedroom Villa Venus, a gorgeously renovated old Portuguese mansion, up for grabs.

Marbella Guest House HOTEL $$$
(☑2479551; www.marbellagoa.com; d/ste from ₹2600/4100; ❋) You might be put off by the name – particularly if you've already noticed the similarities on the sands – but this place hasn't the slightest touch of the Costa del Sol about it. A stunning Portuguese villa filled with antiques and backed by a peaceful courtyard garden, this is a romantic, redolent old-world remnant. Its kitchen serves breakfast, lunch and dinner daily (with some imaginative touches), discounts are given for stays of over seven days, and its penthouse suite is a dream of polished tiles and four-posters. Sadly for kids with a keen sense of style, guests under 12 aren't permitted.

Villa Ludovici Tourist Home GUESTHOUSE $
(☑2479684; Fort Aguada Rd; d incl breakfast ₹900) For 30 years Ludovici's has been welcoming travellers into its well-worn, creaky rooms in a grand old Portuguese villa. This is the place for a four-poster bed on a budget; rooms are vast, if definitely faded, and the hosts (and ghosts) are kind and amiable.

D'Mello's Sea View Home HOTEL $$
(☑2489650; dmellos_sea view_home@hotmail. com; d small/large/sea view ₹1200/1800/2500) Lovely breezy rooms are the principal attraction at D'Mello's, which has the advantage of being just a stone's throw from the beach. A great choice for a simple, serene stay, especially when nearby Dona Florina is fully booked.

Sea Shell Inn GUESTHOUSE $$
(☑2489131; seashellgoa@hotmail.com; Fort Aguada Rd; d without/with AC ₹1600/2100) You won't miss this beautiful white-painted Portuguese mansion, just opposite the massive Newton's supermarket. Its eight plain rooms might come as a bit of a disappointment, however, after visiting the reception; they're in a '70s-style annexe around the back. Still, they're clean, fan-cooled and reasonable value. Rates include breakfast.

Pretty Petals GUESTHOUSE $$
(☑2489184; www.prettypetalsgoa.com; d without/ with AC ₹1200/1500; ❋) Despite the cutesy name, it's not at all twee here. Instead, bright, simply furnished rooms, some with separate kitchenette and dining room, are ranged around a lovely grassy garden, which is just perfect for days when the beach seems too much bother.

Ruffles Beach Resort HOTEL $$
(☑9850752662; www.rufflesgoa.com; d ₹2400; ❋❋) 'Welcome to your abode in Paradise', declares Ruffles' website; that might be a slight overstatement, but this decent place does have a pleasant courtyard pool and well-equipped rooms that are good value.

Horizon Grill & Guesthouse GUESTHOUSE $$
(☑2479727; www.horizonview.co.in; d ₹2000-2500; ❋❋) One of the few midrange places in town catering solely to independent tourists, this small, family-run hotel is a good-value option, with simple rooms set around a small swimming pool. Don't expect luxury, but for the price it can't be beaten. The grill, meanwhile, serves up highly popular English breakfasts.

Vivanta by Taj Fort Aguada HOTEL $$
(☑toll-free 1800111825; www.tajhotels.com; d from ₹9000; ❋@❋) Dominating the headland above Sinquerim Beach, the Taj Group's sprawling beach resort isn't the best the Taj name has to offer, but its service is still top-notch even where its rooms are showing signs of wear and tear. Its Jiva Spa offers a host of soothing balms and palms, and the resort has a gym and pool, and offers adventure sports.

Vivanta by Taj Holiday Village HOTEL $$$
(☑toll-free 1800111825; www.tajhotels.com; cottages from ₹10,000; ❋@❋) Next door to the Taj Fort Aguada, this set of 142 cottages and villas is a smart variation on a five-star theme, possessing all the luxuries you'd expect from this top-end chain. Its Banyan Tree Thai restaurant is well-known for good food in beautiful al fresco surroundings.

✗ Eating

There's a delicious variety of dishes on offer in Candolim, including high-level international cuisine as well as the obligatory all-encompassing beach-shack menus down on the sands. Much of the best on offer is ranged along Fort Aguada Rd, though if you take the side streets to the east you'll also come across local joints for a cheap and tasty breakfast *bhaji-pau* or lunchtime thali.

TOP
CHOICE **Cafe Chocolatti**   CAFE, BAKERY $$
(Fort Aguada Rd; cakes from ₹90; ⊘9am-7pm Mon-Sat) When you're tired of thalis or simply seeking sanctuary, there's nowhere better in Candolim to treat yourself to afternoon tea than this lovely tea room, set in a green garden seemingly light years from the bustle of the beach. The cafe serves up great paninis (go for cheddar and mango chutney), crepes, super salads (the pasta salad is a winner) and simply perfect coffee. Alternatively, simply sit back and indulge in a slice of Victoria Sponge, double chocolate cake, or the best coffee and walnut cake we've ever tasted. Take away a bag of chocolate truffles, homemade by chocolatier-par-excellence, Nazneen Sarosh-Rebelo.

Tuscany Gardens   ITALIAN $$$
(Fort Aguada Rd; mains from ₹255; ⊘closed for lunch Mon) What? I'm not really in Italy, you say? While that's undoubtedly the case, it's easy to drift off into temporary Tuscan reverie whilst dining at Candolim's unbeatably cosy, romantic Italian restaurant, where perfect antipasti, pastas, pizzas and risottos are the order of the day. Try the deliciously inventive *pumpkin insalata* (₹110) – spiced roasted pumpkin on a bed of rocket leaves with caramelised balsamic vinegar – and *penne a la betura* (₹265) – sliced aubergine and mozzarella served over a spicy cream, vodka and tomato sauce.

Bomra's   BURMESE $$$
(Fort Aguada Rd; mains from ₹250) Wonderfully unusual cuisine is on offer at this sleek little place, tucked into a courtyard, and serving interesting modern Burmese cuisine with a fusion twist. Though most dishes are meaty or fishy, vegetarians shouldn't despair: start with a pickled tea-leaf salad or the homemade fried Shan tofu with tamarind soya sauce, and move on to the straw mushroom, lychee, water chestnut, spinach and coconut curry (washed down with a pomegranate margarita) and you'll be very glad you did.

Republic of Noodles   ASIAN FUSION $$$
(Fort Aguada Rd; appetisers ₹250, mains from ₹525; ⊘11am-3.30pm & 7-11pm) For a sophisticated dining experience, the RoN delivers with its dark bamboo interior, Buddha heads and floating candles. Delicious, huge and *Times of India* award-winning noodle plates, including a fabulous phad thai, are the order of the day, with some exciting options for vegetarians.

Banyan Tree   THAI $$$
(Vivanta by Taj Holiday Village; ⊘7.30-10.30pm; mains from ₹600) Refined Thai food is the trademark of the Taj's romantic Banyan Tree, its swish courtyard set, unsurprisingly, beneath the branches of a vast old banyan tree. If you're a fan of green curry, don't miss the succulent, signature version on offer here.

Stone House   MULTICUISINE, STEAKHOUSE $$
(Fort Aguada Rd; mains ₹150-450; ⊘6pm-midnight) Surf 'n' turf's the thing at this venerable old Candolim venue, inhabiting a stone house and its leafy front courtyard, and the improbable-sounding 'Swedish Lobster' tops the list. There's live music most nights of the week, amid the twinkle of fairy lights.

Viva Goa!   GOAN, SEAFOOD $
(Fort Aguada Rd; mains from ₹90; ⊘11am-midnight) This cheap, local-oriented little place, also popular with in-the-know tourists, serves flipping-fresh fish and Goan seafood specialities such as a spicy mussel fry.

L'Orange   MULTICUISINE $$
(Fort Aguada Rd; mains from ₹110; ⊘noon-midnight) A cute, and largely orange, bar, restaurant and art gallery right next to John's Boat Tours. Live music is performed regularly; drop in to find out when.

🍷 Drinking & Entertainment

Candolim's drinking scene is largely hotel-based, but its plentiful beach shacks are a popular place for a relaxed lunchtime beer or a happy-hour sunset cocktail or two.

Sunburn Festival   MUSIC FESTIVAL
(www.sunburn-festival.com) For the last couple of years, Candolim has been the venue for the stellar Sunburn Festival, billing itself as 'Asia's biggest music festival', which has set up camp in Candolim over Christmas and New Year. Check the website for details, and if it continues to run to form, don't miss it for a four-day dance-music extravaganza filled with international DJs and all-day partying.

ANJUNA & NORTH GOA CANDOLIM, SINQUERIM & FORT AGUADA

🛍 Shopping

Fabindia   SOUVENIRS, HOUSEWARES
(Seashell Arcade, Fort Aguada Rd; ⊘10.30am-9pm)
Part of a nationwide chain selling tempting
fair-trade bed and table linens, home furnishings, clothes, jewellery and toiletries.
Fabindia makes for a great, colourful browse,
and is perfect for picking up high-end gifts
or treating yourself to a traditional kurta
(long shirt with short or no collar) or *salwar
kameez* (women's dresslike tunic and trouser
combination) outfit.

Newton's   SUPERMARKET
(Fort Aguada Rd; ⊘9.30am-midnight) If you're
desperately missing Edam cheese or Pot
Noodles, don't delay in dashing to long-
established Newton's, to stock up on homely
goods of all descriptions. This vast supermarket also has a good line of toiletries,
wines and children's toys, and expat folks
travel miles just to peruse its goodies-lined
shelves. Note that if they don't stock what
you're after, a new competitor, Delfino's, has
opened just a few hundred metres south.

Sotohaus   DESIGN
(☑2489983; www.sotodecor.com; Fort Aguada Rd)
Offering cool, functional items dreamed up
by a Swiss expat team, this is the place to invest in a natural-form-inspired lamp, mirror
or dining table, to add a twist of streamlined
India to your pad back home.

ℹ Information

The post office, supermarkets, travel agents,
pharmacies and plenty of banks with ATMs are
all located on the main road, known as Fort
Aguada Rd, which runs parallel to the beach.
Internet outfits change seasonally; ask around
for the year's latest. **Davidair** (☑2489303/4;
www.com2goa.com) is a reputable travel
agency specialising in flights out of Goa and
organised tours throughout India. It prides
itself on its service to foreign tourists, pointing
out sagely on the organisation's website: 'It's a
long way to Goa from Cheltenham, Galliwasted,
Ashby-de-la-Zouch or wherever'.

ℹ Getting There & Around

Buses run about every 10 minutes to and from
Panaji (₹15, 45 minutes), and stop at the central
bus stop near John's Boat Tours. Some continue
south to the Fort Aguada bus stop at the bottom
of Fort Aguada Rd, then head back to Panaji
along the Mandovi River road, via the villages of
Verem and Betim.

Frequent buses also run from Candolim to
Calangute (₹7, 15 minutes) and can be flagged
down on Fort Aguada Rd.

Nerul (Coco) Beach

Nerul Beach (also known as Coco Beach),
located southeast around the coast from
Candolim, affords a great view across the
Mandovi River to Miramar and Panaji in
Central Goa. Despite its rather murky tidal
waters, it makes a nice spot for a quick paddle. With the beaches of the north beckoning, there's no particular reason to stay here,
unless you're checking in to Coco Shamb-
hala (www.cocoshambhala.com; villas €1880 per
week; ❋ 🛜 🏊), a glorious, luxurious collection
of four villas, each of which come with their
own private jetpool, and car and driver.

Along the Mandovi River

If you're looking to truly lose the crowds,
the road that hugs the northern bank of the
broad Mandovi River, just across the slow-
moving waters from state capital Panaji
(Panjim), is the place to do it. It hosts a crop
of unexplored delights, between Fort Aguada, where the river meets the sea, and the
riverside village of Naroa in Bicholim *taluka*
(district) to the east. Exploring under your
own steam, by motorbike, car or scooter, allows you the freedom to meander like the
tributaries of the river itself, stopping off
here and there to seek out the seldom-visited treasures this sleepy stretch has to offer.

REIS MAGOS
☑ 0832
Travelling east from Candolim, after about
5km the road reaches a crossroads at the
small village of Verem, unmistakable because of its colourful Hindu banyan-tree
shrine on the left-hand side of the road. Take
a right here, and the road will lead you up to
tiny Reis Magos (meaning Three Wise Men)
village, with its classic Portuguese fort and
16th-century Reis Magos Church (⊘9am-
noon & 4-5.30pm Mon-Sat, for services Sun), dedicated to St Jerome.

It's easy to appreciate the strategic importance of the fort's site, since it overlooks – and
once afforded protection to – the narrowest
point of the Mandovi River estuary. Built in
1551, after the north bank of the river came
under Portuguese control, it was rebuilt in
1703, in time to assist the desperate Portu-

Along the Mandovi River

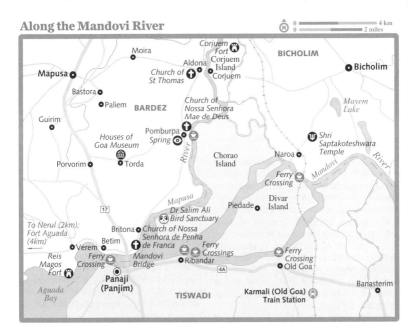

guese defence against the Hindu Marathas (1737–39). It was then occupied by the British army in 1799 when they requisitioned Reis Magos, Cabo Raj Bhavan and Fort Aguada in anticipation of a possible attack by the French.

After the British withdrawal in 1813 the Reis Magos fort gradually lost importance, and was eventually abandoned. Like Fort Aguada nearby, modern Goans have paid homage to Portugal's forts in their own special way: by locking up present-day prisoners within the structure originally designed to keep the naughty folk out. Though it's out of bounds to law-abiding citizens, it makes an imposing sight – from a safe distance – and is worth the trip up here for the excellent views.

The little church standing below the fortress walls is made all the more attractive by the imposing black fort bastions that loom above it. The first church was built in 1555, shortly after the fort itself. A Franciscan seminary was later added, and over the years became a significant seat of learning.

Nowadays the seminary is gone but the church is worth a look, with its steep steps up from the road and fine views of the Mandovi River from the main doors. Outside the church, the lions portrayed in relief at the foot of the steps show signs of Hindu influence (these might, in fact, be evidence of an

early Hindu temple on the same spot), and a crown tops off the facade. The colourful interior of the church contains the tombs of three viceroys, including Dom Luis de Ataide, famous for holding 100,000 Muslim attackers – along with their 2000 elephants – at bay for 10 months in 1570, with his own force of just 7000 men.

Reis Magos nowadays is the scene of a colourful **Reis Magos festival** on 6 January, when the story of the three kings is recreated with young local boys acting the parts of the Magi, complete with gifts for the infant Jesus.

If you're coming here by public transport, buses run regularly between Betim and Candolim or Calangute; coming from either direction, ask to be let off at the Reis Magos junction and then walk to the church and fort.

BETIM

Continuing east from the coast along the course of the Mandovi River, you'll reach the busy village of Betim, which hugs tight to its banks, looking out to Panaji on the other side. Here, you can take a cooking course courtesy of **Holiday on the Menu** (see p117) and fill up on petrol or snacks for your onward travels.

The village can also be reached by passenger **ferry** from Panaji; see p124.

BRITONA & POMBURPA
☑0832

On the opposite side of the NH17 (National Highway 17) from Betim, you'll reach the pretty riverside village of Britona. Its parish church, **Nossa Senhora de Penha de Franca** (Our Lady of the Rock of France), is a grand old dame, occupying a fine location at the confluence of the Mandovi and Mapusa Rivers, looking across to Chorao Island on one side and to the Ribandar Causeway on the other.

Nossa Senhora de Penha de Franca was a Spanish saint who, after one hair-raising voyage in which the sailors saved themselves from certain death by appealing to Nossa Senhora, became associated with seafarers, and thus was favoured by many of those who had survived the voyage to India.

The interior of the church is beautifully decorated, with a high-vaulted ceiling and a simple *reredos* embellished with painted scenes. The church is best visited in the morning and holds one service (in Konkani) on most days.

Britona itself, meanwhile, has plenty of old-fashioned village character, and makes a nice place to stay for the night. **Casa Britona** (☑2416737; www.casaboutiquehotels.com; deluxe/luxury d ₹8000/9000; ✳@✖) is a 300-year-old converted customs warehouse, with luxurious antique-filled rooms, fine outdoor dining beneath the stars and a lovely riverside swimming pool.

Continuing on another 5km to the village of Pomburpa, peek in at its equally beautiful **Church of Nossa Senhora Mae de Deus**

(Our Lady Mother of God), noteworthy for its stunning interior and elaborate gold-leaf *reredos*.

ALDONA
☑0832

Around 5km north of Pomburpa, the large and picturesque village of Aldona is home to the **Church of St Thomas** on the banks of the Mapusa River, which makes a grand sight, particularly when viewed from the village's now-defunct ferry crossing. The church, built in 1596, is attached to a strange, saintly legend. The story goes that one day, as a group of thieves crossed the river to Aldona to strip the church of its riches, they were met by a young boy who warned them to reconsider carrying out their crime. While they were nonetheless attempting to remove valuables, the church bells began to peal; fleeing in a panic, some of the thieves drowned, while the others were captured. As the leader was led sorrowfully away, he recognised the church's statue of St Thomas as the boy who had cautioned him against his misdeeds.

CORJUEM ISLAND

An inland island around 2km northeast of Aldona and now accessible by modern road bridges, here you'll find the only still-intact inland fort, the abandoned and atmospheric **Corjuem Fort**. Around 1705 Corjuem came to mark the easternmost boundary of Portugal's colonial conquest, and the small fort on Corjuem Island was quickly built to protect the territory from raids by the Rajputs and Marathas.

WORTH A TRIP

HOUSES OF GOA MUSEUM

Turning right to take the main highway north just after Britona, it's worth a quick detour away from the Mandovi riverbanks to reach the little village of Torda, where you'll find the interesting **Houses of Goa Museum** (☑2410711; www.archgoa.org; adult/child ₹100/25; ⊙10am-7.30pm Tue-Sun), created by well-known local architect Gerard de Cunha to illuminate the history of Goan homes, apparent statewide in various states of picturesque decreptitude.

Just next door is the **Mario Gallery** (☑2410711; admission free; ⊙10am-5.30pm Mon-Fri, to 1pm Sat) with works by one of India's favourite cartoonists, Loutolim local Mario de Miranda, who died in December 2011 at the age of 85.

Marooned shiplike in the middle of a traffic island, the museum is hard to miss. To find it, turn right at the O'Coqueiro junction and then left at the fork, and you'll find it just there. If you don't have your own transport, a taxi here from Panaji (p111) should cost around ₹300 one-way.

Squat and thick walled, standing alone on a small hillock, the fort has a lonely element of *beau geste* about it, and although there's not a whole lot to see here, it's easy to imagine this place as a solitary outpost in the jungle nearly three centuries ago, filled with homesick Portuguese soldiers just waiting to be overrun by bloodthirsty attackers.

NAROA & SHRI SAPTAKOTESHWARA TEMPLE

For the most scenic entry to the little village of Naroa, clinging to the banks of the Mandovi, venture here by ferry (pedestrians/motorbikes/cars free/₹5/₹12; ☺every 20-30 min) from picturesque Divar Island (p133).

Just 2km from the ferry point, the Shri Saptakoteshwara Temple is tiny, tucked away in a narrow emerald-green valley and undisturbed by anything apart from a few mopeds and the occasional tour bus.

The deity worshipped at the temple is a lingam (a phallic symbol of Shiva, the destroyer), which underwent considerable adventures before arriving here. Having been buried to avoid early Muslim raids, it was recovered and placed in a great Kadamba temple on Divar Island, but when the Portuguese desecrated the spot in 1560 it was smuggled away and subsequently lost. Miraculously discovered again in the 17th century by Hindus, who found it being used as part of a well shaft, it was smuggled across the Mandovi River to safety in the temple. It's said that the great Maratha rebel leader Shivaji used to come here to worship, and personally saw to it that the temple was reconstructed in 1668, creating the small, solid structure that stands here today.

To find the temple, follow the road from the ferry point at Naroa (from Divar Island) for approximately 2km, before forking right down a small tarmac lane. You'll find the temple about 1.5km along, to your left; follow the red and green archaeology arrows until you arrive. You'll know it from its shal-

DEFENDER OF HEARTH AND HOME

Corjuem Fort's most famous Portuguese defender was Ursula e Lancastre, a Portuguese noblewoman who travelled the world disguised as a man, eventually finding herself stationed here as a soldier. It was not until she was suspected and stripped that her secret was discovered. However, this did not put an end to her military career. She promptly went on to marry the captain of the guard, following what was, in retrospect, probably one of the most interesting strip searches in the history of warfare.

low, Mughal-style dome, tall lamp tower, and vaulted arches. Look out for the equestrian mural of Shivaji, above the entrance.

If you don't have your own transport, it's easiest to reach the temple on the GTDC's daily North Goa bus tour (see p230), which departs Panaji at 9.30am and calls first at the temple, then at Mayem Lake before continuing on a whistle-stop tour of North Goa.

MAYEM LAKE

East of Naroa and about 35km from Panaji, glistening Mayem Lake is a pleasant sort of place that's popular among local picnickers, while the GTDC's North Goa bus tour also sets down daily for lunch here. Despite the occasional midday rush, the lake's a quiet spot, offering a lovely bit of R&R, and makes a great place to munch your own packed lunch.

If you're keen to stay for longer than lunchtime, the GTDC's Mayem Lake View (☎0832 -2362144; www.goa-tourism.com; d without/with AC ₹930/1150, ste ₹1890; ✳) is almost certainly the nicest of all the GTDC's hotels. Its rooms are cheerful, clean and good value, particularly those perched at the lake's edge.

Panaji & Central Goa

Includes »

Panaji...............................111
West of Panaji...............124
Old Goa..........................126
Divar Island 133
Goa Velha......................134
Talaulim.........................135
Pilar 135
Ponda 135
Bondla Wildlife
Sanctuary.....................140
Molem & Around 141
Tambdi Surla 142
Hampi............................143
Around Hampi...............148
Hospet...........................149

Best Places to Eat

» Upper House, Panaji (p120)

» Sher-E-Punjab,
Panaji (p120)

» Vihar Restaurant,
Panaji (p121)

» Mango Tree, Hampi (p147)

Best Places to Stay

» Casa Nova, Panaji (p119)

» Backwoods Camp (p142)

» Goa Marriott Resort (p124)

» Mayfair Hotel, Panaji (p118)

Why Go?

However much you do like to be beside the seaside, the attractions of central Goa are as quintessentially Goan as a dip in the Arabian Sea. What hedonism is to the north and relaxation is to the south, culture, scenery and history are to this central portion of the state, eased in between the Mandovi and Zuari Rivers.

Panaji (or Panjim, its former Portuguese name, by which it's still commonly known) is Goa's lazy-paced state capital, perfect for a stroll in the Latin Quarter, while just down the road is Old Goa, the 17th century's 'Rome of the East'.

Top this off with visits to temples and spice plantations around Ponda, two of Goa's most beautiful wildlife sanctuaries, time-untouched inland islands, and India's second-highest waterfall, and it would be possible to spend a week here without making it to a single beach.

When to Go

Central Goa is less about beaches than the south and north of the state, making it less dependent on the high season. October and April are both good, cool, lower-priced times of year to visit Panaji and its surroundings, particularly if you're planning on a lot of sight-seeing; October, moreover, is the best time for wildlife-watching in the region's reserves. If, however, you're looking for ebullient religiosity, Easter, Christmas and the Feast of St Francis Xavier on December 3 make great times to experience Old Goa at its most atmospheric – and most packed.

Panaji

☎ 0832 / POP 98,915

Slung along the banks of the wide Mandovi River, Panaji (also still widely known by its former Portuguese name Panjim), Goa's small and spritely state capital since 1843, boasts its own laid-back brand of originality. Purpose-built neat and tidy by its former Portuguese colonisers, the city's inhabitants have adapted its European-flavoured legacy to suit their affluent and easygoing needs. Nowhere here will you find the rush and hustle of most Indian cities; the Panaji pace is steadfastly stately, its streets are wide and tree-lined and its centre refreshingly free from hawkers and tricksters.

The city's architecture is the surest sign that Goa evolved independently of the rest of India. In the small old quarters of Fontainhas and Sao Tomé, winding alleyways are lined with Portuguese-style houses, boasting distinctive red-tiled roofs, wooden window shutters and rickety balconies decorated with bright pots of petunias. Here, whitewashed churches lurk down laneways, a short wander from technicolour Hindu temples.

History

The land on which Panaji stands today was for centuries little more than a handful of fishing settlements, known to the 12th-century ruling Kadambas as Pahajani, 'the land that does not flood'.

In the late 15th century Goa came under the control of the Muslim sultan Yusuf Adil Shah, who built five hilltop forts and his own fortified summer palace here, protected by 55 cannons and conceived to guard the

mouth of the Mandovi River against attackers. It's thought that Panaji's name might be a derivation of an Urdu reference to these five forts: *panchima afsugani*, 'five enchanted castles'.

When the Portuguese nobleman Afonso de Albuquerque arrived in Goa in 1510, he quickly set about conquering the palace and forts, and by the end of the year it was his. Leaving it almost untouched, however, the conquerors' efforts were instead now concentrated on aggrandising their new capital, Ela (now Old Goa), further east up the river.

For the next 300 years Panaji remained little more than a small and scruffy seafaring village, only notable for its church, where Portuguese sailors stopped off to give thanks to the heavens for having survived the perilous voyage to India. However, as conditions in Old Goa became increasingly desperate (see p126), the land began to support increasing numbers of refugees from the capital, until finally, in 1759 the viceroy moved to Panjim, where he took the old Idalcaon's Palace as his own residence, today the Secretariat.

By the early 19th century the city was taking shape. In 1834 Panjim became known as Nova Goa, and in 1843 was finally recognised by the Portuguese government as Goa's

ABBÉ FARIA

Beside Panaji's Secretariat Building, what looks like a scene from a Hammer House of Horror hit is actually a testament in statue form to one of Goa's most famous exports: 18th-century Candolim-born Abbé Faria, displayed in full dramatic throes, 'pouncing', as Graham Greene once noted, 'like a great black eagle on his mesmerised female patient'.

Abbé Faria, born the son of a monk and a nun in a Candolim mansion in 1756, is one of history's fabulously enigmatic figures, having hovered handsomely on the sidelines of the greatest events of the 18th century and flirted with its main players (the Portuguese royal family, Robespierre, Marie Antoinette and Napoleon being just some of them), somehow ingratiating himself with every successive regime while remaining an elusive outsider, caught in a world of black magic and esoteric pursuits. He was considered the 'father of modern hypnotism' for his explanations on the power of suggestion – uncharted territory at the time. Next time you see a stage hypnotist parading the tricks of the trade, watch too for the ghost of shape-shifting Custodio Faria, flitting restively in the wings.

Panaji & Central Goa Highlights

1 Old-fashioned Portuguese style in **Panaji**, India's cutest state capital (p120)

2 Explore the churches of **Old Goa**, and the remnants of a real saint (p126)

3 Birdwatch to your heart's delight at jungly **Backwoods Camp** (p142)

4 Trek out to **Dudhsagar Falls**, India's second highest. (p142)

5 Hop on a scooter and explore **Divar Island**, a little land that time forgot (p133)

6 Stroll an organic, **spice farm** near Ponda, then stock up on fragrant masalas (p137)

7 See the last of the Kadambas at **Shri Tambdi Surla Mahadeva Temple** (p142)

8 Float in a canoe, spying feathered friends at **Dr Salim Ali Bird Sanctuary** (p125)

9 Wander through vestiges of civilisations past in **Hampi** (p143)

10 Delve into seldom-explored territory by seeking out the **Caves of Khandepar** (p140)

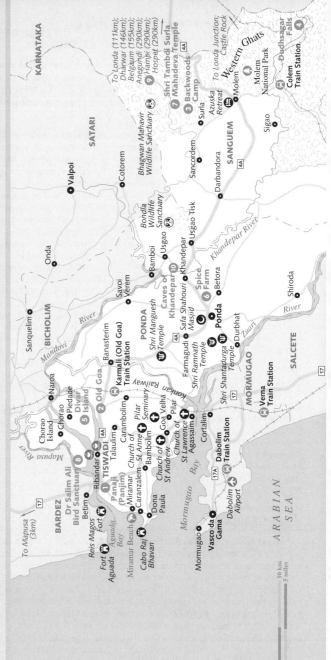

state capital. A spate of building took place; among the public buildings erected were the army barracks (now the police headquarters and government offices) and today's public library. In essence though, Goa was fast becoming a forgotten corner of the Portuguese empire, and lack of money and political interest meant that building work was low key in comparison to the glory days of Old Goa.

Strolling the streets of central Panaji today, you'll find that little has really changed since then. Modern building and development, for the most part, remains reasonably well planned, and the streets are as wide and leafy as they were under Portuguese dominion. Following the final exit of the Portuguese in 1961, the town's name was officially changed to the Maratha title, Panaji, though today most locals still refer to it as Panjim, as it was christened some 500 years ago on Albuquerque's arrival.

◎ Sights

Fontainhas & Sao Tomé AREA

The oldest, and by far the most atmospheric, Portuguese-flavoured districts of Panaji are squeezed between the hillside of Altinho and the banks of Ourem Creek, and make for attractive wandering with their narrow streets, overhanging balconies and quaint air of Mediterranean yesteryear.

Fontainhas, said to take its name from the Fountain of Phoenix spring, which stands near the Maruti Temple, is the larger of the two districts, comprising pastel-shaded houses that head up Altinho hill. The land here was originally reclaimed in the late 18th century by a returning self-made Goan, known as 'the Mosmikar', so-called for the riches he had amassed during a stay in Mozambique.

Located to the north of Fontainhas, the tiny area around the main post office is known as Sao Tomé. The post office was once the tobacco-trading house for Panaji, and the building to the right of it was the state mint. The square that these buildings face once housed the town pillory, where justice turned into spectacle when executions took place. It was here that several conspirators involved in the Pinto Revolt (p102) were put to death, for plotting to overthrow Portuguese rule in 1787.

Secretariat Building HISTORIC BUILDING

The oldest colonial building in Goa is the stolid Secretariat. It stands on the site of the grand summer palace of Goa's 15th-century

CHAPEL OF ST SEBASTIAN

Aside from its general old-world charms, Fontainhas is notable for being home to the pretty **Chapel of St Sebastian** (St Sebastian Rd; ⊘Mass 6.45am daily), built in 1818. This small whitewashed church at the end of a lovely lane contains one of only a few relics remaining as testament to the Goan Inquisition: a striking crucifix, which originally stood in the Palace of the Inquisition in Old Goa. Christ's unusual open eyes are said to have been conceived especially to strike fear into the hearts of 'heretical' suspects brought before the Inquisitors, and awaiting their usually grisly fate.

Nowadays, each mid-November sees a happy street fair set up outside the little chapel to celebrate the Feast of Our Lady of Livrament.

sultan Yusuf Adil Shah, which was originally fortified and surrounded by a saltwater moat.

After falling to the Portuguese in 1510, the palace was further reinforced and used as a customs post, also serving as temporary accommodation for incoming and outgoing Portuguese viceroys. After the viceroys finally abandoned Old Goa to disease and the elements, the building was adopted as their official residence from 1759 until 1918, when they moved on to the grander coastal buildings at Cabo Raj Bhavan (p124).

From this time onwards the building housed the State Assembly, which now meets in the newer, grander **Assembly Complex**, located on the hill across the river. Today, it's home to dry-as-dust government offices, which make for thoroughly unfascinating exploration.

Standing just beside the Secretariat is a far more interesting curiosity: an unusual **statue** of a man appearing to leer tall over a prone and floundering woman. It's a tribute to hypnotist Abbé Faria, one of Goa's most famous sons; see p111.

TOP CHOICE **Church of Our Lady of the Immaculate Conception** CHURCH
(cnr Emilio Gracia Rd & Jose Falcao Rd; ⊘9am-7pm) Panaji's spiritual, as well as geographical, centre is its gleamingly picturesque main church, built in 1619 over an older, smaller 1540 chapel

Panaji (Panjim)

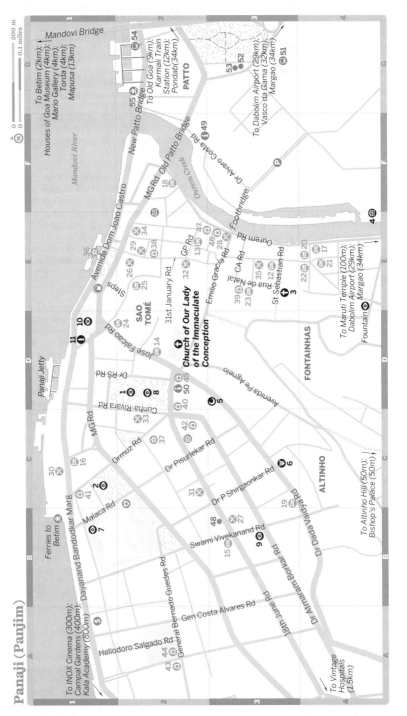

To Betim (2km);
Houses of Goa Museum (4km);
Mario Gallery (4km);
Torda (4km);
Mapusa (13km)

Mandovi Bridge

200 m
0.1 miles

Mandovi River

To Old Goa (9km);
Karmali Train
Station (12km);
Pondab(34km)

PATTO

To Dabolim Airport (29km);
Vasco da Gama (32km);
Margao (34km)

New Patto Bridge

Old Patto Bridge

Dr Alvaro Costa Rd

Ourem Creek

Footbridge

MG Rd

Avenida Dom Joao Castro

GP Rd

Ourem Rd

CA Rd

Emilio Gracia Rd

Rua de Natal

St Sebastian Rd

To Maruti Temple (100m);
Dabolim Airport (29km);
Margao (34km)

Fountain

Steps

SAO TOMÉ

31st January Rd

Jose Falcao Rd

Church of Our Lady
of the Immaculate
Conception

Avenida Pe Agnelo

FONTAINHAS

Panaji Jetty

Dr RS Rd

Cunha-Rivera Rd

MG Rd

Ormuz Rd

Dr Pisurlekar Rd

Dr P Shirgaonkar Rd

ALTINHO

To Altinho Hill (50m);
Bishop's Palace (50m)

Ferries to
Betim

Malaca Rd

Dr Dada Vaidya Rd

Dr Atmaram Borkar Rd

Swami Vivekanand Rd

18th June Rd

Gen Costa Alvares Rd

General Bernado Guedes Rd

Heliodoro Salgado Rd

To INOX Cinema (300m);
Campal Gardens (400m);
Kala Academy (800m)

To Vintage
Hospitals
(1.5km)

Panaji (Panjim)

⊚ **Top Sights**
Church of Our Lady of the
Immaculate Conception D2

⊚ **Sights**
1 Ashokan Pillar D2
2 Azad Maidan... C1
3 Chapel of St Sebastian........................... E3
4 Goa State Museum................................... E4
5 Jama Masjid.. D3
6 Mahalaxmi Temple C3
7 Menezes Braganza Institute B1
8 Municipal Gardens (Church Square)... D2
Panaji Central Library .... (see 7)
9 Public Observatory.................................. B3
10 Secretariat Building................................. D1
11 Statue of Abbé Faria................................ D1

⊕ **Activities, Courses & Tours**
River Cruises .... (see 55)

🛏 **Sleeping**
12 Afonso Guest House................................ E3
Casa Morada .... (see 13)
13 Casa Nova.. E2
14 Casa Paradiso D2
15 Hotel Fidalgo.. B3
16 Hotel Mandovi... C1
17 Hotel Ria Residency E4
18 Hotel Sona F2
19 Mayfair Hotel C3
20 Panjim Inn E4
21 Panjim Peoples E4
22 Panjim Pousada E4
23 Park Lane Lodge E3
24 Republica Hotel.. D2
25 The Crown Goa E2

✗ **Eating**
26 Anandashram.. E2
27 Gujarat Sweet Mart B3

28 Horse Shoe.. E3
29 Hospedaria Venite.................................... E2
30 Quarterdeck.. C1
31 Sher-E-Punjab C2
32 Tea Cafe Goa... E2
33 Upper House.. C2
34 Vihar Restaurant E2
35 Viva Panjim... E3

🎭 **Entertainment**
36 Casino Royale E1
37 Cine Nacional.. C2

🛍 **Shopping**
38 Barefoot E2
39 Bombay Stores E3
Book Fair ....(see 16)
40 Books Books Books D2
41 Fusion Access C1
42 Khadi Gramodyog Bhavan C2
43 Municipal Market......................................A2
44 New Municipal Market A2
45 Singbal's Book House D2
46 Sosa's.. E3
47 Velha Goa Galeria E2

ⓘ **Information**
48 E-zy Travels... B3
49 Goa Tourism Development
Corporation (GTDC) F2
50 Government of India Tourist
Office..D2

ⓘ **Transport**
51 Kadamba Bus Stand G3
Konkan Railway Reservation
Office...(see 51)
52 Paulo Travels G3
53 Private Bus Agents..................................G3
54 Private Bus Stand....................................G2
55 Santa Monica Jetty G2

and stacked like a fancy white wedding cake to the southeast of the ragged municipal gardens. When Panaji was little more than a sleepy fishing village, this place was the first port of call for sailors from Lisbon, who would clamber up here to thank their lucky stars for a safe crossing, before continuing to Ela (Old Goa), the state's capital until the 19th century, further east up the river.

By the 1850s the land in front of the church was being reclaimed and the distinctive criss-crossing staircases were added in the late 19th century. Nowadays, entrance to its gloriously technicolour interior – as gold-plated, floral and multicoloured on the inside as it's perfectly white on the outside – is along the left-hand side wall. The itchy-fingered should note the lead-us-not-into-temptation small sign requesting 'please do not ring the bell' beside a tangle of ropes leading up to the enormous shiny church bell in the belfry, saved from the ruins of the Augustinian monastery at Old Goa and installed here in 1871.

If your visit coincides with 8 December, be sure to head here for the Feast of Our Lady of the Immaculate Conception, which sees a special church service and a lively fair spilling away from the church to mark the date.

Municipal Gardens   PARK

Panaji's central square is the leafy, recently renovated Municipal Gardens, also called Church Square (Largo da Igreja). The Ashokan Pillar at the gardens' centre was once topped by a bust of Vasco da Gama, the first Portuguese voyager to set foot in Goa in 1498, but he was replaced, upon independence in 1961, by the seal of present-day India: four lions sitting back to back, atop an abacus, and the inscription 'Truth Alone Triumphs'.

Jama Masjid   MOSQUE

Nearby, be on the lookout for the tiny Jama Masjid mosque, barely 100m south of the Municipal Gardens, built about two centuries ago. Keep vigilant in your search – it's easy to walk past without even realising it's there. The exterior of the building is plain, its entrance blending in with the small shops on either side, but the interior is extremely ornate in white-marble Islamic style.

Azad Maidan   PARK

To the west of the Municipal Gardens, the grassy Azad Maidan (Freedom Park) wouldn't, sadly, win any prizes at a flower show. It's centred on a small pavilion (whose Corinthian pillars were reclaimed from the rubble in Old Goa), which houses a modern sculpture dedicated to freedom fighter and 'Father of Goan Nationalism' Dr Tristao de Braganza Cunha (1891–1958). The domed edifice formerly held a statue of Afonso de Albuquerque, 1510 Portuguese conqueror of Goa, now relegated to the State Archaeological Museum in Old Goa.

Menezes Braganza Institute & Panaji Central Library   LIBRARY

(⊙9.30am-1.15pm & 2-5.45pm Mon-Fri) At the northwest corner of the Azad Maidan, the Menezes Braganza Institute and the city's Central Library, the oldest public library in India, occupy part of the old buildings that were once the Portuguese army headquarters.

It's worth poking your head in at the building's west entrance, to examine the grand and dramatic *azulejos* (traditional painted ceramic tiles) adorning the wall, which depict scenes from *Os Lusíadas,* a famously epic and glorious Portuguese poem by Luís Vaz de Camões that tells the tale of Portugal's 15th- and 16th-century voyages of discovery, see the boxed text opposite for more on the poet himself.

Much of the upper floor of the building is given over to the Menezes Braganza Institute, which was founded in 1871 as a scientific and literary institution. Originally called the Institute Vasco da Gama, it was renamed in 1963 in honour of the champion of the Goan Independence movement, Luís de Menezes Braganza. The institute has a small art gallery that contains some rare prints and paintings.

FREE Goa State Museum   MUSEUM

(⊠2438006; EDC Complex, Patto; ⊙9.30am-5.30pm Mon-Sat) An eclectic, and not exactly extensive, collection of items awaits visitors to this rather lacklustre museum, in a strangely uncentral area just southwest of the Kadamba bus stand. As well as some beautiful Hindu and Jain sculptures and bronzes, there are a few nice examples of Portuguese-era furniture, some ancient coins and two quirky antique lottery machines. The star exhibit for most, however, is the elaborately carved table and high-backed chairs used by the notoriously brutal Portuguese Inquisition in Goa during its reign of terror.

Maruti Temple   HINDU TEMPLE

Dedicated to the monkey god Hanuman, this modern temple is resplendently lit at night, and affords pleasant views over the city's Old Quarter from its verandah by day. It forms the epicentre of a roughly 10-day festival celebrated in February, when enormous and colourful statues of Hanuman are placed in the street, and festive street stalls are set up throughout the surrounding Hindu quarter of Mala.

Mahalaxmi Temple   HINDU TEMPLE

This modern, technicolour temple off Dr Dada Vaidya Rd is not particularly imposing, but is worth a look inside as the first Hindu shrine established in the city during Portuguese rule, and amply demonstrates that among Panaji's ubiquitous white-washed churches there is a large and thriving Hindu community. The temple was built in 1818 and is devoted to the goddess Mahalaxmi, the Hindu deity of Panaji.

LUÍS VAZ DE CAMÕES

Luís Vaz de Camões (1524–80), who is regarded as Portugal's greatest poet, was banished to Goa in 1553 at the age of 29, after being accused of fighting with, and wounding, a magistrate in Lisbon. He was obviously no soft touch, for he enlisted in the army and fought with some distinction before attracting further official disapproval for publicly criticising Goa's Portuguese administration.

His reward this time was to be exiled to the Moluccas, and he returned to Goa only in 1562 to write his most famous work, *Os Lusíadas,* an epic poem glorifying the adventures of Vasco da Gama, which, classical in style and imperialist in sentiment, has since become an icon of Portuguese nationalism.

A statue of Camões, erected in 1960, stood at the centre of Old Goa until 1983, when many Goans decided that it was an unacceptable relic of colonialism. An attempt by radicals to blow it up met with failure, but the authorities took the hint and removed the statue. It now stands, along with Afonso de Albuquerque and various other disgraced Portuguese colonials, in the State Archaeological Museum in Old Goa.

Altinho Hill AREA

On the hillside above Panaji is the district known as Altinho. Apart from good views over the city and river, the main attraction here is the Bishop's Palace, a huge and imposing building completed in 1893.

The archbishop of Goa came to reside in Panaji early in the 20th century, laying claim to the palatial residence at Cabo Raj Bhavan, on the promontory that looks out over the confluence of the Mandovi and Zuari Rivers. This, however, was not to be: when the Portuguese governor-general realised that it was the best property in Goa, the archbishop was forced to change his plans and settle instead for the palace here in Panaji.

Today, the crumbling mansions of Altinho constitute the most prestigious place to live in Panaji; the pope stayed here at the Bishop's Palace during his visit to Goa in 1999.

Campal Gardens PARK

The road to Miramar from Panaji runs through the Campal district. Just before you reach the Kala Academy, on the seaward side of the road are the strollable Campal Gardens, also known as the Children's Park. The gardens offer a nice view over to Reis Magos Fort (p106) and the boats that cruise along the Mandovi River each evening.

FREE **Public Observatory** OBSERVATORY

(7th fl, Junta House, Swami Vivekanand Rd; ☺7-9pm 14 Nov-31 May) For anyone interested in checking out the incredibly clear night skies over Goa, the local branch of the Association of Friends of Astronomy has a public observatory. The local enthusiasts are only too

happy to welcome visitors and explain what you're looking at. The view of Panaji by night is lovely, especially around dusk.

🎓 Courses

Holiday on the Menu COOKING

(www.holidayonthemenu.com; courses from US$149) London-based Holiday on the Menu offers a range of Goan cooking holidays, ranging from a Saturday 'Curry Morning' and a Thursday 'Vegetarian Morning' to a whole-week program including trips out to a spice plantation and a local market, based in the picturesque village of Betim, just across the river from Panaji. Prices start at US$149 per person for the Saturday Curry Morning, and US$199 for the Thursday Vegetarian Morning, which also includes an ayurvedic massage, in case all that chopping takes a toll.

👉 Tours

It's worth noting that, along with the following listings, you can also take your own free river trip aboard the local ferry that departs frequently (whenever full) all day from the dock next to Quarterdeck and crosses the river to the village of Betim on the other side, and back. Locals have reported seeing river dolphins on evening rides. Avoid rush hour (8am to 9am and 5pm to 6pm) when the boats are crammed.

Mandovi River Cruise RIVER TRIP

The GTDC (see p230) operates a range of entertaining daily hour-long cruises (₹150; ☺dusk cruise 6pm, sundown cruise 7.15pm) along the Mandovi River aboard the *Santa Monica* or *Shantadurga*. All include a live band – sometimes lively (sometimes lacklustre)

CARNIVAL CRAZINESS

Panaji's annual carnival has been hitting the city centre for three chaotic days, sometime in late February or early March, since the 18th century, when it was introduced by the Catholic Portuguese as one last opportunity for excess before the strictures of Lent.

However, the origins of Carnival are far older, dating back as far as the Bacchanalias of ancient Rome, and later enlivened by African slaves in the Portuguese colonies. Once introduced into Goa, of course, an entirely local twist was added to the fun-filled goings on, with the inclusion of *tiatrs*, the satirical folk plays which are still performed throughout Carnival today.

Carnival begins – as it has done for centuries – with the arrival in Panaji of a character called King Momo on *Sabato Gordo* (Fat Saturday), and his instruction to the people of the city to, in essence, 'don't worry, be happy'. Dancing, drinking, processions of floats through the streets, cross-dressing, and *assaltos* (amiable battles) – with sticky mixtures of flour, coloured tikka powder and water – ensue.

Though various criticisms of Carnival have emerged over the years – ranging from its post-Independence shunning due to its 'colonialism', to its recent commercialisation and excuse for the overconsumption of alcohol – Panaji's three days of mayhem are still celebrated by many thousands each year, seeing hotels booked solid, streets filled with revellers, and bars doing a brisk trade. Don't come dressed in your best, and prepare to be soaked to the skin.

performing Goan folk songs and dances. There are also twice-weekly, two-hour **dinner cruises** (incl snacks & buffet dinner ₹500; ☺8.45pm Wed & Sat) and regular two-hour **dolphin-watching trips** (incl refreshments ₹250; ☺8.30am Wed, Sat & Sun). All cruises depart from the Santa Monica Jetty next to the huge Mandovi Bridge. Tickets can be purchased here.

Various other companies offer virtually identical cruises also from Santa Monica Jetty. Head down to the jetty to see what's on offer. In general, though, the GTDC cruises are a little more staid, while others – perhaps because of the promise of 'free beer' – can get a bit rowdier with groups of local male tourists.

Goa by Night bus tour　　　　　BUS TOUR
(₹200; ☺6.30pm Tue & Sun) The GTDC also runs a two-hour Goa by Night bus tour, which leaves in the evening from the same jetty spot and includes a river cruise. As ever, its breakneck speed allows it to pack in as many sights as possible; in this case, in just two hours you'll experience a river cruise, a long string of churches, a palace, a temple and a panoramic view.

Other GTDC trips – of which there are many – depart daily from outside the GTDC Hotel Panaji Residency.

🛏 Sleeping

Panaji's not a city brimming with good budget accommodation, and most of what you'll find at the lower end of the accommodation spectrum is fairly poor quality or, at best, entirely forgettable. If you're looking for rock-bottom budget, the best options run the length of 31st January Rd. Don't expect atmospheric old Portuguese haunts: most consist of nothing much but a cell-like room, no view and a 9am or earlier checkout, with doubles going for around ₹700. Inspect a few before you decide. Some are full of bachelors where it would be a bit odd – and potentially problematic – for women to stay, so if unsure, ask at the reception if the hotel is a 'family' place.

Casa Paradiso　　　　　HOTEL $$
(☑2230092; www.casaparadisogoa.com; Jose Falcao Rd; d/ste ₹1500/2000; ❄) A terrific stay in the heart of the city, just steps away from Panaji's Church of Our Lady of the Immaculate Conception. With friendly staff and modern, well-decorated rooms, the hotel itself makes for a highly comfortable, cosy stay, but it's the central location that really can't be beat.

Mayfair Hotel　　　　　HOTEL $$
(☑2223317; Dr Dada Vaidya Rd; s/d/d with AC from ₹980/1180/1500; ❄) With its bright, cheerful balconies, beautiful ground floor

oyster-shell windows and general, slightly musty air of yesteryear, the Mayfair is an atmospheric central option, doling out old-fashioned hospitality courtesy of its friendly family owners. Not many mod-cons on offer, but it makes a nice, restful and well-priced place to retreat.

Panjim Inn   HOTEL **$$$**
(🖊2226523, 2435628, 2228136; www.panjiminn. com; 31st January Rd, Fontainhas; s/d from ₹2500/3000; 🌣) A long-standing Panaji favourite for its character and charm, this beautiful mansion from the 19th century has 24 spacious, charismatic rooms (go for those in the original old house), a number with four-poster beds and all sporting colonial furniture and individual character. The Panjim Inn people also run Panjim Pousada and Panjim Peoples which, together, comprise by far the most atmospheric choices for a stay in the city. Much of the work gracing the walls of all three is courtesy of the attached Gallery Gitanjali, and is available for purchase.

Panjim Pousada   HOTEL **$$$**
(🖊2226523, 2435628, 2228136; www.panjiminn. com; 31st January Rd, Fontainhas; s/d from ₹2500/3000; 🌣) Down the road from the Panjim Inn, the nine divine, colonial fantasy rooms at Panjim Pousada are set off a stunning central courtyard. Various doorways and spiral staircases lead to the rooms; those on the upper level are by far the best.

Panjim Peoples   HOTEL **$$$**
(🖊2226523, 2435628; www.panjiminn.com; 31st January Rd; d ₹9000; 🌣) Undeniably atmospheric, this lovely option sports a clutch of large, atmospheric rooms with mosaic-covered bathrooms, deep bath tubs, and lots of quaint antiques, arranged around a serene indoor inner courtyard.

Afonso Guesthouse   GUESTHOUSE **$$**
(🖊2222359; St Sebastian Rd; d ₹1500) Run by a friendly elderly gentleman, this lovely place set in a pretty old Portuguese town house offers plain but comfortable rooms, and a little rooftop terrace for sunny breakfasting (dishes ₹20 to ₹30). It's a simple, serene stay in the heart of the most atmospheric part of town, with just two faults: checkout is at 9am (not unusual for Panaji) and it doesn't take bookings.

Park Lane Lodge   GUESTHOUSE **$**
(🖊2227154; St Sebastian Rd; d ₹1000, without bathroom ₹750; 🌣) Set in an old and rambling bungalow near the Chapel of St Sebastian, the Park Lane has been popular with travellers for years, despite its seemingly ever-extending list of rules. Current formidable warnings include 'No Laundry', 'No Internet', 'Gates Closed 10pm' and '8am Checkout'. If that's OK, its six rooms make a characterful, if slightly crumbling, place to stay.

Hotel Fidalgo   HOTEL **$$$**
(🖊2226291-99; www.hotelfidalgo-goa.com; 18th June Rd; d/ste ₹4880/8960; 🌣@🗱) The city's smartest (and rather business-traveller-styled) choice is the Fidalgo, thoroughly modern, with snappy service and a good range of cuisines courtesy of its 'food enclave', including a good vegetarian Indian restaurant, Legacy of Bombay. It's not at all atmospheric, but will guarantee you a very restful, efficient stay. Look out for good deals for booking online via the hotel's website.

The Crown Goa   HOTEL **$$$**
(🖊240 0000; www.thecrowngoa com; Bairo Alto Dos Pilotos, Jose Falcao Rd; d from ₹5500/6500, ste from ₹11,000; 🌣@🗱) Perched high above Panaji, with lovely views from its terrace and small pool, this is a great option for a little bit of luxury in the midst of the city. The price includes breakfast and pick-up/drop-off at the airport or railway station, for stays of more than two nights.

Casa Nova   GUESTHOUSE **$$$**
(🖊9423889181; www.goaholidayaccomodation. com; Gomes Pereira Rd; ste ₹3600) Here's your chance to actually stay in one of Panaji's gorgeous, old Portuguese-style homes – if you can get a booking. Casa Nova consists of just one stylish, exceptionally comfy suite, accessed via a little alley and complete with arched windows, wood-beam ceilings and mod cons like a kitchenette.

Casa Morada   GUESTHOUSE **$$$**
(🖊9822196007, 9881966789; agomes@tbi.in; Gomes Pereira Rd; s/d incl breakfast ₹5000/6000) As fancy as Nova (its sister property) is modern, its two bedrooms and sitting room are full of antique furniture and objets d'art (hence a no-kids policy), with real art on the walls, and floors of pale green marble.

Hotel Mandovi   HOTEL **$$$**
(☏2426270; www.hotelmandovigoa.com; Dayanand Bandodkar Marg; standard s/d ₹3000/3300, executive s/d ₹3900/4000, ste ₹7500; ❀) A Panaji institution (these days with just a touch of the institutional) for more than 50 years, the Mandovi offers comfortable, though dated rooms, many looking out onto the wide Mandovi River. If the urge for sweet things strikes, you'll enjoy A Pastelaria, an old-fashioned cake shop; there's also a little – but well-stocked bookshop (with plenty of titles on Goa) and three restaurants, including the pleasant Quarterdeck just across the road. Check-out, unusually for Panaji, is at noon. Courtesy airport drop-off coach available at scheduled times: ask for the latest departure times.

Republica Hotel   HOTEL **$**
(☏2224630; Jose Falcao Rd; d without/with AC ₹700/1000; ❀) The Republica is a story of unexplored potential, an architectural beauty that's been left to the mercy of the elements. You may not receive a warm welcome or a well-decorated room; indeed, the service is charismatically gloomy and the decor decidedly grim, but that's all part of the charm of this ramshackle wooden Cinderella. If you're not craving comforts, check in for an entirely basic, but atmospheric, stay just brimming with old fashioned Portuguese *saudade* (melancholia).

Hotel Ria Residency   HOTEL **$$**
(☏2220002; Ourem Rd, Fontainhas; d from ₹1300; ❀) In no way spectacular, this place just off the end of 31st January Rd is perfectly acceptable for a comfortable and air-conditioned, if fairly uncharismatic, stay.

Hotel Sona   HOTEL **$$**
(☏2222226; www.hotelsonagoa.com; Ourem Rd; d non-AC/AC₹1300/1400-1700; ❀) With a nice location near the river, in a calm and central part of town, not all of the 30 clinical-but-clean rooms of this four-storey building face the river, so make sure you check out a few first.

✕ Eating

You'll never go hungry in Panaji, where food is enjoyed fully and frequently. A stroll down 18th June or 31st January Rds will turn up a number of great, cheap canteen-style options, as will a quick circuit of the Municipal Gardens. Lots of these are pure-veg, and offer up good thalis, *bhaji-pau* (bread roll

dipped in curry) breakfasts and South Indian snacks.

TOP CHOICE **Tea Cafe Goa**   CAFE **$$**
(5/218 31st January Rd; pastries ₹70; ◷11am-7.30pm) A cute little place tucked away in an old building, dispensing light lunches, pastries, cakes, cupcakes and afternoon treats, with daily specials including zucchini and carrot soup and mushroom quiche, to be enjoyed while reclining in its restful, old-fashioned interior.

Sher-E-Punjab   NORTH INDIAN **$$**
(18th June Rd; mains ₹100-250) A cut above the usual lunch joint, Sher-E-Punjab, recently renovated (and with good ladies' toilets!) caters to well-dressed locals with its generous, carefully spiced Indian dishes. There's a pleasant garden terrace out the back, and an icy AC room if you're feeling sticky. Try the delicious *paneer tikka* (₹165), a zingy veg vindahlo (₹140) but leave room for a bowl of chocolate ice cream (₹60), rich as chocolate mousse.

Upper House   GOAN **$$**
(Cunha-Rivara Rd; mains 95-295; ◷11am-10pm) Fans of Goan seafood and vegetarians alike can rejoice in the food at this relatively new spot specialising in home-style regional dishes. Local favourites such as crab xec xec (cooked in roasted coconut gravy), pork vindahlo and *fish-curry-rice* are done the old-fashioned way (the latter even comes with salt-water mango pickle, rarely found outside Goan mothers' kitchens). The restaurant is on the 1st floor of the building looking out onto the Municipal Gardens.

Viva Panjim   GOAN **$**
(31st January Rd; mains ₹95-220; ◷11.30am-3pm & 7-11pm Mon-Sat, 7-11pm Sun) Though it might be more than a touch touristy these days, this little side-street eatery, with a couple of tables out on the street itself, nevertheless still delivers tasty Goan staples, as well as the standard range of Indian fare, though there are far better places in town for vegetarians. Keep an eye out in the dim interior for Mrs Linda de Souza, restaurant founder and doughty matriarch.

Hospedaria Venite   GOAN **$**
(31st January Rd; mains ₹65-110) Along with Viva Panjim, this is without doubt the lunch address to which most tourists head and, though the food isn't exactly excellent – particularly for the price – the atmosphere

warrants the visit. Its tiny, rickety balcony tables, which look out onto pastel-washed 31st January Rd, make a better place for a beer than a full lunch, though the Goan *chouriços* (spiced sausages; ₹145) and vegetable vindaloo (₹95) are still pretty tasty. Order a cold beer or two, munch on a slightly '70s-style salad (think cold-boiled vegetables in vinaigrette) and watch lazy Panaji slip by.

Quarterdeck
MULTICUISINE **$$**

(Dayanand Bandodkar Marg; mains from ₹80) Watch crammed passenger ferries and hulking casino boats chug by from a waterside table at this open-air multicuisine restaurant perched on the Mandovi banks, run by the venerable Hotel Mandovi across the road. There's a small playground for children and the multicuisine is tasty enough, though the location is without doubt the restaurant's biggest drawcard. Also good for a sundown Kingfisher or two.

Vihar Restaurant
INDIAN, VEGETARIAN **$**

(MG Rd; veg thalis ₹50-80) A vast menu of 'pure veg' food, great big thalis and a plethora of fresh juices make this clean, simple canteen a popular place for locals and visitors alike. Sip a hot chai, invent your own juice combination, and dig into an ice cream for afters.

Gujarat Sweet Mart
SWEETS **$**

(Gujarat Lodge; 18 June Rd; drinks ₹20-50) If you're possessed with a sweet tooth, here's the place to indulge it, with a panoply of Indian confectioneries of the sweet, sweeter and sweetest varieties. Wash all that decadence down with a thick milkshake or lassi, which also come in an array of heavenly, sugary flavours.

Anandashram
INDIAN, GOAN **$**

(thalis from ₹50; ⊙noon-3.15pm & 7.30-10.30pm Mon-Sat) Just opposite the Hospedaria Venite, this teensy little place dishes up simple, mighty-tasty fish curries, and veg and non-veg thalis for lunch and dinner.

Horse Shoe
GOAN **$$**

(Ourem Rd; mains ₹180-350) A well-respected, sweet little Goan-Portuguese place, this is a simple but romantic choice for some traditional dishes and a nice bottle of Portuguese wine.

 ## Drinking

Panaji's drinking scene is centred in the town's tiny, tucked-away bars, mostly equipped with rudimentary plastic tables, a fridge and a rarely turned-off TV. They're great places to mingle with the locals, and generally open up towards lunchtime, closing for a siesta mid-afternoon, and cranking up again come sundown. Though the local clientele is mainly male, women heading out for a drink won't experience any problems, except for perhaps a curious look or two. The river road (Dayanand Bandodkar Marg) and the area surrounding the Municipal Gardens are the best places to instigate a bar crawl.

☆ Entertainment

Panaji doesn't go wild for nightlife, apart from the casino boats that ply the waters of the Mandovi and the quiet imbibing of strong drinks in neighbourhood bars.

Casino Royale
CASINO

(☑02240158888; www.casinoroyalegoa.com; ₹3500 Mon-Thu, ₹4000 Fri-Sun) The newest and largest of Goa's several floating casinos, this upscale floating shrine to all things speculative will have you losing your money all night long. Entry includes a buffet dinner, unlimited drinks, entertainment in the form of live music, and ₹3000 worth of gaming chips. Various age and dress restrictions apply; check the website for details and daily opening hours.

Cine Nacional
CINEMA

(Ormuz Rd; tickets ₹60) If you're feeling up for a bit of grim local grime, you've found the right place at the Nacional. It's dismal, dark and dank, but with unique appeal if you're looking for an unforgettable dose of Bollywood. Just make sure you don't have too much soft drink, as the only filmic quality the toilets possess is their likeness to a certain scene in *Trainspotting*. Films are shown about four times daily; check the posters outside the box office for current screenings.

INOX Cinema
CINEMA

(www.inoxmovies.com; Old GMC Heritage Precinct; tickets ₹180-200) This comfortable, plush multiplex cinema shows Hollywood and Bollywood blockbusters alike. Book online to choose your seats in advance.

Kala Academy
CULTURAL PROGRAMS

(☑2420451; www.kalaacademy.org; Dayanand Bandodkar Marg) On the west side of the city at Campal is Goa's premier cultural centre, which features a program of dance, theatre, music and art exhibitions throughout the year. Many shows are in Konkani, but there are occasional English-language productions; call to find out what's on when you're in town.

 Shopping

Panaji's a decent place for a quick shopping stop, with international brand-name stores such as Wrangler and Tommy Hillfiger dotting Mahatma Gandhi (MG) Rd (at around a third of European prices) and a slew of 'lifestyle stores' selling high-end faux antiques, well-made textiles and richly illustrated coffee-table tomes. For a touch more grit and grime head instead to the municipal markets.

Bombay Stores HOUSEWARES, GIFTS
(☑2230333; Rua de Natal) Selling high-quality gifts, crafts, textiles, beauty products, tea and jewellery, Bombay Stores makes for good gift shopping, with the slightly befuddling slogan 'Treasures to Gift, Gifts to Treasure'.

Fusion Access HOUSEWARES
(☑6650342; www.fusionaccess.com; 13/32 Ormuz Rd) A cool 1st-floor place, filled with some nice furniture, lots of textiles and some richly illustrated books on Goa.

Municipal Market MARKET
(☺from 7.30am) This atmospheric place, where narrow streets have been converted into covered markets, makes for a nice wander, offering fresh produce, clothing stalls and some tiny, enticing eateries. The fish market is a particularly interesting strip of activity.

New Municipal Market MARKET
(☺from 7.30am) Near the Muncipal Market, you'll find everything from fruit and vegetables to tailors, but with a touch less atmosphere than the Municipal Market.

Sosa's CLOTHING
(☑2228063; E245 Ourem Rd) A boutique carrying local labels such as Horn Ok Please, Hidden Harmony and Free Falling, Sosa's is the best place in Panaji to source upscale Indian fashion.

Book Fair BOOKSTORE
(Dayanand Bandodkar Marg; ☺9am-9pm) A small, well-stocked bookshop in the Hotel Mandovi lobby, with plenty of well-illustrated books on Goa.

Singbal's Book House BOOKSTORE
(Church Sq; ☺9.30am-1pm & 3.30-7.30pm Mon-Sat) A good selection of international magazines and newspapers, and lots of books on Goa, are offered at this establishment that, incidentally, had a cameo role in film *The Bourne Supremacy*.

Books Books Books BOOKSTORE
(Church Sq; ☺9.30am-8pm) Hmm, what on earth could they sell here? As it turns out, they offer a good selection of self-help and spiritual titles, novels and children's books.

Velha Goa Galeria HANDICRAFTS
(Ourem Rd; ☺10am-1pm, 3-7pm Mon-Sat) One of several places in town stocking *azueljos* (tinglazed ceramic tiles), this nice place right beside Panjim Inn offers tiles, vases and other ceramic objects reproduced in the old style by Portuguese artist, Anabela Cardosa. Great gifts for parents or grandparents back home.

Barefoot HANDICRAFTS
(31st January Rd; ☺10am-8pm Mon-Sat) Part of Panaji's new wave of high-end shops, specialising in design. Though pricy, it has some nice gifts ranging from traditional Christmas paintings on wood to jewellery and beaded coasters.

Khadi Gramodyog Bhavan HANDICRAFTS
(Dr Atmaram Borkar Rd; ☺9am-noon & 3-7pm Mon-Sat) Goa's only outpost of the government's Khadi & Village Industries Commission has an excellent range of hand-woven cottons, oils, soaps, spices and other handmade products that come straight from (and directly benefit) regional villages.

ⓘ Information

Internet Access

Internet operations change hands thick and fast in Panaji, and you won't have any trouble locating one. Costs range from ₹40 to around ₹60 per hour.

Medical Services
Goa Medical College Hospital (☑2458700; Bambolin) Situated 9km south of Panaji on NH17.

Vintage Hospitals (☑6644401-05, ambulance ☑2232533; www.vintage3.com; Cacula Enclave, St Inez) A couple of kilometres southwest of Panaji, Vintage is a reputable hospital, despite its slightly dubious name.

Money

As with most places in Goa, you can't walk far without finding an ATM, with its usually icy air-conditioning and sleepy security guard. Most take international cards, and you'll find a particularly bumper crop on 18th June Rd.

Thomas Cook (☑2221312; Dayanand Bandodkar Marg; ⊙9.30am-6pm Mon-Sat year-round, 10am-5pm Sun Oct-Mar) Changes travellers cheques commission-free and gives cash advances on Visa and MasterCard.

Post

Hidden in the lanes around the main post office, there are privately run parcel-wrapping services that charge reasonable prices for their artistic services.

Main post office (MG Rd; ⊙9.30am-5.30pm Mon-Fri, 9am-5pm Sat) Offers swift parcel services and Western Union money transfers.

Tourist Information

Goa Tourism Development Corporation office (GTDC; ☑2424001; www.goa-tourism.com; Dr Alvaro Costa Rd; ⊙9.30am-5.45pm Mon-Fri) This GTDC office, just south of the Old Pato Bridge, is a decent place to pick up maps of Goa and Panaji, and to book one of GTDC's host of tours.

Government of India tourist office (☑2223412; www.incredibleindia.com; Communidade Bldg, Church Sq; ⊙9.30am-1.30pm & 2.30-6pm Mon-Fri, 10am-1pm Sat) The staff here are extremely helpful, and can provide a list of qualified guides for tours and trips in Goa. A half-/full-day tour for up to five people costs ₹600/750.

Travel Agencies

There are several travel agencies where you can book and confirm flights; many are along 18th June Rd.

E-zy Travels (☑2435300; www.ezytravels.com; Shop 8-9, Durga Chambers, 18th June Rd) A professionally run travel agent that can book international flights.

⊙ Getting There & Away

Air

Goa's only airport, Dabolim Airport (see p232), is around 30km from Panaji. There are no direct bus services between the airport and Panaji, though some higher-end hotels offer a minibus service, often included in the room tariff.

Prepaid taxis from the airport cost ₹480 and take around an hour. Alternatively, when you step out of the airport building, turn left and walk to the main road, where you can catch a bus to Vasco da Gama (₹4, about every 15 minutes). From the bus stand at Vasco you can take a bus direct to Panaji (₹17, 45 minutes). Buses run between about 7am and 7pm, every 10 to 15 minutes.

Boat

Taking the rusty, chugging passenger/vehicle ferry across the Mandovi River to the fishing village of Betim makes a fun shortcut en route to the northern beaches. It departs the jetty on Dayanand Bandodkar Marg (near the Quarterdeck restaurant) roughly every 15 minutes between 6am and 10pm (passenger/motorcycle free/₹4). From Betim there are regular buses onwards to Calangute and Candolim via Reis Magos.

Bus

All local buses depart from Panaji's **Kadamba bus stand**, with frequent local services (running to no apparent timetable) heading out all over the state every few minutes. Most bus services start at around 6am, running several times an hour until around 10pm. Ask at the bus stand to be directed to the right bus for you, or check the signs on the bus windscreens. Fares range from ₹8 to Old Goa to ₹26 to Margao. To get to the beaches in South Goa, take a bus to Margao (45 minutes) and change; to get to beaches north of Baga, it's best to head to Mapusa and change there (₹12, 50 minutes).

State-run long distance services also depart from the Kadamba bus stand, but since the prices offered by private operators are about the same, and levels of comfort are greater on private lines, it makes sense to go private instead. Many private operators have booths outside the entrance to the Kadamba bus stand (go there to compare prices and times), but most private interstate services depart from the **Interstate bus stand** next to the New Patto Bridge.

One reliable private operator is **Paulo Travels** (☑2438531; www.paulotravels.com; G1, Kardozo Bldg) with offices just north of the Kadamba bus stand. It operates a number of services with varying levels of comfort to Mumbai (₹350 to ₹700, 11 to 15 hours), Pune (₹450 to ₹600, 10 to 12 hours), Hampi (₹450 to ₹650, 10 hours), Bengaluru (Bangalore, ₹450 to ₹750, 14 to 15 hours) and various other long-distance destinations.

Note that the Kadamba bus stand has an internet cafe and ATM.

Train

The closest train station to Panaji is Karmali (Old Goa), 12km to the east. A number of long-distance services stop here, including services to and from Mumbai, and many trains coming from Margao also stop here. Note that Panaji's **Konkan Railway reservation office** (⊙8am-8pm Mon-Sat) is on the 1st floor of the Kadamba bus stand – not at the train station. You can also check times, prices and routes online at www.konkanrailway.com and www.indianrail.gov.in.

🛈 Getting Around

It's easy enough to get around Panaji on foot, and it's unlikely you'll need even as much as an autorickshaw. A taxi to Old Goa costs around ₹300, and an autorickshaw should agree to take you there for ₹150 to ₹200. Lots of taxis hang around at the Municipal Gardens, making it a good place to haggle for the best price. Autorickshaws and motorcycle taxis can also be found in front of the post office, on 18th June Rd, and just south of the church.

West Of Panaji

MIRAMAR
☑0832

Miramar, 3km southwest of the city (follow Dayanand Bandodkar Marg west along the Mandovi waterfront), is Panaji's nearest beach. The couple of kilometres of exposed sand facing Aguada Bay are hardly inspiring compared to other Goan beaches, but are a popular local place to watch the sun sink into the Arabian Sea.

While there's reasonable swimming to be had at Miramar Beach, be warned that the experience might not be an altogether relaxing one. Not many foreigners venture down here, so you'll be something of an attraction – and, in a less-than-modest bathing suit, the most exciting thing that's happened for months.

Along the seafront road, at the start of Miramar Beach, is Gaspar Dias. Originally a fort stood here, designed for defence, directly opposite the fort at Reis Magos on the other side of the Mandovi. There's no fort now, but the most prominent position on the beachfront is taken up by a statue representing Hindu and Christian unity.

Miramar's plush Goa Marriot Resort (☑2463333; www.marriott.com; Miramar Beach; d from ₹11,500; ❄@☎) provides probably the best reason to make the journey here. Luxe and lavish, the Marriot is expertly choreographed, with the five-star treatment beginning in the lobby and extending right up to the rooms-with-a-view. The Waterfront Bar is a great place for a sundowner – whether or not you're staying at the hotel itself – while its on-site casino gets eager pockets jingling.

There are frequent buses to Miramar from Panaji's Kadamba bus stand, and from various points along the Panaji riverfront (₹4, 20 minutes), setting you down near Miramar's main roundabout. Buses then continue on southwards to Dona Paula.

DONA PAULA
☑0832

Situated on the headland that divides the Zuari and Mandovi Rivers, 9km southwest of Panaji, Dona Paula allegedly takes its name from Dona Paula de Menenez, a Portuguese viceroy's daughter who threw herself into the sea from the cliff top after being prevented from marrying a local fisherman. Her tombstone, attesting to her grisly fate, still stands in the chapel at nearby Cabo Raj Bhavan. Though the views out over Miramar Beach and Mormugao Bay are nice enough, the drab village and persistent hawkers could, given enough time, inspire you to consider a fate similar to that of dear Dona.

For the last 40 years, Baroness Yrsa von Leistner's (1917–2008) whitewashed *Images of India* statue has graced a mock acropolis on an outcrop of rock at the end of the Dona Paula road. It portrays a couple looking off in different directions, the man towards the past and the woman towards India's future. Ain't it always the way.

Meanwhile, on the westernmost point of the peninsula stands an old fortress, Cabo Raj Bhavan (Cabo Raj Niwas; www.rajbhavangoa. org; ☉chapel Mass 9.30-10.30am Sun, Christmas, Easter & feast days), nowadays the official residence of the Governor of Goa. Plans to build a fortress here, to guard the entrance to the Mandovi and Zuari Rivers, were first proposed in 1540 and, although the 16th century had become the 17th before work on the fortress began, a chapel was raised on the spot almost immediately. The fortress was subsequently completed and the chapel extended to include a Franciscan friary. The fort itself, though equipped with several cannons, was never used in defence of Goa, and from the 1650s was instead requisitioned as a grand and temporary residence for Goa's lucky archbishop.

From 1799 to 1813 the site (along with Fort Aguada and Reis Magos Fort, to the north) was occupied by the British who, during the Napoleonic Wars, deemed it necessary in order to deter the French from invading Goa. Now all that remains of the British presence is a forlorn little British cemetery, with gravestones spanning just over a century. It's tucked away behind the Institute of Oceanography – look for the hand-painted sign to the cemetery and the clam-shaped Oceanography Institute roof. It's off the main roundabout, heading from Dona Paula to Miramar. Cabo Raj Bhavan's 500-year-old chapel also draws thousands of locals to its Feast of the Chapel for prayers and festivities each 15 August.

After the departure of the British, the buildings were once again inhabited by the archbishop of Goa, but didn't remain long in his possession: in 1866 the Portuguese viceroy took a shine to the buildings, and had them refurbished and converted into the governor's palace, packing the poor old archbishop off to the hilltop Bishop's Palace in Panaji.

🍴 Sleeping & Eating

Though there's no particular need or reason to stay there, the Dona Paula vicinity offers several options for higher-end sleeping. They're popular with wealthy domestic tourists and package-holidayers but not especially enticing, unless you've the need to stick close to Panaji. All three have decent restaurants, in case you're craving lunch; for something rather cheaper, there's a cluster of quite standard cafes all along the seafront.

O Pescador HOTEL $$$
(☎2453863; www.opescador.com; d without/with AC/ste ₹3200/5500/7500; ❄🐶) Also known as the Dona Paula Beach Resort, O Pescador's site has been well used to create well-decorated mock-Portuguese villas with a nice view of the 'private' (though no beach in Goa is legally private) beach. It's a firm favourite among the UK package-holiday crowd.

Cidade de Goa HOTEL $$$
(☎2454545; www.cidadedegoa.com; d from ₹10,000; ❄@🛜🐶) Indulgence is the order of the day at this swanky village-style place, designed by renowned local architect Charles Correa, located 1km down the coast from Dona Paula at Vanguinim Beach. All the usual opulence is on offer, including pool, spa and casino, with eight restaurants to satisfy your culinary requirements. Chow down at Portuguese-themed Alfama, complete with wandering minstrels to serenade you as you dine, or drop in for a cool sundowner at the Bar Latino.

Prainha HOTEL $$$
(☎2453881-3; www.prainha.com; r/cottages from ₹4500/6800; ❄@🛜🐶) Lovely beachside cottages and pleasant rooms in peaceful gardens, all with good views of a little sandy beach.

ℹ️ Getting There & Away

Frequent buses to Dona Paula depart the Kadamba bus stand in Panaji (₹5, 20 minutes), running along riverfront Dayanand Bandodkar Marg, and passing through Miramar along the way.

You can also make the fun journey across Mormugao Bay, from Dona Paula to Mormugao – just north of Vasco da Gama – on a rusty, old **ferry** (pedestrians/motorbikes/cars free/₹10/20), which departs several times daily.

Panaji to Old Goa

RIBANDAR

The old riverside road joining Panaji to Old Goa, via the quaint village of Ribandar, seems to have changed little since it was first built, on land reclaimed from marshes, some 400 years ago. Driving this route towards Old Goa gives you – despite the modern touches – the distinct impression that time has stood still here. Ribandar makes a nice place to pause, and provides one of several access points, by ferry (pedestrians/motorbikes/cars free/₹4/12;⏰every 30min from 8.30am to 8pm), to Chorao (p125) and Divar (p133) Islands, beautiful islands supporting old-fashioned communities and a glorious bird sanctuary.

CHORAO ISLAND

Lazy Chorao Island, accessible by ferry from Ribandar or Divar Island, is only known for its beautiful bird sanctuary. But if you arrive here under your own steam, to while away the hours spotting chirping, cheeping things, it's worthwhile also taking a detour into little Chorao village itself, with its handful of whitewashed village churches and picturesque Portuguese homes.

Dr Salim Ali Bird Sanctuary

Named after the late Dr Salim Moizzudin Abdul Ali, India's best-known ornithologist, this serene sanctuary on Chorao Island was created by Goa's Forestry Department in 1988 to protect the birdlife that thrives here and the mangroves that have grown up in and around the reclaimed marshland. Apart from the ubiquitous white egrets and purple herons, you can expect to see colourful kingfishers, eagles, cormorants, kites, woodpeckers, sandpipers, curlews, drongos and mynahs, to name just a few. Marsh crocodiles, foxes, jackals and otters have also been spotted by some visitors, along with the bulbous-headed mudskipper fish that skim

VISITING OLD GOA

As Goa's top historical attraction and a focal point for pilgrims and domestic bus tours, Old Goa can get very crowded on weekends and feast days. The best time to visit is on a weekday morning, when you can take in Mass at Sé Cathedral or the Basilica of Bom Jesus and explore the rest of the site before the afternoon heat sets in. Remember to cover your shoulders and legs when entering the churches and cathedral, and take notice of 'No Photography' signs.

across the water's surface at low tide. There's a birdwatching tower in the sanctuary that can be reached by boat when the river level, dependent on the tide, is not too low.

Even for those not especially interested in the birds themselves, a leisurely drift in dugout canoe through the sanctuary's mangrove swamps offers a fascinating insight into life on this fragile terrain, while a peek at the farming and fishing activities of the island is a fascinating contrast to the pace of modern life in nearby Panaji.

The best time to visit is either in the early morning (around 8am) or in the evening (a couple of hours before sunset), but since the Mandovi is a tidal river, boat trips depend somewhat on tide times. You'll find boatmen, in possession of dugout canoes to take you paddling about the sanctuary, waiting around at the ferry landing on Chorao Island; the going rate is anywhere between ₹350 and ₹700 for a 90-minute trip, while entry to the sanctuary – payable to the forest officer – costs another ₹50. Don't forget to bring binoculars and a field guide to all things feathered if you're a keen birdwatcher.

To get to Chorao Island by bus, board a bus from Panaji bound for Old Goa and ask to be let off at the Ribandar ferry crossing (₹4, 15 minutes).

Old Goa

🎵 0832

Picture the scene. It's 1760, and you're lucky enough (and pious enough, given the dark penchants of the Inquisition) to be living in the most glorious city in all of Asia – the Rome of the East – filled with ornate cathedrals soaring at heights unimaginable

to most people on the subcontinent. Then, suddenly, disaster strikes. All around, people fall ill, eyes bleeding, mouths foaming. Your neighbours die in their dozens, and then your parents, your cousins, your friends. You rush to the cathedral to beg God for help, but the deaths continue. The smell of decay hangs heavy in the hot, breathless air, and it's an all-too-familiar scene. It happened 10 years ago, and 15 years before that.

But this time, you decide it's worse. Scrabbling together what you can carry of your belongings, you scoop up your children, praying it's not already too late, and flee the glorious city of dreaming spires. You cast a final glance back as the towers and turrets recede into the distance, and put your mind to the future, and onwards to Panaji.

Life in Old Goa, the principal city of the Portuguese eastern empire from 1510 until its abandonment in 1835, was anything but dull. Its rise was meteoric. Over the course of the century following the arrival of the Portuguese in Goa, the city became famous throughout the world. One Dutch visitor compared it with Amsterdam for the volume of its trade and wealth. However, its fall was just as swift, and eventually, plagued by epidemic after deadly epidemic – cholera, malaria and typhoid among them – the city was completely abandoned.

These days in Old Goa, 9km east of Panaji on the course of the broad Mandovi River, only a handful of imposing churches and convents remain in a city that was once so grand and so powerful it rivalled Lisbon.

History

The first records of a settlement on the site of Old Goa date back to the 12th century and a Brahmin colony, known as Ela. Though continuously occupied, it wasn't until the 15th century that Ela rose to prominence, with the Muslim Bahmani rulers choosing it as the site for a new Goan capital, in place of the ransacked and silted-up port capital of Govepuri (today Goa Velha).

Within a short time the new capital was a thriving city. Contemporary accounts tell of the magnificence of the city and of the grandeur of its royal palace, the city enlarged and strengthened with ramparts and a moat. It became a major trading centre and departure point for pilgrims to Mecca, and also gained prominence for its shipbuilding.

With the arrival of the Portuguese in the 16th century, Ela became the new Portuguese capital and a base for the shipment

Old Goa

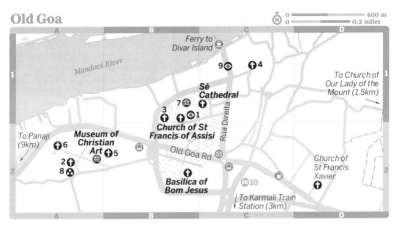

Old Goa

⊙ Top Sights
Basilica of Bom Jesus	B2
Church of St Francis of Assisi	B1
Museum of Christian Art	A2
Sé Cathedral	C1

⊙ Sights
1	Archaeological Museum	B1
2	Chapel of St Anthony	A2
3	Chapel of St Catherine	B1
4	Church & Convent of St Cajetan	C1
5	Church & Convent of St Monica	B2
6	Church of Our Lady of the Rosary	A2
7	Kristu Kala Mandir Art Gallery	B1
8	Ruins of the Church of St Augustine	A2
9	Viceroy's Arch	C1

🛏 Sleeping
10	Old Goa Heritage View	C2

of spices back to the Old World. Soon came missionaries (including the young Francis Xavier; see p195), intent on converting the natives, and in 1560 the Inquisition (see p192), to put paid to the legendary licentious behaviour of both locals and colonials. Though their methods were gruesome, the behaviour they were targeting was widespread: despite the proliferation of churches and cathedrals, Old Goa was a city of drunkenness and adultery, even the clerics themselves sometimes keeping harems of slave girls, and death from syphilis was rife.

Syphilis, however, wasn't to be Old Goa's most widespread disease. The city had been built on swamps, a breeding ground for mosquitos and malaria, while water sources tainted with sewage caused cholera to sweep its streets. Moreover, by the end of the 16th century the Mandovi River was silting up and Portuguese supremacy on the seas had been usurped by the British, Dutch and French. The city's decline was accelerated

by another devastating cholera epidemic, which struck in 1635. Finally, by 1759, the Portuguese had had enough, and the Viceroy moved his official residence to Panjim.

In 1843 Panjim was officially declared the new capital, and by 1846 only Old Goa's convent of Santa Monica was in regular use, though that was also eventually abandoned, leaving the shadow of a grand and desolate city behind.

From the late 19th century until the mid-20th century, Old Goa remained a city of ghosts, empty but for one or two buildings used as military barracks. When archaeological interest started to increase, work was done to clear the area, and some buildings were returned to their former uses. But for many of the once-glorious buildings, plundered for building materials or simply falling victim to the elements, the reprieve came too late; the starkest reminder of this is the skeletal tower of the Church of St Augustine, which can be seen for miles around.

OLD GOA'S ARCHITECTURE

In order to make the most of what you encounter in Old Goa, it's worth brushing up quickly on its architectural heritage.

Most churches are made of laterite, a local red and highly porous stone, which was traditionally coated in white lime wash, mixed with crushed clam shells, in an effort to prevent erosion. Some were embellished with harder-wearing basalt, much of it quarried from Bassein, near Mumbai, though some is thought to have been brought as ballast by ships from Portugal.

Built in an era of glorious colonialism, much of what's on display today is staunchly European, inspired by the building fashions of late-Renaissance Rome. The pinnacle of building here (in the early 17th century) collided with the rise, in Europe, of the baroque movement, characterised by its love of dripping gilt, scrollwork and ornamentation. This pomp and splendour served an important purpose for its priests and missionaries, as it kept the locals awed into submission, feeling dwarfed and vulnerable when confronted with an immense gold altarpiece.

The second style evident at Old Goa is more wholly Portuguese, known as Manueline, after its main patron King Manuel I. This vernacular approach saw the embellishment of buildings with symbols reflecting Portuguese might; anchors, ropes and other maritime motifs represent Portugal's ascendency on the high seas. Though not too much Manueline architecture has survived the test of time, the Church of Our Lady of the Rosary remains a well-preserved example.

◉ Sights

Sé Cathedral   CATHEDRAL

At over 76m long and 55m wide, this is the largest church in Asia. Building work commenced in 1562, on the orders of King Dom Sebastiao of Portugal, to replace the older church of St Catherine, which had until then served as Old Goa's far less grandiose cathedral. Progress was slow, and beset with financial difficulties; work on the building wasn't completed until 1619 and the altars weren't finished until 1652, some 90 years after their construction had first been ordered.

The exterior of the cathedral is notable for its plain style, in the Tuscan tradition. Also of note is its rather lopsided look resulting from the loss of one of its bell towers, which collapsed in 1776 after being struck by lightning. The remaining tower houses the famous **Sino de Ouro** (Golden Bell), the largest in Asia and renowned for its rich tone, which once tolled to accompany the Inquisition's notoriously cruel *autos-da-fé* (trials of faith), held out the front of the cathedral on what was then the market square.

The huge interior of the cathedral is also surprisingly plain. To the right as you enter is a small, locked area that contains a font made in 1532, said to have been used by St Francis Xavier. Two small statuettes, inset into the main pillars, depict St Fran-

cis Xavier and St Ignatius Loyola. There are four chapels on either side of the nave, two of which have screens across the entrance. Of these, the **Chapel of the Blessed Sacrament** is outstanding, with every inch of wall and ceiling gorgeously gilded and decorated – a complete contrast to the austerity of the cathedral interior.

Opposite, to the right of the nave, is the other screened chapel, the **Chapel of the Cross of Miracles**. The story goes that in 1619 a simple cross (known as the *Cruz dos Milagres*) made by local shepherds was erected on a hillside near Old Goa. The cross grew bigger and several witnesses saw an apparition of Christ hanging on it. A church was planned on the spot where the vision had appeared and while this was being built the cross was stored nearby. When it came time to move the cross into the new church it was found that it had grown again and that the doors of the church had to be widened to accommodate it. The cross was moved to the cathedral in 1845, where it soon became, and remains, a popular place of petition for the sick.

Towering above the main altar is the huge gilded *reredos* (ornamental screen), its six main panels carved with scenes from the life of St Catherine, to whom the cathedral is dedicated. She was beheaded in Alexandria, and among the images here are those showing her awaiting execution and being carried to Mt Sinai by angels.

Mass takes place from Monday to Saturday at 7am and 6pm; on Sunday it's at 7.15am, 10am (High Mass) and 4pm.

Kristu Kala Mandir Art Gallery GALLERY
(₹10; ⊙9.30am-5.30pm Tue-Sun) This gallery, sandwiched between the Church of St Francis of Assisi and Sé Cathedral, is located in what used to be the archbishop's house, and contains a hodgepodge collection of contemporary Christian art and religious objects.

Church of St Francis of Assisi CHURCH
West of the Sé Cathedral, the Church of St Francis of Assisi is no longer in use for worship, and consequently exudes a more mournful air than its neighbours.

The church started life as a small chapel, built on this site by eight Franciscan friars on their arrival in 1517. In 1521 it was replaced by a church consecrated to the Holy Ghost, which was then subsequently rebuilt in 1661, with only the doorway of the old building incorporated into the new structure. This original doorway, in ornate Manueline style, contrasts strongly with the rest of the facade, the plainness of which had become the fashion by the 17th century. Maritime themes – unsurprising given Old Goa's important port status – can be seen here and there, including navigators' globes and coats of arms, which once adorned ships' sails.

The interior of the church, though now rather ragged and faded, is nevertheless beautiful, in a particularly 'folk art' type style. The walls and ceiling are heavily gilded and decorated with carved wood panels, with large paintings depicting the works of St Francis adorning the walls of the chancel. Look out for the huge arch that supports the choir, painted vividly with floral designs, and the intricately carved pulpit. The *reredos* dominates the gilded show, although this one is different from others in Old Goa, with a deep recess for the tabernacle. The four statues in its lower portion represent apostles, and above the *reredos* hangs Christ on the cross. The symbolism of this scene is unmistakable: Jesus has his right arm free to embrace St Francis, who is standing atop the three vows of the Franciscan order – Poverty, Humility and Obedience.

Like many other Old Goa churches, tombstones of long-gone Portuguese gentry are laid into the floor, while the more unusual font, situated just beside the door, is made partly from a fragment of an old pillar from a Hindu temple.

Note, too, the sign inside that reads 'No Photography of Persons'. Presumably, they've no problem with you clicking pictures of any heavenly hosts that decide to put in an appearance.

Archaeological Museum MUSEUM
(⊙9am-6.30pm Sat-Thu) Part of the Franciscan monastery at the back of the Church of St Francis of Assisi is now an archaeological museum, housing some lovely fragments of sculpture from Hindu temple sites in Goa, and some Sati stones, which once marked the spot where a Hindu widow committed suicide by flinging herself onto her husband's funeral pyre. Also here you'll find two large bronze statues: one of the Portuguese poet Luís Vaz de Camões (p117), which once stood more prominently in the central grassy area of Old Goa, and one of Afonso de Albuquerque, the Portuguese conqueror and first governor of Goa, which stood in the Azad Maidan in Panaji, before being moved here after Independence.

Upstairs, a gallery contains portraits of some 60 of Goa's Portuguese viceroys, spanning more than 400 years of Portuguese rule. Not particularly exciting in terms of portraiture, they're an interesting insight into Portugal's changing fashions, each as unsuitable for the tropical heat as the last.

Chapel of St Catherine CHURCH
About 100m to the west of the Church of St Francis of Assisi stands the small Chapel of St Catherine. An earlier chapel was erected on this site by Portuguese conqueror Afonso de Albuquerque in 1510 to commemorate his triumphant entry into the city on St Catherine's Day. In 1534 the chapel was granted cathedral status by Pope Paul III and was subsequently rebuilt; the inscribed stone added during rebuilding states that Afonso de Albuquerque actually entered the city at this spot, and thus it's believed that the chapel stands on what used to be the main gate of the Muslim city, then known as Ela. The chapel is currently empty and unused, and thus rarely open to visitors. Check the doors to see if you're in luck.

[TOP CHOICE] **Basilica of Bom Jesus** CHURCH
Famous throughout the Roman Catholic world, the imposing Basilica of Bom Jesus

PANAJI & CENTRAL GOA OLD GOA

contains the tomb and mortal remains of St Francis Xavier, the so-called Apostle of the Indies (p195), a former pupil of St Ignatius Loyola, founder of the Society of Jesus (the Jesuits). St Francis Xavier's missionary voyages throughout the East became legendary – and, considering the perilous state of transport at the time, were nothing short of miraculous.

Construction on the basilica began in 1594 and was completed in 1605, to create an elaborate late-Renaissance structure, fronted by a facade combining elements of Doric, Ionic and Corinthian design, with pillars carved from basalt brought from Bassein, some 300km away. Prominent in the design of the facade is the intricately carved central rectangular pediment, embellished with the Jesuit emblem 'IHS', an abbreviation of the Latin 'Iesus Hominum Salvator' (Jesus, Saviour of Men).

This is the only church in Old Goa not plastered on the outside, the lime plaster having been stripped off by a zealous Portuguese conservationist in 1950. Apparently his notion was that exposed to the elements, the laterite stone of which the basilica is built would become more durable and thus the building would be strengthened. Despite proof to the contrary, no one has got around to putting the plaster back yet; hence, some of the intricate carving is eroding with the dousing of each successive monsoon.

Inside, the basilica's layout is simple but grand, contained beneath a simple wooden ceiling. The huge and ornate gilded *reredos,* stretching from floor to ceiling behind the altar, takes pride of place, its baroque ornament contrasting strongly with the classical, plain layout of the cathedral itself. It shows a rather portly St Ignatius Loyola, protecting a tiny figure of the infant Jesus. His eyes are raised to a huge gilded sun above his head, on which 'IHS' is again emblazoned, above which is a representation of the Trinity.

To the right of the altar is the slightly grisly highlight for the vast majority of visitors: the body of St Francis Xavier himself. The body was moved into the church in 1622, and installed in its current mausoleum in 1698 courtesy of the last of the Medicis, Cosimo III, Grand Duke of Tuscany, in exchange for the pillow on which St Francis' head had been resting. Cosimo engaged the Florentine sculptor Giovanni Batista Foggini to work on the three-tiered structure, constructed of jasper and mar-

ble, flanked with stars, and adorned with bronze plaques that depict scenes from the saint's life. Topping it all off, and holding the shrivelled saint himself, is the casket, designed by Italian Jesuit Marcelo Mastrili and constructed by local silversmiths in 1659, whose sides were originally encrusted with precious stones which, over the centuries, have been picked off.

Crowds are heaviest at the basilica during the **Feast of St Francis Xavier**, held annually on 3 December and preceded by a nine-day devotional novena, with lots of lighthearted festivity alongside the more solemn open-air Masses. Once every 10 years, the saint is given an exposition, and his body hauled around Old Goa before scores of pilgrims; the next is scheduled for 2014.

Passing from the chapel towards the sacristy there are a couple of items relating to St Francis' remains and, slightly further on, the stairs to a **gallery** of highly dubious and infinitely missable modern art.

Next to the basilica is the **Professed House of the Jesuits**, a two-storey laterite building covered with lime plaster. It actually pre-dates the basilica, having been completed in 1585. It was from here that Jesuit missions to the east were organised. Part of the building burned down in 1633 and was partially rebuilt in 1783.

Mass is held in the basilica in Konkani at 7am, 8am and 6pm Monday to Saturday, at 8am and 9.15am on Sunday, and at 10.15am in English on Sunday. Confession is held daily in the sacristy from 5pm to 6pm.

Church & Convent of St Cajetan   CHURCH

Modelled on the original design of St Peter's in Rome, this church was built by Italian friars of the Order of Theatines, sent here by Pope Urban VIII to preach Christianity in the kingdom of Golconda (near Hyderabad). The friars, however, were refused entry to Golconda, so settled instead at Old Goa in 1640. The construction of the church began in 1655, and although it's perhaps less interesting than the other churches, it's still a beautiful building and the only domed church remaining in Goa.

Though the altar is dedicated to Our Lady of Divine Providence, the church is named after the founder of the Theatine order, St Cajetan (1480–1547), a contemporary of St Francis Xavier. Born in Vicenza, St Cajetan spent his whole life in Italy, establishing the Order of Theatines in Rome in 1524. He was known for his work in hospitals and with 'incurables', and for his high moral stance in an increasingly corrupt Roman Catholic church. He was canonised in 1671.

The facade of the church is classical in design and the four niches on the front contain statues of apostles. Inside, clever use of internal buttresses and four huge pillars have given the interior a cruciform construction, above the centre of which is the towering dome. The inscription around the inside of the base of the dome is a verse from the Gospel of St Matthew. The largest of the altars on the right-hand side of the church is dedicated to St Cajetan himself. On the left side are paintings illustrating episodes in the life of St Cajetan; in one it appears, quite peculiarly, that he is being breastfed at some distance by an angel whose aim is remarkably accurate. Traditionally, the last mortal remains of deceased Portuguese governors were kept in the church's crypt, beneath the *reredos,* in lead coffins until their shipment home to their final resting place. The last few, forgotten for more than three decades, were finally sent back to Lisbon in 1992.

Adjoining the church, the Convent of St Cajetan is nowadays a college for recently ordained priests; next door, immediately to the west, you'll see a freestanding basalt doorway, atop five steps, which is the only remains of the grand palace of Goa's 16th-century Muslim ruler Adil Shah. This was later converted into the notorious Palace of the Inquisition, in whose dungeons countless 'heretics' languished, awaiting their dreadful fate. The palace was torn down in the 18th century and its materials repurposed for building in Panaji.

Ruins of the Church of St Augustine   RUIN
Standing on Holy Hill (Monte Santo) is perhaps the most mournful memorial to Old Goa's fallen might. All that's left today of the Church of St Augustine is the 46m-high tower, which served as a belfry and formed part of the church's facade. The few other remnants are choked with creepers and weeds, making picking your way among them rather difficult.

The church was constructed in 1602 by Augustinian friars who had arrived in Old Goa in 1587. It was abandoned in 1835, mostly due to the repressive policies of the Portuguese government that resulted in the eviction of many religious orders from Goa. As Old Goa emptied due to a continual series of deadly epidemics, the church fell into neglect and the vault collapsed in 1842. In 1931 the facade and half the tower fell down, followed by more sections in 1938. The tower's huge bell was moved in 1871 to the Church of Our Lady of the Immaculate Conception in Panaji, where it can be seen (and heard) today.

Church & Convent of St Monica   CHURCH
Work on this three-storey laterite church and convent, also standing on the hill, commenced in 1606 and was completed in 1627, only to burn down nine years later. Reconstruction began the following year and it's from this time that the current buildings date. Once known as the 'Royal Monastery' because of the royal patronage that it enjoyed, the building comprised the first nunnery in the East but, like the other religious institutions, it was crippled by the banning of the religious orders and, though it didn't immediately close, it was finally abandoned when the last sister died in 1885. During the 1950s and '60s the buildings housed first Portuguese and then Indian troops, before being returned to the church in 1968.

PANAJI & CENTRAL GOA OLD GOA

WHEN A MAN LOVES A WOMAN

Sex and scandal aren't solely a modern fascination – Old Goa, in particular, at one time was full of it – and the graves of Garcia de Sá and Caterina a Piró, in Old Goa's demure Church of Our Lady of the Rosary, have their own lascivious tale to tell.

Caterina a Piró, a 'commoner' by birth, was the first Portuguese woman to arrive in the new colony of Old Goa, apparently departing Portugal in an attempt to flee the scandal surrounding her affair with a Portuguese nobleman named Garcia de Sá. The star-crossed pair, however, were destined to meet again, when de Sá was made one of Goa's earliest governors.

Under pressure from the newly arrived St Francis Xavier, de Sá was finally persuaded to do the honourable deed and marry Caterina, who, unfortunately, was already on her deathbed at the time. Her finely carved tomb, at a 'respectful' distance from Garcia's, might suggest to some that the relationship was never *exactly* true love.

CHURCH OF OUR LADY OF THE MOUNT

There is one other church in Old Goa, often overlooked due to its location on a wooded hilltop, some 2km east of the central area. Approached by a long and overgrown flight of steps (locals will warn you not to go solo – the site is a bit remote), the hill on which the church stands commands an excellent view of the whole of Old Goa down below. The church was built by Afonso de Albuquerque, completed in 1519, and has been rebuilt twice since; it now makes the perfect, suitably sorrowful place to watch the sunset over the ruins of once-mighty Old Goa. Usually locked, you can gain entry during the Feast of St Francis Xavier in December, and the Monte Music Festival in February, when concerts are held here.

The building is now used by nuns of the Mater Dei Institute, and visitors are welcomed if they're suitably dressed. The high point of a visit is a peek at the 'miraculous' cross behind the high altar, said to have opened its eyes in 1636, when blood began to drip from its crown of thorns.

Museum of Christian Art
MUSEUM

(http://christianartmuseum.goa-india.org; adult/child ₹30/free; ⊙9.30am-5pm) This excellent museum, in a stunningly restored space within the 1627 Convent of St Monica, contains a collection of statues, paintings and sculptures, though the setting warrants a visit in its own right. Interestingly, many of the works of Goan Christian art made during the Portuguese era, including some of those on display here, were produced by local Hindu artists; this might explain a tiger-skin-wrapped John the Baptist, fitted out in the style of Hindu god Shiva.

Church of Our Lady of the Rosary
CHURCH

Passing beneath the buttresses of the Convent of St Monica, about 250m further along the road is the Church of Our Lady of the Rosary, which stands on the top of a high bluff. It's one of the earliest churches in Goa; legend has it that Albuquerque surveyed the action during his troops' attack on the Muslim city from this bluff and

vowed to build a church there in thanks for his victory. It's also thought to be here that St Francis Xavier gave his first sermon upon his arrival in Old Goa.

The church, which has been beautifully restored, is Manueline in style and refreshingly simple in design. There are excellent views of the Mandovi River and Divar Island from the church's dramatic position, but unfortunately the building is frequently locked.

The only ornaments on the outside of the church are simple rope-twist devices, which bear testimony to Portugal's reliance on the sea. Inside the same is true; the *reredos* is wonderfully plain after all the gold decorating those in the churches down in the centre of Old Goa, and the roof consists simply of a layer of tiles. Set into the floor in front of the altar is the tombstone of one of Goa's early governors, Garcia de Sá, and set into the northern wall of the chancel is that of his wife, Caterina a Piró.

Chapel of St Anthony
CHURCH

Opposite the ruins of the Church of St Augustine is the Chapel of St Anthony, which is now partly in use as a convent. The chapel, dedicated to the saint of the Portuguese army and navy, was one of the earliest to be built in Goa, again on the directions of Afonso de Albuquerque in order to celebrate the assault on the city. Like the other institutions around it, St Anthony's was abandoned in 1835 but was brought back into use at the end of the 19th century. St Anthony's statue inside the church was afforded the honorary rank of army captain and, for many years before the church's abandonment, was paraded out each year to collect its military wages.

Viceroy's Arch
MONUMENT

Perhaps the best way to arrive in Old Goa is the same way that visitors did in the city's heyday. Approaching along the wide Mandovi River (and probably giving thanks for having made it at all), new arrivals would have first glimpsed the city's busy wharf just in front of the symbolic arched entrance to the city.

This archway, known as the Viceroy's Arch, was erected by Vasco da Gama's grandson, Francisco da Gama, who became viceroy in 1597. On the side facing the river the arch (which was restored in 1954 following a collapse) is ornamented with the deer emblem on Vasco da Gama's coat of arms. Above it in the centre of the archway is a statue of da Gama himself. On the side facing the city is a sculpture of a European woman wielding a sword over an Indian, who is lying under her feet. No prizes for guessing the message here, as the Inquisition made its way liberally across the city. The arch originally had a third storey with a statue of St Catherine.

The road running from the dock through the Viceroy's Arch and into the city was known as the Rua Direita (so-named for being the only straight, 'direct' street in the city), and was lined, in its prime, with shops, a bazaar, a customs house, foundry and other businesses. The waterfront was fully built-upon, with the whitewashed, red-roofed homes of wealthy merchants thronging its shores, all now figments of a long-vanished past.

🛏 Sleeping & Eating

There's no particular reason to stay overnight in Old Goa when Panaji is so close by, and the city can be easily accessed as a day trip from elsewhere in the state. If you're feeling peckish, a string of little tourist restaurants near the bus stop offer snacks, chai and thalis, and some vend beer, too.

Old Goa Heritage View   HOTEL **$**
(Old Goa Residency; ☑2285327, 2285013; d without/with AC ₹770/990; ❋) If you find you need, for any reason, to spend the night in Old Goa, the GTDC's offering may not be exciting, but it's reasonably good value and is a comfortable distance from everything you're here to see in Old Goa.

❶ Information

Old Goa has no tourist office, but willing tour guides linger outside the main churches. You can also enquire at the Archaeological Museum, which stocks books on Old Goa, including S Rajagopalan's excellent booklet *Old Goa,* published by the Archaeological Survey of India. One of the most comprehensive is *Old Goa: the Complete Guide* by Oscar de Noronha (2004).

❶ Getting There & Away

There are frequent buses from Old Goa (₹8, 25 minutes) to the Kadamba bus stand at Panaji; buses from Panaji to Ponda also pass through Old Goa. Buses to Panaji or Ponda leave when full (around every 10 minutes) from either the main roundabout or the bus stop/ATM just beside the Tourist Inn restaurant. Alternatively, Old Goa has plenty of free parking if you're coming under your own steam.

Divar Island

Stepping off the ferry from Old Goa onto beautiful little riverine Divar Island, you have the distinct feeling of entering the land that time forgot. Its marshy waters, crisscrossed with sleepy single-lane roads, make for lovely, languid exploration, and though there's not much particularly to see, it's a wonderful, and seldom-visited place to drink in the atmosphere of old-time Goa.

The largest settlement on the island, Piedade, is sleepy but picturesque; filled with lazy old Portuguese palaces, and ladies gossiping at the roadside. But Divar, whose name stems from the Konkani *dev* and *vaddi* (translated as 'place of the Gods'), has an important Hindu history that belies its modern day tranquillity.

Before the coming of the Portuguese, Divar was the site of two particularly important temples – the Saptakoteshwara Temple (moved across the river to Bicholim when the Portuguese began to persecute the Hindus), as well as a Ganesh temple that stood on the solitary hill in Piedade. The former contained a powerful Shivalingam (phallic symbol representing the god Shiva) which was smuggled during the Inquisition to Naroa on the opposite side of the river, just before more than 1500 Divar residents were forcibly converted

---

BUT WHERE ARE THE MEN?

Most of the inhabitants of Divar Island, whom you'll see out and about on its sleepy streets, are women, since a large number of Divar's male population have left their home turf to seek their fortunes on the construction sites of the Middle East and elsewhere in Asia. Each year, in January, they return home to celebrate the Festa das Bandeiras (Flag Festival), during which they parade around Piedade, waving flags from their adoptive homes. The tradition is thought to stem from an ancient pagan Harvest Festival, during which the villagers marked the boundaries of their land by marching about it, wielding weapons. Today the most dangerous part of the proceedings is the brandishing of pea-shooters, an only mildly hazardous part of the gleeful event.

to Christianity. It's likely that the Ganesh temple, meanwhile, was destroyed by Muslim troops near the end of the 15th century, since the first church on this site was built in around 1515.

The church that occupies the hill today, the **Church of Our Lady of Compassion**, is in fine condition. It combines an impressive facade with an engagingly simple interior. The ceiling is picked out in plain white stucco designs, and the windows are set well back into the walls, allowing only a dim light to penetrate into the church; the views alone, however, make Piedade and its church worth the trip.

Just behind the church, a small **cemetery** offers one of only a few fragments of the once grand Kadamba dynasty (see p191). The small chapel in its grounds was converted from an older Hindu shrine, and the carving, painted plaster ceiling and faint stone tracery at the window all date from before the death of the Kadamba dynasty in 1352. Look around for the priest, who'll unlock the chapel for you to take a look.

If you're enchanted enough with the island to want to stay awhile, rest your weary feet at the **Divar Retreat** (☑9823993155, 992010027; www.divarretreat.com; r incl breakfast, lunch & dinner ₹5000; 🛜🏊), a nice little guesthouse in an old Portuguese home, with the somewhat mystifying website slogan, 'A real spaced out life that every individual comes in search to Goa'.

Divar Island can only be reached by one of three ferry services. A boat from Old Goa (near the Viceroy's Arch) runs to the south side of the island, while the east end of the island is connected by ferry to Naroa (p109) in Bicholim *taluka* (district). Another ferry operates to Ribandar from the southwest of the island. All ferries run every 30 minutes, from around 7am to 8pm, and are free for pedestrians, ₹5 for motorbikes and scooters, and ₹12 for cars.

Goa Velha

☑0832

Though it's hard to believe it today, the small and sleepy village of Goa Velha – nowadays just a blur of roadside buildings on a trip south towards Margao along the national highway NH17 – was once home to Govepuri, a grand international port and capital city, attracting Arab traders who settled the surrounding area, rich from the spoils of the spice trade.

Before the establishment of Old Goa (then known as Ela) as Goa's Muslim capital around 1472, Govepuri, clinging to the banks of the Zuari River, flourished under the Hindu Kadamba dynasty. It was only centuries later, long after grand Govepuri had fallen, that the place was renamed Goa Velha by the Portuguese, to distinguish it from their new capital, Old Goa, known to them simply as Goa.

The city, which in its heyday was southwest India's wealthiest, was established by the Kadambas around 1054, but in 1312 was almost totally destroyed by Muslim invaders from the north, and over the following years was repeatedly plagued by Muslim invasions. It wasn't until Goa came under the control of the Hampi-based Vijayanagar Empire in 1378 that trade revived, but by this time the fortunes of the old capital had declined beyond repair, due to both its crushing destruction and the gradual silting-up of its once lucrative port. In 1472 the Muslim Bahmani sultanate took Goa, destroyed what remained of Govepuri, and moved the capital to Old Goa.

Just off the main road at the northern extent of Goa Velha is the **Church of St Andrew**, which hosts an annual festival. On the Monday a fortnight before Easter, 30 statues of saints are taken from their storage place in Old Goa and paraded around the roads of the village. The festivities include a small fair, and the crowds that attend this festival are so vast that police have to restrict movement on the NH17 highway that runs through the village.

The procession has its origins in the 17th century when, at the prompting of the Franciscans, a number of lavishly decked-out life-sized statues were paraded through the area as a reminder to locals of the lives of the saints and as an attempt to curb the licentiousness of the day. Originally the processions started and ended at Pilar, but in 1834 the religious orders were forced to leave Goa and the statues were transferred to the Church of St Andrew. Processions lapsed and many of the original sculptures were lost or broken, but in 1895 subscriptions were raised to obtain a new set, which is still used today, and the procession was reinstated with gusto.

Buses running between Panaji and Margao pass through Goa Velha and Agassaim. They leave from the Kadamba bus stand in Panaji (₹5, 20 minutes).

CHURCH OF ST LAWRENCE, AGASSIM

About 3km south of Goa Velha, at the south end of the small village of Agassim, is the **Church of St Lawrence**, a plain and battered-looking building that houses one of the most flamboyantly decorated *reredos* (ornamental screen) in Goa. The heavily gilded construction behind the altar is unique not only for its wealth of detail but also for its peculiar design, which has multitudes of candlesticks projecting from the reredos itself. The panelled blue-and-white ceiling of the chancel sets the scene. Also interesting are the Jesuit IHS motifs set into the tiled walls, representing, as at Old Goa's Basilica of Bom Jesus, 'Iesus Hominum Salvator' (Jesus, Saviour of Men).

Talaulim

About 5km north of Goa Velha, in the small village of Talaulim, the massive **Church of St Anne** (known to the local people simply as Santana) is an imposing 17th-century structure which, though spectacular, has suffered gravely from years of rain and neglect. A handpainted sign by the side door still boasts the claim made by some observers that this is one of the greatest churches of its type (baroque, with Indian influences). However, it's hard to feel anything other than sorry for the appalling state it's in now. Even so, mildewed and languishing as it is, the place is still undeniably impressive. Its massive five-storey facade is covered in intricate carving, and if you peek through the doors you can see that the interior – largely dating from the 18th and 19th centuries – is still intact, though with more than a touch of the ghostly about it. If you find the chapel locked, tug on the church bell to summon the key-holder.

It's easiest to get here under your own transport, or to ask around at the Kadamba bus stand for a bus from Panaji.

Pilar

A few kilometres north of Goa Velha, and 12km southeast of Panaji, set on a hill high above the surrounding countryside, is **Pilar Seminary**, one of four theological colleges

built by the Portuguese. Only two of these seminaries still survive, the other being Rachol Seminary (p158) near Margao. The hill upon which the seminary stands was once the site of a large and ancient Hindu temple, dedicated to Shiva; it's thought that this was the Goveshwar Mandir, from whose name Goa is thought to have derived. The college was established here in 1613 by Capuchin monks, naming it Our Lady of Pilar, after the statue they brought with them from Spain.

Abandoned in 1835 when the Portuguese expelled the religious orders, the seminary was rescued by the Carmelites in 1858 and became the headquarters of the Missionary Society of St Francis Xavier in 1890. The movement gradually petered out and in 1936 the buildings were handed over to the Xaverian League. Today the seminary is still in use, these days as a training centre for missionaries, and is also the site of local pilgrimages by those who come to give thanks for the life of Father Agnelo de Souza, a director of the seminary in the early 20th century who was beatified after his death.

Aside from the beautiful views afforded from its roof terrace, the seminary is home to a small **museum** (admission free; ☺8am-1pm & 3-6pm Mon-Sat), which holds some of the Hindu relics discovered on-site, as well as some lovely religious paintings, carvings and artefacts. The 1st floor of the building houses a small, but brilliantly lit, chapel.

At the bottom of the hill is the old **Church of Our Lady of Pilar**, which still contains the original statue brought from Spain, along with lots of tombstones of Portuguese nobility, the grave of the locally famed Father Agnelo, and some attractive paintings in an alcove at the rear of the chapel.

Getting to Pilar is easiest with your own transport; alternatively, take a bus to Goa Velha and bargain hard for a taxi or autorickshaw to take you the couple of kilometres up to Pilar Seminary.

Ponda

☑0832
Workaday Ponda is the urban gateway to Goa's interesting Hindu temple heartland, as well as to the fragrant spice plantations that pepper the countryside all around. As such, the pleasant but unremarkable town makes a useful stopping-off point for a quick lunch, an ATM cash stop or a hot shot of chai on the way out to view temples and vanilla groves.

Ponda & Around

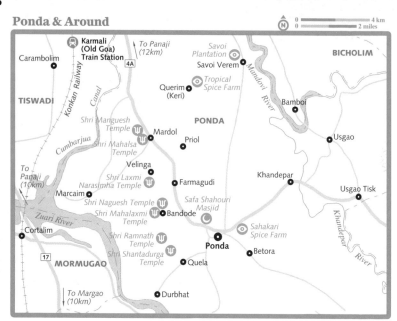

If you've time to kill in Ponda take a look at the **Safa Shahouri Masjid** (also known as the Safa Masjid), Goa's oldest remaining mosque, 2km from the town centre, on Ponda's northern outskirts. Built by Bijapuri ruler Ali Adil Shah in 1560 (and conveniently close to today's NH4A highway for a quick visit) it was originally surrounded by gardens, fountains and a palace, and is said to have matched the mosques at Bijapur in size and quality. Today little remains of the mosque's former grandeur, despite attempts at restoration by the Archaeological Survey of India. But what it lacks in sights, it makes up for in legend: it's said that it's connected, by way of an underground passage, to a ruined hilltop fort, some 2km away. The passage hasn't been discovered yet, though this shouldn't discourage those with a flashlight and a penchant for adventure.

🛏 Sleeping & Eating

Given that Ponda is just 30km from Panaji, there's little reason to stay overnight. In case you do decide you want to, a scattering of unremarkable hotels are ranged along the main road, with budget rooms priced from ₹200 to ₹300; wander along and take your pick of a fairly dingy crop.

Hotel Sungrace   HOTEL $
(☎2311238; s/d/ste with AC ₹600/700/1500, s/d without AC ₹500/600; ❄) At the heart of town, the Sungrace advertises itself as 'the Elegant Hotel in Ponda' and, in contrast with the rest of Ponda's offerings, it's not far wrong. Clean, efficient and bright modern rooms are stacked atop a busy restaurant, serving up the usual range of Indian and Chinese dishes. It's wise to book ahead during festival and holiday periods, as its 28 rooms are frequently filled with Indian tourists. The Sungrace is located one road to the left of the main road if you're coming into Ponda from the south.

Cafe Bhonsle   INDIAN $
(thalis from ₹45; ⏰7am-10pm Mon-Sat, to 3pm Sun) This all-vegetarian restaurant, on the right-hand side of the main road when entering town from the south, makes a great all-day stop in the midst of Ponda, whipping out high-speed thalis to a hungry lunchtime crowd, with an extensive menu of Indian and Chinese food – and a mean *bhaji-pau*. Clean, quick and efficient, it's sure to satisfy.

Sumudra Pub & Family Restaurant INDIAN $
(⏰11am-3pm & 7-11pm) Near the popular Bhonsle, this is another good option for a cheap and tasty lunch, with the added ad-

vantage of a 1st-floor open-air eating area offering a pleasant bird's-eye view of Ponda's busy main road.

ℹ Getting There & Away

There are regular buses, via Old Goa, between Panaji and Ponda (₹18, 1½ hours), and to and from Margao (₹15, one hour). To explore the region's surrounding temples and spice farms, you'll need your own transport, or to take one of the GTDC's lightning day trips (see p230).

Around Ponda

For nearly 250 years after the arrival of the Portuguese in 1510, Ponda *taluka* remained under the control of Muslim or Hindu rulers, and many of its temples came into existence when Hindus were forced to escape Portuguese persecution by fleeing across its district border, bringing their sacred temple deities with them as centuries-old edifices were destroyed by the new colonial regime.

Here the temples remained, safe from the destruction that occurred in the Velhas Conquistas (Old Conquests), and by the time that Ponda itself came under Portuguese control, increased religious tolerance meant that no threat was posed to the temples.

But despite the temples' intrepid history, true temple junkies may be disappointed with the area's architectural collection. Most were built during the 17th and 18th centuries, making them modern compared to those elsewhere in India. Nevertheless,

what they lack in ancient architecture they make up for with their highly holy ancient deities, salvaged on devout Hindus' flights from probable death at the hands of the Inquisition.

The temples are clustered in two main areas: the first in the countryside 5km west of town, and the second north along the route of the NH4A highway. If you're not a true temple-traipser, the two with most appeal are the Shri Mahalsa and Shri Manguesh temples, both near the villages of Priol and Mardol. Close to the busy highway, they are easy to reach by bus; take any bus between Panaji and Margao that runs via Ponda and ask your driver to drop you off near the temples. To get to other temples of the region, it may be easiest to visit with your own car or motorbike, or negotiate a day rate with a taxi from Panaji, Ponda or Margao.

The other reason to visit Ponda *taluka* is to visit one of the aromatic spice plantations that await in the heart of the countryside, welcoming you with lavish lunches, elephants and informative tours.

SHRI MANGUESH TEMPLE

Around 9km north of Ponda, this temple is one of the most visited of Goa's Hindu temples, admirably combining two key features of Goan Hinduism: first, it's dedicated to a solely Goan deity (in this case the local god Manguesh), and second, it exhibits the mixture of architectural styles that typifies the region's temples.

SPICE UP YOUR LIFE

Though there are several spice plantations in the general Ponda area, one of the most popular is the Tropical Spice Farm (☎0832-2340329; www.tropicalspiceplantation.com; ₹400; ☉9am-4pm), 5km north of Ponda. An entertaining 45-minute tour of the spice plantation, followed by a banana-leaf buffet lunch, is included in the price, and elephant rides/bathings are available for ₹600 extra.

Nearby, the 200-year-old Savoi Plantation (☎2340272; www.savoiplantation.com; ☉9am-4.30pm), whose motto is 'Organic Since Origin', is less touristy, elephant-free and the cream of the crop, where you'll find a warm welcome from knowledgeable guides keen to walk you through the 40-hectare plantation at your own pace. Local crafts are for sale, and you're welcomed with fresh pomegranate juice, cardamom bananas and other organic treats. If the peace appeals, there are a couple of recently-added cottages (d incl meals ₹5000).

Two further options are the heavily touristed Sahakari Spice Farm (☎0832-2312394; www.sahakarifarms.com; ☉daily), just 2km from Ponda near the village of Curti, equipped with elephants and enthusiastic staff, and the quieter, organic Spice Farm (☎2427705; ₹400, children half price; ☉9am-4pm), 7km from Ponda, where there's also an elephant available for rides (for ₹600) and buffet lunch is included in the entry price.

The temple's original location was on the south side of the Zuari River, near the present-day village of Cortalim. When the Portuguese took control, its ancient Shivalingam stone was brought to Priol and installed in a new temple (enlarged later in the mid-18th century), an effort that saw Hindus from Portuguese-held districts risking death, arriving in the dead of night to worship here. Today the temple has grown to encompass a substantial complex that includes accommodation for pilgrims and administrative offices.

Architecturally, Shri Manguesh shows the influences of both Christian and Muslim styles. There's evidence of Christian influence in the octagonal tower above the sanctum, the pillared facade of the impressive seven-storey *deepastambha* (lamp tower), the largest in Goa, and the balustrade design around the roof, while the domed roofs indicate a Muslim influence. The tank (reservoir) in front of the temple is the oldest part of the complex. If you walk down to the right-hand side of the temple you can also see the giant *raths* (chariots) that are used to parade the deities during the temple's festival, which takes place in the last week of January or the first week of February.

Manguesh, the temple's god, is said in Goan Hindu mythology to be an incarnation of Shiva. The story goes that Shiva, having lost everything to his wife Parvati in a game of dice, came to Goa in a self-imposed exile. When Parvati eventually came looking for him, he decided to frighten her and disguised himself as a tiger. In horror, Parvati cried out *'trahi mam girisha!'* (Oh lord of mountains, save me!), whereupon Shiva resumed his normal form. The words *mam girisha* became associated with the tale and Shiva's tiger incarnation, with time, became known as Manguesh. The Shivalingam left to mark the spot where all this happened was eventually discovered by a shepherd, and a temple was built to house it at the temple's original location near Cortalim.

SHRI MAHALSA TEMPLE

The Mahalsa Temple, 1km down the road from the Shri Manguesh Temple, is in the tiny village of Mardol. This temple's deity originally resided in an ancient shrine in the village of Verna in Salcete *taluka* in the south. The buildings were reputedly so beautiful that even the Portuguese priest whose job it was to oversee their destruction requested that they should be preserved and

converted into a church. Permission was refused, but before the work began in 1543 the deity was smuggled away to safety.

Again, Mahalsa is a uniquely Goan deity, this time an incarnation of Vishnu in female form. Various legends suggest how Mahalsa came into being. In one, Vishnu, who was in a particularly tight corner during a struggle with the forces of evil, disguised himself as Mohini, the most beautiful woman ever seen, in order to distract his enemies. The trick worked and Mohini, with her name corrupted to Mahalsa, was born. To complicate matters, Mahalsa also fits into the pantheon as an incarnation of Shiva, the destroyer. In general, however, she is regarded by her devotees as a representative of peace; for this, and for her multifaceted identity, she has many devotees.

Once you pass through the entrance gate, off the busy side street, the temple is pleasantly peaceful. The inner area is impressive, with huge wooden pillars and slatted windows and, like most of the other temples in this area, an ornamented silver frame surrounds the doorway to the sanctum. Walk around to the back of the main building and peer through the archway to the water tank; the combination of the ancient stonework, palm trees and paddy fields beyond is quite a sight.

In front of the temple stands a large *deepastambha* and a 12.5m-high brass oil lamp that is lit during festivals; it's thought to be the largest such lamp in the world.

In addition to the annual chariot procession held in February for the **Zatra festival**, the temple is also famous for two other festivals. Jasmine flowers are offered in tribute to the god Mahalsa during the **Zaiyanchi Puja festival**, which falls in August or September. The full-moon festival of **Kojagiri Purnima** is also celebrated here; on this particular night (usually in September) the goddess Lakshmi (Laxmi) descends to earth to bestow wealth and prosperity on those who stay awake to observe the night-time vigil.

SHRI LAXMI NARASIMHA TEMPLE

Almost immediately after leaving the village of Mardol on the main road, a side road to the right takes you up a hill towards the little village of Velinga and the Laxmi Narasimha Temple, one of the most attractive and secluded temples around Ponda. It's dedicated to Narasimha or Narayan, a half-lion half-human incarnation of Vishnu,

GOA'S TEMPLE ARCHITECTURE

Though Goa's temples often exhibit a strange and colourful blend of traditional Hindu, Christian and Muslim architectural elements, several of their key components remain constant.

On entering a temple, you'll first reach the *prakara* (courtyard), which surrounds the whole complex, often encompassing a *tirtha* (water tank), in which worshippers bathe before continuing into the temple. Next you'll pass one or two pillared *mandapas* (assembly halls), used for music, dancing and congregational prayer.

Through these, you'll arrive at the *antaralya* (main shrine), surrounded by a *pradak-shena* (passage) for circumambulation, and flanked by two shrines of the temple's lesser deities. Within the main shrine is the *garbhagriha* (shrine room), which houses the *devta* (sacred deity) – in elaborate statue or simple stone form – and forms the most sacred part of the temple. Only high-caste Brahmin priests are admitted to the shrine room, where they perform regular ritual purifications. Topping off the shrine room is the *shikhara* (sanctuary tower), which symbolises the Divine Mountain, the source of the sacred River Ganges.

Just as Goan food is a heady mix of influences, so too is its architectural fusion, and Goa's temples also sport some features specific to the sunny state. Sanctuary towers tend to have been influenced by Portuguese church trends (despite the fact that those same conquerors were responsible for the destruction of many of the originals), often resulting in octagonal towers topped by a copper dome. *Mandapa* roofs are often terra-cotta-tiled, decorated with oriental images imported from Macau, another Portuguese colony, and embellished with Muslim motifs. The most distinct of all, however, are the Maratha-conceived *deepastambhas* or *deepmals* (lamp towers) – multistoreyed pago-das usually standing beside the temple's main entrance, whose multiple cubby holes hold dozens of oil lamps stunningly illuminated on special occasions and during the weekly ceremonial airing of the *devta*.

which he created to defeat a formidable adversary. The deity was moved here from the district of Salcete in 1567, and the most picturesque part of the temple is the old water tank, to the left of the compound as you enter, spring-fed and entered via a cer-emonial gateway. Although the temple has a sign by the door announcing that entry is for the 'devoted and believers only', respect-ful nonbelievers will probably be allowed to have a look. If ushered out, however, you'll get the best overall view of the place from the gateway to the tank, looking through the *mandapa* (pillared assembly hall) to the in-ner area and the sanctum beyond.

SHRI NAGUESH TEMPLE

A short distance further south, in the vil-lage of Bandode, is the small and peaceful Naguesh Temple. The most striking part of the temple is the ancient water tank, with its overhanging palms, fishy depths and weath-ered stones together making an attractive scene. Also of note are colourful images in relief around the base of the *deepastambha,* and the frieze of Ramayana scenes running inside along the tops of the pillars. Unlike

its neighbours, this temple was in exist-ence well before Albuquerque ever set foot in Goa, but the buildings you see today are newish and rather uninteresting. The tem-ple is dedicated to Shiva, known in this in-carnation as Naguesh, and is particularly rich in animal representation. Note Shiva's Nandi bull lying at the entrance porch, the subsidiary shrine to elephant god Ganesh, and the peacocks and elephant heads adorn-ing the corners of the *shikhara* (sanctuary tower) roofs.

SHRI MAHALAXMI TEMPLE

Only 4km outside Ponda, and a stone's throw from the Naguesh Temple, is the relatively uninspiring Mahalaxmi Temple. The god-dess Mahalaxmi, looked upon as the mother of the world, was particularly worshipped by the Shilahara rulers and by the Kadambas, and thus has featured prominently in the Hindu pantheon in southern India. Here she wears a lingam (phallic symbol of Shiva) on her head, symbolising her connection with Shiva.

THE CAVES OF KHANDEPAR

If all those temples are making you see heavenly constellations, a trip out to the small village of Khandepar – especially if you're an archaeological enthusiast or spelunker – will prove rewarding.

Khandepar is 5km northeast of Ponda on the NH4A national highway. Set back in the dense forest behind the Mandovi River you will find (with some persistent asking around) four small rock-cut caves believed to have been carved into the laterite stone around the 12th century, though some archaeologists date their origin back as early as the 9th century. Thought to have been used by a community of Buddhist monks, each of the four caves consists of two simple cells, with tiered roofs added in the 10th or 11th centuries by the Kadamba dynasty who, it's thought, appropriated the caves and turned them into Hindu temples. The fourth cave supports the Buddhist theory, containing a pedestal used for prayer and meditation. There are also niches in the walls for oil lamps, and pegs carved for hanging clothes. The first cave, meanwhile, has a lotus medallion carved into its ceiling, typical of the later Kadambas.

These are among Goa's oldest remaining historical treasures, and yet (herein lies the excitement) they were only rediscovered in 1970.

Don't be surprised if no one knows what you're talking about when you get to the Khandepar junction (preferably with your own transport). Be persistent and ask around until you find someone knowledgeable enough to take you to the site; it's worth the effort to get here before it becomes a prime tourist attraction.

SHRI RAMNATH TEMPLE

Though undoubtedly one of Ponda's all-round uglier temples, Shri Ramnath is notable for the impressive and extravagant silver screen on the door to the sanctum. Although other temples have similar finery, the work here is exceptional, in particular the two unusual scenes depicted at the top of the lintel. The lower of the two depicts kneeling figures worshipping a lingam, while the upper one shows Vishnu lying with Lakshmi, his consort, on a couch made up of the coils of a snake. The lingam installed in the sanctum was brought from Loutolim in Salcete *taluka* in the 16th century.

SHRI SHANTADURGA TEMPLE

Surrounded by forest and paddy fields, the Shri Shantadurga Temple is one of the most famous shrines in Goa and is consequently packed with those who come to worship, as well as day trippers brought in by the bus load. Hustle past the rows of roadside hawkers to get a look at this heavily European-inspired creation, built in 1738, 200 years after its deity had been smuggled in from Quelossim, not far from present-day southern Colva.

The goddess Shantadurga is another form taken by Parvati, Shiva's consort. As the most powerful of the goddesses, Parvati could either adopt a violent form, Durga, or she could help to bring peace, as Shanta.

The legend goes that during a particularly savage quarrel between Shiva and Vishnu she appeared in her Durga form and helped to make peace between the two gods – thus embodying the contradiction that the name Shantadurga implies. In Goa she has come to be worshipped as the goddess of peace and has traditionally had a large following.

Features to look out for here are the lavishly decorated interior, complete with marble, chandeliers and an intricately worked silver screen, while outside you'll find massive *raths* (chariots) used in the annual Yatra festival held here each February, and a beautiful, six-storey *deepastambha*.

Bondla Wildlife Sanctuary

Small and hard-to-get-to Bondla Wildlife Sanctuary (entry ₹5, motorcycle/car ₹50/100, camera/video camera ₹25/100; ⊙9am-5.30pm Fri-Wed) is undeniably beautiful, but its out-of-the-way location makes it only an option for those with their own transport or those committed public-transport-travelling naturalists with plenty of time on their hands. Its location remains even more hidden due to a dearth of signposts as to its whereabouts, off the main, truck-blown NH4A road from Ponda to Molem.

You're unlikely to see animals just by wandering around the sanctuary, though the park's jungly reaches are home to wild boar, gaurs (Indian bison), monkeys, jackals and deer, but it's a butterfly-spotter and birdwatcher's paradise, and a great place to peaceably stake out both if you're staying at nearby Backwoods Camp (see p142). Entry to the park's forlorn little zoo, nature interpretation centre and botanical gardens (none of which are worth the trip out here in themselves, unless you've a penchant for caged animals and ornamental lawns) are all included in your sanctuary entrance fee.

If you're opting to reach the park by public transport, there are buses from Ponda to Usgao village (₹5), from which you'll need to take a taxi (₹200) the remaining 10km.

Molem & Around

✆0832

If you're keen to visit Goa's largest protected wildlife area, the state's oldest temple, or the second-largest waterfalls in the whole of India, chances are you'll end up in Molem, a dusty, truck-blown village on the main road east into Karnataka state. Despite the tourist magnets at its dishevelled doorstep, Molem does little in the way of cashing in on its advantages.

Accessible by bus from Ponda and by private car or motorbike along the NH4A, the drive out here is made quite unpleasant by the constant stream of wagons emerging from iron ore mines in the area, and shuddering, like *Dark Crystal* beasts of burden, along heavily pot-holed roads. This can make the journey excruciatingly slow, and the eventual arrival in Molem even more anticlimactic.

Bhagwan Mahavir Wildlife Sanctuary (₹5, motorcycle/car ₹10/30, camera/video camera ₹30/130; ☺8.30am-5.30pm) lies a stone's throw from Molem and, with an area of 240 sq km, this is the largest of Goa's four protected wildlife areas; it also encompasses the 107-sq-km Molem National Park. Unless you're on a guided tour, however, you might also have problems actually gaining access to the park's quiet, shady, unmarked trails. In theory, tickets are available at the Forest Interpretation Centre, 2km before the park entrance, close to Molem town. In practice, though, there are usually only a couple of bewildered-looking men sitting about, who will have enough trouble interpreting your request to purchase a ticket, let alone finding the keys to the park gates. Beware, too,

that aside from the top-end Dudhsagar Spa Resort, Molem is unequipped with anywhere to stay.

But, along with dogged persistence, there are three distinct ways to gain access to the sanctuary. The first, organise a tour through a travel agent, hotel or tour guide, and head out here on a day trip, most of which confine themselves to Dudhsagar Falls and the Devil's Canyon. The second, hop aboard the GTDC's lightning tour of the region, which again only involves a trip to the falls. And the third, spend a plush night or two at Azuska Retreat, where staff can arrange trips into the park's seldom-trodden jungly interior.

If you do make it into the thick of the park, you'll be rewarded with lush and deserted tracts of forest populated by jungle cats, Malayan giant squirrels, gaurs, sambars, leopards, chitals (spotted deer), slender loris, Malayan pythons and cobras. Though the wildlife is confoundedly shy and hard to spot, with wildlife numbers still recovering from devastation during Goa's colonial rule, there's an observation platform a few kilometres into the park. The best time to see wildlife is in the early morning or late evening.

Molem's sole and upscale accommodation option, **Dudhsagar Spa Resort** (✆2612319; www.dudhsagarsparesort.com; d/tent incl breakfast ₹3250/5000; ❄@≋) is a relatively new and luxurious series of bungalows and huge luxury tents, set up around a lovely, if slightly municipal-feeling, garden. The tents are a delight, with huge beds, sleek modern furnishings and gorgeous deep baths, set on the quiet side of the site amid tall trees brimming with monkeys. It's situated near the Molem forest checkpoint. The highly obliging folks here can organise all sorts of excursions into the park, including elephant rides, night-time forest forays, along with trips out to Dudhsagar Falls. There is also a spa with steam baths and sauna (and even teeth-whitening on offer!), three restaurants and a nice garden pool, and a range of ayurvedic and detox treatment programs.

Molem and the gateway to the sanctuary lie 55km east of Panaji (54km from Margao), with its main entrance on NH4A. To reach here by public transport, take any bus to Ponda, then change to a bus to Belgaum or Londa (both in neighbouring Karnataka state), getting off at Molem (₹10, two hours).

DUDHSAGAR FALLS

Situated in the far southeastern corner of the Bhagwan Mahavir Wildlife Sanctuary, Goa's most impressive waterfalls splash down just west of the border with Karnataka state, and at 603m are the second highest in India after Jog Falls (see p186). They're best visited as soon after monsoon as possible (October is perfect), when the water levels are highest and the cascades earn their misty nomenclature, Dudhsagar meaning, in Konkani, 'Sea of Milk'.

Aside from taking a day trip, it's not all that difficult to reach the falls. First, you need to get to the village of Colem, around 7km south of Molem, either by car or by the 8.13am train from Margao (p151). It's best to check return train times at the Margao railway station in advance, since they vary seasonally. From Colem, pick up a shared jeep (₹4000 per jeep, divided by up to six people) for the highly scenic, highly bumpy, approximately 45-minute journey. After this, it's a quick clamber up over the rocks to reach the falls themselves.

The jeep takes you into the sanctuary, through a number of extremely scenic jungle and forest areas (there are three streams to be forded, which would make this trip tricky – though not impossible – by Enfield or other motorbike). En route, you might be driven past Devil's Canyon, a beautiful gorge with a river running between the steep-sided rocks. Though some intrepid souls do don their costumes and take a dip, locals say it's named through being a dangerous spot to swim, with strong underwater currents and the odd 'mugger' crocodile.

At the falls themselves swimming is quite possible and very refreshing, but don't picture yourself taking a romantic swim on your own – there'll be plenty of other bathers joining in. You can also walk the distance to the head of the falls (though it's unwise without a local to guide you), a real uphill slog, but affording beautiful views, and really earning you the pleasure of the swim at the end of it.

If all this seems like too much hard work, the GTDC (p230) runs one of its trademark whirlwind tours, the 'Dudhsagar Special' (with/without AC ₹800/700) to the waterfall, throwing in, for good measure, Old Goa, Ponda and lunch at Molem (not included in the cost), with a visit to the Shri Tambdi Surla Mahadeva Temple on the return leg. Tours depart Calangute, Mapusa, Panaji or Miramar on Wednesdays and Sundays, departing 9am and returning 6pm. Alternatively, check out the 'Jungle Book' tours offered by Goa Eco Tourism (www.goaecotourism.com), which has an overnight trip out here, with elephant rides and encounters with local villagers.

Tambdi Surla

If you're a history or temple buff, don't miss the atmospheric remains of the unusual little Hindu Shri Mahadeva Temple at Tambdi Surla, 12km north of the truck-stop town of Molem. Built around the 12th century by the Kadamba dynasty, who ruled Goa for around seven centuries, it's the only temple of dozens of its type to have survived both the years and the various conquerings and demolishings by Muslim and Portuguese

---

WORTH A TRIP

BACKWOODS CAMP

In a forest in the Mahaveer Sanctuary full of butterflies and birds, Backwoods Camp (☑9822139859; www.backwoodsgoa.com) could not be a more magical, serene spot. The camp is around 1km from Tambdi Surla temple, in the village of Matkan, and for birdwatching enthusiasts it offers Goa's richest source of feathered friends, with everything from Ceylon frogmouths and Asian fairy bluebirds, to puff-throated babblers and Indian pittas putting in a regular appearance. Accommodation comes in the form of tents on raised forest platforms, bungalows, and farmhouse rooms (all with attached bathroom), and the camp makes a valiant attempt to protect this fragile bit of the Goan ecosystem, through measures including waste recycling, replanting indigenous tree species, and employing local villagers. One-, two- and three-day birdwatching excursions, including guide, transport from Ponda, accommodation at the camp and all meals, cost from ₹4000, ₹6000 and ₹8000 per person, respectively.

forces, and probably only made it thus far due to its remote jungle setting, only accessible, until recently, after trekking through dense jungle.

No one quite knows why this spot was chosen, since historically there was no trade route passing here and no evidence of there having been any major settlement nearby. Furthermore, the high-quality, weather-resistant black basalt of which the temple is constructed must have been brought a considerable distance – probably all the way across the Western Ghats themselves – since rock of this sort isn't generally found in Goa. Consequently the origins of the temple are something of a mystery, and although it hasn't survived completely unscathed – the headless Nandi bull in the *mandapa* (pillared pavilion) is evidence of some desecration – it remains a beautiful insight into a long lost world.

The temple itself is very small, facing eastward so that the rays of dawn light up its deity. At the eastern end, the open-sided *mandapa* is reached through doorways on three sides. The entrance to the east faces a set of steps down to the river, where ritual cleansing was carried out before worship. Inside the *mandapa* the plain slab ceiling is supported by four huge **carved pillars**. The clarity of the designs on the stone is testimony not only to the skill of the artisans, but also to the quality of the rock that was imported for the construction; look out for the image on one of the bases of an elephant crushing a horse, thought to symbolise Kadambas' own military power at the time of the temple's inauguration.

The best examples of the carvers' skills, however, are the superb lotus-flower **relief panel** set in the centre of the ceiling, and the finely carved pierced-stone **screen** that separates the outer hall from the *antaralya* (main shrine), flanked by an image of Ganesh and several other deities. Finally, beyond the inner hall is the *garbhagriha* (shrine room), where the lingam resides.

The exterior of the temple is plain, with a squat appearance caused by the partial collapse of its *shikhara* tower. On the remains of the tower are three relief carvings depicting the three most important deities in the Hindu pantheon: on the north side (facing towards the access road) is Vishnu, to the west is Shiva and to the south is Brahma. On the level above are three further carvings, depicting each of the deities' consorts.

THE DHANGARS

Goa's green eastern reaches are home to the Dhangars, one of the state's nomadic tribes who have lived, for centuries, on buffalo-herding. Their lifestyle, like that of many other nomadic tribes, is today threatened (in their case by deforestation and high levels of alcoholism), and many have been forced to move to cities in search of work, or attempt settled forms of agriculture. You might, however, still see them in far-flung stretches of the park, tending their lowing, leathery livestock as they have for centuries.

Given its somewhat out-of-the-way location, Tambdi Surla makes the easiest day trip with your own wheels (though GTDC tours also stop here). It's a scenic drive, and quite well signposted, from Molem. Otherwise, take a bus to Molem from Ponda, and negotiate a taxi fare from there. If you roll up on a weekday, when it's not inundated with quick-stopping, fast-snapping day trippers, this remote place remains a solitary and stirring memorial to a once grand and glorious era.

FURTHER AFIELD

Hampi

☑ 08394

Unreal and bewitching, the forlorn ruins of Hampi, around 330km from Goa, make a highly worthwhile, and popular, side trip from the coast. They lie scattered over a landscape that leaves you spellbound: heaps of giant boulders perch precariously over miles of undulating terrain, their rusty hues offset by jade-green palm groves, banana plantations and paddy fields, while the azure sky painted with fluffy white cirrus adds to the magical atmosphere. A World Heritage Site, Hampi is a place where you can lose yourself among the ruins, or simply be mesmerised by the vagaries of nature, wondering how millions of years of volcanic activity and erosion could have resulted in a landscape so fascinating.

Hampi is a major pit stop on the traveller circuit, with the cooler months of November to March being the peak season. While it's

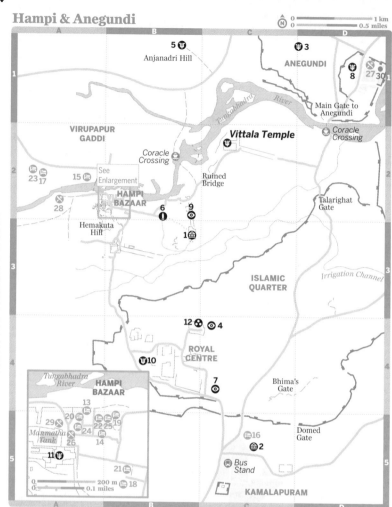

possible to see the main sites in a day or two, this goes against Hampi's relaxed grain; plan on lingering for a while.

Hampi Bazaar and the southern village of Kamalapuram are the two main points of entry to the ruins. Kamalapuram has a government-run hotel and the archaeological museum. But the main travellers' scene is Hampi Bazaar, a village crammed with budget lodges, shops and restaurants, all towered over by the majestic Virupaksha Temple. The ruins are divided into two main areas: the Sacred Centre, around Hampi Bazaar; and the Royal Centre, towards Kamalapuram. To

the northeast across the Tungabhadra River is the historic village of Anegundi.

History

Hampi and its neighbouring areas find mention in the Hindu epic Ramayana as Kishkinda, the realm of the monkey gods. In 1336 Telugu prince Hariharaya chose Hampi as the site for his new capital, Vijayanagar which, over the next couple of centuries, grew into one of the largest Hindu empires in Indian history. By the 16th century it was a thriving metropolis of about 500,000 people, its busy bazaars dabbling in interna-

Hampi & Anegundi

◎ **Top Sights**
  Vittala Temple C2

◎ **Sights**
  1 Achyutaraya Temple B3
  2 Archaeological Museum C5
  3 Durga Temple D1
  4 Elephant Stables C4
  5 Hanuman Temple B1
  Lotus Mahal .... (see 12)
  6 Nandi Statue B2
  7 Queen's Bath C4
  8 Ranganatha Temple D1
  9 Sule Bazaar B2
  10 Underground Shiva Temple B4
  11 Virupaksha Temple A5
  12 Zenana Enclosure B4

◎ **Sleeping**
  13 Archana Guest House A4
  14 Gopi Guest House A5

  15 Hema Guest House A2
  16 Hotel Mayura Bhuvaneshwari C5
  17 Mowgli A2
  18 Padma Guest House B5
  19 Pushpa Guest House B5
  20 Rama Guest House A5
  21 Ranjana Guest House B5
  22 Rocky Guest House A5
  23 Shanthi A2
  24 Shanthi Guest House A5
  25 Vicky's B5

◎ **Eating**
  26 Durga Huts A5
  27 Hoova Craft Shop & Cafe D1
  28 Mango Tree A2
  29 New Shanthi A5

◎ **Information**
  30 Kishkinda Trust D1

tional commerce, brimming with precious stones and merchants from faraway lands. All this ended in 1565, when a confederacy of Deccan sultanates razed Vijayanagar to the ground, striking it a death blow from which it never recovered.

A different battle rages in Hampi today, between conservationists bent on protecting Hampi's architectural heritage and the locals who have settled there. A master plan is being prepared to classify all of Hampi's ruins as protected monuments, while resettling villagers at a new commercial-cum-residential complex away from the architectural enclosures. However, implementation is bound to take time, given the resistance from the locals who fear their livelihoods might be affected by the relocation process. Global Heritage Fund (www.globalheritagefund.org) has more details about Hampi's endangered heritage.

◎ **Sights**

Virupaksha Temple   HINDU TEMPLE
(₹2; ⏰dawn-dusk) The focal point of Hampi Bazaar is the Virupaksha Temple, one of the city's oldest structures. The main *gopuram* (gateway tower), almost 50m high, was built in 1442, with a smaller one added in 1510. The main shrine is dedicated to Virupaksha, a form of Shiva.

If Lakshmi (the temple elephant) and her attendant are around, she'll bless you on the forehead for a coin. The adorable Lakshmi takes her morning bath at 8.30am, just down the way by the river ghats.

Hemakuta Hill   HISTORIC SITE
To the south, overlooking Virupaksha Temple, Hemakuta Hill has a scattering of early ruins, including monolithic sculptures of Narasimha (Vishnu in his man-lion incarnation) and Ganesh. It's worth the short walk up for the view over the bazaar.

Nandi Statue   STATUE
At the east end of Hampi Bazaar is a Nandi statue, around which stand some of the colonnaded blocks of the ancient marketplace. This is the main location for Vijaya Utsav, the Hampi arts festival held in November.

Vittala Temple   HINDU TEMPLE
(Indian/foreigner ₹10/250; ⏰8.30am-5.30pm) From the eastern end of Hampi Bazaar, a track, best covered on foot, leads left along the riverbank to the Vittala Temple, about 2km away. The undisputed highlight of the Hampi ruins, the 16th-century temple is in fairly good condition, though a few cement scaffolds have been erected to keep the main structure from collapsing.

Work possibly started on the temple during the reign of Krishnadevaraya (1509–29) but it was never finished or consecrated. Yet, the temple's incredible sculptural work remains the pinnacle of Vijayanagar art. The

OUT OF HARM'S WAY

Hampi is generally a safe, peaceful place. However, don't wander around the ruins after dark or alone, as it can be dangerous terrain to get lost in, especially at night. Note that alcohol and narcotics are illegal in Hampi, and possession can get you into trouble.

outer 'musical' pillars reverberate when tapped, but authorities have placed them out of tourists' bounds for fear of further damage, so no more do-re-mi. Don't miss the temple's showcase piece: the ornate **stone chariot** that stands in the temple courtyard, whose wheels were once capable of turning.

Retain your ticket for same-day admission into the Zenana Enclosure and Elephant Stables in the Royal Centre.

Sule Bazaar & Achyutaraya Temple   HISTORIC SITE
Halfway along the path from Hampi Bazaar to the Vittala Temple, a track to the right leads over the rocks to deserted Sule Bazaar, one of ancient Hampi's principal centres of commerce. At the southern end of this area is the Achyutaraya Temple. Its isolated location at the foot of Matanga Hill makes it quietly atmospheric, doubly so since it is visited by few tourists.

Royal Centre   HISTORIC SITE
While it can be accessed by a 2km foot trail from the Achyutaraya Temple, the Royal Centre is best reached via the Hampi-Kamalapuram road. It's a flatter area compared to the rest of Hampi, where the boulders have been shaved off to create stone walls. A number of Hampi's major sites stand here, within the walled ladies' quarters called the Zenana Enclosure (Indian/foreigner ₹10/250; ⊙8.30am-5.30pm). There's the Lotus Mahal, a delicately designed pavilion which was supposedly the queen's recreational mansion. The Lotus Mahal overlooks the Elephant Stables, a grand building with domed chambers where state elephants once resided. Your ticket is valid for same-day admission to the Vittala Temple.

Further south, you'll find various temples and elaborate waterworks, including the Underground Shiva Temple (⊙8.30am-5.30pm) and the Queen's Bath (⊙8.30am-5.30pm), deceptively plain on the outside but amazing within.

Archaeological Museum   MUSEUM
(Kamalapuram;₹5; ⊙10am-5pm Sat-Thu) The archaeological museum has well-displayed collections of sculptures from local ruins, Neolithic tools, 16th-century weaponry and a large floor model of the Vijayanagar ruins.

🛏 Sleeping

There's little to choose between many of the basic guesthouses in Hampi Bazaar and Virupapur Gaddi, some of which have lately undergone refitting to attract upmarket travellers. The only government-run hotel (with a legal beer bar and a non-veg restaurant) is in Kamalapuram. Note that prices can shoot up by 50% or more during Christmas, and drop just as dramatically in the low season (April to September) and that, since many Hampi Bazaar guesthouses are tiny operations, it can be a good idea to book in advance.

HAMPI BAZAAR

TOP CHOICE Padma Guest House   GUESTHOUSE $
(☎241331; padmaguesthouse@gmail.com; d from ₹700; ❊) In a quiet corner of Hampi Bazaar, the astute and amiable Padma has been quietly expanding her empire since we were last here. The basic but squeaky clean rooms are a pleasant deviation from Hampi's usual offerings, and those on the first floor have good views of the Virupaksha Temple. New rooms have been added to the west, with creature comforts (TV and AC) previously unheard of in Hampi. Well done, says 'Lovely Planet'.

Gopi Guest House   GUESTHOUSE $
(☎241695; kirangopi2002@yahoo.com; d ₹450-1200; ❊@) Centrally located amid the bustle of Hampi Bazaar, this pleasant dive continues to provide commendable service to travellers. The new block is quite upscale by Hampi's standards, with en suite rooms fronted by a sun-kissed terrace. The rooftop cafe – with a lovely view of the Virupaksha Temple – is a nice place to hang out.

Pushpa Guest House   GUESTHOUSE $
(☎241440; d from ₹600) This place was putting finishing touches to its terrace rooms during research, many of which already sported flowery pink walls and tiled floors. There is an extremely cordial family playing host, and a lovely sit-out on the 1st floor.

Shanthi Guest House   GUESTHOUSE $
(☎241568; s/d ₹300/350, without bathroom ₹250/400) An oldie but a goodie, Shanthi offers a peaceful courtyard with a swing chair,

and has plastic creepers and colourful posters of a hundred gods decorating its basic rooms. There's a small souvenir shop at the entrance that operates on an honour system.

Ranjana Guest House GUESTHOUSE $
(☑241696; d with/without AC ₹900/700; ✳) Almost on a par with Padma next door, this place also prides itself on well-appointed rooms; those on the terrace have killer views. There are a few cheapies adjoining the family quarters downstairs.

Rama Guest House GUESTHOUSE $
(☑241962; d ₹500-700) Sitting close to the river, this place seems a popular option with Bengaluru's young weekenders. Some rooms are a little low on light, though adequately appointed for a budget dig.

Vicky's GUESTHOUSE $
(☑241694; vikkyhampi@yahoo.co.in; d ₹450; @) A large operation done up in pop purple and green, with tiled floors, internet access and rooftop cafe. Fix the rate firmly while booking.

Rocky Guest House GUESTHOUSE $
(☑241951; rockyhampi@yahoo.co.in; d ₹500) A comfy option opposite Gopi, with clean rooms, friendly management and a travel desk.

Archana Guest House GUESTHOUSE $
(☑241547; addihampi@yahoo.com; d from ₹600) A quiet and cheerful establishment at the end of a lane, with decent rooms.

VIRUPAPUR GADDI
Many travellers prefer the tranquil atmosphere of Virupapur Gaddi, across the river to the north of Hampi Bazaar. A small boat (₹10) frequently shuttles across the river from 7am to 6pm. During the monsoon, the river runs high and ferry services may be suspended.

Hema Guest House GUESTHOUSE $
(☑9449103008; d ₹350) Laid-back and happening, this is one of Virupapur Gaddi's most popular spots, with rows of cute and comfy cottages in a shady grove. The informal river-view cafe is perpetually full with lazing tourists.

Shanthi GUESTHOUSE $
(☑9449260162; shanthi.hampi@gmail.com; cottage ₹800-1500; @) Shanthi's earth-themed, thatched cottages have rice-field, river and sunset views, with couch swings dangling in their front porches. The restaurant does good thalis and pizzas.

Mowgli GUESTHOUSE $$
(☑9448217588; hampimowgli@hotmail.com; d ₹600-1400; ✳@) A cluster of lilac cottages scattered around a sprawling garden complex with soothing views across the rice fields, Mowgli is a top-class chill-out spot this side of the river. It can fill up quickly over weekends, so book early.

KAMALAPURAM
Hotel Mayura Bhuvaneshwari HOTEL $$
(☑08394-241474; d from ₹1400; ✳) This tidy government operation, about 3km south of the Royal Centre, has well-appointed rooms (adorned with corny murals), a much-appreciated beer bar, a good multicuisine restaurant and ayurvedic sessions (from ₹1500) on request.

✗ Eating

Due to Hampi's religious significance, meat is usually off the menu and alcohol is banned; most establishments are open from 7am to 10pm.

 Mango Tree MULTICUISINE $
(mains ₹80-120) Creativity blends with culinary excellence at this rural-themed chill-out joint, spread out under the eponymous mango tree by the river. Walk through a banana plantation to get here, and try the special vegetable curry (₹100), the banana fritters (₹60) or the spaghetti with cashew nuts and cheese

DANCES WITH BEARS

About 15km south of Hampi, amid a scrubby undulated terrain, lies the **Daroji Sloth Bear Sanctuary** (₹25; ◷9.30am-6pm), which nurses a population of around 40 free-ranging sloth bears. It's possible to drive through the sanctuary and sight these furry creatures, along with leopards, wild boars, hyenas, jackals and others animals, as well as some exotic birds. Accommodation is in luxury cottages at the **Daroji Sloth Bear Resort** (per person incl full board Indian/foreigner from ₹3000/€70; ✳), located on the sanctuary's periphery. Book through **Jungle Lodges & Resorts Ltd** (☑080-25597944; www.junglelodges.com; Shrungar Shopping Complex, MG Rd, Bengaluru; ◷10am-5.30pm Mon-Sat). The resort can arrange pick-up and drop off from Hampi.

PANAJI & CENTRAL GOA HAMPI

(₹100). The terraced seating is perfect for whiling away a lazy afternoon, book in hand.

New Shanthi MULTICUISINE $
(mains ₹90-140) A hippie vibe, complete with trance music and acid-blue lights, hangs over this popular option serving Mexican, Italian and Indian regulars, with cookies and crumbles on the side. A good range of teas (jasmine, lemongrass and herbal) are on offer.

Durga Huts CAFE $
(mains ₹70-90) Clearly a hit with music lovers. Prem Joshua's fusion tracks get heavy airplay here, and there are a few guitars and drums on standby for an impromptu jam session. The food is of passable quality.

❶ Information

Aspiration Stores (◷10am-1pm & 4-8pm) Good for book guides. Try *Hampi* by John M Fritz and George Michell, a good architectural study.

Canara Bank (◷11am-2pm Mon-Tue & Thu-Fri, 11am-12.30pm Sat) Changes currency and has an ATM.

Hampi Heritage Gallery (◷10am-1pm & 3-6pm) Books and photo albums on Hampi's history and architecture, plus walking tours for ₹250.

Sree Rama Cyber Cafe (per hr ₹40; ◷7am-11pm) Has printing and data burning facilities.

Tourist office (☏241339; ◷10am-5.30pm Sat-Thu) Arranges guides for ₹300/600 for a half/full day.

❶ Getting There & Away

From Goa, private buses to Hampi (with a variety of comfort levels) run regularly throughout high season from Panaji, Margao and a number of beach resorts. Drop into a local travel agent for your most up-to-date options. Prices are around the ₹800 range and most buses are sleepers, though don't expect much sleep, what with potholed roads and tea stops throughout the night.

Some of these buses will drop you at the bus stand in Hampi Bazaar itself, but others may drop you in Hospet, a chaotic, workaday Indian town if ever there was one. From here, you can take a bus to Hampi Bazaar. The first bus from Hospet (₹12, 30 minutes, half-hourly) is at 6.30am; the last to Hospet leaves Hampi Bazaar at 8.30pm. Alternatively, an autorickshaw between Hospet and Hampi costs around ₹200.

Hospet is also Hampi's nearest train station.

❶ Getting Around

Once you've seen the main sights in Hampi, exploring the rest of the ruins by bicycle is the thing to do. The key monuments are haphazardly signposted all over the site; while they're not quite adequate, you shouldn't get lost. Bicycles cost about ₹30 per day in Hampi Bazaar; mopeds can be hired for around ₹250, plus petrol (₹70 per litre). To cross the river, load your vehicle onto a boat for an extra ₹10.

Walking is the only way to see all the nooks and crannies, but expect to cover at least 7km just to see the major ruins. Autorickshaws and taxis are available for sightseeing, and will drop you as close to each of the major ruins as they can. A five-hour autorickshaw tour costs ₹500.

Organised tours depart from Hospet; see opposite for details.

Around Hampi

ANEGUNDI

Across the Tungabhadra River, about 5km northeast of Hampi Bazaar, sits Anegundi, an ancient fortified village that's part of the Hampi World Heritage Site but pre-dates Hampi by way of human habitation. Gifted with a landscape similar to Hampi, quainter Anegundi has been spared the blight of commercialisation, which is why it remains a chosen getaway for those who want to soak up the local atmosphere without having to put up with the touristy vibe.

❂ Sights & Activities

Mythically referred to as Kishkinda, the kingdom of the monkey gods, Anegundi retains many of its historic monuments, such as sections of its defensive wall and gates, and the Ranganatha Temple (◷dawn-dusk) devoted to Rama.

Hanuman Temple HINDU TEMPLE
(◷dawn-dusk) The whitewashed Hanuman Temple, accessible by a 570-step climb up the Anjanadri Hill, has fine views of the rugged terrain around. Many believe this is the birthplace of Hanuman, the Hindu monkey god who was Rama's devotee and helped him in his mission against Ravana. The hike up is pleasant, though you'll be courted by impish monkeys, and within the temple you'll find a large group of chillum-puffing sadhus.

Kishkinda Trust CULTURAL PROGRAMS, OUTDOOR ADVENTURE
(TKT; ☏08533-267777; www.thekishkindatrust.org) The Kishkinda Trust, an NGO that promotes sustainable tourism in Anegundi, organises soft adventure activities such as rock-climbing, camping, trekking and boating around the village. Equipment and trained instructors are provided. A slew of

THE KISHKINDA TRUST

Since 1995, the Kishkinda Trust (www.thekishkindatrust.org) has been involved in promoting rural tourism, sustainable development and women's empowerment in Anegundi, as well as preserving the architectural, cultural and living heritage of the Hampi World Heritage Site. The first project in 1997 created a cottage industry of crafts using locally produced cloth, banana fibre and river grass. It now employs over 600 women, and the attractive crafts produced are marketed in ethnic product outlets across India.

For the benefit of tourists, TKT has a team featuring some of the best guides in the region, who are fluent in English and know the terrain like the back of their hands. Exploring the region while riding pillion on their motorcycles can be a truly enriching experience. Guides charge ₹300/600 for a half/full day. Contact the trust for details.

cultural programs, including performing arts sessions, and classical and folk music concerts are also conducted from time to time.

🛏 Sleeping

Anegundi has several homestays managed by The Kishkinda Trust. Contact the trust for bookings. Guesthouses listed can provide meals upon prior notice.

Naidile Guest House GUESTHOUSE **$$**
(d ₹1700) A charmingly rustic air hangs over this renovated village home in the heart of Anegundi, where you can savour all the sights and sounds of the ancient village. It can sleep up to five people.

Peshagar Guest House GUESTHOUSE **$**
(d incl breakfast ₹900) Six simple rooms done up in rural motifs open around a pleasant common area in this new guesthouse. There's also a sumptuous breakfast platter available.

Champa Guest House GUESTHOUSE **$**
(d incl breakfast ₹800) Champa offers basic but pleasant accommodation in two rooms, and is looked after by an affable village family.

Hoova Craft Shop & Café CAFE **$**
(mains ₹50-70; ⏱9.30am-5pm Mon-Sat, to 2pm Sun) A lovely place for an unhurried meal. You can also shop for sundry souvenirs made by the village's women.

ℹ Getting There & Away

Anegundi can be reached by crossing the river on a coracle (₹10) from the pier east of the Vittala Temple. The concrete bridge that was being erected across the river has mysteriously collapsed, taking with it all hopes of cycling across, though you can take your bike on a coracle for an extra ₹10.

You can also reach Anegundi by taking a bus (₹25, one hour) from Hospet.

Hospet

📞08394 / POP 164,200

This busy regional centre is the transport hub for Hampi; some travellers find themselves a little overwhelmed by the chaos upon exiting, tired and sore, their night bus from Goa. The Muslim festival of **Muharram** brings things to life in this otherwise dull transit town; otherwise, with Hampi barely 30 minutes away, there's really no reason to linger here.

ℹ Information

SBI, HDFC Bank and ICICI Bank have ATMs along the main drag and Shanbagh Circle. Internet joints are common, with connections costing ₹40 per hour.

KSTDC tourist office (📞221008; Shanbagh Circle; ⏱10am-5.30pm Mon-Sat) Offers an uninspiring Hampi tour (₹250) for groups of 10 or more.

ℹ Getting There & Away

Bus

Hospet's bus stand has services to Hampi from Bay 10 every half-hour (₹12, 30 minutes). Some overnight buses to and from Goa pick up and drop off passengers here.

Train

Hospet's **train station** is a ₹20 autorickshaw ride from town. To reach here from Goa, the Howrah Express, which runs every Tuesday, Thursday, Friday and Saturday leaves Vasco da Gama at 7.10am, and Margao at 7.45am, and arrives in Hospet at 2.53pm (sleeper/3AC/2AC ₹170/447/609).

The Amaravathi Express runs on Tuesday, Thursday, Friday and Saturday, departing Hospet at 6.30am and arriving in Magdaon (Margao) at 1.55pm and Vasco da Gama at 3pm. The Kcg Ypr Express runs Tuesday to Sunday, departing Hospet at 6.35am and arriving in Magdaon at 1.55pm and Vasco da Gama at 3pm.

Palolem & South Goa

Includes »

Margao 151
Vasco Da Gama 161
Colva 166
Benaulim 169
Varca, Cavelossim &
Mobor 171
Chaudi 177
Palolem 177
Colomb 181
Patnem 182
Rajbag 183
Cotigao Wildlife
Sanctuary 183
Galgibag 183
Polem 184
Gokarna 184

Best Places to Eat

» Home, Patnem (p182)

» Capo Nero, Colomb (p181)

» Blue Whale, Mobor (p174)

Best Places to Stay

» Micky's Huts & Rooms, Patnem (p182)

» Casa Susegad, Loutolim (p158)

» Park Hyatt, Arossim (p164)

» Sevas, Palolem (p179)

Why Go?

South Goa, bounded to the north by the wide Zuari River and to the south by the neighbouring state of Karnataka, is the quieter, shyer sister of her older, party-friendly North Goa sibling. Though resorts have made it here too – uncharming Colva and package-holiday-friendly Cavelossim being the two biggest – the pace never reaches the frenetic levels of Calangute or Candolim further north, and resorts still peter out quickly into palm groves and paddy fields.

Along this stretch you'll still be able to find the beach solitude you're seeking, along with busy, beloved, crescent-sanded and easy-paced Palolem. The coast is punctuated with top-end five-star resorts which, for all their sins, have managed to keep the shoreline free from midrange con-crete-block development. Inland you'll find some fabulous historic sights, bucolic bliss and Goa's most easily accessible wildlife reserve, making the south a redolent, rewarding and re-energising place to base yourself.

When to Go

From November to February, the weather in Goa's balmy south is just perfect. Not too hot, a light breeze, cloudless days and warm evenings bring the bulk of the tourists to the area. If you want to embrace the crowds, festivities, and high, high prices (think double high-season rates or more) come for Christmas and New Year. If you prefer low-key, come in October or March, or brave the increasing heat of April and May, when tourist services are shutting up shop, but the monsoon is still to come.

Margao

📞 0832 / POP 94,400

The capital of Salcete province, Margao (also known as Madgaon) is, along with coastal Vasco da Gama, the main population centre of South Goa and is a happy, bustling market town of a manageable size for getting things done. If you're basing yourself in Goa's south, it's a useful place for shopping, organising bus and train tickets, checking emails or simply enjoying the busy energy of big-city India in manageable small-town form.

Though the modern town favours commerce over culture, this wasn't always the case. Before the Portuguese conquests of the 16th century onward, Margao was a centre for both pilgrimage and learning, with dozens of Hindu temples and a library of thousands upon thousands of volumes. However, all traces were destroyed by the Portuguese, as Margao became absorbed into their 17th-century Novas Conquistas (New Conquests).

Today, it nevertheless makes for a nice wander, while its small Shiva temple, just south of the covered market, still attracts Hindus each evening, to light candles and incense, and leave offerings of garlanded marigolds and coconuts to the ever-popular god. If you happen to be in town towards Christmas, Margao's Christians also hold a large fair to celebrate the Feast of Our Lady of the Immaculate Conception around 8 December.

Margao's town centre, ranging around the Municipal Gardens, is quite small and compact, with its shops, restaurants, ATMs and covered market all within easy reach. To the north of town, the old Portuguese-flavoured Largo de Igreja district, with its Church of the Holy Spirit, is worth a stroll; about 1km north further is the main (Kadamba) bus station.

About 1.5km southeast of the Municipal Gardens is Margao's train station (also known as Madgaon train station), a main stop on the north-to-south Konkan Railway (see p233), which replaced the now-defunct Old Margao train station, just to the east of the flyover on the south end of town.

⊙ Sights & Activities

Church of the Holy Spirit   CHURCH

Margao's main church also comprises probably its most interesting attraction, first built in 1565, on the site of an important Hindu temple. Before demolition started on the temple, local Hindus managed to rescue the statue of the god Damodara, to whom the building was dedicated. It was secretly moved to a new site in the village of Zambaulim, around 30km southeast, where there is still a large temple today.

However, the new church didn't last long and was burned to the ground by Muslim raiders the same year it was built. It was soon replaced and a seminary was established, but both were subsequently destroyed, again by Muslim forces, after which the seminary was moved to Rachol, to the northeast.

The present church, built in 1675, has lasted rather longer. It remains in use as a parish church and is finely decorated inside. The impressive *reredos* (ornamental screen) is dedicated to the Virgin Mary, rising from ground level to the high ceiling, made more distinguished by the gilded and carved archway that stands in front of it. The church doors are usually unlocked throughout the day, and access is via the side entrance on the northern side. Outside, in the centre of a dusty square, nowadays most often used for volleyball games, stands a 17th-century cross, atop a pedestal carved with images depicting the story of Easter.

Largo de Igreja   AREA

Largo de Igreja, the area around the Church of the Holy Spirit, features a number of traditional old Portuguese mansions, in various states of decay or repair. The most famous is the grand, 1790 Sat Burnzam Ghor (Seven Gabled House). Originally, as its name suggests, there were seven of the distinctive high-peaked gables, of which only three remain, though it remains an impressive edifice. Built by Sebastiao da Silva, private secretary to the viceroy, it sports an especially beautiful private chapel, dedicated to St Anna, and noteworthy for being the first private chapel in which a Goan family was permitted to privately perform Mass. Its upstairs salons are filled with a stunning assortment of porcelain, chandeliers, marble and damask. Though it's not open daily to the public, your best bet to arrange a visit is to contact the GTDC (p230) about a tour.

Monte Hill   AREA

Located about 500m southeast of Sat Burnzam Ghor and a fair climb up Monte Hill, Margao's only hill, Mount Church is a simple whitewashed building, faced by a

PALOLEM & SOUTH GOA MARGAO

Palolem & South Goa Highlights

1 Laze the weeks, or months, away on upbeat **Palolem Beach** (p177)

2 March around **Margao's market** to pick up spices, coffee, bangles and stop off for a chai or two (p156)

3 Stay the night in one of **Loutolim's historic homes** (p158)

4 Hunker down on low-key **Patnem Beach**, far quieter than its Palolem neighbour (p182)

5 Linger in **Agonda** on silent sands, where even the nightlife goes to bed just after sunset (p176)

6 Head out into the hinterland to seek out the **Usgalimal Rock Carvings** (p160)

7 Explore a colonial *palácio* (palace) relic or two in the village of **Chandor** (p159)

8 Spend the afternoon with four-legged friends, playing with the puppies at the **GAWT dogs' home** in Curchorem (p172)

9 Seek out your own patch of empty sands at Mobor's **Blue Whale** (p174)

10 Head on down to pilgrim-heavy **Gokarna** for a just-out-of-state adventure (p184)

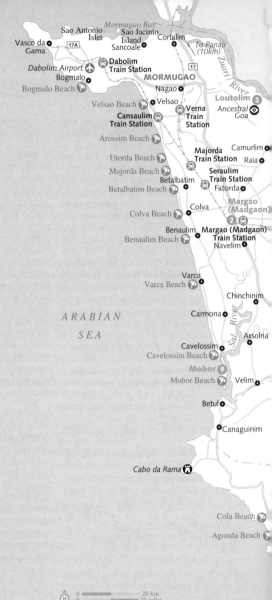

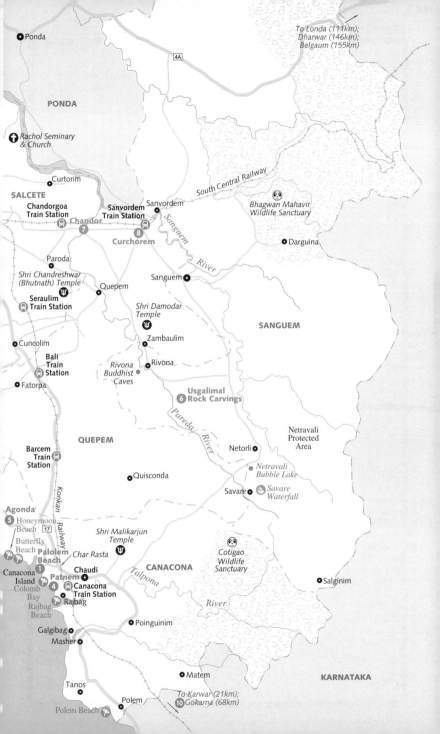

Margao (Madgaon)

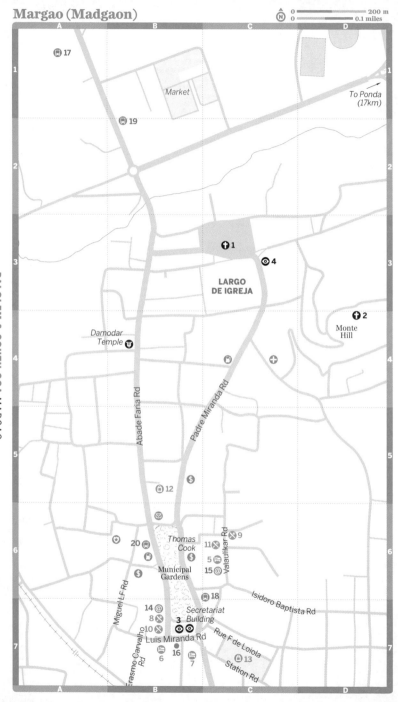

PALOLEM & SOUTH GOA MARGAO

Margao (Madgaon)

◉ Sights
1 Church of the Holy Spirit C3
2 Mount Church D4
3 Municipal Library B7
4 Sat Burnzam Ghor C3

🛏 Sleeping
5 Hotel Tanish C6
6 Margao Residency B7
7 Om Shiv Hotel B7

✕ Eating
8 Casa Penguim de Gelados..................... B7
9 Gaylin... C6
10 Longhuino's B7
11 Tato... C6

🛍 Shopping
12 Golden Heart Emporium B5
13 MC New Market...................................... C7

ℹ Information
14 Cyberlink B7
15 Grace Cyber Cafe.................................. C6
16 Maharaja Travels................................... B7

ℹ Transport
17 Bus Stand.. A1
18 Buses to Palolem, Colva,
   Benaulim & Betul C6
19 Kadamba Bus Stand B2
20 Old Bus Stand.. B6

similarly diminutive piazza cross. A detour up here is worth it for the view: from the shade of a grove of palm trees in front of the church, it's possible to see straight across the coastal plain to the beaches of Colva and Benaulim.

Municipal Library   LIBRARY
(⊙8am-8pm Mon-Fri, 9am-noon & 4-7pm Sat & Sun) On the west side of the Secretariat Building, you'll find respite from the sun in the dusty Municipal Library, which houses some good books about Goa. Don't miss the library's newspaper reading room, in which you're required to collect your newspaper at the counter and then sit in the seat designated only for readers of that particular paper; you'll be pleased to know it's a 'No Spitting and No Smoking Zone'.

Canopy Ecotours   TOURS
(⌚2710650, 9764261711, 9764052225; www.canopy goa.com; trips per person from ₹1000) If you're a fan of our feathered friends, are keen to spot crocs, or are interested in getting to grips with Goan heritage, venture out into the wilds to meet them with Canopy, an environmentally sensitive operation based in Margao, also offering unusual butterfly-spotting, dragonfly-spotting and wildlife photography trips. Its outings will take you to remote corners of the Western Ghats, and are highly recommended for an alternative – and ecologically minded – introduction to the Goan countryside. Canopy also runs a set of 10 rustic huts on the outskirts of Bhagwan Mahavir Wildlife Sanctuary, and can organise rock climbing, rappelling and other adventure activities.

🛏 Sleeping

Margao doesn't have the range of accommodation that you'd expect in a town of this size, and with the beaches of the south beckoning, there's really no pressing reason to stay here. Most of the budget options in town are really of the rock-bottom variety: a few are strung between the Municipal Gardens and an area near the old train station, in case you're feeling hardy enough to inspect a few. Otherwise, the three choices listed present solid value for a night's sojourn.

Hotel Tanish   HOTEL $$
(⌚2735656; hoteltanishgoa@gmail.com; Reliance Trade Centre, Valaulikar Rd; s/d without AC ₹900/1100, deluxe r/suite ₹1500/1800) Without doubt the best place to stay in town, this top-floor hotel offers great views of the surrounding countryside, with stylish, well-equipped rooms. Suites come with a bathtub, a big TV and a view all the way to Colva; just make sure you get an outside-facing room, as some overlook the mall interior.

Om Shiv Hotel   HOTEL $$
(⌚2710294; www.omshivhotel.com; Cine Lata Rd; s/d/ste with AC from ₹1200/1400/2500; ❄) In a bright yellow building tucked away behind the Bank of India, Om Shiv does a fine line in 'executive' rooms, which all have air conditioning and balcony. It's mostly worth recommending, however, for the suites, which have exceptional views, or as a back-up if Hotel Tanish happens to be full.

PALOLEM & SOUTH GOA MARGAO

Margao Residency
HOTEL $$

(☎2715528; Luis Miranda Rd; s/d ₹1075, d with AC ₹1220; ❋) The omnipresent GTDC's outfit in town, this is an at-a-push reasonable mid-range choice, with clean, fairly comfy rooms and a great central location just opposite Longhuino's. Other GTDC hotels and a vast range of tours can be booked at reception.

✗ Eating

TOP CHOICE Longuinho's
MULTICUISINE $

(Luis Miranda Rd; mains ₹80-170) Every day since 1950, quaint old Longhuino's has been serving up tasty Indian and Chinese dishes, popular with locals and tourists alike. To thoroughly hark back to the '50s, order the tongue roast for ₹95 (and that doesn't mean a very spicy masala) and follow it up with a rum ball (₹25) or a 'Bolo sans Rival' cream cake (₹25), and look out for daily Goan specials, which include *ambot tik* (a slightly sour but fiery curry dish) and *balchao* (a spicy meat curry). The food might not be tip-tip-top (though the Chinese is pretty good) but the atmosphere is well worth it.

Casa Penguim de Gelados
SNACKS, INDIAN $

(opposite Municipal Gardens; veg thali ₹50; ⊙8.30am-8pm Mon-Sat) Tea and ice creams are really the thing here, but this clean, fan-cooled place also does a decent vegetarian thali and an array of dosas and *idlis* (South Indian spongy, round, fermented rice cakes). If you're hungry, go for the special veg thali for ₹75.

Tato
INDIAN $

(Apna Bazaar Complex, off Valaulikar Rd; thalis from ₹60; ⊙Mon-Sat) Down a small street east of the Municipal Gardens is this excellent, and highly fragrant, vegetarian restaurant popular with lunching locals. If you're indecisive, order a thali (traditional South Indian all-you-can-eat meal served on a stainless-steel dish), though the *paneer chilli* (spicy Indian cheese) is the manager's personal favourite. It costs slightly more to eat upstairs in the icy air-conditioning, but the fan-cooled ground floor is perfectly fine too.

Gaylin
CHINESE $

(Valaulikar Rd; mains from ₹60; ⊙noon-3pm & 6.30-11pm) Hidden behind opaque glass doors decorated with dragon motifs, you'll find generous, garlicky renditions of Chinese favourites dispensed by friendly Darjeeling-derived owners, with recipes suitably spiced up to cater to resilient Indian palates.

Shopping

TOP CHOICE Golden Heart Emporium
BOOKSTORE

(☎2734250; Confidant House, Abade Faria Rd; ⊙10am-1.30pm & 4-7.30pm Mon-Sat) One of Goa's very best bookshops, crammed with fiction, nonfiction, children's books, and illustrated volumes on the state's food, architecture and history. It also stocks otherwise hard-to-get titles by local Goan authors. It's situated down a little lane off Abade Faria Rd, on the right-hand side as you're heading north.

MC New Market
MARKET

Margao's crowded, covered canopy of colourful stalls (perfect for self-caterers) is a fun place to wander around, sniffing spices, sampling soaps and browsing the household merchandise.

🛈 Information

There are plenty of banks offering currency exchange and 24-hour ATMs ranged around the Municipal Gardens, and on the western extension of Luis Miranda Rd. GTDC trips (see p230) can be booked at the front desk of the Margao Residency hotel, also on Luis Miranda Rd.

Cyberlink (Caro Centre, Abade Faria Rd; per hr ₹40; ⊙8.30am-7.30pm Mon-Sat) Reasonably swift internet access on the central square. Be sure to heed the notice that requests you to 'Register yourself before sitting on the PC'. Fax and international call services are also available.

Grace Cyber Cafe (1st fl, Reliance Trade Centre, Valaulikar Rd; per hr ₹20; ⊙9.30am-7.30pm Mon-Sat) A spanking new place in the centre of town, Grace has reliable, fast connections and a number of other services including CD writing and DVD direct from USB.

Apollo Victor Hospital (Hospicio; ☎2705664; Padre Miranda Rd) Has a casualty department and a well-stocked 24-hour pharmacy. It's about 500m northeast of the Municipal Gardens.

Maharaja Travels (☎2732744; Luis Miranda Rd; ⊙9am-1pm & 3-6pm Mon-Sat) A great hole-in-the-wall place for long-distance bus tickets; note that opening hours are very, *very* flexible.

Main post office (⊙9am-1.30pm & 2.30-5pm Mon-Sat) On the north side of the municipal gardens. The post office can also arrange Western Union money transfers.

Thomas Cook (☎2714768; Mabai Hotel Bldg; ⊙9.30am-6pm Mon-Sat) A reliable place to change money and perform money transfers, on the eastern side of the Municipal Gardens.

TAKE THE LOW ROAD

Take your moped, your Enfield Bullet, your Ford Ambassador taxi or your little hired Hyundai and hit the open road – avoiding cows, pedestrians, careening trucks, chickens, dogs, bicycles, pigs, water buffalo and the assorted other obstacles that make Goan roads something of a thrilling ride. Take your time, take a hot chai here and there, and savour the stunning scenery – and a local lunch at your own, newly discovered roadside cafe – on one of the state's most gorgeous southern stretches of pot-hole-plentiful tarmac.

» **Cavelossim to Agonda** Hop aboard the rusty rub-a-dub ferry at Cavelossim (p172), and meander the coastal road – with stunning views down to the sea – stopping off at windswept Cabo da Rama fort (p175), all the way down to sleepy, seaside Agonda (p176).

» **Cotigao Wildlife Sanctuary** Though its roads are bumpier than most, a trip out along the lanes of this sanctuary (p183), towards the Western Ghats, takes you through tiny villages, tracts of forest and farmland, and miles of untouched countryside, complete with haystacks and oxen pulling the plough.

» **Quepem to Usgalimal** Delve deep into the Goan hinterland with a drive out from busy little Quepem's Portuguese palace (p160) to Usgalimal's ancient rock carvings (p160), hidden away along the course of a lazy stream.

» **Colva to Velsao** Head north from busy beachfront Colva (p166), up the scenic coast road past dozens of crumbling Portuguese palaces. Stop off here and there to discover deserted stretches of beach, and climb up to Velsao's Our Lady of Remedios chapel (p164) for the view back down.

» **Vasco da Gama to the NH17** Hug tight to the southern bank of the Zuari River, heading east from Vasco da Gama (p161) to take an interesting drive past shipbuilders, rusting trawler hulks and a couple of tiny riverine islands.

» **Heading east to Netravali** Embrace the spirit of adventure, with a jaunt down south off the NH17 highway to the 'bubble lake' and a hidden waterfall at Netravali (p182). You'll likely get lost several times along the way, but getting there, through thick forest, is more than half the fun.

❶ Getting There & Around

Bus

Local buses arrive and depart from the **Kadamba bus stand** about 2km north of the Municipal Gardens. Many services also stop at the old bus stand in the town centre. Buses to Palolem, Colva, Benaulim and Betul stop both at the Kadamba bus stand and at the bus stop on the east side of the Municipal Gardens. Services run to no particular timetable, but are cheap and frequent.

Though there are daily public buses to Mumbai (₹800, 16 hours), a better bet is to take a long-distance private bus, which is more comfortable, quicker and costs about the same. You'll find booking offices all over town; Maharaja Travels is one helpful choice.

Private buses to Mumbai (AC/non-AC ₹850/750, 12 hours) and Hampi (sleeper/luxury ₹850/750, eight hours) all leave from the bus stand opposite the Kadamba bus station.

Taxi

Taxis are plentiful around the Municipal Gardens and Kadamba bus stand, and are a quick and comfortable way to reach any of Goa's beaches, including Palolem (₹700), Calangute (₹1000), Anjuna (₹1100) and Arambol (₹1700). Be sure to wear your best bargaining cap for negotiating your fare.

Train

Margao's well-organised train station (also known as Madgaon train station), about 2km south of town, serves both the Konkan Railway and local South Central Railways routes, and is the main hub for trains from Mumbai to Goa. Its **reservation hall** (⊙8am-2pm & 2.15-8pm Mon-Sat, 8am-2pm Sun) is on the 1st floor. See p233 for details of Konkan Railway services. It's also very useful for journeys by rail to the seaside pilgrim town of Gokarna (see p186); it's less than a two-hour hop if you take the train.

Outside the station you'll find a very useful pre-paid taxi stand; use this to get to your beachside destination and you'll be assured a fair price. Alternatively, a taxi or autorickshaw to or from the town centre to the station should cost around ₹80.

Around Margao

As tempting as it is to head directly west to the beach from Margao, the area to the east and northeast of town is a rich patchwork of rice paddy fields, lush countryside, somnolent rural villages, superb colonial houses, and a smattering of historical and religious sites. With a day to spare and a hired motorcycle, car or taxi, you can cover most of the sights of interest, and still get back to the beach in time for your happy-hour cocktail.

RACHOL SEMINARY & CHURCH

Built in 1580 atop an old Muslim fort, the Rachol Seminary and Church stands near the village of Raia, 7km from Margao. Although it's not officially open to visitors, you'll likely be able to find a trainee priest to show you around its beautiful church and cloistered theological college.

Built by the Jesuits, the seminary soon became a noted centre of learning, graced with one of India's first printing presses. Among the seminary's most famous members were Father Thomas Stevens, who by 1616 had busily translated the Bible into Konkani and Marathi, to help with the conversion of the locals, and Father Ribeiro, who produced the first Portuguese-Konkani dictionary in 1626.

Work on the church (dedicated to Jesuit founder St Ignatius Loyola) began in 1576, four years before the founding of the seminary, and it has been maintained in excellent condition. Its splendid gilded *reredos* fills the wall above the altar, featuring an image of St Constantine, the first Roman emperor to convert to Christianity; fragments of St Constantine's bones are on display near the main doorway. One of the side altars also displays the original Menino Jesus (see p168), which was first installed in the Colva church, before being taken up to Rachol amid much controversy and general hoo-hah.

Not much evidence remains of the old Muslim fort, though the archway spanning the road up to the seminary is one remnant, as is the still-discernible old moat at the bottom of the hill. Bits of Hindu sculpture also grace the hallways of the theological college, as does an ancient water tank beneath its central courtyard.

LOUTOLIM
☎ 0832

Architectural relics of Goa's grand Portuguese heritage can be seen around the unhurried village of Loutolim, some 10km northeast of Margao. The village hosts a number of impressive Portuguese mansions but just one, Casa Araujo Alvares (₹125; ☺10am-6pm), which was built in 1757, is officially open to the public. It may not be as brimming with atmosphere as some of the other examples you'll find scattered across the state, but it's still well worth looking in on. Though Loutolim's other mansion masterpieces (Miranda House, Roque Caetan House and Salvador Costs House among them) aren't officially open to the public, you never know – linger longingly for long enough outside the great wrought gates, and you might just be invited inside. Start out up at the central village square, with its scruffy, brooding whitewashed church, and wander from there.

If you're keen for high kitsch, be sure to drop in at Ancestral Goa (☎2777034; ₹20, camera ₹10; ☺9am-6.30pm), which encompasses a host of attractions including – but not limited to – 'Big Foot', a wishing rock, Mini Goa (as if the full-sized version weren't mini enough), and the 'longest laterite sculpture' in India.

Big Foot aside, the best reason to visit Loutolim is to bask in slow, sleepy Goan village life and gaze at the privately owned jewels of mansions scattered along the foliage-thick lanes. Without your own wheels, Loutolim is best accessed by taxi from Margao; a one-way fare should be about ₹140.

🛏 Sleeping

TOP CHOICE Casa Susegad GUESTHOUSE $$$
(☎6483368; www.casasusegad.com; s/d from ₹3750/5000; ✸☀) With just four lovely, antique-filled rooms, this place run by a friendly British couple makes a wonderful place to wind down, with an organic vegetable garden supplying delicious dinners. Parakeets, monkeys, cats and dogs (they're keen supporters of the worthy Goa Animal Welfare Trust) inhabit the extensive gardens, while a swimming pool glitters on the terrace.

Villa Verde VILLA $$$
(☎6484667; www.villaverdegoa.com; s/d ₹3000/5000; ✸@☀) A beautiful Portuguese villa, lovingly restored to house just five lucky guests in three bedrooms, travellers rave about the gracious hospitality (provided by the lovely Carmita), along with the surroundings, the pool, the home-cooked meals

and the generally magical feel of this beautiful, tranquil place. Sadly, however, small children aren't allowed.

CHANDOR

About 15km east of Margao, on the border between Salcete and Quepem *talukas* (districts), stands the small village of Chandor, a higgledy-piggledy collection of once-grand Portuguese mansions, arranged along a dusty main road, which now sees more long-distance trucks than grand, embroidered palanquins. It's a photographer's dream, with its paint-peeling gables – many topped with typically Portuguese carved wooden roosters – dripping ivy and the looming white Nossa Senhora de Belem church.

A kilometre east past the church, and open to the public, is the Fernandes House (☎2784245; ₹200; ⊙9am-6pm), whose original building dates back more than 500 years, while the Portuguese section was tacked on by the Fernandes family in 1821. The secret basement hideaway, full of gun holes and with an escape tunnel to the river, was used by the family to flee attackers.

Despite modern appearances, Chandor was once far more than a picturesque, but decrepit, countryside village. Between the late 6th and mid-11th centuries it was better known as Chandrapur, the most spectacular city on the Konkan coast. This was the grand seat of the ill-fated Kadamba dynasty (see p191) until 1054 when the rulers moved to a new, broad-harboured site at Govepuri, at modern-day Goa Velha. When Govepuri was levelled by the Muslims in 1312, the Kadambas briefly moved their seat of power back to Chandrapur, though it was not long before Chandrapur itself was sacked in 1327, and then its glory days were finally, definitively, over.

Few signs remain of once-glorious Chandrapur, though the village has an archaeological site, where the foundations of an 11th-century Hindu temple and a headless stone Nandi bull (the vehicle of Shiva) still mark the spot.

The best way to reach Chandor is with your own transport, or by taxi from Margao (₹350, round trip, including waiting time). On 6 January, Chandor hosts the colourful Feast of the Three Kings, during which local boys re-enact the arrival of the three kings from the Christmas story.

PALOLEM & SOUTH GOA AROUND MARGAO

CHANDOR'S COLONIAL JEKYLL & HYDE

Braganza House, built in the 17th century and stretching along one whole side of Chandor's village square, is possibly the best – and worst – example of what Goa's scores of once grand and glorious mansions have today become. Granted the land by the King of Portugal, the house was divided from the outset into the east and west wings, to house two sides of the same big family.

The West Wing (☎2784201; ⊙10am-5pm) belongs to one set of the family's descendants, the Menezes-Braganças, and is filled with gorgeous chandeliers, Italian marble floors and antique treasures from Macau, Portugal, China and Europe. The elderly, rather frail, Mrs Aida Menezes-Bragança nowadays lives here alone, but will show you around with the help of her formidable assistant. Between them, they struggle valiantly with the upkeep of a beautiful but needy house, whose grand history oozes from every inch of wall, floor and furniture.

Next door at the East Wing (☎2784227; ⊙10am-6pm), prepare for a shock. Owned by the Pereira-Braganza family, descendants of the other half of the family, it's as shabby and decaying as the other is still grand. Paint peels from windows; ceilings sag; antiques are mixed in willy-nilly (and atmospherically) with a jumble of cheap knick-knacks and seaside souvenirs. The high point here is the small family chapel, which contains a carefully hidden fingernail of St Francis Xavier (see p129), and even this – the chapel, not the fingernail – is beginning to show signs of neglect. You're unlikely to see a more stark architectural contrast at such close quarters for quite a while. It's a moving, if somewhat melancholy, experience.

Both homes are open daily, and there's almost always someone around to let you in. Though there are no official entry fees, the owners rely on contributions for the hefty costs of maintenance: ₹100 per visitor per house is reasonable, though anything extra would, of course, be welcome.

CURTORIM

About 5km north of Chandor is the small village of Curtorim, another of Goa's many peaceful pastoral places. If you're passing through, stop to have a look at the Church of St Alex, a large whitewashed affair with a rusty tin-roofed porch and a lovely, lavish interior, which looks out serenely onto a vast lily-studded lake. It's one of Goa's oldest churches and makes a grand spot to break a countryside journey.

QUEPEM

About 8km southeast of Chandor, in the busy small town of Quepem, stands the Palácio do Deão (☑2664029/9823175639; www.palaciododeao.com; ◷10am-5pm Sat-Thu). This recently renovated 18th-century palace, just opposite the Holy Cross Church, was once the home of the town's founder himself, and sits on the banks of the small Kushavati River, a tributary of the Pareda River.

Plans are afoot to create a cultural centre here, but for now the house and its beautiful, serene gardens make a great place for a stop-off between Chandor and the Usgalimal rock carvings further south. Call ahead to book a tour or arrange a delicious Portuguese-inspired lunch or afternoon tea on its lovely terrace. All donations are used to continue restoration work and eventually create a cultural centre here. Stop by the Church of the Holy Cross – the small, pretty church – across the way, while you're here.

A taxi from Margao, 14km away, will cost ₹550 round trip, including waiting time; the bus (₹10, every few minutes) stops just a few minutes' walk down the road.

SHRI DAMODAR TEMPLE

Approximately 12km southeast of Chandor and 22km from Margao, on the border of Quepem and Sanguem *talukas,* is the small village of Zambaulim, home to the Shri Damodar Temple.

Though the temple itself is uncompromisingly modern, the deity in its sanctum is anything but, having been rescued in 1565 from the main temple in Margao, which was destroyed by the Portuguese to make way for their Church of the Holy Spirit.

The ablutions area, built 200m back from the main buildings on the banks of the Kushavati River, is an ancient Hindu site, and its water – if you're feeling simultaneously brave and under the weather – is said to have medicinal properties.

RIVONA BUDDHIST CAVES

Continuing south from Zambaulim for about 3km, the road passes through Rivona, which consists of little more than a few houses spread out along the roadside. As the road leaves the village, curling first to the left and then right, there is a small sign on the left, pointing to Shri Santhsa Gokarn. A short way up the dirt track, which comes to an end at a tiny temple, the Rivona Buddhist caves (also called Pandava caves) are on the left. Look out for strips of red cloth, hung auspiciously from an old tamarind tree nearby. The main cave's entrance is just beside an ablutions tank and small well.

It's thought that the caves were occupied by Buddhist monks, who settled here some time in the 6th or 7th century AD. There's little to see, but the tiny compartments are an interesting reminder that religions other than Hinduism, Islam and Christianity also made it to Goa. There's a small staircase cut through the rock between the upper and lower levels of the caves. If you plan to have a poke about inside, you'll need a torch and be mindful to keep a very sharp eye out for snakes – the caves are teeming with these modern-day tenants.

USGALIMAL ROCK CARVINGS

One of Goa's least visited but most fascinating sights is tucked far into the depths of the countryside at Usgalimal, seeing only a teeny trickle of adventurous visitors and, so far, no busloads of tour groups whatsoever.

Make the effort to head out here and you'll be rewarded not only with some beautiful countryside driving, but also with a series of prehistoric petroglyphs (rock art), carved into the laterite-stone ground on the banks of the Kushavati River, and depicting various scenes including bulls, deer and antelope, a dancing woman, a peacock and 'triskelions' – a series of concentric circles thought by some archaeologists to have been a primitive means of measuring time.

These underfoot carvings are thought to be the work of one of Goa's earliest tribes, the Kush, and were only discovered by archaeologists in 1993, after being alerted to their existence by locals. The images are thought to have been created some 20,000 to 30,000 years ago, making them an important, if entirely unexploited, prehistoric site. In order for you to make out the carvings better, you'll likely have a helping hand from a local, who sits patiently at the site waiting to drizzle water from a plastic bottle into the grooves; he appreciates a tip for his efforts.

To get here, continue past Rivona for about 6km and keep an eye out for the circular green-and-red Archaeological Survey of India signs. An unsealed road off to the right of the main road leads 1.5km down to the river bank and carvings, passing a large abandoned ore pit to the left, its flood waters deep and luminescent.

SHRI CHANDRESHWAR (BHUTNATH) TEMPLE

Approximately 14km southeast of Margao near the village of Paroda, a number of hills rise out of the plain, the highest of which is Chandranath Hill (350m). At the top, in a small clearing stands the Shri Chandreshwar (Bhutnath) Temple, a small but attractive 17th-century building in a lovely, solitary setting.

Although the present buildings date from the 17th century, legend has it that there has been a temple here for almost 2500 years, since the moment a meteor hit the spot. The site is dedicated to Chandreshwar, an incarnation of Shiva who is worshipped here as 'Lord of the Moon'. Consequently it's laid out so that the light of the full moon shines into the sanctum and illuminates the glittering gold deity. At the rear of the shrine, two accessory stone deities keep Chandreshwar company: Parvati (Shiva's consort) to the west, and Ganesh (his son) to the east. It's said that when the moonlight falls on it, the shrine's lingam (phallic symbol of Shiva) oozes water.

Leaving through the side entrance there is another small shrine standing separately that is dedicated to the god Bhutnath, who is worshipped in the form of a simple stone pinnacle that sticks out of the ground.

To get here, you'll need your own transport, since buses don't service this road. Head to Paroda, and ask there for the turnoff that takes you up the narrow, winding hillside road. There's a small parking area near the top, from which the approach to the temple is via a steep flight of steps.

Vasco Da Gama

☑ 0832 / POP 150,000

Industrial Vasco da Gama is a busy port town, and was once a major transport hub for travellers until its train station was eclipsed by Margao's, further south. Situated at the base of the isthmus leading to Mormugao Harbour, Vasco sports both an oil refinery and Goa's biggest red-light district at Baina, where there's also a small (dirty) beach and a steady influx of sailors and truck drivers. The city also has a reputation for being the crime centre of Goa, largely because of its outlying shanty towns, inhabited by migrant workers looking for employment in its port, iron-ore and barge-building industries.

All that said, it's really not an unpleasant place, and the city centre is actually quite nice by workaday Indian town standards. But with no sights of interest, it's just that there's really no compelling reason, as a visitor to Goa, to come here.

In case you do, though, Vasco da Gama's city centre is arranged along three parallel roads, bordered to the south by the railway line and to the north by Mormugao Bay. All the services you need, including ATMs, pharmacies, plenty of cheap *udupi* (South Indian vegetarian) restaurants, and even a Baskin Robbins for ice cream, are arranged along the most southerly of the three roads, Swatantra Path. Next, to the north, you'll find Pe José Vaz Rd, and further again, FL Gomes Rd, off which, to the north again, is the fruit and vegetable market and a minibus stand. About 200m south of the minibus stand you'll find Vasco da Gama train station on Swatantra Path; from here the main bus stand is 400m east.

🛏 Sleeping & Eating

Vasco Residency   HOTEL $$

(☑2513119; Swatantra Path; d without/with AC ₹1000/1375; ❋) Secure, central and bland as they come, the GTDC's Vasco offering is serviceable if, for some reason, you find yourself stuck in Vasco. British visitors might feel at home with a trip to its Little Chef bar and restaurant.

Hotel La Paz Gardens   HOTEL $$

(☑2512121; www.hotellapazgardens.com; Swatantra Path; s/d standard ₹1700/2200, premium ₹2300/2800, deluxe ste ₹4600/5200; ❋) This is the top place in town; a comfortable but unexceptional business hotel comprising 72 rooms with air-con and satellite TV. Other facilities include a gym, sauna and three restaurants, including the locally popular Chinese restaurant, Sweet-n-Sour. Free airport transfers are included in the room rates.

Welcome Restaurant   INDIAN $

(Swatantra Path; thali ₹60; ☉7am-10pm) Considered by many locals to be the best restaurant in Vasco, this all-veg *udupi,* just a couple of doors down from La Paz Gardens, churns out dosas (paper-thin lentil-flour pancakes) and *idlis* in the morning, thalis and *puri-bhajis* (deep-fried puffy dough circles, served with a small chickpea curry for dipping) at lunch, and a full Indian menu come dinnertime. If the warm beetroot-coconut concoction is included in your thali, you're in for a real treat.

❶ Getting There & Away

Express minibuses run nonstop from the minibus stand off FL Gomes Rd to Margao (₹20, 45 minutes) and Panaji (₹25, 45 minutes). There are also regular buses from here to the airport (₹8) and Bogmalo (₹10). Long-distance state buses don't depart from here, but private buses to Mumbai (₹400) depart daily from outside the train station, where you'll find booking agents' offices. At the eastern end of Swatantra Path is a second bus stand, from which you can flag down eastbound buses.

A taxi from the airport costs around ₹150 and an autorickshaw ₹80.

Around Vasco Da Gama

SAO ANTONIO ISLET

If you've the taste for truly local flavour on a Sunday afternoon, venture about 6km east from Vasco da Gama, on the riverside road that takes you to the NH17 highway, where you'll find the tiny Sao Antonio islet in the middle of the Zuari estuary, joined by a thin isthmus to the main land. Here, at low tide, hundreds of locals converge to pick clams, wading waist-deep into the muddy tidal waters, accompanied by copious quantities of *feni* (liquor distilled from coconut milk or cashews) and general merry-making.

SAO JACINTO

Another 1km along from Sao Antonio, you'll reach Sao Jacinto, a second little river island connected to the mainland by a causeway where you'll find an old lighthouse and two small whitewashed chapels. It's home to a small village of mostly fishermen and toddy (palm beer) tappers, and makes a pleasant place to pause for a few minutes, to have a quick look around.

SANCOALE

A mournful monument to Portugal's past glories is on display at Sancoale, another 1km past Sao Jacinto, where you'll find all that's left of Nossa Senhora de Saude (Our Lady of Health), a once-impressive 1566 church, built to commemorate the spot where the first Jesuits touched down in Goa in 1560. A fire ravaged the church in 1834, and all that's left now is a highly decorative part of the facade, worth stopping off to see by following the Archaeological Survey of India sign that leads the way off the main road.

Bogmalo to Betalbatim

The northern section of South Goa's coastline extends from Bogmalo, just a few kilometres south of Dabolim Airport, down to Mobor, perched on the headland above the mouth of the Sal River. The main village-based resorts

FADING FISHERIES

Somewhere in the region of 50,000 Goans are dependent on fishing for their family income, but Goa's once-abundant waters are today facing a serious threat from overfishing, and locals now reminisce about their younger days when *ramponkars* (fishermen), in their simple wooden outriggers, would give away 60cm-long kingfish because they had so many to spare. These days it's difficult to buy fish direct from boats, and even local markets offer slim pickings because much of the best fish is sold directly to upmarket hotels, exported, or shipped to interstate markets where the best prices are fetched. Naturally this has driven up the price of seafood, not only for tourists, but for Goans who rely on their staple *fish-curry-rice*.

Overfishing has become a phenomenon since modern motorised trawlers, owned and operated by wealthy businessmen, started to eclipse the simple traditional fishing methods of the *ramponkars* in the 1970s. Despite a law limiting trawlers to beyond a 5km shoreline 'exclusion zone', trawlers stay relatively close to the shore, adversely affecting the *ramponkars'* catch, while their use of tightly knit nets, which don't allow juvenile fish to escape (these are either thrown away or used for fertiliser) has further dwindled fish stocks. Although the *ramponkars* continue to press for change, Goan state legislature seems helpless in the face of powerful trawler owners, while the seas slowly empty and irreversible damage is done to maintaining this precious resource.

here are Colva and Benaulim, both rather lacklustre compared to the smaller villages dotting the coastal road, but nevertheless equipped with decent facilities and a good range of restaurants. Colva, in particular, tends to attract a domestic and package-holidaying crowd, while Benaulim is a lower-budget, marginally more atmospheric choice. Meanwhile, Cavelossim, further south, is another firm favourite on package-holiday itineraries, with a scruffy village, quietly buzzing nightlife and a long, uninterrupted beach.

To experience the beauty of this area, head to the deserted stretches of beach between the local villages and sprawling five-star resorts between Velsao and Betalbatim, where you'll find little other than seabirds floating on the thermals and scuttling sand crabs to keep you company.

BOGMALO
📞 0832

So close and yet so far, Bogmalo is a world away from the hubbub of Dabolim Airport and its polluted surroundings, though in fact it's just a 4km, 20-minute taxi ride. The roar of the surf is, however, accompanied by the roar of arriving and departing planes, both from the civilian airport and from its military neighbour. Its beach is a small, pretty bay, tragically marred by the '70s-style, 'five star' Bogmalo Beach Resort, which somehow evaded the restriction requiring all hotels to be built at least 500m from the high-tide line and plonked its fancy concrete skirts down right on the beach itself.

It makes a decent stop if you've got an hour or two to kill before a flight, or if you're keen to experience Goa's underwater scene, courtesy of its highly respected diving outlet. Otherwise it's not especially appealing, cramped with ragtag stalls, beach cafes and spluttering busloads of excitable domestic day-trippers.

Note that if you're looking for cash, there's a reliable ATM machine at the entrance to the Naval Aviation Museum.

⊙ Sights & Activities
Though there's not an extensive range on offer, there are usually a couple of jet skis available for hire on the beach, along with a kayak or windsurfer or two. Ask around, or wander along the beach to find a vendor and negotiate a price.

Full Moon Cruises   BOAT TRIPS
(📞 9764625198, 9764762988; rahul54293@gmail. com; Full Moon Cafe; boat trip per couple ₹4500). Despite the name, these boat trips aren't held at full moon, and nor are they really cruises. They're daily boat trips, tailored to their customers' requirements, usually involving a spot of dolphin-watching, a bit of fishing and a visit to Bat Island (the name giving you a clue to its sole inhabitants), which floats, lush and calm, just off the Bogmalo coast. Trips usually last from 9am to 12pm, but affable organiser Rahul will throw in more time for free if you'd like to stay out longer. Contact him at the Full Moon Cafe at the southern end of Bogmalo Bay.

Goa Diving   DIVING
(📞 2555117, 2538204; www.goadiving.com) Goa Diving is an internationally respected outfit (with the distinction of having been the first dive school in the whole of India), with a range of dives to suit novices and would-be Jacques Cousteaux alike. Its booth is at the southern entrance to the beach, diagonally opposite the Full Moon Cafe. It offers lots of courses; some off local Grande Island, where you can explore the remains of the British-built SS *Mary,* and others at Pigeon Island, 85km to the south. Local dives start at ₹2000 for a one-tank dive; five dives plus transfers and one night's accommodation near Pigeon Island comes to ₹15,000. An introductory dive costs ₹3000, an advanced course costs ₹13,000 and an open-water course costs ₹18,000.

Naval Aviation Museum   MUSEUM
(📞 5995525; adult/child ₹20/5, camera/video ₹20/50; ⊙10am-5pm Tue-Sat) If you've exhausted your options or your patience for hawkers down on Bogmalo Beach, the Naval Aviation Museum at the naval base on the road above the beach makes an interesting diversion. Full of men idling about, especially around its Cockpit Cafe, the museum offers a neat and interesting presentation of India's naval history, and its connection to machines of the air. Make sure to turn left into the museum gates, rather than heading on straight ahead, where you'll likely encounter a goose-stepping naval officer complete with snow-white socks pulled up to his knees, intent on making sure you don't get much further.

🛏 Sleeping & Eating
If you've got a particularly early flight from nearby Dabolim Airport, you might consider spending a night at Bogmalo. Otherwise, there's no pressing reason to check in here. For lunch, there are three beach shacks – each offering a standard Indian menu and decent seafood – in a row: take your pick

from the Full Moon Cafe, Stiff Waves and Dom's Sea Cuisine.

Coconut Creek   COTTAGES $$$
(☎2538090, 2358100; www.coconutcreekgoa.com; cottages with/without AC ₹6250/5500; ❄@🛜🏊) Stylish cottages set up largely for package tourists are set around a pool in a coconut grove, for the best, most laid-back, but nevertheless rather overpriced, stay in Bogmalo. Rates include transfer to/from Dabolim Airport and a hearty 'American breakfast'.

Joets Guest House   GUESTHOUSE $$$
(☎2538036, 2538090; joets@sancharnet.in; d ₹3950; 🛜) Down on the beachfront, this clean and simple guest house, run by the same operators as Coconut Creek, offers simpler rooms, but has nice views out over the bay. Rates also include airport transfers, that same American breakfast, and free use of the swimming pool and fitness room at Coconut Creek.

Sarita's Guest House   GUESTHOUSE $$
(☎2538965; saritasguesthouse@rediffmail.com; d ₹1500) Sarita's has clean but unremarkable and, like everything in Bogmalo, overpriced rooms, with a common balcony offering an unimpeded view of the beach.

❶ Getting There & Away
An irregular bus service runs between Bogmalo and Vasco da Gama (₹9, 25 minutes). Buses depart from the car park in front of the entrance to the Bogmalo Beach Resort. Taxis and autorickshaws wait around in the same area; a taxi to the airport should cost ₹250 and an autorickshaw will be around ₹150.

VELSAO
☑0832
South from Bogmalo, Velsao marks the northerly starting point of South Goa's beautiful beaches. Despite the gloomy presence of the vast and looming Zuari Agro chemical plant to the north, Velsao's beach makes a quiet place to get away from it all, in the company of just a lifeguard, a scattering of tourists and a flock or two of milling seabirds.

The beach road travels through thick coconut groves past dozens of old bungalows, while the coastal road around this stretch makes for a delicious countryside drive, fringed with lily-pad-studded lakes and paddy fields and coconut groves stretching gently down to the sea.

If you're travelling the coast under your own steam, it's the view, rather than the plain little chapel itself, that should entice you to take the steep road east off the coastal road up to **Our Lady of Remedios** at the top of the hill. On clear days, you'll have a gorgeous, camera-clicking view south along the calm, quiet sands – studiously ignoring the uglier northerly and easterly views up towards the monstrous fertiliser factory and surrounding industrial sprawl.

AROSSIM
☑0832
Quiet and clean Arossim, like Velsao to its north, is a good place to settle into solitude with a good book, particularly if you studiously ignore the chemical plant lurking on the northern headland. Here, the simple **Starfish Beach Shack** (mains from ₹110) is the only place for a drink or lunch, and is extremely popular with British and Russian package holidayers from the nearby Heritage Village Club Hotel. Its sun beds and beach umbrellas occupy a very quiet patch, and its snapper is snapped up as soon as the catch comes in. To get to the beach, follow signs for the Heritage Village Club hotel, then hop across the sandbags, over an extremely desultory creek.

On Arossim Beach's approach road you'll also find the wonderful **The Treasure** (☎2754228; thetreasure@rediffmail.com; Arossim Beach Rd, near Heritage Village Club), set in a beautiful, rambling old heritage home. If you're a fan of the gorgeous Goan vintage furniture you'll see gracing many of the state's old homes and higher-end hotels, pick up your own pieces here from a selection that ranges from dripping chandeliers to carved four-poster beds (they regularly ship internationally). Don't miss the small shrine-like chapel on this mansion's staircase, a feature that graces the very best of Goa's colonial homes.

The top sleeping option in Arossim is the 18-hectare **Park Hyatt Resort & Spa** (☎2721234; www.goa.park.hyatt.com; d from ₹12,000; ❄@🏊) Rooms here are lavish and large, and the resort has plenty of features that would entice even the most adventurous to stay put. Its Sereno Spa is spread over a series of stunning outdoor pavilions, offers a magical *Abhyanga* – 'four-hands' massage – performed simultaneously by two therapists. Gorgeous upmarket Goan cuisine is dished up at fantastic **Casa Sarita** (mains from ₹625; ☺lunch&dinner), offering the piquant flavours of Goa in all their glory. Make for the *vindalho* (a fiery dish in a marinade of vinegar and garlic) or the mushroom *xacuti* (a spicy dish incorporating coconut milk and flesh). You won't be disappointed.

UTORDA
📞0832

A clean, if slightly characterless, stretch of beach, approached on sandbag stepping-stones and rickety bridges over a series of fairly stagnant pools, Utorda makes for a pleasant afternoon on its sands, taking your pick from a ragtag bunch of beach shacks, many of whose sun beds you can use. Though the pretty coast is offset by the hulking Zuari Agro chemical plant further north, it's still popular with holidaymakers from the surrounding swish resorts, and the beach has the added bonus of an on-duty lifeguard.

Daily **fishing and dolphin-watching trips** are in no short supply in Utorda. Take your pick from the seasonal offerings sold in and around the beach shacks that line the main stretch of sands.

🛏 Sleeping & Eating

Zeebop by the Sea   SEAFOOD $
(dishes from ₹80; ⏱10.30am-11.30pm) Renowned for its excellent seafood – or 'underwater treasures', as the restaurant itself describes its cuisine – simple Zeebop, just back from Utorda's main beach and opposite Kenilworth, is a firm favourite with locals in the know. Closed Good Friday.

Dom Pedro's Haven   GUESTHOUSE $$
(📞9890191147, 9922909432; www.dompedroshaven.com; r with/without AC ₹1800/1500; ❄) A down-to-earth option (unusual on this strip of coast) on the left-hand side at the entrance to the Utorda beach road. It's a simple six-room affair run by a local family; note that it closes down annually between June and September.

Royal Orchid Beach Resort   HOTEL $$$
(📞2884400; www.royalorchidhotels.com; d from ₹6000; ❄@🛜☎) Highly recommended by travellers, the Royal Orchid is a lush, flash, plush place gracing Utorda's nice sands. Its Aristo Spa offers lots of natural treats, including a yoghurt-turmeric body wrap, just in case you've ever wondered how a paneer tandoori tikka feels.

Kenilworth   HOTEL $$$
(📞6698888; www.kenilworthhotels.com; d from ₹12,000; ❄@☎) The other of Utorda's two ritziest resorts is an upmarket affair backing onto the beach with all the standard five-star bells and whistles. Its Mallika restaurant, open from 7pm till 11pm, offers 'Northern frontier' fine dining, with succulent kebabs, thick fluffy tandoori-oven breads, and other Punjabi- and Kashmiri-inspired delights.

MAJORDA
📞0832

Approached through pleasant, leafy Majorda village, Majorda Beach is a smarter, more-organised option than neighbouring Utorda. Here, the stagnant streams and puddles that blight the division between road and beach have been arranged to form a moat, which flows round into a pleasant stream, forded by small, bamboo bridges. The beach itself has about half-a-dozen Russian-oriented beach shacks, all serving up the standard beach fare with menu boards chalked up in Cyrillic. To get here, take the left-hand curve of the beach approach (the right-hand curve takes you down to the swish Majorda Beach Resort); you'll find souvenir stalls, simple grocery shops, a few decent guesthouses and a range of little cafes serving up snacks.

🏃 Activities

Horse Riding   HORSE RIDING
(📞9822586502; 20-min beach ride ₹350) Keen equestrians shouldn't pass up the chance for a sunset or sunrise ride along Goa's sands, and Majorda is currently the only place in the state to do it. Bookings with Frank, the proprietor, are essential, for rides ranging from beginner to advanced. The horses are often tethered outside Greenland Bar & Restaurant (see p166).

Treat Yourself Health Centre   EXERCISE, MASSAGE
(📞9822586502; ⏱6am-9pm) Under renovation and expansion at the time of research, this spick and span little place in the heart of Majorda village offers a well-equipped gym, swimming pool and ayurvedic massage centre, run by a British expat. Rates for the gym and pool start at ₹150 per day, while massages begin at ₹750 for an hour-long session. Take a left-hand turn off the beach approach road.

🛏 Sleeping

You'll find a number of small guesthouses and rooms-to-let in Majorda if you wander the road down towards the beach. The Majorda Beach Resort, down beside the sea, bills itself as a 5-star resort 'where fun never sets', but has recently been getting poor reviews from travellers, who deem it expensive and in need of a major overhaul.

TOP CHOICE Vivenda Dos Palhacos   BOUTIQUE HOTEL $$$
(📞9881720221; www.vivendagoa.com; d from ₹5750; @☎) No beach bar or five-star facilities here, but this upmarket boutique hotel,

PALOLEM & SOUTH GOA BOGMALO TO BETALBATIM

run by a British brother-and-sister team whose family brews the superstrength Hayward's 5000 beer (an Indian truck-driver favourite), is a gem of the south Goan coast. Rooms inhabit an old Portuguese mansion and older Hindu house, with sparkling courtyard pool and resident basset hound. There's also a top-end tent and self-contained cottage on offer.

Rainbow's End   GUESTHOUSE $
(☑2881016; r from ₹600) A great value place for those looking to stay for a while, these simple self-contained units, situated in a characterful building amid a lovely garden, are on the left-hand side as you turn down towards the beach road.

🍴 Eating & Drinking

TOP
CHOICE **Greenland Bar &**
Restaurant   MULTICUISINE $
(mains from ₹100; ☺10am-10pm) On Majorda's southern 'Cabana Beach', across a little bamboo bridge, you'll find cute Greenland, run by a lovely British couple from Kent (who are proud of keeping the toilets spotlessly clean). The Indian chef cooks up a range of local specialities including *xacutis* and *vindalhos,* along with yummy banana fritters. There's plenty to keep children entertained while you're munching, and you'll find Frank's steeds (see p165) resting up just outside the restaurant. Sunday evenings from 6pm see a traditional roast dinner served up, immensely popular with all who sample it.

Raj's Pentagon Restaurant &
Garden Pub   DRINKING, INDIAN $
(mains from ₹120; ☺till midnight) On the right-hand side as you head to the beach, there's decent garden dining at this large, friendly place, worth visiting for a filling lunch or evening drink. Live music hits the stage here every night: on Wednesday it's 'slow rock and tease' courtesy of Ralph and Cedric; the Friendly Brothers put in an appearance on Sundays; and on Mondays the restaurant revels in country music provided by Raul the One Man Band.

Fusion   MULTICUISINE $$$
(www.fusiongoa.com; mains from ₹220; ☺6.30pm-10.30pm) Proud winner of the *Times of India* Food Award in 2011 for best European restaurant in Goa, this swish place on the left as you head down the beach road dishes up a whole mixture of Euro-slanted dishes, from stroganoff and bourguignon through to

gnocchi, carpaccio and Greek dolmas. They are exceptionally proud of their Brazilian chef in charge of the grill, and have a decent (if predictable) variety of vegetarian options.

BETALBATIM
☑0832

Though the beaches along this entire strip – from Mobor in the south right up to Velsao further north – are actually just different patches of one long and continuous stretch of sand, each place manages to retain its own very distinct and individual character. Betalbatim, just to the north of Colva, is a good example of what a difference a few hundred metres can make, as calm, quiet and pastoral as Colva is touristed and dust-blown. And even Betalbatim itself consists of several different smaller strips of beach – try Sunset Beach or Lovers' Beach, which is suitably lovely, though the only lovers to be seen when we visited were a pair of wheeling seagulls, along with the odd solitary dog and a lone lovelorn sea eagle. To get to Lovers' Beach, follow signs from the main road, passing a less lovely rash of time-shares on the way.

As well as Sunset and Lovers', there are a couple of other entrance points onto Betalbatim beach from the village, all more or less guaranteeing peace and quiet.

A local legend and also popular with Indian tourists, Martin's Corner (www.martin scornergoa.com; mains from ₹90; ☺11am-3pm & 6.30-11pm), near Sunset Beach, is a great place to try out Goan cuisine, in a relaxed and quite upmarket setting. The *xacutis* and *vindalhos* here are superb, and there are plenty of tasty vegetarian options on offer. There's live music most nights from 8pm. Plump for, or avoid, Wednesday, depending on your relationship with karaoke.

If you decide to stay, check into the swish new Alila Diwa (☑2746800; www.alilahotels. com; r from ₹9600; ❋☀☎), a new five-star hotel with a tremendous pool, a good spa and chic, minimalist rooms.

Colva
☑0832 / POP 10,200

If it's a beach paradise you're after, you'll probably be disappointed with what's awaiting you in Colva. A large concrete roundabout marks the end of the beach road and the entrance to the beach, filled with day-trippers, package tourists and listless hawkers. The main beach drag is lined with

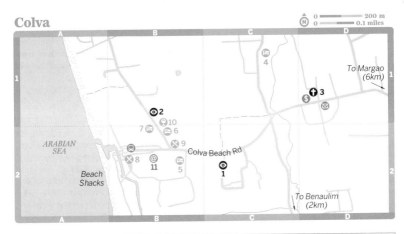

Colva

◎ Sights
1 Friends of Goa Animal Welfare
  Trust Shop...C2
2 Goa Animal Welfare Information
  Centre & Office B1
3 Our Lady of Mercy Church...................D1

▣ Sleeping
4 Casa Mesquita..C1
5 La Ben...B2
6 Skylark Resort.......................................B2

7 Soul Vacation...B2

◎ Eating
8 Café Coffee Day......................................B2
9 Sagar Kinara B2

◎ Drinking
10 Leda Lounge & Restaurant....................B1

❶ Information
11 Hello Mae Communications...................B2

dreary stalls and shabby cafes; sure, it's got all the material needs you're seeking, but as far as atmosphere goes it's sorely lacking.

Perhaps the biggest reason to stay at Colva (or Benaulim, a touch south) is its central location if you're keen to explore this part of the coast (which stretches north as far as Velsao and south as far as the mouth of the Sal River at Mobor), which in many parts is empty and gorgeous. The inland road that runs this length is perfect for gentle scootering, with lots of picturesque Portuguese mansions and whitewashed churches along the way.

◎ Sights & Activities

Colva's beach entrance throngs with young men keen to sell you **parasailing** (per ride ₹700), **jet-skiing** (15 min ₹800) and **dolphin-watching trips** (per person around ₹400). There's little to choose between operators, which gives you significant leeway in terms of haggling for the best deal.

⬈ Friends of Goa Animal Welfare Trust (GAWT)   WELFARE SHOP
(www.gawt.org; ◔10am-12.30pm & 5-7pm Mon-Sat) One place to stop off is at the Goa Animal Welfare Trust (GAWT) in Colva, just beside the Leda Lounge, where you can borrow books from its lending library, or peruse the new and secondhand goods for sale, all proceeds of which go toward helping out Goa's four-legged friends. Books and saleable items (for the shop) and towels and sheets (for the dog shelter) are accepted as donations.

⬈ GAWT Information Centre & Office   WELFARE SHOP
(◔9.30am-1pm & 3-5pm Mon-Sat) The GAWT Information Centre & Office, also in Colva and located just below the Infant Jesus Church Hall, is the place to go to find out more about the work of this organisation. Also see p172 for more information.

🛏 Sleeping

It's hard to recommend many budget or midrange options in Colva, since the majority are either horribly overpriced or, more simply, horrible. Indeed, since there's barely anything midrange up-to-scratch enough to include here, unless you're lying low in one of the town's groovier top-end choices you're far better off heading down to Benaulim or pushing on further south.

Skylark Resort   HOTEL $$$

(☎2788052; www.skylarkresortgoa.com; r without/with AC from ₹2300/3000; ✳☀) By far the best on offer in Colva, Skylark's clean, fresh rooms are graced with bits and pieces of locally made teak furniture and block-print bedspreads, while the pool makes a pleasant place to lounge. It's a quick five-minute stroll to the beach.

La Ben   HOTEL $$

(☎2788040; www.laben.net; r with/without AC ₹1800/1400; ✳) Calling itself a 'budgeted hotel', this place gets high marks from travellers for its neat, clean rooms and helpful management. Its rooms certainly represent reasonable value, considering the area, if you're not desperately seeking anything with character.

Casa Mesquita   GUESTHOUSE $

(₹300) With just three rooms that go beyond simple and no telephone for bookings, this atmospheric old mansion on the main coast road is certainly the place to go if you thrive on the atmosphere that Colva lacks. Goodness knows when the rooms were last cleaned; nevertheless, the elderly owners are friendly, the paint's suitably peeling and the ghosts of better days linger lovingly in the shadows.

COLVA'S MENINO JESUS

If the only miracle you've experienced in Colva is finding a nice budget bed, the village's 18th-century Our Lady of Mercy Church has been host to several miracles of its own, of the rather more celestial kind.

Inside, closely guarded under lock and key, lives a little statue known as the 'Menino' (Baby) Jesus, which is said to miraculously heal the sick. Legend has it that the statue was discovered by a Jesuit priest named Father Bento Ferreira in the mid-17th century, after he was shipwrecked somewhere off the coast of Mozambique. The plucky missionary swam to shore, to see vultures circling a rocky spot. On closer inspection, he discovered the statue, apparently washed ashore after having been tossed overboard as worthless by Muslim pirates.

When he was posted to Colva in 1648, Father Ferreira took the Menino Jesus along with him, and had it installed on the high altar, where it promptly began to heal the sick and soon acquired some serious local celebrity. It wasn't long before it was worshipped with its own special Fama de Menino Jesus festival, which still occurs each year on the second Monday in October.

However, all was not smooth sailing for the Menino. When the Portuguese suppressed many religious orders in 1836, the Jesuits were forced to flee Colva, and took the Menino with them to their seminary in Rachol (see p158), where both they – and it – were safe. Colva's residents weren't pleased with the removal of their miracle-worker, and petitioned the head of the Jesuits in Rome, then the viceroy, then the king of Portugal himself for its return.

Finally they got the answer they hoped for, orders for the statue to go back to Colva. However, the Jesuits didn't quite seem to get around to returning it, and finally the Colvan villagers clubbed together and had their own replica made, furnished with a diamond ring that had fallen off the finger of the original Menino during the move to Rachol. Meanwhile, in Rachol, the first statue slowly appeared to lose its healing powers, while the newcomer healed away merrily, prompting the delighted villagers to claim it had been the ring, and not the statue, that was the source of its miraculous powers all the while.

These days, the distinctly unmiraculous Menino is still kept at Rachol Seminary, while its more successful successor only sees the light of day during the annual Fama festival. Then, the little image is removed from deep within the church's vaults, paraded about town, dipped in the river, and installed in the church's high altar for pilgrims to pray to, hoping for their own personal miracle.

Soul Vacation HOTEL **$$$**
(☑2788144, 2788147; www.soulvacation.in; d incl breakfast from ₹7366; ✳🌐✖) Thirty sleek, white rooms arranged around nice gardens and a pool are the trademarks of Soul Vacation, set 400m back from Colva Beach, but recently receiving less-than-stellar reviews from travellers, for its lackadaisical service, slipping standards and rising prices.

✗ Eating & Drinking

There are plenty of beach shacks lining the Colvan sands, offering the extensive standard range of fare, and you'll spot this season's best by the crowds already dining within. For simpler eating, head up to the roundabout just before the church, where tourist joints are replaced by simple chai shops and thali places, and there are plenty of fruit, vegetable and fish stalls for self-caterers. At night, *bhelpuri* (crisp fried thin rounds of dough with lentils, puffed rice and onions) vendors set up camp here, dishing up big portions of the fried noodle snack.

Sagar Kinara INDIAN **$**
(mains ₹80-150) A pure-veg restaurant upstairs (non-veg is separate, downstairs) with tastes to please even committed carnivores, this great place is clean, efficient and offers cheap and delicious North and South Indian cuisine all day long.

Café Coffee Day CAFE **$**
(cakes & coffees from ₹50; ⊙8am-midnight) A pleasant enough place to escape the heat, this wannabe sleek joint offers a half-decent cappuccino (₹58) along with a range of cakes, including the suitably '70s black forest gateau (₹52), reminiscent of the era when Colva was still cool. Just next door is a branch of Subway, in case you're craving those famous foot-longs from back home.

Leda Lounge &
Restaurant CONTINENTAL, BAR **$$**
(mains ₹125-200; ⊙7.30am-midnight) Somewhat pricey Western favourites (pizzas, salads, sandwiches) meet fancy drinks (Mojitos, Long Island iced teas) at this comfy, cosmopolitan cafe-lounge. It's a hip environment (relative to Colva), and there's often live music too.

❶ Information

Colva has plenty of banks, ATM machines and travel agents strung along Colva Beach Rd, and a post office on the lane that runs past the eastern end of the church.

Hello Mae Communication Centre (Colva Beach Rd; internet per hr ₹50; ⊙8am-10pm) Internet access and money exchange. Keep in mind the stern warning: 'No Surfing of Porn Websites'.

❶ Getting There & Away

Buses run from Colva to Margao roughly every 15 minutes (₹15, 20 minutes) from 7.30am to about 7pm, departing from the parking area at the end of the beach road.

Benaulim
☑0832

A long stretch of largely empty sand, peppered with a few hawkers and stray dogs, laid-back, windswept Benaulim has the distinct feeling of a Welsh seaside resort, were global warming ever to get that far. That said, it's a reasonable-enough place to relax on the sands, with a lifeguard present and plenty of sunbed-equipped beach shacks lining the stretch to the north of the main beach entrance.

Benaulim also has a special place in Goan tradition: legend has it that it was here that the god Parasurama's arrow landed when he fired it into the sea to create Goa. Modern-day archers, however, might choose a prettier spot.

Most accommodation, eating options, grocery shops and pharmacies are concentrated along the Vasvaddo Beach Rd along the stretch around the crossroads and football ground.

◉ Sights

Goa Chitra Museum MUSEUM
(☑6570877; www.goachitra.com; St John the Baptist Rd, Mondo Vaddo, Benaulim; ₹200; ⊙9am-6pm Tue-Sun) Artist and restorer Victor Hugo Gomes first noticed the slow extinction of traditional objects – from farming tools to kitchen utensils to altarpieces – as a child in Benaulim. But it wasn't until he was older that he realised the traditional, and especially agricultural, knowledge was disappearing with them. He created this ethnographic museum from the more than 4000 cast-off objects that he collected from across the state over 20 years (he often had to find elderly people to explain their uses). In addition to the organic traditional farm out the back, you'll see tons of tools and household objects, Christian artefacts and some fascinating farming implements, including a massive grinder for making coconut oil,

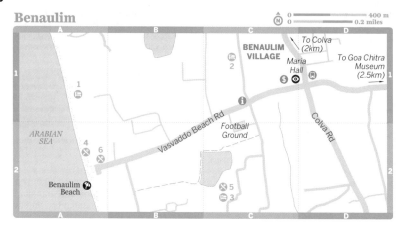

Benaulim

🛏 Sleeping

1 Anthy's Guesthouse A1
2 D'Souza Guest House C1
3 Palm Grove Cottages C2

🍴 Eating

4 Johncy A2
5 Malibu Restaurant C2
   Palm Garden Restaurant .... (see 3)
6 Pedro's Bar & Restaurant A2

which, ingeniously, attaches to a bull who does all the hard work. Goa Chitra is 3km east of Maria Hall, a large building at the corner of the main turn off to Benaulim's beach, which houses the Bank of Baroda.

🏃 Activities

Pele's Water Sport   WATER SPORTS

(☏9822080045, 9822686011) Water sports in Benaulim are not as prevalent as they are at more-crowded Colva, though some operators hang around the beach shacks. One of the most prolific is Pele's Water Sport; jet skis cost ₹600 per 10 minutes, parasailing costs ₹600 per ride, and dolphin trips are ₹350 per person. You'll find someone from Pele's down on the beach, if he doesn't find you first.

🛏 Sleeping

Lots of budget rooms for rent throng the main road towards the beach, and the lanes around it: walk around, shop around and bargain if you're even slightly outside high season (Christmas and New Year). Prices have slowly crept up, but there are still lots of family-run places with just a handful of rooms with bargain-basement prices.

Palm Grove Cottages   HOTEL $$

(☏2770059; www.palmgrovegoa.com; d without/with AC from ₹1700/2100; ❄) Old-fashioned, secluded charm is on offer amid the dense foliage at Palm Grove Cottages, hidden among a thicket of trees on a road winding slowly south out of Benaulim. Guest rooms are atmospheric, and the ever-popular Palm Garden Restaurant graces the garden.

D'Souza Guest House   GUESTHOUSE $

(☏2770583; d ₹900) As you may guess from the name, this traditional blue-painted house is run by a local Goan family and comes with bundles of homely atmosphere, a lovely garden and just three spacious, clean rooms – making it best to book ahead.

Anthy's Guesthouse   BEACH HUTS $$

(☏9922854566; anthysguesthouse@rediffmail.com; r ₹1300-1800) One of just a handful of places lining Benaulim's beach itself, Anthy's is a firm favourite with travellers for its good restaurant, and its well-kept, if bland, chalet-style rooms, which stretch back from the beach surrounded by a garden. Ayurvedic massage is available here for ₹600.

Taj Exotica   HOTEL $$$

(☏6683333; www.tajhotels.com; d from US$300; ❄@🏊) If your budget runs to it, here's one of Goa's plushest resorts, set in 23 hectares of tropical gardens 2km south of Benaulim, though traveller feedback suggests that some rooms could really do with some TLC.

✗ Eating

The beach road is filled with places to eat, which change frequently. Choose a place crowded (with locals, if possible) and you won't go far wrong.

Malibu Restaurant   INDIAN, ITALIAN **$$**
(mains from ₹150) This place offers one of Benaulim's more sophisticated dining experiences in its secluded garden setting just a short walk back from the beach. It does great renditions of Italian favourites and has live jazz and blues on Tuesday evenings.

Pedro's Bar &
Restaurant   INDIAN, MULTICUISINE **$$**
(mains ₹90-250; ⊘9am-midnight) Set amid a large, shady garden on the beachfront and popular with local and international travellers alike, Pedro's offers standard Indian, Chinese and Italian dishes, as well as Goan choices and 'sizzlers'. You can also book a variety of day trips from here.

Johncy   INDIAN, MULTICUISINE **$$**
(mains ₹85-220; ⊘9.30am-1am) Like Pedro's beside it, Johncy dispenses standard beach-shack favourites from its location just back from the sand. Staff are obliging and the food, if not exciting, is fresh and filling.

ⓘ Information

Bank of Baroda (Maria Hall, Vasvaddo Beach Rd) Just west from the junction of the Colva Rd, the ATM here professes to be 24-hour, but in reality is sometimes locked. Since this is the only machine in town, it might be wise to stock up on cash in Cavelossim, Margao or Colva, just in case.

GK Tourist Centre (✐2770476, 2771221, 2770471; gktouristcentre@hotmail.com; Vasvaddo Beach Rd)

ⓘ Getting There & Around

Buses from Margao to Benaulim are frequent (₹15, 15 minutes); some continue on south to Varca and Cavelossim. Buses stop at the crossroads quite a distance from the main action and beach; you might prefer to hail an autorickshaw (₹50) for the five-minute ride to the sea.

Varca, Cavelossim & Mobor

✐0832
Heading south from Benaulim, you'll travel a road lined with beautiful Portuguese relics, paddy fields, whitewashed churches and farmland, encountering first the town of Varca – a sleepy village outside which several five-star resorts have sprung up. Next up is Cavelossim, an ever-increasing (but still quite pleasant and friendly) strip of stalls, malls, and midrange to top-end hotels running parallel to the beautiful white-sand beach. Finally, where the Sal River meets the ocean, you'll find little Mobor, dominated by the presence of the Leela, one of Goa's costliest hotels, and the peninsula tipped by a tiny fishing settlement of poor migrant fishermen from Orissa state.

These three destinations back a 10km stretch of beautiful, pristine beach, where it's little effort to find a comfy sun lounge or a deserted patch of virgin sands, depending on your preference. Luckily, the presence of these luxury residences (and the high precedent set for the price of sea-facing real estate here) seems to have saved this swathe of sands from tacky, midrange development. Even if you're not staying at one of the swanky addresses along it, with your own transport you've got plenty of opportunity to enjoy the sands (which belong to everyone, despite what some hotels might assert). Moreover, many resorts employ their own staff to keep the beachfront litter-free.

Locals report that some hotels have a nasty habit of assuring their comfortably cocooned guests that there's nothing to see and nowhere to go in the vicinity and that, if you do venture out far from its pearly gates, you'll likely be mugged – or worse. But wander the beaches or back lanes a little, and you'll likely come across a great places for a *bhaji-pau* (bread roll dipped in curry) breakfast (₹10), a perfect spot for a cold beer or a friendly fisherman willing to take you out on his sunset adventures.

There are regular buses that serve the main coastal road, from Margao, via Colva or Benaulim, all the way down to Mobor. They run daily, every few minutes between around 8am and 10pm, and can be flagged down along the road. The furthest stop south drops you outside the grounds of the Leela, from which it's an easy walk to the beach or the Blue Whale, for a bite to eat.

VARCA
A seemingly endless palm-backed strip of sand punctuated, here and there, by the grounds of a luxury resort or a whitewashed Christian shrine, Varca is quiet, calm and almost entirely hawker-free, making it easy to find a quiet spot all to

yourself. Outside the resorts, one good access point is the portion known as Zalor Beach. Follow signposts from Varca village, near the church. When you arrive a final sign declares: 'You are being watched. No Spitting or Abusing Children'.

CAVELOSSIM

Cavelossim village – a straggling strip of jewellery shops, souvenir shops, ATMs and one quite swish department store, and with a strange proliferation of dentists – is a place of large, down-at-heel hotels and time-share complexes strung along the main road. It's here that holidayers shop for sandals and sarongs, and the two-week brigade settle in to their plain back-from-the-beach abodes. For all that, though, the beach remains long, wide and beautiful, dotted with water-sports vendors and beach shacks, and makes a nice place for a paddle.

Look out, on the road south, for the Old Anchor Hotel, allegedly the first ever resort in South Goa (a questionable accolade in itself). This place is worth at least a glance solely for its extreme Las Vegas-style kitsch, shaped to resemble a huge boat. Ahoy there, me hearties.

🏃 Activities

Betty's Place Boat Trips   BOAT TRIPS
(☎2871456, 2871038; www.bettysgoa.com; ⊙restaurant 7-11pm) A restaurant by night, Betty's offers a wide range of boat cruises by day, including a full day combined dolphin-watching and birdwatching trip (₹750 including lunch and drinks), fishing trips, sunset boat rides (₹300), and a two-hour birdwatching trip on the River Sal (₹350; departs daily at 4pm). Drop in or call in advance to book your boat trip. Meanwhile, the restaurant is known for its seafood and tandoori dishes (tiger prawns are ₹550) and hosts frequent live music.

IT'S A DOG'S LIFE

The small town of Curchorem, situated inland in Goa about 6km past Chandor, is as sleepy and unremarkable as they get – except in one way. Here, housed in the old police station on the right-hand side of the main road, is the main dogs' home of the Goa Animal Welfare Trust (GAWT; ☎2653677; www.gawt.org) where southern Goa's sick and stray animals find rare solace.

GAWT (along with International Animal Rescue in the north; see p31) tries its best to help the animals out, providing veterinary help for sick animals, shelter for puppies and kittens, sterilisation programs for street dogs and low-cost veterinary care (including anti-rabies injections) for Goan pets. It also deals with animal cruelty cases, and runs school 'pet awareness' programs.

The shelter is open daily from 9am to 5pm and volunteers are welcome, even just for a few hours on a single visit, to walk or play with the dogs. Items such as your old newspapers – all those copies of the *Times of India* and the *Herald* you've bought from beach vendors – can be used for lining kennel floors, as will old sheets, towels and anything else you might not be taking home.

Secondhand goods and old books are sold at the GAWT Information Centre & Charity Shop (see p167) in Colva.

It is possible – though lengthy and expensive – to take street dogs with you back home. You'd need to satisfy quarantine requirements, which vary from country to country, but there are plenty of ways to do it if you're determined. The Trust can probably provide you with advice, and phone numbers of people who undertake animal transportation regularly. If all that seems too difficult, you can also adopt (and name) one of the shelter's long-term residents for about £50 per year.

GAWT is happy to take long-term volunteers (though it can't provide housing or meals); there is also the chance for a male veterinary volunteer to work alongside its own current vet. It's a great volunteering opportunity for the recently veterinarily qualified, wanting to rack up some pro-bono experience.

For further information about GAWT and other volunteering opportunities with organisations in Goa, see p30.

Ferry

FERRY

(pedestrians/motorbikes/cars free/₹4/7; ⊘8am-8.30pm, every 30 min) For a slightly less sophisticated watery experience, hop on the 10-minute ferry across the Sal River to Assolna. To reach it, turn east at the ferry timetable sign, near Cavelossim's whitewashed church, then continue on for 2km to the river. Outside operational hours, you can charter the ferry to reach the opposite shore for a princely ₹55.

🛏 Sleeping

Cavelossim is squarely aimed at package tourists, and most midrange places have little interest in renting rooms separately to individual travellers. Unless you're really keen to stay here, consider instead basing yourself either to the north or further south.

Holiday Inn Resort
HOTEL $$$

(☑2871303; www.holidayinngoa.com; d from ₹10,200; ✷@✲) On the road south towards Mobor, you'll reach the Holiday Inn, a sleek beachfront place gleaning generally excellent traveller reviews, with great service, a large pool and plenty of Thai and ayurvedic spa treatments on offer.

Casa de Cris
GUESTHOUSE $$

(☑2685909; www.casadecris.com; d from ₹2500; ✷@) A very smart newish option, this place, near Sao Domingo's, has crisply painted, well-maintained rooms, with nice homely touches. A great choice for a relaxed, comfortable stay.

Radisson Blu Resort
HOTEL $$$

(☑6726666; www.radissonblu.com; d/ste ₹9000/12,500; ✷🛜✲)This large new place with easy beach access, captures a large portion of the package-tour market, with its 132 suites and rooms. It gets good traveller feedback for its pool, Aura Spa, free wi-fi, unusual for a large chain hotel, and general neat-and-tidiness.

Sao Domingo's Holiday Home
HOTEL $$

(☑2871461; www.saodomingosgoa.com; d without/with AC ₹2000/2300; ✷) Down a laneway opposite Goan Village, this tidy hotel is in a pleasant area of coconut palms just a few minutes' walk from the River Sal. Rooms have balconies and hot water, and some have air-con. If it's full, there are a further eight rooms on offer, with similar prices and facilities, at its neighbouring complex, Luciana's Residency.

GOA'S FERRIES

One of the joys of day-tripping in Goa is a quick ride on one of the state's slowly shrinking selection of passenger ferries, which, until the recent addition of road bridges to span Goa's wide and wonderful rivers, formed a crucial means of transport for locals.

Though slowly disappearing altogether, and often in rather bad, rusty, fume-ridden condition, they're still a great way to see Goa's waterways without the need to sign up for an organised boat trip, and make a fab, thrifty way of getting about. Most ferries run every half an hour or so from around 7am to 8pm, some stopping between 1pm and 2pm for lunch. Pedestrians travel free; motorbikes and scooters cost ₹4; and cars are ₹7 to ₹12. Hop aboard, and experience life on the water the truly local way.

» Querim to Terekhol Fort (p75)
» Dona Paula to Mormugao Bay (p124)
» Old Goa to Divar Island (p133)
» Divar Island to Naroa (p109)
» Cavelossim to Assolna (p173)
» Ribandar to Chorao Island (p125)
» Panaji to Betim (p111)

🍴 Eating

There are plenty of decent beach shacks strung along the beach, including the popular Mike's Beach Oasis Shack, owned by the village-based Mike's Place. All serve up the usual mix of seafood, traveller favourites and Indian dishes.

Papa Joe's
GOAN, INDIAN $

(mains from ₹90; ⊘daily) 'Nothing fancy, just friendly', say the Papa Joe folks who serve great, spicy Goan cuisine in an open-air restaurant at Orlim, situated just north of Cavelossim on the right-hand side of the coastal road. Even the seafood seems happy to be there: their lively specialities include 'laughing squid' and 'jumping prawns'. And if their publicity blurb is to be believed, they've been chefs to the stars: 'Lovely Music Best Food', allegedly said 'David Beckam [sic] of UK'. On occasion, it may be closed if there's a family wedding, christening or funeral under way.

Rice Bowl   CHINESE **$**
(mains from ₹80; ⊙10am-3pm & 6-9pm) A simple, small place with an extensive Chinese
menu, Rice Bowl offers tasty fuel for a day
on the beaches of Cavelossim, with great
chow mein and vegetable Peking rice.

Mike's Place   MULTICUISINE, BAR **$**
(mains from ₹110) A popular place for evening
meals and drinks, Mike's Place arranges live-
music nights in its easygoing restaurant/bar
and beach parties every Wednesday.

MOBOR

Little Mobor comprises the spit of land that
licks down to the banks of the Sal River.
Drive the road to its culmination and you'll
pass the fancy entrances of the Holiday Inn
and Leela on your right-hand side, and the
picturesque fishing-boat-lined Sal estuary
on your left. Here you'll get a good glimpse
of Goa's opposing faces: the gated decadence
of the Leela – with its 12-hole golf course
and gourmet Italian restaurant – and the
poverty-stricken migrant fishermen who
wake each morning at 3am to ply the seas
and make ends meet.

🛏 Sleeping & Eating

⎡TOP⎤
⎣CHOICE⎦ **Blue Whale**   INDIAN, MULTICUISINE **$**
(mains from ₹60) Stray beyond the Leela to
the very end of the Mobor peninsula, and
you'll be rewarded with one of the most
picture-perfect spots in the whole of Goa, at
this simple beach shack with an extensive
all-day menu, run by friendly local Roque
Coutinho. Wander to the spot where the
River Sal meets the sea, and you'll be guaranteed beachside bliss.

🏖 **Bamboo House Goa**   BEACH HUTS **$$$**
(☎976649369, 9822385270; www.bamboohouse
goa.com; huts ₹3400) Just 10 huts set behind
the Blue Whale at the end of the Mobor pe-
ninsula, this quiet, simple place is perfect to
hole up away from the crowds. With its eco-
credentials (composting, solar energy, inno-
vative sewage treatment) and its total sepa-
ration from the rather hectic pace of Cavelos-
sim just down the road, you'll feel as rested
and rejuvenated from the outside world as if
you'd alighted on a desert island. Ask about
discounts for stays of longer than a week, or
if you're booking more than one hut.

Leela Goa   HOTEL **$$$**
(☎6621234; www.theleela.com; r from ₹25,000;
❄@☎) If you have the taste for luxury, the

opulent Leela is the place to indulge it. Set
amid 30 hectares of land, this enormous ex-
panse of manicured Goan perfection has its
own 12-hole golf course, and various rooms
of varying degrees of decadence. Go for upmarket Indian and Goan cuisine at its signa-
ture Jamavar restaurant, or alfresco at Riverside, on the banks of the River Sal, which
serves delicious Italian dishes along with a
good dollop of *la dolce vita*.

❶ Getting There & Away

To the south of Mobor is the mouth of the Sal
River. To continue down along the coast of
South Goa you'll either need to backtrack and
head north via Benaulim for the NH17 national
highway or take the small road leading east from
Cavelossim, cross by ferry to Assolna, and then
continue down the coast road.

Assolna to Agonda

One of the most beautiful roads in Goa is the
coastal stretch between Assolna, on the south
side of the Sal River, and the village of Agonda, some 20km south, and is perfect to explore if you've got your own transport. Hilly,
winding and highly scenic, the road takes
you into tiny villages, past *palácios* (palaces),
through thick patches of coconut grove, and
up to some stunning vistas out over the sea.
Take a detour out to windswept Cabo da
Rama fort along the way, of which little remains but the ghosts of conquerors past.

ASSOLNA

If you get to Assolna by ferry from Cavelossim, turn left and follow the road to the T-
junction, then right here, and you'll arrive at
the village of Assolna, which has a lovely little
collection of old-fashioned *palácios*. Though
none are open for visiting, you won't miss
the Casa dos Costa Martins a little further
on, on the right-hand side of the road, an
older home that was converted to Portuguese
style during the 17th century. You'll still see
a nod to its earlier Hindu incarnation in the
oyster-shell peacock-tail motif (a typical Hindu symbol) above the front door.

BETUL

Continuing southwards from Assolna, opposite the narrow Mobor peninsula is the
ramshackle fishing village of Betul. Few
foreign tourists stay here and, apart from
getting local boatmen to take you out on
the river or watching the fishermen unload
their catch at the harbour, there's not much

to do, but it's a great place to wander along the tangle of fishing huts and boats of the bay and estuary. When the tide's in, you'll see seabirds diving for fish; when it's out, you'll see locals in the mud searching for crabs and other seafood. If you're feeling energetic, climb up to the cross-topped Baradi Hillock viewpoint at the south end of the village, especially nice at sunset, to see the glorious southern beach stretching off into the distance.

CABO DA RAMA

The laterite spurs along the coastline of Goa, providing both high ground and ready-made supplies of building stone, were natural sites for fortresses, and there was thus a *fortress* at Cabo da Rama long before the Portuguese ever reached Goa.

Named after Rama of the Hindu Ramayana epic, who was said to have spent time in exile here with his wife Sita, the original fortress was held by various rulers for many years. It wasn't until 1763 that it was obtained by the Portuguese from the Hindu Raja of Sonda and was subsequently rebuilt; what remains today, including the rusty cannons, is entirely Portuguese.

Although the fort saw no real action after the rebuild, it was briefly occupied by British troops between 1797 and 1802 and again between 1803 and 1813, when the threat of French invasion troubled the British enough to move in. Parts were used as a prison until 1955, before the whole thing was allowed to fall into ruin.

There is little to see of the old structure except for the front wall, with its dry moat and unimposing main gate, and the small church that stands just inside the walls, but the views north and south are worth coming for. Services are still held in the chapel every Sunday morning.

To get to the fort from the coast road between Betul and Agonda, turn west at the red-and-green signposted turn-off about 10km south of Betul. The road dips into a lush valley then winds steeply up to a barren plateau punctuated by farmhouses and wandering stock. The fort is at the end of this road, about 3km from the turn-off.

There are local buses direct from Margao or Betul (₹10, around 40 minutes) several times daily but since there's nothing to do once you've explored the fort, make sure you check on times for returning buses. There are a couple of simple cafes outside the fort entrance, serving snacks and ice-cold drinks to while away some time while waiting for a bus.

A return taxi to Cabo da Rama costs around ₹800 from Palolem, including waiting time.

GOA'S FORTS

It's well worth making time during your stay in Goa to head on up to one of its several surviving forts, which in their heyday topped windy bluffs all along the coast, and stood watch for several centuries over strategically important estuaries. Built by the Portuguese (but frequently on the sites of older defensive structures) soon after their 16th-century arrival into Goa, the forts were made of locally mined laterite, a red and porous stone that proved, in most instances, a good match for the forces pitted against it.

Under the supervision of Italian architect Fillipo Terzi, the Portuguese developed their Goan bastions to be able to withstand the forces of gunpowder and cannonballs, their low walls thick and filled with earth 'cushions' to deflect cannon fire. Meanwhile, their bastions were built to be good swivelling spots for Portugal's own massive revolving cannons.

Inside the strong fort walls, the buildings were often carved directly out of the stone itself, with storerooms for supplies and weaponry connected by a maze of subterranean tunnels. Sometimes these tunnels led down as far as to the sea itself and hidden mooring points, which would prove vital to supply the forts during any lengthy times of siege.

Though the forts were made to withstand attacks from the sea by Portugal's main trade rivals, the Dutch and the British, they were never the sites of full-scale warfare, and as the threat of maritime invasion slowly faded during the 18th and 19th centuries, most forts fell into disrepair. Some, such as Cabo da Rama, Reis Magos and Fort Aguada, found favour as prisons, while others became army garrisons or plundering sites for building materials. Today, they're atmospheric relics of a bygone age, with the advantage of some picture-perfect views down over the coast they once guarded so closely.

AGONDA
☑ 0832

Twelve kilometres south of the turn-off to Cabo da Rama (and 8km north of Palolem), the coast road passes the small village and spectacular beachfront of Agonda, a gorgeous 2km of white sand and a favourite with visiting olive ridley marine turtles, who are protected courtesy of a forestry department-staffed beach shack, and whose buried eggs are cordoned off for their safety.

Over the last few years Agonda has experienced a sharp rise in popularity, with ever more beachfront shack and hut operations lining its coconut groves behind the beach. But compared to somewhat hectic Palolem further south, the pace remains slow and the wide beach relatively empty – partly because the surf here can be fierce and is rarely good for swimming. Indeed, it's almost, these days, a taste of Palolem Past.

If you're looking for the ultimate laid-back experience, spending most of your time with a book or upside-down in a yoga asana and with little-to-no nightlife, Agonda's an ideal place to be. There's lots of foreigner-run yoga, meditation and ayurveda set-ups, and you'll find no end of daily classes and courses on offer. Keep an eye out for signs detailing the season's latest offerings posted around the Fatima Restaurant, and on lamp posts and telegraph poles the length of the beachside road. It is worth noting that there's nowadays an ATM in Arambol, just beside the church crossroads.

🍴 Sleeping & Eating

You'll find dozens and dozens of sleeping options in Agonda but, since most is of the beach-hut variety, the management, prices and quality can vary vastly from season to season. It pays to walk along the beach and see what takes your fancy, but listed here are some dependable, longer-standing options. Most beach huts have good restaurants, with parachute silk and floor cushions in abundance, and many are atmospherically candlelit come nightfall.

TOP CHOICE ⟩ **Fatima Thali Shop**   GOAN, MULTICUISINE $
(veg thali ₹65) Beloved by locals and visitors alike, teensy Fatima, with just four tables and set a few doors down from the church, is an Agonda institution, with a long and tasty menu whipped up inside its improbably small kitchen. The vegetable thalis are very popular, and can easily become a habit, whilst the Israeli salads, fish dishes, scrambled eggs, fruit salads and spaghetti all offer comfort-food options, washed down with a nice big chai.

La Dolce Vita   ITALIAN $
(mains from ₹120; ⊙ daily from 6.30pm) Fantastic Italian food is dished out daily at Dolce Vita, an Italian-run place with gingham tablecloths, a long, sprawling blackboard menu, and plenty of passionate yelling and gesturing when the place gets busy. The pizzas are thin, the pastas are entirely yummy and the

A HIDDEN HOTEL

Tucked away in the jungle towards the south end of Agonda, and rising like Greystoke from the tree line, is the eerie concrete shell of the abandoned Seema Hotel. In the early 1980s, the story goes, a handful of absentee landlords sold the palm groves in the southern portion of the beach to a hotel, allegedly backed by the former PM Rajiv Gandhi, who was later assassinated in 1991.

Agonda's toddy tappers, however, angered by the destruction of their livelihood, refused to move as building work got under way for a luxury hotel, with helipad, golf course and luxuriant swimming pool. The toddy tappers remained adamant, threatening to use force if necessary, and painting a rock in the bay with the ominous slogan, 'Your tourists will never be safe here'.

For reasons still unclear, the project collapsed soon after. Some claim it was this local pressure that caused the building work to be abandoned, others that one of Gandhi's business partners was involved in some dodgy dealings and ran out of funds, others still that the partners quarrelled to the point of no return.

Today the huge site remains in the hands of receivers, and the hotel's shell is home to troupe upon troupe of screeching monkeys, as well as a small team of round-the-clock security guards. They won't mind you wandering through, if you can pick your way through the jungle thickets, to take a closer look at the resort that never was.

THE SOUTH'S HIDDEN COVES

On the coastal strip around Palolem and Agonda, three tiny coves, accessible only by hiking there or taking a fishing boat, grace the lovely coastline. The most northerly is Cola Beach, accessible from the main coastal road a couple of kilometres north of Agonda; look out for the small signpost and make the trek down to this beautiful spot, home to a couple of beach hut operations.

Further south, you'll find Honeymoon Beach and then Butterfly Beach, two lovely coves, the latter named for its lepidopterous inhabitants. If you're planning on walking to Butterfly Beach (we recommend taking a boat from Palolem instead), it's a stiff one-hour jaunt with a steep ascent then descent to the beach, so allow plenty of time to get there and back. Bear in mind there's nowhere to buy a cold drink when you get there, so come equipped with sustenance.

tiramisu is well worth saving space for. Take a left on the beach road (heading south) to find it.

Fatima Guesthouse   GUESTHOUSE $
(☑2647477; d downstairs/upstairs ₹600/700) An ever-popular guesthouse with clean rooms, a pool table and highly obliging staff, situated on the southern stretch of Agonda's beach road. Staff will oblige in booking day trips, and there's usually some yoga going on here too.

Abba's Gloryland   GUESTHOUSE $
(☑2647822; hut/r ₹800/1000) On the opposite side of the road from the beach, this friendly, family-run place offers cool, tiled rooms with a lockable cupboard and attached bathroom, and nice, light huts with cool slate floors. And in case you need to brush up on your Ten Commandments, there's a framed poster to remind you.

Sandy Feet   BEACH HUTS, MULTICUISINE $$
(☑7875231781, 8806703636; whatsup.sandy-feet4u@gmail.com; huts from ₹1500) A popular beach hut operation situated towards the north end of Agonda, the huts here are comfy and close to the sands, but the best reason to come is for the fantastic Nepali food, especially the vegetable *momos* (dumplings; ₹105) and lip-smackingly spicy peanut salad (₹95). Laid-back staff, good music and strong cocktails make this a great place to unwind, while if you're part of a group (or just feeling thirsty) go for a Sandy Bowl (₹500), your choice of cocktail in a portion big enough to serve four.

Chattai   BEACH HUTS $$
(☑9423812287; www.chattai.co.in; hut ₹1600) Towards the north end of the beach, Chattai offers lovely, airy huts on the sands, with a touch more muslin-draped sophistication than most.

ℹ **Getting There & Away**
It's quite easy to hire a scooter or motorbike from private vendors along the beach road, if you're planning on doing a bit of travelling about. Otherwise, autorickshaws depart from the main T-junction near Agonda's church, and cost ₹220 to Palolem, and ₹250 to Patnem, and local buses run from Chaudi sporadically throughout the day (₹10), also setting down at the T-junction.

Chaudi
☑0832

Also known as Canacona, the bustling small town of Chaudi, with all its essential services along its single main street (which is also the NH17 highway), is the place to come to get things done if you're staying in Palolem, Agonda, Patnem or around. Here you'll find several banks and ATM machines, pharmacies, doctors, a supermarket of sorts, a post office, a stationery and toy shop, mobile phone vendors, and a good fruit and vegetable market and bakeries for stocking up on self-catering essentials.

Chaudi also has the south's biggest railway station (Canacona), about 1.5km northeast of town and the gateway, by rail, to Palolem.

Palolem

Well, we suppose we knew it had to happen eventually, and happen it has. We hereby (with a sniffle) officially declare Palolem...100% mainstream.

Palolem's long and stunning crescent beach was, as recently as 15 years ago, another of Goa's undiscovered, unlittered gems, with few tourists and even fewer facilities to offer them. It then slowly became a magnet for in-the-know backpackers, a lovely, languid bolthole with a few beach hut operations and a distinctly alternative vibe, until some three years ago it was just reaching saturation point. Nowadays, it's no longer quiet or hidden or especially mellow, with development picking up the pace, swarms of holidayers come high season, and prices rising breathtakingly year after year.

Some people are less fond of the recent developments in the area, dismissively labelling the Palolem of today 'Pálaga', making reference to a certain Spanish concrete-block holiday destination – and it's true that it's becoming increasingly rare to get an inch of sand to yourself. With the advent of cheap charter flights from Britain you might also see signs of the stag-weekend phenomenon: groups of lads, in football shirts and fairy wings, escorting a sozzled groom-to-be down Palolem's main strip.

With all these caveats in mind, however, Palolem's still a great place to be, outside the choc-a-bloc calamity that is Christmas and New Year. The nightlife remains mostly low-key, aside from the occasional late-night beach bar and 'silent party' (see the boxed text, opposite). If you're looking for a good place to lay up, rest a while, swim in calm seas and choose from an infinite range of yoga, massages and therapies on offer – without expecting a quiet, rustic beachside scene – Palolem may well be the ideal destination for you.

Activities

Palolem is the place to be if you're keen to fill your days with yoga, belly dance, reiki, t'ai chi or tarot, among many, many other things in varying degrees of esotericism. There are courses and classes on offer all over town, with locations and teachers changing seasonally. Meanwhile, massage and ayurveda are everywhere, and it's best to ask around to see whose hands-on healing powers are hot this season.

Kayaks are available for hire on Palolem Beach; an hour's paddling (occasionally with a life jacket included) will cost ₹400. Finally, Palolem is slowly cottoning on to a demand for Indian cookery classes. Keep your eyes peeled for fliers and posters, since a number of guesthouse and beach-hut chefs are now offering courses in how to make a mighty fine masala.

Tours

At the north end of Palolem Beach, you'll find no end of local fishermen willing to take you out on dolphin-spotting and fishing expeditions, trips up to nearby the Butterfly and Honeymoon Beaches, or boating on the estuary.

Palolem

To Dreamcatcher (300m);
Ordo Sounsar (400m)

To Banyan
Tree (100m)

To Chaudi (2km);
Canacona Train
Station (3km);
Agonda (8km);
Cotigao Wildlife
Sanctuary (9km)

ARABIAN
SEA

Mosque

To Patnem
(700m)

Palolem

Sleeping
1 Bhakti Kutir..B2
2 Ciaran's...A1
3 Luke's Residence.......................................B2
4 Oceanic Hotel...B2
5 Palolem Guest House..............................B2
6 Sevas...B2
7 Village Guesthouse...................................B1

Eating
8 Cafe Inn..A1

9 Cheeky Chapati...A1
10 German Bakery..A2
11 Hira Bar & Restaurant.............................A1
12 Shiv Sai...A1
13 Smugglers' Inn...A1

Shopping
14 Butterfly Bookshop...................................A1

SILENCE – I'M DANCING!

Some years ago, new government regulations came into force which ordered that all loud music be switched off at 10pm sharp. Though in other parts of the state this signalled the death knell of the party scene, one enterprising group of individuals decided to do something inventive about it. To circumvent the ban, this international group, known as Silent Noise, recently brought to Goa several hundred sets of wireless headphones, to reinstate all-night partying – only this time without the noise.

The basic premise of a 'silent party' is to don your headphones, often with two channels of music on offer, and then party the night away to your choice of DJ, in inner bliss but outer silence, the only noise being an occasional whoop when a popular tune comes on. Silent parties are fast catching on, but Silent Noise's remain the original and best. Check their website for details, and be suspicious of impersonators: you have to cough up a hefty deposit to take a set of headphones for the evening, and we've had reports that one unscrupulous operator has a hard time parting with the capital at the end of the silent evening's partying.

Information on Palolem's original 'silent parties' can be found at Silent Noise's www. silentnoise.in

Goa Jungle Adventure   OUTDOOR ADVENTURE
(☑9850485641; www.goajungle.com; trekking/ canyoning trips from ₹1200/1500) Run by a couple of French guys, this adventure outfit gets rave reviews from travellers for its trekking and canyoning trips. Trips run from a halfday to several days, and rafting trips are also occasionally offered. Shoes can be rented for ₹150 per day.

🛌 Sleeping

Most of Palolem's accommodation is of the simple beach-hut variety, with little to distinguish where one outfit stops and next door's begins, particularly as huts become annually closer and closer packed together. Since huts are dismantled and rebuilt with each passing season, standards can vary greatly from one year to the next: it's best to walk along the beach and check out a few before making your decision. A simple hut without attached bathroom will usually cost upwards of ₹600, while something more sophisticated can run to ₹2500 and well beyond. Colomb also has some good options, and you'll still be within walking distance to Palolem. Note that many beach huts operations these days offer free wi-fi.

TOP
CHOICE **Sevas**   BEACH HUTS **$**
(☑2639194, 2643977; www.sevaspalolemgoa.com; huts ₹500-1500; @) Next door to Bhakti Kutir, Sevas offers a comparably atmospheric experience for a far lower price. Huts and cottages are well maintained and set in pretty grounds; the family-sized cottage is a partic-

ular treat for folks travelling with children, with its wrap-around corridor, perfect for those games of hide-and-seek. Staff are generally friendly, there are a number of daily yoga classes, and the simple menu is healthy and good.

Dreamcatcher   BEACH HUTS **$$**
(☑2644873; www.dreamcatcher.in; huts & cottage ₹1000-7700) Eye-catching huts are on offer at Dreamcatcher, set just back from the beach and running alongside the small river at the north end of Palolem Beach. The beauty here is in the riverside restaurant, the attention to detail in the spacious huts (each of which is individually named), the bubbling central fountain, and the wide range of holistic treatments and massage on offer, with daily drop-in yoga and reiki courses available.

Fernandes   BEACH HUTS **$$$**
(☑9637398149; www.fernandeswoodencottages. com; huts ground fl/1st fl ₹2500/3000) Situated right beside Banyan Tree (and convenient for its yummy Thai food), this smart wooden beach hut operation offers the added bonus of 1st-floor huts above the restaurant, with fabulous views out to sea. A great, very mellow option on an otherwise quite busy bit of beach.

Palolem Guest House   HOTEL **$**
(☑2644879; www.palolemguesthouse.com; d from ₹700; ❄) If you pale at the thought of another night in a basic beach hut, this splendid place offers lots of plain but comfortable rooms with solid brick walls ranged around

a nice leafy garden. And all just a quick walk from the beach.

Bhakti Kutir   COTTAGES $$$
(☏2643472; www.bhaktikutir.com; cottages ₹3500-4500; @) Ensconced in a thick wooded grove between Palolem and Colomb Beaches, Bhakti's well-equipped rustic cottages are a little on the pricey side these days, and have lost some of their original charm, but still offer a unique jungly retreat if you don't mind bucket showers, tree frogs in the toilet, and the occasional rustle in the undergrowth. There are daily drop-in yoga classes, and the outdoor restaurant, beneath billowing parachute silks, turns out imaginative, healthy meals.

Ciaran's   BEACH HUTS $$$
(☏2643477; www.ciarans.com; huts incl breakfast ₹4000; ❈☎) Ciaran's has worked hard to keep its distinction over the years, so much so that the cottages these days can really no longer be called 'huts'. Rooms are very pleasant, set around a pretty garden, and all with their own verandah area. There's also an inviting restaurant that churns out barbecued seafood at candlelit tables under white umbrellas, and wi-fi is free.

Ordo Sounsar   BEACH HUTS $$
(☏9822488769; www.ordosounsar.com; huts with/without private bathroom ₹2500/1800) Set almost as far north up Palolem Beach as it's possible to go, across a rickety bridge spanning a wide creek, this hidden place makes a cool, quiet alternative to some of the elbow-to-elbow options further on down the sands. Its huts may not be top-quality and the whole site, at the time of research, had a bit of a scruffy aura, but it's undeniably away from the crowds.

Oceanic Hotel   HOTEL $$$
(☏2643059; www.hotel-oceanic.com; d from ₹3500; ❈@☒) This nice white building, set a fair distance from the beach on the road between Palolem and Patnem, is an ever-popular six-room place, made particularly appealing by its small swimming pool and patio restaurant perched alongside.

Village Guesthouse   GUEST HOUSE $$$
(☏2645767; www.villageguesthousegoa.com; d from ₹2750; ❈@☎) Billing itself as 'Palolem's first boutique guesthouse', the Village's eight lovely doubles are a cut above the (sometimes motley) rest. Nicely furnished with sparkling new bathrooms, four-poster beds,

and homely touches, it makes a terrific-value place to be based, despite being set back considerably from the beach. Rates include breakfast.

Luke's Residence   GUESTHOUSE $$$
(☏2643003; www.lukesresidence.com; d without/with AC ₹2500/3000; ❈☎) Set in a quiet, green part of Palolem, about 10 minutes' walk from the beach, Luke's is praised by its oft-returning guests for its warm, helpful hospitality and great food. The beds are comfy; most rooms would easily fit three or four beach huts inside. Rates include a simple breakfast.

🍴 Eating

Palolem's beach is lined with beach shacks, offering all-day dining and ultrafresh seafood as the catch comes in and the sun goes down. As with accommodation, places here change hands and quality seasonally, and are generally much of a muchness, but we've listed a few well-established options. Colomb has some decent choices too.

Cafe Inn TOP CHOICE   CAFE $$
(light meals ₹70-240) If you're craving a cappuccino, roam for foam no further than Coffee Inn, which grinds its own blend of beans to perfection. Its breakfasts are immense, as are its scrummy sandwiches (try the smoked mozzarella) and piled-high salads, but it's the evening barbeque (from 6pm to 10pm) that will really blow you away.

Hira Bar & Restaurant   INDIAN $
(breakfast from ₹12; ☺breakfast & lunch) The very best place to start the morning in Palolem with a simple *bhaji-pau* and a glass of chai, along with locals and long-staying foreigners. It looks a little desolate, but persevere: that's all part of the in-the-know charm.

Banyan Tree   THAI, MULTICUISINE $$
(mains from ₹135) One of the best beach bets for Thai specialities, the simple Banyan Tree cooks up tasty Thai curries of the green, red, yellow and potato-and-peanut-rich Massaman varieties, with banoffee pie and Lavazza coffee for afters.

Shiva Sai   INDIAN $
(veg thali ₹40-50; ☺breakfast & lunch) A thoroughly local lunch joint, knocking out tasty thalis of the veggie, fish and Gujarati kinds, and a good line in breakfasts, such as banana pancakes (₹40). Look out, too, for a number

of other nearby local holes-in-the-wall that dispense similar great grub at lunchtime.

Cheeky Chapati   MULTICUISINE, BRITISH **$$**
(mains from ₹150) The best time to visit this woodsy, British-run place is after 7pm on a Sunday, when old-fashioned roasts (including a scrummy veggie option, with gravy) grace the menu, and plates arrive at tables piled high with potatoes, vegetables and all the trimmings.

Smugglers' Inn   BRITISH **$$**
(mains from ₹150) If you're craving full English breakfasts or Sunday dinner with all the trimmings, the Smugglers' Inn, with its football on TV and weekly quiz nights, provides that little bit of Britain in the midst of beachside India.

German Bakery   BAKERY, MULTICUISINE **$**
(pastries ₹25-80, mains ₹95-170) Tasty baked treats are the stars at the Nepali-run German Bakery, but the breakfasts are excellent too. It also occasionally has yak cheese from Nepal, and is set in a peaceful garden festooned with flags.

🛍 Shopping

Butterfly Bookshop   BOOKSTORE
(Palolem Beach Rd; ⊙9am-9.30pm) The best of several good bookshops in town, this cute and cosy place (with resident cat) stocks best sellers, classics, and a good range of books on yoga, meditation and spirituality.

ℹ Information

Palolem's beach road is lined with travel agencies, internet cafes and places to change money. There are no ATM machines near Palolem's beach, but there's one on the road to Chaudi and three in Chaudi itself. An autorickshaw from Palolem to Chaudi costs ₹100.

Sun-n-Moon Travels (per hr ₹40; ⊙8am-midnight) Fast internet and recommended travel services.

ℹ Getting There & Away

There are hourly buses to Margao (₹30, one hour) from the bus stop on the corner of the road down to the beach. There are also buses every 15 minutes to nearby Chaudi (₹5), from which you can get frequent buses to Margao and Panaji. The closest train station is Canacona in Chaudi.

An autorickshaw from Palolem to Patnem costs ₹50; an autorickshaw from Palolem to Chaudi costs ₹100. A prepaid taxi from Dabolim Airport to Palolem costs ₹1000.

Colomb

☑0832

Around the headland south from Palolem is a small, rocky bay named Colomb, connected to the southern end of Palolem beach by pathways including one over the rocky beach-hut-filled headland itself. Here rustic restaurants and local homes shelter among a peaceful clump of coconut trees. The rocky bay is probably better suited to paddling than swimming (but wear rubber shoes of some description to avoid laceration), but the short walk to Palolem to the north and Patnem to the south makes this a good low-key choice. It's a good place for long-stayers to seek out simple village homes, available for rent by the month or season, or anyone looking for a more tranquil alternative to the Palolem bustle.

🛏 Sleeping & Eating

TOP
CHOICE **Capo Nero**   ITALIAN **$$**
(pizzas ₹190-230) Giving every other Italian place in South Goa a serious run for its money is this restful, as yet undiscovered option on the Colomb Bay road. The pizza oven gets fired up nightly at 6.30pm for thinnest-of-thin-crust delights, which can be parcelled up for takeaway, if a sunset picnic is in the planning. Try the mixed olive pizza which, with lots of onions and just the right touch of seasoning, is completely delicious.

Laguna Vista   BEACH HUTS **$**
(☑2644457; huts from ₹800) A variety of decent huts are on offer at this secluded, relaxed place; prices rise according to the size, view and facilities of the hut in question. Many people come here for the food, with great Tibetan *momos* (dumplings) and Nepali thalis on offer, along with live music on weekend evenings. Its French co-owner also runs informal cooking courses in gourmet French cuisine. Ask staff for details.

Boom Shankar   SEAFOOD, MULTICUISINE **$**
(mains ₹70-150; ⊙8.30am-3.30pm, 5.30pm-10.30pm) As popular for its view over the bay as for its cuisine. The Indian, Goan, Chinese, Thai and Western food here is good value (diverse specials include goulash and seafood tempura in wasabi soya), but it's the sunset cocktails, and attendant happy hour, that draw long-staying visitors here day after week after month.

NETRAVALI BUBBLE LAKE

If you're in the mood for some adventure, arm yourself with your own set of wheels and some serious determination, and set off into the South Goa countryside to track down the mysterious Netravali 'bubble lake', actually the bathing tank of the small Hindu Gopinath temple.

It's known in Konkani as the *Budbudyanchi Talli*. Streams of bubbles constantly bob up to the lake's surface, the streams getting faster if you clap your hands close to the lake's surface, but no one knows quite why.

And if you manage to make it out here, reward yourself with a trip to the nearby waterfall at the village of Savare, a 45-minute walk through dense jungle, after which you can cool off with a refreshing dip in the waterfall's pool.

It's hard to give directions for how to get to Netravali, since we're not quite sure how we managed it – through trial and error – ourselves. Suffice to say, the bubble mystery is real, and the journey through the countryside (including along some very steep roads through the wild Forestry Department-managed tract of forest known as the Netravali Protected Area) is stunning. Coming from Palolem or Chaudi on the NH17, turn off at the Forest Checkpoint on the left-hand side, and prepare for a true voyage of discovery.

Patnem

☑ 0832

Much smaller and far less crowded than Palolem to the north, pretty Patnem makes a much quieter and friendly alternative. The surf here is lively, making it great for swimming some days, and impossible on others, when an equally lively undertow is present, though these days there are life guards present in high season and flags posted on the beach for reference. Its main beach road hosts a string of stalls selling the usual variety of clothes, Kashmiri jewellery and trinkets, without the attendant hard-sell of Palolem, while its beach is backed by a line of huts and shacks, offering happy hours, all-day menus and a whole host of hut accommodation.

🏃 Activities

Harmonic Healing Centre   YOGA, ALTERNATIVE THERAPIES

(☑ 2512814; www.harmonicingoa.com) Set high on a hill at the northern end of Patnem Beach and with regular classes, workshops and treatments – including reiki, yoga, massage, tarot readings and chiropractic treatments – Harmonic is a one-stop centre for all things calming and curative. Consult the website for up-to-date listings on how to get yourself harmonious; drop-in yoga classes cost ₹350, while treatments start at ₹1300 for an hour.

🛏 Sleeping & Eating

Long-stayers will revel in Patnem's choice of village homes and apartments available for rent. A very basic house can cost ₹10,000 per month while a fully equipped apartment will go for ₹40,000 or even more. There are lots of beach hut operations (all with attached beachfront restaurants) lining the sands; many change annually, so walk along to find your perfect spot.

TOP CHOICE Micky Huts & Rooms   BEACH HUTS $

(☑ 9850484884; huts ₹800) By far the best accommodation bargain on the whole of Patnem Beach, run by the friendliest and most obliging local family you could imagine, and set deep beneath a huge stand of bamboo which twinkles with fairy lights come evening. Micky also has the massive advantage of being the only place on Patnem Beach to stay open come low season (they only close during August and September) giving intrepid off-season travellers rest, respite, a good meal and the whole of lovely Patnem beach almost to themselves.

TOP CHOICE Home   CONTINENTAL $$

(☑ 2643916; home.patnem@yahoo.com; mains from ₹100) This hip, relaxed restaurant run by a lovely British couple serves up unquestionably the best food in Patnem. Go for fresh salads with bold, rustic flavours, dine finely on risottos, specials involving volcanic ash-rolled goats cheese and yummy bowls of pasta, or simply stop in for coffee and the best chocolate brownies in India (be sure to tell Richard we sent you!). Home also rents out eight nicely decorated, light rooms (₹1000 to ₹3500). Email to book or ask at the restaurant.

Mamoos
MULTICUISINE **$**

(📞9422059876; huts small/large ₹1000/3000)
A huge sigh of relief comes from those who
mourned the closing of Mamoos in Palolem
a couple of years ago. But a big hoorah for
its new location on the Patnem Beach road,
where they're still dishing up the same delicious *aloo gobi* (cauliflower and potato curry) and killer tandoori paneers. The huts, set
back from the road in a lush, green garden,
make a great change from the beach parade.

Papaya's
BEACH HUTS **$$**

(📞9923079447; www.papayasgoa.com; huts
₹3000) Rustic huts constructed with natu-
ral materials head back into the palm grove
from Papaya's popular restaurant, which
does several versions of all the beachfront
classics. Each hut is lovingly tended to and
the staff are keen to please. There's also a
larger family hut available for ₹3500, and a
two-bedroom house for ₹6000.

❶ Getting There & Away
The main entrance to Patnem Beach is reached
from the country lane running south from Pal-
olem (past the Oceanic Hotel), then turning right
at the (rather misleadingly named) Hotel Sea
View. Alternatively, walk about 20 minutes along
the path from Palolem via Colomb Bay, or catch a
bus heading south (₹4).

Rajbag
📞0832

Quiet little Rajbag is a small sandy cove,
one beach south from Patnem and accessi-
ble both by road and with a nice short walk,
from Patnem Beach to the north, clambering
across the rocks along the way. Like many
beaches in this area, however, beware of the
treacherous undertow when swimming.

Though dominated by a hulking five-star,
it's a nice place to linger on the sands, and
is usually quite quiet (unless said five-star
happens to be hosting a massive wedding or
providing backdrop for a Bollywood block-
buster-in-the-making). Rajbag is also worth
visiting just to track down one of the best,
teeny, local restaurants in south Goa.

🛏 Sleeping & Eating
A number of locals have apartments and
houses geared to long-stayers up for grabs
in Rajbag; ask around for leads. Meanwhile,
venture down to the end of the main Rajbag
road, which ends abruptly at the banks of
the Talpona River, to get your *feni* fix from
one of the local bars.

TOP CHOICE Vernekar Restaurant
INDIAN **$**

(mains from ₹30; ☾dinner). Seek out this stellar
place and we promise you won't be disap-
pointed. A good bet is to ask local rickshaw
drivers how to get to this little place, down
a lane back from the main road opposite the
Intercontinental. It offers a mean tandoori
chicken and the world's finest *aloo gobi* for
less than the price of a Coke at the hotel
itself. It might be simple, but it serves up
some of the very best grub in South Goa.

Intercontinental Goa Lalit
MULTICUISINE **$$$**

(📞2667777; www.ichotelsgroup.com; d from
US$160; ❋@☎) These days Rajbag is domi-
nated by the presence of this massive five-
star, and most of its visitors are consequently
hotel guests. The hotel is particularly popular with well-heeled domestic and Russian
tourists, but is generally a bit lackadaisical
and not terribly well maintained.

Cotigao Wildlife Sanctuary
About 9km east of Palolem, and a good day
trip, is the beautiful, remote-feeling Cotigao
Wildlife Sanctuary (📞2965601; admission/
camera ₹5/25; ☾7am-5.30pm), Goa's second-
largest sanctuary and easily its most accessible, if you have your own transport.

Don't expect to bump into its more exotic
residents (including gaurs, sambars, leopards and spotted deer), but frogs, snakes,
monkeys, insects and blazingly plumed birds
are in no short supply. Trails are hikable; set
off early morning for the best sighting prospects from one of the two forest watchtowers, though heed the park warden's recent
warning: 'Don't climb too high, madam, for
ladder is under repair.' The watchtowers are
6km and 9km from the park entrance, so to
get there in time to see the creatures at their
most active, get going from Palolem, Patnem
or nearby at the crack of dawn.

Galgibag
Picture a postcard-perfect beach, backed
by swaying pine trees and flanked by two
twinkling rivers. Add some sea eagles riding
the currents high overhead, a beach shack
or two at the northernmost reach, and the
nesting places of the rare, long-lived olive ridley marine turtles, and you've got Galgibag,
around 16km from Chaudi and accessed by a
lovely road that runs along the south shores
of the Talpona River.

PALOLEM & SOUTH GOA RAJBAG

Don't come to Galgibag to swim – undertows and currents are strong – but it's unsurpassed for a quiet, nature-immersed walk. Stop off for sustenance at the fabulous family-run **Surya's Beach Café** (vegetable curry ₹50), nestled at its southern end in the trees, just before the river, specialising in seafood, mussels and oysters. Even top British celebrity chef Gordon Ramsay has allegedly dined at – and recommended – this place, as Surya's business card proudly notes.

Polem

In the very far south of the state, just a hop, skip and a jump to Karnataka, lies Goa's southernmost beach, set around a small bay on the seafront of the village of Polem. Though the village itself seems to have been lumbered with an unsavoury reputation – due to its secretive, lucrative line in interstate liquor smuggling – it's actually a fine spot for a seaside stroll or a picnic on the pristine sands, with a beautiful view of a cluster of rocky islands out towards the horizon. Tourist development thankfully hasn't yet made it as far as Polem, and the beach retains a local feel, with a few fishermen bringing in their catch to the northern end and nothing much else to keep you company except scuttling crabs and circling seabirds.

For a fishy lunch so fresh it's still quivering, stop off at the **Kamaxi Hotel** (⊙lunch & dinner) in among the palms, run by the eccentric local, Laxaman Raikar. He stocks Kingfisher, if you're in need of something cold and frothy, and also has three exceedingly basic, somewhat grim and grotty rooms for rent – in case you get seriously stranded – for ₹200 apiece.

To get to Polem, take a bus from Chaudi (₹12, 50 minutes) and get off at the bus stop, around 3km after the petrol station. The stop is directly opposite the turn-off to the beach. Then it's a 1km walk to the village and beach.

FURTHER AFIELD

Gokarna

✒ 08386

Heading south out of Goa and into the neighbouring state of Karnataka, a major stopping-off point for travellers and Indian pilgrims alike is Gokarna, which sits on a secluded seaside spot around 90km south of

Palolem. A mix of Hindu rituals and a medieval way of life is on show at this village, whose ambience is heightened during **festivals** such as Shivaratri and Ganesh Chaturthi. While the main village is conservative in its outlook, a few out-of-town beaches are custom-made for carefree sunbaking.

◉ Sights & Activities

Temples   HINDU TEMPLES

Foreigners and non-Hindus are not allowed inside Gokarna's temples. However, there are plenty of colourful rituals to be witnessed around town. At the western end of Car St is the **Mahabaleshwara Temple**, home to a revered lingam (phallic representation of Shiva). Nearby is the **Ganapati Temple**, while at the other end of the street is the **Venkataraman Temple**. About 100m further south is **Koorti Teertha**, the large temple tank (reservoir) where locals, pilgrims and immaculately dressed Brahmins perform their ablutions next to washermen on the ghats.

Beaches   BEACH

Gokarna's 'town beach' is dirty, and not meant for casual bathing. The best sands are due south, and can be reached via a footpath that begins south of the Ganapati Temple and heads down the coast (if you reach the bathing tank, or find yourself clawing up rocks, you're on the wrong path).

A 20-minute hike on the path brings you to the top of a barren headland with expansive sea views. On the southern side is **Kudle** (pronounced kood-lay), the first of Gokarna's pristine beaches. Basic snacks, drinks and accommodation are available here, and it's a nice place to chill. South of Kudle Beach, a track climbs over the next headland, and a further 20-minute walk brings you to **Om Beach**, with a handful of chai shops, shacks and large groups of local tourists on weekends.

South of Om Beach lie the more isolated **Half-Moon Beach** and **Paradise Beach**, which come to life only between November and March. They are a 30-minute and one-hour walk, respectively.

Depending on demand, fishing boats can ferry you from Gokarna Beach to Kudle (₹100) and Om (₹200). An autorickshaw from town to Om costs around ₹200.

Don't walk around after dark, and not alone at any time; it's easy to slip on the paths or get lost, and muggings have occurred. For a small fee, most lodges in Gokarna will safely store valuables and baggage while you chill out on the beach.

Ayurveda

Well-trained masseurs at **Ayur Kuteeram** (☏9480575351; Gokarna Beach; ⊘9am-8pm) can work magic on those knotty muscles. An *Abhayanga* treatment costs a mere ₹700. Quality ayurvedic therapies and packages are also available at specialist ayurvedic centres at the SwaSwara resort and Om Beach Resort.

🛌 Sleeping

With a few exceptions, the choice here is between a beach shack or a basic but more comfortable room in town. Some guesthouses in town cater to pilgrims, and may come with certain rules. Prices can increase during festivals or the high season.

BEACHES

Both Kudle and Om beaches have shacks offering budget huts and rooms. Places open up on Half-Moon and Paradise beaches from November to March. Most places provide at least a bedroll; bring your own sheets or sleeping bag. Padlocks are provided and huts are secure. Communal washing and toilet facilities are simple.

SwaSwara

HOTEL $$$

(☏257132, 0484-3011711; www.swaswara.com; Om Beach; d 7 nights Indian/foreigner ₹115,000/€2015; ❄@≋) This amazing health resort sits on the hill overlooking Om Beach. No short stays on offer here, but you can relax at this superbly designed red-laterite-brick resort for a full week, and enjoy a holiday based around yoga and ayurvedic treatments. There's an interactive kitchen here, and the artists in residence can help you hone your creative skills. Rates include full board, transport, leisure activities and daily yoga sessions. Weeklong ayurvedic treatment packages kick off at around US$600.

Namaste Café

GUESTHOUSE $

(☏257141; Om Beach; huts from ₹800; ❄@) In and out of season, Namaste is the place to hang. What's better, the place has upped its luxuries since the last time we were here, and now offers air-con and internet on its serene Om Beach premises. The restaurant-bar cooks up great bites and is the premier Om chill-out spot. In season, it also offers basic huts (₹150) at Paradise Beach and cottages at Namaste Farm (from ₹500) on the headland.

Hotel Gokarna International Kudle Resort

HOTEL $$

(☏257843; Kudle Beach; d ₹1600; ❄) Run by the same management that owns Hotel Gokar-

na International in town, this midrange option has smart rooms and a lovely garden up front. The waves wash up to its gates during high tide, and seal the deal in its favour.

Nirvana Café

GUESTHOUSE $

(☏329851; Om Beach; d ₹350; cottage ₹450) Located on the southern end of Om, this extremely pleasant guesthouse featuring huts within a shady garden should be done renovating by now.

GOKARNA

Om Beach Resort

HOTEL $$

(☏257052; www.ombeachresort.com; Bangle Gudde; d incl breakfast Indian/foreigner ₹2800/ US$105; ❄@) This little jewel sits on a headland 2km out of Gokarna, off the Om Beach road. Set amid lawns and shady trees, its red-brick cottages are excellently designed, and its restaurant serves good seafood to go with the booze. There's a professional ayurvedic centre on site, with seven-night treatment packages starting from US$490 per person.

Kamat Lodge

GUESTHOUSE $

(☏256035; Kamat Complex, Main St; s/d ₹250/350, d with AC ₹1300; ❄) A value-for-money place on Gokarna's main drag, this hotel offers clean rooms with fresh sheets and large windows. But don't expect room service and other such extras.

Nimmu House

GUESTHOUSE $

(☏256730; nimmuhouse@yahoo.com; s/d from ₹300/600; @) A pleasant option off Gokarna's main beach, run by a friendly family.

Vaibhav Lodge

GUESTHOUSE $

(☏256714; off Main St; d ₹250, s/d ₹200/250; @) A backpackers' dig, with mosquito nets, hot water in the morning and a rooftop restaurant.

Shastri Guest House

GUESTHOUSE $

(☏256220; Main St; s/d/tr ₹200/300/450) A hostel-like place with good, airy doubles in the new block out the back. The singles are cramped, though.

🍴 Eating

The chai shops on all of the beaches rustle up basic snacks and meals.

Namaste Café

CAFE $

(Om Beach, mains ₹80-100; ⊘7am-11pm) Om Beach's social centre serves some excellent Western staples such as pizzas, burgers and shakes. But the real draws are its tasty seafood dishes, especially the grilled calamari

WORTH A TRIP

WALK ON THE WILD SIDE

Located in the jungles of the Western Ghats about 100km from Goa, emerging Dandeli is a wildlife getaway that promises close encounters with exotic wildlife, such as elephants, panthers, sloth bears, Indian bisons and flying squirrels. It's a chosen birding destination too, with resident hornbills, golden-backed woodpeckers, serpent eagles and white-breasted kingfishers. Also on offer are adventure activities ranging from kayaking to bowel-churning white-water rafting on the swirling waters of the Kali River.

Kali Adventure Camp (per person incl full board Indian/foreigner from ₹2300/€70; ❄) offers accommodation in tented cottages and rooms, done up lavishly while adhering to ecofriendly principles. Book through Jungle Lodges & Resorts Ltd (☏080-25597944; www.junglelodges.com).

Frequent buses connect Dandeli to both Hubli (₹45, two hours) and Dharwad (₹35, 1½ hours), where there are onward connections to Goa, Gokarna and Hospet.

and the pomfret preparations. Dinners are particularly enjoyable, later in the evening when it is quieter.

Prema Restaurant MULTICUISINE $
(Gokarna Beach; mains ₹80-110; ⊙10am-8.30pm) A decent menu comprising Continental improvisations and colourful ice-creams. Spice packs and herbal oils for sale at the counter.

Pai Restaurant SOUTH INDIAN $
(Main St; mains ₹50-80; ⊙6.30am-9.30pm) Serves a fantastic veg thali for ₹55.

Pai Hotel INDIAN $
(Car St) A popular and freshly renovated eatery with an excellent vegetarian menu.

ⓘ Information

SBI (Main St) Has an ATM.

Shama Internet Centre (Car St; per hr ₹40; ⊙10am-11pm) Fast internet connections.

Sub post office (1st fl, cnr Car & Main Sts; 10am-4pm Mon-Sat)

ⓘ Getting There & Away

Bus

From the **bus stand**, buses roll to Karwar (₹33, 1½ hours), which has connections to Goa. Frequent direct buses run to Hubli (₹107, four hours), where you can change for Hospet and Hampi.

Train

Travelling by train is by far the most pleasant way to reach Gokarna from Palolem, and makes a nice quick less-than-two-hour journey. Various express trains run between Margao's Madgaon station in South Goa and **Kumta station**, which is 25km away from Gokarna itself. You can also pick up the latter two of the following trains at Canacona station in Chaudi, if you're travelling between Palolem and Gokarna.

The *Maru Sagar Express* (train no 12978) departs Madgaon on Fridays at 1.25pm, reaching Kumta at 2.46pm. It departs Kumta on Sundays at 8.44am and arrives at Margao at 10.55am.

The *Poorna Express* (train no. 11097) departs Madgaon on Saturdays at 1.15pm, reaching Kumta at 2.46pm. It departs Kumta on Mondays at 12.12pm and arrives at Madgaon at 3pm.

The *Matsyagandha Express* (train no. 12619) departs Madgaon at the less friendly 1.35am, arriving at Kumta at 3.12am. This service, however, runs daily. On the return leg, it departs Kumta at 6.40pm and arrives in Madgaon at 8.30pm.

Fares all cost around ₹309 for a 2nd class AC ticket, ₹240 for a 3rd class AC ticket, and ₹140 for a simple sleeper ticket. Many hotels and small travel agencies in Gokarna can book tickets. Autorickshaws charge ₹250 from Gokarna to Kumta station; a bus costs ₹15.

Jog Falls
☏08186

Nominally the highest waterfalls in India, the Jog Falls only come to life during the monsoon. At other times, the Linganamakki Dam – further up the Sharavati River – limits the water flow. The tallest of the four falls is the Raja, which drops 293m.

For a good view of the falls, bypass the area close to the bus stand and hike to the foot of the falls down a 1200-plus step path. Watch out for leeches during the wet season.

Hotel Mayura Gerusoppa (☏244732; d ₹650), near the car park, has a few enormous and musty doubles. Stalls near the bus stand serve omelettes, thalis, noodles and rice dishes, plus hot and cold drinks.

Jog Falls has three buses daily to Karwar via Kumta (₹51, three hours), where you can change for Gokarna (₹16, one hour). A return taxi from Gokarna costs ₹1500.

Understand
❯ Goa & Mumbai

GOA TODAY 188

With growth and modernisation afoot, just how is Goa doing in that delicate balancing act of past, present and future?

HISTORY 190

From the Mauryans to the Portuguese, many civilisations have added their own coat of paint. Here's how best to view the resulting masterpiece.

THE WAY OF LIFE 197

When it comes to living, Goans take *susegad* seriously. But there's more to progressive Goa than the art of relaxation.

ARTS & ARCHITECTURE 203

Architecture, music and dance form the beating heart of Goa, where cultural melanges have created fascinating art forms.

FOOD, GLORIOUS FOOD 206

Never go hungry beside the Arabian Sea, with sizzling seafood, Portuguese-inspired hotpots and South Indian vegetarian treats aplenty.

MARKETS & SHOPPING 212

Stretch your rucksack seams with booty from market stalls, lifestyle shops, bookstores, antiques emporia...and even a magic shop or two.

WILDLIFE & THE ENVIRONMENT 215

Behind the beach fronts, a greener, quieter, kingfisher-filled Goan world exists. But how best to keep it that way?

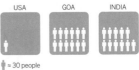

population per sq km

USA   GOA   INDIA

👤 ≈ 30 people

Goa Today

Paradise Found

Goa was a solitary Portuguese outpost in India for almost 500 years and the influence of colonial rule can still be seen everywhere: in the exquisite, crumbling architecture; in the East-meets-West cuisine; and in the siesta-saturated *joie de vivre* that Goans themselves call *susegad*.

Little wonder, with all these charms, that just about everybody wants – or wanted at some point in history – to come here. The state has had her fair share of would-be conquerors, from the Mauryans and the Marathas, to the British, Dutch and Portuguese. Today pinkish package tourists throng the northern beaches; upwardly mobile internationals lounge beside infinity pools; well-heeled Russians party through the evenings; and young Israelis soak away the stresses of military service.

But international travellers aren't the only non-Goans who arrive in the state in search of the good life. Domestic tourists from across India flock here for an annual dose of sun and fun, outnumbering international visitors five-to-one. Moreover, Goa enjoys one of India's highest per-capita incomes and comparatively high health and literacy rates, factors which attract a good scattering of folks from other parts of India who arrive looking for work and that magical *susegad* they've heard so much about.

» Population: 1.34 million

» Annual tourists: 2.6 million (12% of tourists to India)

» Average annual income per capita: ₹34,000 (US$683)

» Literacy rate: 82% (national average: 65%)

The Darker Side

Despite its myriad charms, Goa is not a perfect paradise. Goa's large homeless population is mostly migrants, driven from their homes often due to water shortages, and hoping life here will treat them more kindly. Almost inevitably, it doesn't.

Meanwhile Goa suffers from a sorely stressed environment, burdened by the effects of logging, iron-ore mining, relentlessly expanding tour-

Top Books

» **Maximum City: Bombay Lost and Found** (Suketu Mehta) Mumbai in all its gritty glory

» **Goa and the Blue Mountains** (Richard Burton) Classic account of Goa, written in 1851

» **Goa Traffic** (Marissa de Luna) Thriller set in Goa's party scene

» **Reflected in Water: Writings on Goa** (Jerry Pinto) Collected writings by literary luminaries

» **Houses of Goa** (Pandit/Mascarenhas) Beautifully illustrated book on Goa's mansions

Goan Music

» **Goa Trance** (www.goatrance radio.com) Goan psy-trance

» **Goan Fusion** (www.remomusic. com) Legend Remo Fernandes

» **Konkani radio** (www.live365 .com/stations/61664) Traditional Goan music of all kinds

belief systems
(% of population)

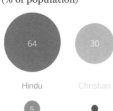

64
Hindu

30
Christian

5
Muslim

1
Other

if 100 people visited Goa

83 would be Indian

ism and uncontrolled industrial growth. Rare turtle eggs have traditionally been considered a delicacy but in recent years have been trampled underfoot on increasingly busy beaches; plastic bottles lie in vast glaciers that approach as the real kind recede; and vagrant cows feast on refuse from noisome rubbish bins.

Poverty, prostitution, a shady drugs trade, violent crime and police corruption all also remain pressing problems, just as they do in Mumbai. Animal shelters overflow with unwanted domestic creatures and children's homes struggle to provide shelter, safety and education for the state's shockingly large population of at-risk and orphaned children. A number of charities address some of these issues; though, as they'll attest, their level best is seldom enough.

A Silver Lining?

Nevertheless, if a healthy economy is any indication of a state's ability to weather the storm, then the picture isn't all bleak. Goa's active economy has given rise to a healthy Gross Domestic Product of around US$3 billion annually, about 2½ times India's national average.

And though, in 2008 and 2009, tourism to Goa plummeted, due to the global economic downturn combined with fears of terrorism spawned by the 2008 Mumbai (Bombay) attacks, locals held on tight, and by 2012 tourism appeared to have recovered.

Meanwhile, enterprising locals slowly lead the way toward to a cleaner, more sustainable future, instigating small local recycling initiatives, volunteering on turtle-egg protection duties, or working with local green organisations, such as the Goa Foundation and Green Goa Works. With luck, such efforts will go forth and multiply, to ensure Goa's charms keep their place on travel itineraries for centuries to come.

» Size: length 105km, width 65km

» Staple lunch dish: *fish-curry-rice*

» Strangest historical relic: St Francis Xavier's finger-nail, Chandor

» Best hidden sight: Netravali Bubble Lake

Dos

» Refill plastic water bottles with filtered water

» Consider buying souvenirs from cooperatives or charity concerns

» Support businesses that support the environment

» Use shower water sparingly to avoid shortages affecting locals

Don'ts

» Sunbathe nude or topless; it's not welcomed in Goa

» Wear shoes inside local Goan houses

» Sport bikinis and shorts outside beach resorts; they're not considered appropriate

Green Resources

» **Goa Forest Department** (www.goaforest.com)

» **Goa Foundation** (www.goafoundation.org)

» **Green Goa Foundation** (www.greengoafoundation.com)

» **Green Goa Works** (www.greengoaworks.in)

History

A quick 100,000-year skip through the history of little, lush Goa offers you a keen insight into some of the region's most mysterious and alluring archaeological and historic remains, and into the Goan psyche itself. The state's story is one of conflicts and conquests, with suitors throughout history vying for her delicate hand.

The greatest lasting influence you'll notice is the mark of her most recent conquerors, the Portuguese, who ruled Goa from 1512 to 1961, yet they weren't the first to arrive here. Archaeologists now believe even Goa's earliest inhabitants were settlers from elsewhere, arriving to tame this brilliant patch of emerald and aquamarine from the opposite side of the Western Ghats. Thus it's not hard to see why Goans are generally so welcoming to successive waves of foreign visitors, having started out as visitors – albeit in prehistory – themselves.

For a whiz through Mumbai's history, see p39.

> Head out to remote Usgalimal in South Goa to examine the petroglyphs (rock art), including images of a peacock and a dancing woman inscribed into the laterite river rocks by the earliest Goans.

Prehistoric Beginnings

According to Hindu legend, Goa was created by Parasurama, the sixth incarnation of the Hindu god Vishnu, who shot an arrow into the Arabian Sea and commanded the tide to retreat, to create a peaceful spot for his Brahmin caste to live.

A trip out into the Goan hinterland, however, to the riverside rock carvings of Usgalimal offers an alternative picture of the first Goans, hunter-gatherer tribes who inhabited the hinterland sometime between 100,000 BC and 10,000 BC. No one really knows where they originally came from; some believe they were migrants from Africa, others that they hailed from eastern Asia, or were a northern tribe forced southwards by instability in their homeland.

TIMELINE	100,000– 10,000 BC	2400– 700 BC	AD 420
	Hunter-gatherer tribes inhabit the Goan interior, evident in the impressive rock carvings at Usgalimal and stone implements discovered at the Zuari River, near Dudhsagar Falls.	Goa experiences at least two waves of Aryan immigration from the north, bringing with them improved farming techniques and the first elements of what would become Hinduism.	Goa's home-grown Hindu rulers, the Kadambas, rise to power over their distant overlords, and install their own royal family, ushering in a period of religious tolerance, prosperity and innovation.

Early Wranglings

Goa's history becomes less of a mystery around the 3rd century BC, when it became part of the mighty Buddhist Mauryan empire. Ashoka, probably the greatest Mauryan emperor, sent a Buddhist missionary to convert the locals; the monk set up shop in a rock-cut cave near modern-day Zambaulim, preaching nonviolence and urging the tribes to give up their nasty habit of blood sacrifice. Though he had some success, introducing the plough and spreading literacy, his liturgy fell largely on deaf ears, and following the rapid demise of the Mauryans after the death of Ashoka in 232 BC, Goa turned to Hinduism, commingled with its old tribal practices.

The next seven centuries saw Goa ruled from afar by a succession of powerful Hindu trading dynasties, which sent Goan goods and spices to Africa, the Middle East and Rome. However, continued wrangling between these dynasties offered the opportunity for a homespun dynasty to quietly emerge: in AD 420 the local Kadamba clan declared independence, and created their very own 'royal family'.

Another Hindu legend relates that Goa's name came from Lord Krishna, who was so enchanted by the place that he named it after the cows ('Go' in Sanskrit) belonging to the charming milkmaids he encountered here – for whom Krishna had quite the famous predilection.

Kadamba Prosperity

Finally, Goa had some stability. By the late 6th century, the Kadambas had found their stride, and in contrast with what was to come, the Kadamba rule was a period of tolerance. Muslim merchants from Arabia and East Africa were encouraged to settle, Hindu temples were constructed statewide and prestigious academic institutions were inaugurated.

Yet, like all good things, it was not to last. The success of the Kadambas signalled their own downfall, with Muslim Bahmani sultans from the Deccan in South India, keen on getting their hands on Kadamba wealth, pouring into Goa from the 10th century onwards. Today, the sole Kadamba structure to survive the troubled years to follow is the melancholy Tambdi Surla Mahadeva temple, saved from a grisly fate only because of its remote jungle location.

In 1352, the Bahmanis triumphed, and years of religious tolerance were brought to an abrupt and painful end. The new rulers immediately set about a harsh regime of Hindu persecution, destroying the grand Kadamba temples and killing their priests. They reigned intermittently, ousted by rival kingdoms from time to time, until the late 1400s, when a force far bigger than their own was to sail merrily over the horizon.

Traces of the Kadambas

» Caves of Khandepar

» Tambdi Surla

» Goa's Kadamba bus company logo (featuring the roaring-lion Kadamba dynastic crest)

Portugal Ahoy!

In 1498 Vasco da Gama, a Portuguese sea captain, landed south of Goa at Calicut (present-day Kozhikode) on the Malabar Coast, 'seeking Christians and spices', with a view to superseding the Arab monopoly of the

1054	1352	1498	1534
Goa's capital shifts from Chandrapur (modern-day Chandor) to Govepuri (now Goa Velha). Wealth and trade skyrocket, with locals building vast homes and places of worship with the profits of the spice trade.	After suffering three centuries of Muslim raids, Goa comes under the rule of Muslim Bahmanis and almost all trace of the Kadambas' Hindu legacy is quickly destroyed, except for the Tambdi Surla Mahadeva temple.	Portuguese captain Vasco da Gama arrives in Goa, making him the first European to reach India via the Cape of Good Hope. The Portuguese hope this will allow them to dominate Eastern trade routes.	Portugal gains the islands that form modern-day Mumbai from the Muslim sultans of Gujarat. They name the area 'Bom Bahia'. A century later, the British government takes possession.

overland spice trade. He didn't have much luck finding Christians, but there were certainly spices in abundance.

It was to take 50 years of Muslim-Christian fighting, however, before Portugal was able to claim those spices as its own, establishing firm territorial borders in Goa – now known as the Velhas Conquistas (Old Conquests) – that stretched from Chapora Fort in the north to Cabo da Rama Fort in the south.

GOAN HOUSE OF HORRORS

Of all Portugal's alleged abuses of its Goan subjects, the terrors to which the population was subjected under the iron rule of the Inquisition – also known as the Holy Office or Santo Officio – were undoubtedly the worst.

The Inquisition was dispatched to Goa on royal command, originally conceived to target 'New Christians' (Cristianos Nuevos), the forcibly converted Jews and Muslims of Portugal who had fled to the country's colonies and 'lapsed' back to their original faiths. By the time the Inquisition arrived, life was already becoming increasingly difficult for the region's Hindus, who for some years had been enduring a slowly eroding official tolerance to their faith. Idols had already been banned, temples closed and priests banished. Now, with the arrival of the Inquisitors, matters went from bad to worse: refusing to eat pork became a crime punishable by imprisonment, as was possession of turmeric, incense and other items used in traditional Hindu worship.

Though the genuinely louche and licentious Portuguese gentry were generally above the law, the lower, indigenous classes soon found themselves at risk of imprisonment in the fearsome dungeons of the Palace of the Inquisition, the *Orlem Ghor* (big house), of Old Goa, with tortures such as the rack, flesh-eroding quicklime, burning sulphur and thumbscrews awaiting their arrival.

Once a 'confession' of heresy had been extracted, the prisoner then languished in a windowless cell, awaiting one of the Inquisition's famous *autos-da-fé* (trials of faith). During these morbidly theatrical 'trials', dozens of prisoners, dressed in tall mitres and robes emblazoned with macabre images of human beings engulfed in flames, would be marched across the city of Old Goa, from the Palace of the Inquisition to the Church of St Francis of Assisi, amid crowds of onlookers and to the solemn tolling of the Sé Cathedral bell.

Inside the church, following a lengthy sermon, the judgments were read to the accused.

The luckiest ones were to endure slavery abroad. Victims who refused to recant their 'heresy' were usually burned at the stake; those willing to admit to it were thoughtfully strangled before the pyre was lit.

In the period between 1560 and 1774 (after which records become sketchy) a total of 16,176 people were arrested by the Inquisition, mostly Hindus, though more than two-thirds of those burned alive were Jews who had been forcibly converted as Cristianos Nuevos. In 1814 the Inquisition was finally repealed, as part of an Anglo-Portuguese treaty, and most of its later records destroyed.

1543	1560	1612	1643
Goa's Muslim sultan cedes areas of Goa to Portugal, to stop it from supporting a rival contender for the throne. Portugal now owns land from Chapora Fort in the north to Cabo da Rama Fort in the south.	Portugal's Tribunal of the Holy Office (the Goan Inquisition) arrives in Goa to begin its brutal 200 years of suppression of religious freedoms, executing hundreds of 'heretics', and instilling fear into Goan hearts.	British East India Company ships defeat a Portuguese fleet off the coast of Western Gujarat, starting the end of Portuguese hold. The Dutch soon outmanoeuvre Portuguese ships with their superior technology.	The Ponte de Linhares, (now Ribandar Causeway) is built by the Portuguese to join the capital Old Goa to the little port at Panjim, a step which, 200 years later, will help it supersede the older, plague-ridden capital.

The Inquisition Arrives

Initially, Portugal's approach to its new subjects was relatively enlightened: Hindus were considered friends against Portugal's Muslim foe, and 'conversion' was largely confined to allowing Portuguese soldiers to marry local women, so that their children would be raised Christian.

But in 1532 Goa's first Vicar General arrived, and the age of tolerance was over. Increasingly stringent laws were passed to forbid Hindu worship, and to allow only Christians rights to land. Then, in 1560, the terrifying Portuguese Tribunal of the Holy Office – otherwise known as the Goan Inquisition – came to Goa.

Establishing itself at the old sultan's palace in what is now Old Goa, the tribunal soon began flexing its ecclesiastical muscles. But astonishingly, the subsequent two centuries of Portuguese religious terrorism still failed to completely eradicate Hinduism from Goa. Many Hindus fled across the Mandovi River, into the region around modern-day Ponda, smuggling their religious statuaries to safety and secretly building temples to house them.

The 'Inquisition Table', around which sat its dreaded interrogators, is now housed at the Goa State Museum in Panaji. A crucifix that once stared down, with open eyes, at the Inquisitors' victims, now also lives in Panaji, at the Chapel of St Sebastian.

HISTORY THE INQUISITION ARRIVES

Goa's Golden Age

Not all religious orders, however, came tarred with the same cruel and zealous brush as the Inquisitors. By the mid-16th century, Franciscan, Dominican and Augustinian missionaries, along with Jesuits and others, were present in Goa, establishing hospitals and schools, and teaching alternative methods of farming and forestry.

When they weren't busy converting the masses, they were masterminding much of Goa Dourada's (Golden Goa's) glorious ecclesiastical building boom. Levies from the lucrative international spice trade financed work on the Sé Cathedral and the Basilica of Bom Jesus, and soon Old Goa's population stood at 300,000, larger than London or Lisbon itself. Though life remained perilous – many would-be immigrants perished at sea en route, or succumbed to bouts of malaria, typhoid and cholera that swept the city – in Goa it seemed truly golden.

On encountering Francis Xavier's 'incorrupt' body in 1634, a Portuguese noblewoman named Dona Isabel de Caron was allegedly so anxious to obtain a relic that she bit off the dead saint's little toe... and it gushed fresh blood into her mouth.

Portuguese Struggles

Just as 'Goa Dourada' and its magnificent edifices were in their ascendancy, however, Portugal's own fortunes were beginning to wane.

In 1580, bankrupted by a disastrous campaign in North Africa, Portugal was annexed by Spain, and it wasn't until 1640 that the Portuguese regained independence. Wranglings followed over Goa, both with Britain and with the last of the mighty Maratha Empire, led by Shivaji, whose homeland lay in the Western Ghats. Finally, a May 1739 treaty between the Portuguese and the Marathas forced the Portuguese to hand over

1664	1739	1781–88	1787
The Hindu Marathas, under the leadership of legendary, fearsome warrior Shivaji, temporarily take parts of Goa, alerting the Portuguese to the dangers lurking in eastern, as well as western, powers.	The Portuguese sign a treaty with the Marathas, handing over large tracts of their northern territory near Mumbai in exchange for full Maratha withdrawal from Goa.	The Novas Conquistas (New Conquests) sees Portugal add to its Goan territory, delineating, by 1788, the confines of the state as we see it today.	The first serious local attempt to overthrow the Portuguese, the Pinto Revolt, is attempted; it's unsuccessful and its leaders are either tortured and executed, or shipped to Portugal.

large tracts of their northern territory, near Mumbai (Bombay), in exchange for a full Maratha withdrawal from Goa.

And though Portugal succeeded in adding more territory to Goa during the 18th century – four *talukas* (districts), including Ponda, Quepem and Canacona, known as the Novas Conquistas, or New Conquests, the grand age of Portuguese Goa was on the decline. The effects of the Inquisition, coupled with plague after horrendous plague sweeping Old Goa, meant that by 1822 Old Goa had been completely abandoned, its monuments lost in a tangle of jungle. The senate moved to Panjim (present-day Panaji) in 1835, which soon after became Goa's official capital.

Meanwhile Portugal continued to struggle with troublemakers within and without. In 1787 the short-lived Pinto Revolt, whose conspirators were largely Goan clerics, sought to overturn their overlords' rule. The revolt was discovered while it was still in the planning, and several of the leaders were tortured and put to death, while others were imprisoned or shipped off to Portugal (see p102).

Visit Goa's Forts

» Fort Tiracol (Terekhol)

» Chapora Fort

» Fort Aguada

» Reis Magos Fort

» Cabo da Rama Fort

» Corjuem Fort

End of an Empire

The 19th century saw increasing calls for Goan freedom from Lisbon. Uprisings and rebellions became common, and by the 1940s the Goan leaders were taking their example from the Independence movement across the border in British India. But despite widespread demonstrations, on 10 June 1947 the Portuguese Minister of Colonies, Captain Teofilo Duarte, warned that the 'Portuguese flag will not fall down in India without some thousands of Portuguese, white and coloured, shedding their blood in its defence'.

Portugal's dictator Dr Antonio de Oliveira Salazar attempted to lobby world leaders into condemning India's claims over Goa: he even managed to persuade John F Kennedy to write to Nehru, advising him against the use of force on the issue.

The March to Independence

When overtures by the newly independent Indian government were made to the Portuguese in 1953, it became clear that the Portuguese had no intention of withdrawing. On 11 June 1953 diplomatic relations between the two countries were broken off.

Within Goa, protests continued, often met with violent retaliation from Portuguese forces. Meanwhile India manoeuvred for international support. Finally, however, Indian Prime Minister Jawaharlal Nehru found himself pushed to the brink when, in November 1961, Portuguese troops stationed 10km south of Goa opened fire on Indian fishing boats. On the night of 17 December 1961 Operation Vijay finally saw Indian troops crossing the border. They were met with little resistance and by evening of the following day the troops reached Panaji.

At 8.30am on 19 December, troops of the Punjab Regiment occupied the Panaji Secretariat Building and unfurled the Indian flag, signifying

1835	**1843**		**1926**
Goa's senate moves from Old Goa to a healthier capital at Panjim (today's Panaji). Goa's viceroy, Dom Manuel de Portugal e Castro, levels the dunes and drains the swamps to make it a habitable alternative.	Panjim becomes Goa's new capital, and Old Goa is left almost uninhabited. British adventurer Richard Burton soon describes Old Goa as a place of 'utter devastation'.		Portugal declares itself a republic, and dictator Dr Antonio de Oliveira Salazar takes the helm, refusing to relinquish control over the country's colonies.

HUW JONES / LONELY PLANET IMAGES ©

» Old Goa (p126)

the end of the 450-year Portuguese occupation of Goa. The Portuguese left quietly shortly afterwards.

Post-Independence

Initially, India's self-proclaimed 'liberation' of Goa was met with a luke-warm response from Goans themselves. Some feared a drop in their relatively high standard of living, and saw in themselves few similarities with their Indian neighbours. Others feared the loss of their cultural identity, and that Portuguese plutocrats would simply be replaced by an army of Indian bureaucrats.

Nevertheless, the first full state government was operating in Goa by the end of December 1962. On 31 May 1987 Goa was officially recognised as the 25th state of the Indian Union, and in 1992, its native tongue, Konkani, was recognised as one of India's official languages.

INCORRUPTIBLE OLD ST FRANCIS

Goa's patron saint, Francis Xavier, was born in Spain in 1506. A founding member of the Society of Jesus (the Jesuits), he embarked on a number of missionary voyages from Goa between 1542 and 1552, before dying off the coast of China just before Christmas, 1552.

After his death (so the story goes) several sackfuls of quicklime were emptied into his coffin, to consume Xavier's flesh in preparation for the return of the mortal remains to Goa. Yet, two months later, the body remained in perfect condition – 'incorrupt' despite all that quicklime. The following year, it arrived back in Goa, where its preservation was declared a miracle.

The church, however, wanted proof. In 1554 the viceroy's physician performed a medical examination, and declared all internal organs intact and that no preservatives had been used. He then asked two Jesuits in attendance to insert their fingers into a small wound in Xavier's body. 'When they withdrew them,' he noted, 'they were covered with the blood which I smelt and found to be absolutely untainted.'

It took until 1622 for Francis Xavier to be canonised for his posthumous efforts. But by then, holy relic hunters had corrupted the incorruptible: his right arm had been removed and divided between Jesuits in Japan and Rome (where it could allegedly still sign its name), and by 1636 parts of one shoulder blade and internal organs had been scattered throughout southeast Asia. Even his diamond-encrusted fingernail was re-moved, and is now squirrelled away at the Pereira-Braganza house in Chandor (p159).

At last, at the end of the 17th century, the body reached an advanced state of desic-cation and the miracle appeared to be over. Nowadays the parched remains of Francis Xavier are kept in a glass coffin in the Basilica of Bom Jesus in Old Goa. But once every decade on Xavier's feast day, 3 December, the coffin is paraded through Old Goa for closer examination by the masses. The next airing will take place in 2014.

1940s	1955	1961	1967
Goa's independence movement gains ground. On 18 June 1946, a demonstration in Margao leads to the arrest of independence activist Dr Ram Manohar Lohla. In the aftermath, 1500 campaigners are jailed.	On 15 August a huge satyagraha is called. Portuguese troops open fire on protestors; many are arrested, beaten, imprisoned and exiled to Africa.	On 17 December, Indian troops cross the border into Goa; by 19 December, an Indian flag flies atop Panaji's Secretariat Building.	A Goan opinion poll shows that the state's residents don't want Goa to be assimilated into its neighbouring state, Maharashtra, despite Maharashtra pressing for this.

For most of the 1990s political instability plagued the young state: between 1990 and 2005, Goa had no fewer than 14 governments. Corruption became rife, and policymaking impossible. One of the parties to benefit from the chaos was the right-wing Hindu nationalist Bharatiya Janata Party (BJP). In March 2006 anti-Muslim riots broke out in Sanvordem, in the interior of Goa. Since then, attacks on Hindu temples and shrines have risen alarmingly, amid constant calls to maintain the religious tolerance Goans themselves are famous for. Anti-Muslim sentiments, in the extreme Hindu camp, have also been running dangerously high.

A small faction within Goa still advocates independence of Goa from India; learn more at www.freegoa.com. Meanwhile, to keep abreast of developments in India, check BBC News' Country Profile, at www.bbc.co.uk/news/world-south-asia-12557384.

Goa Today

In an age of extremists, it remains to be seen whether Goa can escape unscathed. Recently a Hindu group publicly threatened to attack Western women seen drinking alcohol in Goan pubs. Violent crime frequently makes newspaper headlines, police corruption is still considered rife, and the November 2008 terrorist attacks on Mumbai's hotels and restaurants rattled Goans, who feared they'd be the next hard hit. Over Christmas and New Year 2008–2009, sandbagged machine-gun posts were maintained on Goa's beaches and public parties cancelled, for fear that the spectre of global terrorism would destroy the tourist industry on which the state depends. Happily this didn't come about, but Goans remain vigilant, fearing it's only a matter of time before the troubles of the outside world, once again, interfere with Goa's workings.

1987	1996	2008	2009
On 31 May, Goa is officially declared India's 25th state by Prime Minister Rajiv Gandhi, in a landmark ruling for the state's generations of armed supporters.	Bombay's name is officially changed to Mumbai, the name derived from the goddess Mumba who was worshipped by early Koli fisherfolk in the area.	Goa's tourism industry is hit hard by the global recession and the threat of terrorism against tourists, with a sharp drop in visitors after the Mumbai terrorist attacks of 26–29 November, known as '26/11'.	India takes to the polls in countrywide elections. On 22 May the new government is sworn in, with the Indian National Congress party's Prime Minister Manmohan Singh in for a second consecutive term.

The Way of Life

Goan Identity

With the constant comings and goings of the sultans, kings, governors and colonising cultures over the last several thousand years, Goans have grown adept at clinging tight to their indigenous traditions while blending in the most appealing elements of each successive visitation. Goans today take substantial pride in their Portuguese heritage – evident in their names, music, food and architecture – combining this seamlessly with Hindu festivals, Konkani chatter, Christmas parties, a keen interest in the English football leagues and, with the recent influx of Russian travellers to Goa's shores, an uncanny ability to rustle up a good bowl of borscht.

Modern Goa, moreover, is a place where the hippies of the '60s have gone native, and where children of a whole host of cultures, alongside centuries-old Goan families, now deem themselves part of the cultural landscape. Here 'local' can mean a hole-in-the-wall *feni* (liquor distilled from coconut milk or cashews) joint where patrons chat in Konkani and gaze at Bollywood music videos, or a chic boutique hotel whose patrons are simultaneously British and fourth-generation inhabitants of India. Local can also mean a gleeful beach party with young Goans dancing the night away with international travellers, or a whitewashed Catholic church rubbing shoulders with a Hindu shrine, where Christian wakes are held by candlelight in honour of Hindu deities.

But whether Catholic Goan, Hindu Goan, Muslim Goan or 'new' Goan, some things unite everyone native to the eclectic state. Everyone has a strong opinion about the constantly changing faces of Goa, and of what it means, in essence, to be Goan. Everyone possesses a set of nostalgic memories of 'the way things used to be', whether this means the opulent

SUSEGAD

You won't get far in Goa without spotting references to *susegad* or *sossegado*, a *joie de vivre* attitude summed up along the lines of 'relax and enjoy life while you can'. Originating from the Portuguese word *sossegado* (literally meaning 'quiet'), it's a philosophy of afternoon naps, long, lazy evenings filled with *feni* (liquor distilled from coconut milk or cashews) and song, and generally living life with a smile. On the 25th anniversary of Goan Independence, even Prime Minister Rajiv Gandhi described how 'an inherent non-acquisitiveness and contentment with what one has, described by that uniquely Goan word *sossegado*, has been an enduring strength of Goan character'.

In essence, it is *susegad* that makes a visit to Goa so special, with people ready to smile and say hello, to let you onto a crowded bus or to simply sit and chat the warm tropical hours away.

landowning days of Portuguese dependence, the trippy free-love '60s, or the calm before the package-holiday storm. And above all, Goans across the state are eager to ensure, each in their own individual way, that Goa doesn't lose its alluring, endearing, ever-evolving distinctiveness in the decades to come.

Lifestyle

Compared to the rest of the country, Goa is blessed with a relatively high standard of living, with healthcare, schooling, wages and literacy levels all far exceeding the national average. Its population of somewhere around 1.5 million is divided almost exactly down the middle between rural and urban populations, and many people continue to make their living from tilling the land or raising livestock.

However, there are still those who fall desperately far below the poverty line. You'll notice slums surrounding the heavy industry installations as you drive south on the national highway from Dabolim Airport. Many migrant workers, attracted to Goa by the hopes of benefiting from its tourist trade, end up begging on its beaches, and hundreds of homeless children from surrounding states are supported by local and international charities (see p30).

Another acute local problem, linked both to poverty and Goa's liberal attitude to drinking, is alcoholism. There are tens of thousands of registered alcoholics in the state, and many more unregistered sufferers; you're sure to witness the fallout of too many *fenis* in those stumbling about outside local bars at some time during your visit.

Traditional Culture

Though many cultural traditions overlap and mingle, particularly within Goa's Christian and Hindu communities, you'll find some traditional practices still going strong in Goa.

Marriage

Though 'love matches' are increasingly in vogue in Goa in Christian and Hindu circles alike, both communities still frequently use a matchmaker or local contacts to procure a suitable partner for a son or daughter. If all else fails, you'll find scores of ads listed in the newspaper classifieds, emphasising the professional qualifications, physical attributes and 'wheatish' complexion of the young, eligible individual.

Generally, following Hindu marriages, the young wife will leave her family home to live with her husband's family. However, this is not always the case, and many young couples today are choosing to branch off to begin their own family home. Dowries are usually still required by the groom's family in both Christian and Hindu weddings, either helping facilitate a match or hindering it; a mixed-caste marriage will become much more acceptable if there's a good dowry, but a high-caste girl from a poor family can find it very difficult to secure a partner of a similar 'status'.

Hindu weddings in Goa are lengthy, gleeful and colourful, while Christian wedding ceremonies are more sombre (though the party afterwards usually kicks up a storm) and similar to those in the West, with some elements, such as the ritual bathing of the bride, borrowed from Hinduism. *Chudas,* green bracelets traditionally worn by married women, are donned by both Hindu and Christian brides, and tradition dictates that, should her husband die before her, the widow must break the bangles on his coffin.

Embracing the digital age, Goans, like almost everyone else, are taking to the internet in search of love. Popular sites – allowing would-be brides and grooms (and their parents) to scour the whole of India for suitable matches include www. bharatmatrimony. com and www. shaadi.com.

Death

Death, as everywhere, is big business in Goa, and you'll spot plenty of coffin makers, headstone carvers and hearse services on your travels. In the Christian community, personal items are placed with the deceased in the grave, including (depending on the habits of the deceased) cigarettes and a bottle of *feni,* while most Hindus are cremated. Annual memorials, wakes and services for the dead are honoured by Christians and Hindus alike.

There are numerous superstitions in the Hindu and Christian communities about restless spirits – particularly of those who committed suicide or died before being given last rites – and a number of measures are undertaken at the funeral to discourage the spirit from returning. The clothing and funeral shroud are cut, and a needle and thread are placed in the coffin. The spirit of the deceased who wishes to come back must first repair its torn clothing, a task that takes until daylight, at which time departure from the grave is impossible.

For a glimpse of *Six Feet Under,* Goan style, swing by the corner Abade Faria Rd, close to the Church of the Holy Spirit, in Margao, where a busy funeral director and coffin making industry churns out memento mori, stacking spare coffins photogenically in an abandoned building across the road.

THE WAY OF LIFE LIFESTYLE

Contemporary Issues

Women in Goan Society

Generally, the position of women in Goa is better than that elsewhere in India, with women possessing property rights, education options and career prospects not shared by their sisters in other states. The result of Goa's progressive policies today is that women are far better represented than elsewhere in professions and positions of influence. While men undoubtedly still predominate and many women still choose to fulfil traditional household roles, around 15% of the state's workforce are women, many of whom fill roles as doctors, dentists, teachers, solicitors and university lecturers, and 30% of panchayat (local government council) seats are reserved for women.

GOAN HEROINES?

Goa is no stranger to Bollywood sensation, providing a picturesque backdrop for many movies each year. But the 2011 hit *Dum Maaro Dum,* a crime thriller directed by Rohan Sippy, prompted more than a raised eyebrow or two. It's set amid Goa's seamier side, with a plot involving cocaine smuggling, parties and the Russian mafia, and one song lyric in particular caused offence when actress Bipasha Basu trilled, 'Over here, liquor is cheap, but women are even cheaper...'

Public outcry quickly followed in Goa, with locals decrying this representation of their women. A petition filed at the Goa Bench of the Mumbai High Court sought a permanent ban on the movie, stating that the portrayal might attract sex offenders, drug traffickers and criminals to Goa.

The Shiv Sena political party, too, found itself up in arms. 'Goa has already been sold. Half of the land in Goa...has been sold to outsiders including those in the Bollywood film industry,' said local Shiv Sena politician Philip d'Souza; 'Now, stop selling the daughters of Goa.' Pramod Salgaocar, former chair of the Goa State Women's Commission, added that the movie's trailer was exploiting the character of Goan women simply to sell a movie, while Victoria Fernandes, Member of the Legislative Assembly, said she would take the matter up with the Indian cabinet. 'Who is tolerating this,' she asked, 'and why?'

The film, nevertheless, grossed $10 million upon release. Yet overall it received lukewarm critical reviews, not so much for its portrayal of women – Goan or otherwise – but for a lacklustre pace. In the words of critic Raja Sen, 'As can be said the morning after a party with too much cocaine, all that eventually remains are a couple of good lines.'

For a peek at what the fuss is all about, check out the official trailer for *Dum Maaro Dum* on YouTube.

Female Foeticide

Throughout India, baby boys frequently remain favoured over baby girls, particularly among the poor, and largely for what are seen as practical reasons. Girls require dowries when they get married, and then generally leave home to support their husband and his family. Conversely, boys, so the logic goes, will stay close to home, supporting their parents through old age.

In a bid to counter the practice of aborting female foetuses, the determination of sex of the unborn child has been made illegal under India's Prohibition of Sex Selection Act. But despite the law, the number of girls born continues to fall significantly short of the number of boys, and although Goan girls don't suffer ill-treatment to the same extent as girls in other regions of India, Goan organisations remain committed to actively promoting equality, and you'll pass plenty of posters cheerfully declaring 'Girl or Boy, Small Family is Joy'.

Religion

At the Church of Our Lady of Miracles in Mapusa, which was built on the site of an ancient Hindu temple, the church's annual feast day, held 16 days after Easter, is celebrated by Christians and Hindus together.

On paper, at least, it's clear: roughly 30% of Goa's population is Christian, 65% Hindu and 5% Muslim. But statistics alone don't reveal the complex, compelling religious concoction that typifies the population's belief.

Religious Hybrids

During the fierce, Inquisition-led imposition of Christianity by the Portuguese, many Hindus fled to safety in parts of the state still considered safe, while others converted to the new faith and remained in Portuguese territory. Thus, for generations, many Goan families have contained both Catholics and Hindus.

The distinction was further blurred by the ways in which Christianity was adapted to appeal to the local population. As early as 1616 the Bible was translated into Konkani, while in 1623 Pope Gregory permitted Brahmin families to retain their high-caste status after converting to Catholicism, and allowed the continuance of a number of local festivals and traditions.

GOA'S CASTE SYSTEM: HINDU & CHRISTIAN ALIKE

Every Hindu is born into an unchangeable social class, a caste or varna, of which there are four distinct tiers, each with its own rules of conduct and behaviour.

These four castes, in hierarchical order, are the Brahmins (Bamons in Konkani; priests and teachers), Kshatriyas (Chardos in Konkani; warriors and rulers), Vaisyas (merchants and farmers) and Sudras (peasants and menial workers). Beneath the four main castes is a fifth group, the Untouchables (Chamars in Konkani; formerly known as 'Harijan', but now officially 'Dalits' or 'Scheduled Castes'). These people traditionally performed 'polluting' jobs, including undertaking, street sweeping and leather working. Though discrimination against them is now a criminal offence in India, it's nevertheless still an unfortunate part of life.

While the caste system doesn't play as crucial a part in life in Goa as elsewhere in India, it's nevertheless still recognised and treated in a uniquely Goan way, and holders of public office remain largely of the Bamon or Chardo castes.

The Christian community also quietly adheres to the caste system, a situation that can be traced back to Portuguese rule since, as an incentive to convert to Catholicism, high-caste Goan families were able to keep their caste privileges, money and land. Even today, in village churches, high-caste Christians tend to dominate the front pews and the lower castes the back of the congregation, and both Hindus and Christians carefully consider questions of caste when selecting candidates for a suitable marriage match.

Today this fusion of these religions is still extremely evident. In Goa's numerous whitewashed churches, Christ and the Virgin Mary are often adorned with Hindu flower garlands, and Mass is said in Konkani. Christians and Hindus frequently pay respects to festivals of the others' faith, with both Christmas and Diwali being a source of celebration and *mithai*-giving (sweet-giving) for all.

But that's not to say that Goa is free from religious tensions. In 2006 anti-Muslim riots, beginning with the destruction of a makeshift village mosque in Sanvordem, shook Goa's religiously tolerant to the core. Moreover, spates of robberies of relics from churches and Hindu temples continue to spark public debate on religious tolerance, ultimately, and happily, reinvigorating the fervour with which the majority respect different faiths.

Hinduism

Though Hinduism encompasses a huge range of personal beliefs, the essential Hindu belief is in Brahman, an infinite being, or supreme spirit, from which everything derives and to which everything will return. Hindus believe that life is cyclical and subject to reincarnations (avatars), eventually leading to moksha, spiritual release. An individual's progression towards that point is governed by the law of karma (cause and effect); good karma (through positive actions such as charity and worship) may result in being reborn into a higher caste and better circumstances, and bad karma (accumulated through bad deeds) may result in reincarnation in animal form. It's only as a human that one can finally acquire sufficient self-knowledge to achieve liberation from the cycle of reincarnation.

Hindus have long worshipped animals, particularly snakes and cows, for their symbolism. The cow represents fertility and nurturing, while snakes are associated with fertility and welfare. Cows take full advantage of their special status in Goa, lazing in the middle of even chaotic highways, seemingly without a care on this mortal coil.

Christianity

Christianity has been present in Goa since the arrival of the Portuguese in the 16th century, who enforced their faith on Goa's Muslim and Hindu population by way of the Goan Inquisition. By the time Hindus and Muslims were once again able to practise freely, Catholicism had taken root and was here to stay.

For the last 30 years or so, a form of faith known as 'Charismatic Christianity' has being gaining ground in Goa. Worship involves lots of dancing, singing and sometimes 'speaking in tongues', with readings from the New Testament allegedly used to harness the power of the holy spirit, heal the sick and banish evil forces. Unlike mainstream Catholicism, Charismatic Christianity's services are usually in the open air, and its priests reject all notions of caste, understandably making the movement particularly popular among Goa's lower castes.

Islam

Brought to Goa in the 11th century by wealthy Arab merchants, who were encouraged by local rulers to settle here for reasons of commerce, Islamic rule predominated in the region for large chunks of medieval Goan history.

With the arrival of the Portuguese, Islam all but disappeared from Goa, and now remains in only small communities. Most Goan Muslims today live in Goa's green heartland, around Ponda, in the vicinity of the state's biggest mosque, the Safa Masjid.

THE WAY OF LIFE RELIGION

Goan Hindu homes are identifiable by the multicoloured *vrindavan* (ornamental container) that stands in front of the house. Growing inside it is the twiggy tulsi plant, sacred to Hindus since in mythology the tulsi is identified as one of the god Vishnu's lovers, whom his consort, Lashmet, turned into a shrub in a fit of jealousy.

Goa's Most Colourful Churches

» Church of Our Lady of the Immaculate Conception, Panaji

» Basilica of Bom Jesus, Old Goa

» Church of the Holy Spirit, Margao

Sport

The official soccer season runs from January to May; tickets to the matches generally cost less than ₹30 and can be bought at the ticket kiosks outside the Jawaharlal Nehru Stadium in Margao on match days.

Just about everyone knows how seriously Indians take the pursuit of cricket, but it may come as a surprise to learn that Goa's top sport is football (soccer), another legacy left over from the days of Portuguese rule. Every village has at least one football team, and sometimes several – one team for each *waddo* (ward) of the village – and league games are fiercely contested.

This has seen the creation of several teams that regularly perform at National Football League (NFL) level, and these days there are even Goan players in the national football squad. The main Goan teams to watch are Salgaonkar SC from Vasco da Gama, Dempo SC from Panaji, and Churchill Brothers SC from Margao, and matches are played out at the Jawaharlal Nehru Stadium, near the Margao bus station, regularly attracting up to 35,000 fans. Goans are also keen cricketers and you'll see plenty of dusty playing fields being used for local matches. Volleyball, too, is a firm local favourite, with regular matches played at sunset on beaches and on almost every village green.

Arts & Architecture

Music & Dance

Listen carefully beyond the Bob Marley, lounge and techno jumble of the beach shacks, and you'll hear Goa's own melodies, which, like most other things in the state, are a heady concoction of East and West.

The most famous kind of Goan folk song is the *mando,* also known as 'the love song of Goa', a slow melody with accompanying dance, which sees its largely Catholic participants dance in parallel lines, flourishing paper fans and handkerchiefs. You might catch a glimpse of this if you pass a Christian wedding or feast day in progress.

Though increasingly rare, the melancholy, haunting *fado* can still be heard here and there in Goa, whose songs lament lost love, or the longing for a Portuguese home that most singers, in fact, have never seen. Listen out for the late, great folk singer Lucio de Miranda, or Oslando, another local folk and *fado* favourite.

Local Konkani pop is a strange and sometimes wonderful combination of tinny, trilly musical influences – African rhythms and Portuguese tunes, with a bit of calypso thrown in – and you'll catch its twangy melodies from passing cars, buses and taxis, and in local Goan lunch spots. A classic, old-school performer to look out for, who has influenced a whole new generation of local musicians, is the much-loved Lorna, 'the Goan nightingale'.

Aside from local celebrations (to which tourists are often extended a warm welcome), the best places to find traditional music and dance performances are at Panaji's Kala Academy and Calangute's Kerkar Art Complex.

REMO FERNANDES

Known in the West and worshipped in India, Remo Fernandes is famous for his ability to fuse cultural influences in both his music and his image.

Remo was born in Siolim in 1953. After studying architecture in Bombay and hitch-hiking around Europe and Africa (busking along the way), he returned to Goa. Several rejections from Indian labels made him record his first (and arguably one of his best) albums, *Goan Crazy,* at home in Siolim. From there, Remo shot to success with more hit albums, movie score offers, awards, product endorsements and titles like 'the Freddie Mercury of India'.

Remo is loved in Goa, not only for the versatility of his talent but also for never cutting his Goan roots along his path to fame. When Remo turned 50 in May 2003, he celebrated with a free 4½-hour concert in Goa.

Look out for *Old Goan Gold* and *Forwards into the Past,* which has arrangements by Remo and vocals by the late, *fado*-famed Lucio de Miranda. Remo, meanwhile, still lives and records in Siolim, and you might catch a concert if you're in the village during its exuberant Zagor festival in December (see p79 for more).

The Western music scene in Goa still thumps – albeit less incessantly than in recent years – to the hypnotic rhythms of Goa trance, or psytrance, which came to prevalence in the early 1990s. Its most famous exponent remains Goa Gil, who DJs trance parties worldwide. Go to www.goagil.com to see where he's next appearing – though these days it's unlikely to be in Goa.

Pop into Margao's Golden Heart Emporium, the book stores around Panaji's Municipal Gardens, or one of Calangute's several bookshops for an especially good selection of the most up-to-date local Goan literary releases.

Literature

Although it can be difficult to get hold of Goan literature (books go out of print very quickly), a decent amount of Konkani literature is available in English translation.

Some mainstays of Goan literature include *Angela's Goan Identity,* a fictional work by Carmo D'Souza, which offers a fascinating insight into a girl's struggle to define her Goan identity towards the final years of the Portuguese era in Goa, while Frank Simoes' engaging *Glad Seasons in Goa* offers an affectionate account of Goan life.

Perhaps the greatest classic of Goan literature, though, is *Sorrowing Lies My Land,* by Lambert Mascarenhas, first published in 1955, which deals with the struggle for Goan Independence launched in Margao in 1946. Meanwhile, Victor Rangel Ribeiro weaves together Goan vignettes in his award-winning first novel *Tivolem,* and Mario Cabral E Sa's *Legends of Goa,* illustrated by one of Goa's best-known artists, Mario de Miranda, is a colourful reworking of some of Goa's best folk tales and historical titbits.

Architecture

Goa's most iconic architectural form is likely the slowly crumbling bungalow mansion, with its wrought-iron balconies, shady front *balcãos* (pillared porches), oyster-shell windows and central *saquãos* (inner courtyards), around which family life traditionally revolved.

Stroll the lanes of Chandor, Siolim or the coastal villages between Velsao and Mobor for a treasure trove of Portuguese mansions in various stages of decay. Meanwhile visit Calizz in Candolim or the Houses of Goa museum at Torda to get up to speed on Goa's architectural heritage.

Most were built in the early 18th century, as rewards to wealthy Goan merchants and officials for their services to the Portuguese. The architecture was inspired by European tastes, but the materials – red laterite stone, wood, terracotta, and oyster shells used instead of glass for windows – were all local. The wealthiest of these homes also contained a locally crafted wooden chapel or oratory, which housed gilded and golden relics, altars and images of Catholic saints as the focal point for family prayers.

Churches, too, bear the hallmark of Portugal, many of them cruciform and constructed of whitewashed laterite stone. Even the humblest of village churches usually sports a sumptuous interior, with an elaborate gilt *reredos* (ornamental screen), and lots of carving, painting and chandeliers. Goan temples are yet another form of architectural hybrid, enfolding both Muslim and Christian elements into traditional Hindu designs. Domed roofs, for example, are a Muslim trait, while balustraded facades and octagonal towers are borrowed from Portuguese church architecture. Their most unusual and distinctive features, however, are their 'light towers', known as *deepastambhas,* which look a little like Chinese pagodas and are atmospherically decorated with oil lamps during festival periods. For more on Goan temple architecture, check the boxed text on p139. Meanwhile, for details on Mumbai's incredible spread of architectural gems, see p40.

Painting

Although there's no style that is particular to Goa, some of the state's most historically significant artistic output can be seen in the murals at Rachol Seminary (p158), in the ornately decorated churches across Goa, and adorning the portraiture-heavy walls of Goa's grand mansion homes.

Out and about in Goa, the two artists you're most likely to come across are Dr Subodh Kerkar, whose work fills the Kerkar Art Complex in Calangute (p94), and the late, much-loved artist and illustrator Mario Miranda, who died in 2011 but whose distinctive style continues to adorn everything from books to billboards to the walls of Café Mondegar (p60) in Mumbai.

Mumbai is an architectural paradise, filled with Victorian Gothic fantasies, including the High Court, Chhatrapati Shivaji railway station, and the Taj Mahal Palace Hotel. Don't miss, too, the modern engineering of the Global Pagoda, and the serene spirituality of Haji Ali's Mosque.

Cinema

The Indian film industry is the largest on the planet, with around 800 movies produced annually, most of them elaborate, formulaic, melodramatic Bollywood montages that celebrate romance, violence and music, with saccharine lip-synched duets and fantastic dance routines, all performed by Indian megastars who are worshipped like deities countrywide. It's absolutely imperative, during any stay in Goa, to see at least one of these incredible creations of high camp, and Panaji is the place to do so, with the comfortable INOX Cinema (p121) and the far more gritty and atmospheric Cine Nacional (p121) the best cinematic destinations.

The INOX also plays host to Goa's grand and glittering annual International Film Festival of India (IFFI; www.iffi.gov.in), the country's largest festival, which sees Bollywood's greatest and most glorious jetting in for preening and partying all along the red carpet.

For more on Bollywood, see p50.

Theatre

Goa's theatre scene is dominated by the unique local street plays known as *tiatr* and *khell tiatr* (a longer form of *tiatr* performed only during festivals such as Carnival and Easter). The *tiatrs,* almost all of which are in Konkani, provide a platform for satire on politics, current affairs and day-to-day domestic issues.

Since 1974 Panaji's Kala Academy (p121) has held an annual festival (all performed in Konkani) each November, showcasing the work of well-known *tiatr* writers.

Food, Glorious Food

Goan cuisine, with its manifold combinations of coconut, chillies, vinegar, rice and spice, is one of the world's original fusion foods, rich in Portuguese and South Indian heritage. '*Prodham bhookt, magi mookt*', say the locals in Konkani; 'You can't think until you've eaten well', and Goans take the sating of their appetites extremely seriously.

Typically, unlike in much of India, Goan dishes come with a meaty or fishy accent, the most delicious of which are set aside for feast days, saints' days and weddings. Hunt about in local haunts, however, and your search will be rewarded with mouth-watering Goan curries galore, such as *xacutis, vindalhos, cafrials* and *balchãos*. Meanwhile, in the sweet department, creations are cooked up in combinations of sugar, cardamom, coconut and jaggery (dark palm sugar): they might not be bikini-conducive, but they sure do taste divine.

Staples & Specialities

Given Goa's seaside location, it's little wonder that the local lunchtime staple is *fish-curry-rice,* crisp fried mackerel steeped in a thin coconut, tamarind and red chilli sauce and served with a mound of rice; you'll find it on any 'non-veg' restaurant's menu, and it's a cheap and tasty way to fill up at midday.

Aside from things aquatic, chicken and pork are the flesh of favour (you'll see the live versions gadding about in every Goan farmyard), and the latter makes for another local lunchtime favourite, served up in the form of a piled plate of Goan *chouriços*. These air-dried spicy red pork sausages (similar to Spanish chorizo) are flavoured with *feni* (liquor distilled from coconut milk or cashews), toddy (palm sap) vinegar and chillies, and strung in desiccated garlands from streetside stalls, to be rehydrated, fried up and served with fresh *pau,* fluffy white bread rolls that are part of Portugal's lasting legacy to the state.

According to linguists, there's no such thing as an Indian 'curry' – the word, an anglicised derivative of the Tamil word *kari* (black pepper), was used by the British as a term for any dish including spices.

Sauces

Look out for *xacuti,* a spicy Goan sauce – pronounced sha-*coo*-tee – which combines coconut milk, freshly ground spices and red chillies. Chicken and seafood are frequently served basted with *rechead,* a spicy marinating paste, which sees its host fried, grilled or baked in a tandoori oven. Dry-fried chicken might otherwise be served spicy *cafrial* style, marinated in a green masala paste and sprinkled with toddy vinegar. Meanwhile, the original *vindalho* – far from being the sole preserve of British curry house lads – is a uniquely Goan derivative of Portuguese pork stew that traditionally combines *vinho* (wine vinegar) with *ahlo* (garlic) and spices. You'll find most sauces are used to cook some sort of meat or fish, but vegetarians should always enquire about the availability of a 'veg' version: vegetarian *vindalho* is especially delicious.

Spices

Head to one of Goa's divinely scented spice farms to find evidence of the sought-after spices that kept conquerors coming back to Goa for centuries. South India still produces the very best of the world's black-pepper crop, an essential ingredient in savoury dishes worldwide, while locally produced turmeric, coriander and cumin, combined with garlic, chillies, tamarind and *kokum* (a dried fruit used as a spice) form the basis of many a Goan curry.

Rice

Rice is by far the most important staple in India, providing most meals for most people throughout most of their lives, and Goa is no exception. In its more sophisticated guises, rice is cooked up to make *pulao* (pilau; aromatic rice casserole), or a Muslim biryani, with a layer of vegetable, chicken or mutton curry hiding under a ricey surface. Both these dishes are prevalent on Indian menus throughout the state, and make a great change whenever you're tired of the plain white variety.

Dhal

Vegetarian or omnivorous, Christian, Hindu or Muslim, India is united in its love for dhal (lentils or pulses). Most commonly in Goa, you'll find three types of dhal gracing the menu: thin, spicy *sambar*, served with many breakfast dishes; 'dhal fry', which is yellow, mild and has the comforting consistency of a thick soup; and 'dhal makhani', richer and darker, spiked with *rajma* (kidney beans), onions and another handful or two of some of the 60 types of pulses grown in the country. Various other pulses, including *kabuli chana* (chickpeas) and *lobhia* (black-eyed beans), also turn up regularly in that delicious Goan breakfast staple, *bhaji-pau*.

Left-handers beware: when out and about in non-Western restaurants, try to eat only with your right hand; the left is considered unclean and for the purposes of ablution only. If you're invited to dine with a family, always take off your shoes and wash your hands before dining.

FOOD, GLORIOUS FOOD STAPLES & SPECIALITIES

GOAN NUTS

Swaying coconut palms form the very essence of the Goan landscape, but they're far more than just a photogenic sunset sight. Goans alone get through something approaching 40 million coconuts every year, and the simple coconut is responsible for the livelihoods of around 18% of the state's population.

Coconut flesh, known as copra, gives flavour and substance to almost every Goan speciality dish, savoury and sweet alike, as well as providing oil for use in other sorts of cooking, soap manufacture, hair oil and cosmetics. The hairy outer shell of the coconut is spun into water-resistant coir rope, and used by Goan fishermen to secure their boats.

But the humble coconut's usefulness doesn't stop there. Its sap, known as toddy, is collected by toddy tappers, who shinny up their swaying trees two or three times daily. It's then fermented and made into that killer liquor, *feni*, which is drunk widely. Coconut wood is used for timber, and its leaves provide roofing for many a lean-to shelter and simple traveller beach hut.

Out and about on the Goan beach, you're bound to be approached by coconut vendors keen to cut open a fresh fruit, so that you can sip on the vitamin-rich milk. It makes a refreshing change from an everyday soft drink, and offers up a true, unadulterated taste of Goa. Just don't, whatever you do, set up your sleeping bag beneath a coconut palm: a few victims a year meet their maker by way of fruit that go bump in the night.

Seafood

Among the most famous Goan fish dishes are *ambot tik,* a slightly sour curry; *caldeirada,* a mild seafood stew with vegetables flavoured with wine; and the Portuguese-inflected *recheiado* which sees a whole fish, usually a mackerel or pomfret, slit down the centre, stuffed with a spicy red sauce, and fried up in hot oil. Another regular on Goan menus is *balchão,* a rich and tangy tomato and chilli sauce, often used to cook tiger prawns or fish.

Dairy products

Goa abounds with milk products. A small pot of glistening white *dahi* (curd) is served with most meals, most traditionally in an unfired clay pot; paneer (cheese) is a godsend for the vegetarian majority; lassi (yoghurt and iced-water drink) is popular in both sweet and savoury forms; ghee (clarified butter) is a traditional cooking medium; and the best local sweets are made with milk.

Recently Goa has also seen a rise in the number of European-style cheeses on offer. Maia Cheese, based in Palolem, was founded by a Russian expat and makes tasty mozzarella, feta, and ricotta, among others. Kodaicanal and Auroville dairies, both in nearby states, have also branched out into cheesemaking; their products can be bought at grocery shops statewide, and are found gracing many a beachside pizza.

Sweets

Look out for *bebinca,* the most famous of Goan sweets, a rich 16-layer coconut pancake-type cake, whipped up with sugar, nutmeg, cardamom and egg yolks. Also be sure to sample *batica,* a squidgy coconut cake best served piping hot from the oven; *doce* made with chickpeas and coconut; and *dodol,* a gooey fudgelike treat, made from litres of fresh coconut milk, mixed with rice flour and jaggery.

Drinks

Nonalcoholic Drinks

There's nothing more refreshing on a tropical day than a steaming glass of chai (tea), boiled for hours with milk, sugar and masala spices, and served piping hot, sweet and frothy.

Coffee is less widely consumed by local Goans, but you'll have no problem finding the instant kind; 'milk coffee', as it's sold in beach shacks, is usually a boiling hot cup of steamed milk, with a spoonful of Nescafé sprinkled on top. Goa is increasingly finding its way into the speciality coffee market, and fragrant loose beans can be bought at local markets, while high-end coffee stands are popping up in tourist hot spots.

Aside from India's tooth-jarringly sweet selection of carbonated drinks, 'lime-soda' is a standard cold option (soda water mixed with freshly squeezed lime juice); ask for it 'plain' if you don't want sugar or salt added.

Alcoholic Drinks

Goans love to drink – a fact sadly attested to by the state's high level of alcoholism. The tipple of choice is beer, and Kingfisher and Kings are the two local favourites.

Next comes *feni,* the local moonshine, made either from a palm sap or cashew base, which is fermented and distilled to around 30% to 35% proof. *Feni* first-timers might decide to mix it with a soft drink, or just close their eyes and take their medicine: a shot in a local bar costs from ₹20 to ₹40.

COOKING COURSES

Informal cooking courses held by locals, especially in Palolem, Arambol and Anjuna, can often be found advertised on hotel and cafe noticeboards. The UK-based company India on the Menu (www.indiaonthemenu.com) runs cooking courses from its purpose-built kitchen near Panaji.

Hard liquor, known in India as IMFL – Indian-made foreign liquors – is largely cheap, and palatable if mixed with something soft, sweet and bubbly. You'll have fun choosing from the names on offer; opt for a Honeybee or an Old Monk depending on your inclination.

Wine, though not India's strong point, is slowly gaining ground, but you'll pay dearly for choosing the grape over the grain: bought at a liquor store, even a mediocre bottle of local wine costs around ₹500 (safe bets are Sula, Chateau Indage and Grover). Unless you're a fan of the sickly sweet, avoid Madeira – though when drunk cold on ice, it tastes a bit like dessert wine – and local port wines.

Celebrations

Goans need only the flimsiest excuse to celebrate and almost every month has a festival that requires feasting.

Weddings are occasions to indulge gastronomic fantasies, including dishes such as *sorpotel,* a combination of meat, organs and blood, diced and cooked in a thick, spicy sauce flavoured with *feni.* Seafood also features at feasts, tables groaning under the weight of dishes such as fish aspic (set in gelatine), oyster pie, stuffed and grilled *surmai* (mackerel) and curried or fried prawns. Desserts might include *bebinca* and *leitria* (an elaborate coconut covered by a lacy filigree of egg yolks and sugar syrup).

Hindu festivals, too, are synonymous with feasting. *Karanjis,* crescent-shaped flour parcels stuffed with sweet *khoya* (milk solids) and nuts, are synonymous with Holi, the most boisterous Hindu festival, as are *malpuas* (wheat pancakes dipped in syrup), *barfis* (fudgelike sweets) and *pedas* (multicoloured pieces of *khoya* and sugar). Pongal (Tamil for 'overflowing'), the south's major harvest festival, produces a dish of the same name, made with the season's first rice along with jaggery, nuts, raisins and spices.

Where to Eat & Drink

Goa's eating-out options are divided into the 'local' and 'nonlocal' varieties: the local serving up Indian cuisine of one sort or another, and the nonlocal encompassing everything from Tibetan kitchens to French fine dining.

Goan Cookbooks

Great Goan Cooking: 100 Easy Recipes – Maria Teresa Menezes

Savour the Flavour of India – Edna Fernandes

Goan Recipes and More – Odette Mascarenhas

THE MOST IMPORTANT MEAL OF THE DAY

Keen breakfasters will delight in the range of options on offer in Goa, from the 'banana-honey-porridge' of the beach shacks to the South Indian treats of the Goan breakfast table.

Don't miss the classic *bhaji-pau,* a white bread roll *(pau)* served ready to dunk into a spicy side curry *(bhaji).* Washed down with a glass of hot chai, it's simply one of the world's best and simplest breakfasts, and will set you back a mere Rs15 or so. Each establishment has its own take on the *bhaji* that makes up *bhaji-pau:* most are dhal-like and potato-based; others include black-eyed beans, chickpeas and caramelised onions. In some more adventurous establishments, try a cashew nut *bhaji,* or swap your *pau* for *paratha* (a griddle-fried, pancake-like bread). In Mumbai, *bhaji-pau* is known as *pav-bhaji,* and is a variation on the same theme, generally with a thicker, more lentil-heavy, tomato-based sauce.

Mouth-watering *masala dosas* (thin pancakes of rice and lentil batter, fried and folded, and often served with masala-spiced potato filling) are also served up for breakfast, as are the other southern specialities of *idli* (round steamed rice cakes often eaten with *sambar* and chutney) and *vada* (also spelled 'wada'; potato and/or lentil savoury doughnut, deep-fried and served with *sambar* and chutney). Whatever combination you choose, cornflakes will never seem the same again.

VEGETARIAN STAPLES

Here are a few old faithfuls you'll see gracing most menus, perfect for a clear-conscience dinner.

Aloo Gobi Potato and cauliflower in a thick masala sauce

Dhal Makhani Black lentils and red kidney beans cooked up in a rich creamy sauce

Vegetable Korma Vegetables cooked in a mild coconut sauce, usually far less heavy than the kind at the curry house back home

Malai Kofta Vegetable dumplings steeped in a rich, sweet-yet-savoury sauce

Tandoori Paneer Tikka Indian cheese coated in hot and sour paste, and oven-baked with accompanying vegetables

Channa Masala Chickpeas marinated in a spicy, tomato sauce

The simplest local restaurants, often known as 'hotels' – though they have no rooms on offer – come either in 'veg' or 'non-veg' varieties, and are the best destinations for a cheap breakfast or a filling lunch.

Midrange Indian restaurants, meanwhile, generally serve one of two basic genres of Indian food: South Indian (the vegetarian food of Tamil Nadu and Karnataka) and North Indian (richer, and often meatier, Punjabi-Mughlai food). The final (and rarest) type of local restaurant is that serving Goan cuisine itself.

Away from the beach shacks and chic coastal lounges, the best place for a tipple is a hole-in-the-wall local bar. Dingy walls, plastic chairs and an ever-playing TV are all prerequisites; many close for a siesta after lunch, reopening around sunset, but make up for lost time by staying open well into the wee hours.

Food & Drink Online

» www.ifood.tv/network/goan_/recipes

» www.indianfoodforever.com/goan/

» www.indianwine.com

» www.goanfoodrecipes.com

Street Food

Whatever the time of day, people are boiling, frying, roasting, peeling, juicing, simmering or baking food in streetside stalls to lure passersby. You'll encounter samosas (deep-fried pyramid-shaped pastries filled with spiced vegetables and sometimes meat) and *aloo tikka* (mashed potato patties), along with *puri* (also spelt 'poori'; thin puffed-up deep fried breads) and *bhelpuri,* an addictive Mumbai snack made from thin rounds of dough, with rice, lentils, lemon juice, onion, herbs and chutney.

In general, don't be frightened to tuck into street food. A good rule of thumb is that if locals are eating at a streetside stand, it's a pretty safe bet, so follow your nose and the evening buzz to street food tasty as any gourmet's offerings, yet on sale for peanuts.

Vegetarians & Vegans

Tens of millions of Indian vegetarians can't be wrong – India has the world's best breadth of choice for those who abstain from fish, flesh and fowl. You might experience some challenges if you're vegan, since it's sometimes hard to work out whether food has been cooked in ghee (clarified butter) but a quick peek into the kitchen will usually clear things up. Vegetarian joints serving up South Indian cuisine are locally known as *udupis.*

FOOD GLOSSARY

ambot tik	sour curry dish made with meat or fish and flavoured with tamarind
balchão	fish or prawns cooked in a rich, spicy tomato sauce
balchão de porco	the same as balchão, but made with pork
bebinca	richly layered, pancake-like Goan dessert made from egg yolk and coconut

cafrial	method of preparation in which meat, usually chicken, is marinated in a sauce of chillies, garlic and ginger and then dry-fried
caldeirada	a mild curry of fish or prawns layered in a vegetable stew
caldin	mild meat or vegetable dish cooked in spices and coconut milk
chai	sweet, spiced tea
chouriço	spicy air-dried pork sausages, fried up and served for lunch
dhaba	basic restaurant or snack bar
doce	sweet made with chickpeas and coconut
dodol	traditional fudgey Christmas sweet made with rice flour, coconut milk and jaggery
dosa	paper-thin lentil-flour pancake, eaten for breakfast
feni	Goa's most famous drink, a liquor distilled from coconut-palm toddy or juice of cashew apples
fish-curry-rice	Goa's staple dish, a simple concoction of mackerel in spicy, soupy curry, served with rice
kokum	dried fruit used as a spice
sanna	steamed rolls or cakes made with rice flour, ground coconut and toddy
sorpotel	pork liver, heart or kidney cooked in thick, slightly sour, spicy sauce and flavoured with *feni*
thali	a selection of curries, salad, pickle and rice, served on a metal platter, making for a cheap and filling lunch option
udupi	vegetarian cafe or canteen, selling South Indian–style snacks and thalis; also known as an udipi
uttapam	griddle-fried rice-flour pancake
vindalho	hot and sour curry, usually using pork, spiced with chillies, vinegar and garlic; completely unlike the Western curry-house killer, vindaloo
xacuti	spicy sauce made with coconut milk, lemon juice and plenty of red chilli

Markets & Shopping

Where to Shop

Without a doubt, one of the best places to shop in the whole of India is Mumbai, where handicraft emporia, antique shops, designer boutiques and gritty, grimy markets are all part of the retail landscape. Set aside at least an afternoon, if not a day, to devote to the fine art of Mumbai shopping – you'll undoubtedly leave heavier of suitcase and lighter of wallet. For detailed information, see p63.

Although Goa can't compete in terms of the range of goods available, that's not to say there isn't plenty on offer. The state itself isn't known for specific products of any sort, but tourism lures market traders from all over India. While this means that you're unlikely to take home much that is genuinely Goan – apart from bottles of *feni* (liquor distilled from coconut milk or cashews) and packets of locally grown spices – it also means that you can find almost anything from Kashmiri carpets to Karnatakan carvings.

Panaji, meanwhile, has a growing number of upscale 'lifestyle boutiques' vending high-end household goods and gorgeous Goan coffee table books. Craft shops, department stores and clothes shops line the 18th June Rd and MG Rd and there's even a Wrangler shop in case your jeans give up the ghost. Calangute, too, hosts a selection of sleek boutiques, souvenir shops and big-name brands. Most stores are situated on the roads leading down its beaches, and on the main Calangute–Candolim road.

Goa's Best Bookstores

» Other India Bookstore, Mapusa

» Book Palace, Calangute

» Rainbow Bookshop, Vagator

» Golden Heart Emporium, Margao

» Butterfly Bookshop, Palolem

Markets

Mumbai's markets are manifold, as you'll find if you walk into the labyrinthine bazaars just north of the Chhatrapati Shivaji Terminus (Victoria Terminus). Shop alongside locals at Crawford Market or Bhuleshwar Market, both vending foodstuffs and household goods, or trawl Mangaldas Market for silks and fabrics. For clothing, try the stalls on MG Rd between Azad and Cross maidans, and for Indian jewellery, including thousands of glass bangles, go to Zaveri Bazaar.

In Goa, the markets are either aimed specifically at visitors or specifically at locals. For local shopping, try the municipal markets in Panaji and Margao, with plenty of colour and a good line in spices, bangles and posters of Indian gods, or head to Mapusa, whose massive market is most vibrant on Fridays. For tourist markets, Anjuna's Wednesday Flea Market, though somewhat commercialised, is still quite fun to stroll, while two Saturday night markets – Mackie's and Ingo's – operate throughout high season (November to March) just outside Calangute and Baga.

The roads down to the beach in Palolem and Arambol, too, are packed with stalls selling silver jewellery, drums, hammocks, embroidered bed-sheets, sandals, and all the usual lines in Indian souvenirs. But if you prefer the goods to come to you, never fear: sit for 15 minutes on almost any stretch of beach, and migrant sales-ladies will appear bearing jewellery, fabrics, and an excellent line in hard-sell.

Those craving home comforts should head to Anjuna or Candolim, both of which possess Western-style supermarkets filled to the brim with Western goods at Western prices. Shredded Wheat, Vegemite, Cheshire Cheese or Ribena, anyone?

What to Buy

Antiques

You'll find a concentration of antiques on Mutton St in Mumbai, though you'll need to determine the real from the reproduction. For genuine antiques at genuine antique prices, try Phillips in Colaba, a Mumbai institution that's been around for the last century and a half.

In Goa, you'll find a couple of knick-knack-style antiques shops in Mapusa near the Municipal Gardens, along with antique-furniture shops scattered here and there across the state. But before you fall in love with that four-poster, bear in mind that not all antiques stores are clued up as to how to ship it back to your bedroom, back home.

Carpets

It may not surprise you that India produces and exports more handcrafted carpets than Iran, but it probably is more of a surprise that some of them are of virtually equal quality. India's best carpets come from Kashmir, and can be found in usually Kashmiri-run shops throughout Goa.

Leatherwork

Indian leatherwork is not made from cowhide but from buffalo, camel, goat or some other form of animal. Chappals, the basic sandals found all over India, are the most popular buy.

Papier-Mâché

Probably the most characteristic Kashmiri craft, basic papier-mâché articles are made in a mould, then painted and polished in layers until the final intricate design is produced. Items include bowls, jewellery boxes,

For an unusual gift for that budding Houdini, or to provide means to pass time on a long bus journey, seek out rabbits in hats and enchanted handkerchiefs at Shamin Khan's Star Magic Shop in Baga, which also has a weekly stall at the Anjuna Flea Market.

THE ART OF HAGGLING

The friendly art of haggling is an absolute must in most parts of Goa and Mumbai, unless you don't mind paying above market value. Traders in towns and markets are accustomed to tourists who have lots of money and little time to spend it, meaning that a shopkeeper's 'very good price' might in fact be a rather bad one.

If you have absolutely no idea what something should really cost, a good rule of thumb is to bank on paying half of what you're originally quoted. The vendor will probably look aghast and tell you that this is impossible, as it's the very price they had to pay for the item themselves. This is when the battle for a bargain begins and it's up to you and the salesperson to negotiate a price. You'll find that many shopkeepers lower their so-called final price if you head out of the shop and tell them that you'll think about it.

Don't lose your sense of humour and sense of fairness while haggling – it's not a battle to squeeze every last rupee out of a poor trader, and not all vendors are out to make a fool of you. In essence, the haggle itself is often the very spirit, and the fun, of the Indian shopping experience.

tables and lamps; a little bowl might cost only ₹50, while a large, well-made item may approach ₹1000.

Textiles

This is still India's major industry and 40% of the total production is at village level, where it is known as *khadi* (homespun cloth). Bedspreads, tablecloths, cushion covers or fabric for clothing are popular *khadi* purchases. In Gujarat and Rajasthan heavy material is embroidered with tiny mirrors and beads to produce everything from dresses to stuffed toys to wall hangings; tie-dye work is popular in Rajasthan and Kerala; and in Kashmir embroidered materials are turned into shirts and dresses.

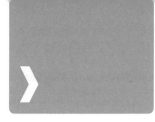

Wildlife & the Environment

For the four decades since Goa's Portuguese overlords finally left its shores, Goa has experienced phenomenal, and flawed, growth in tourism, industry and population, sometimes taxing to the limit its stunning, diverse, yet fragile environment.

The Land

Goa occupies a narrow strip of the western Indian coastline, approximately 105km long and 65km wide, but within this relatively tiny area exists an incredibly diverse mixture of landscapes, flora and fauna.

Western Ghats

To the east of the state lie the gorgeous green Western Ghats, whose name derives from the Sanskrit for 'sacred steps'. This mountain range runs along India's entire west coast, but in Goa is made up of the Sahyadri Range, comprising around one-sixth the state's total area. The ghats are the source of all seven of Goa's main rivers, the longest of which, the Mandovi, meanders for 77km to the Arabian Sea.

This lush deciduous region, responsible for channelling much-needed water down onto the plains, is in definite danger. Logging threatens its forests, while soil erosion, the result of deforestation, represents a flood danger to the midland region beyond the mountains.

Midland Region

Goa's grassy hinterland is made up mostly of laterite plateaux, with thin soil covering rich sources of iron and manganese ore. The midland has thus become the scene of large-scale open-cast mining, evident in the red gashes in Goan hillsides, and the relentless lines of iron-ore trucks chugging along like colonies of worker ants.

In areas not affected by mining, spice, fruit, cashew (Goa's principal cash crop) and areca nut plantations still predominate. Terraced orchards make efficient use of limited water sources, to support coconut, jackfruit, pineapple and mango groves.

Coastal Plain

Though just a fraction of the state's total area, Goa's coast is its claim to fame. Here mangroves line tidal rivers, providing shelter for birds, marine animals and crocodiles, while vivid green paddy fields, coconut groves and the seas and estuaries provide the majority of the population's food.

These 180 sq km of coastal lands, however, are probably the most threatened of all. The beaches, and sea waters beyond them, have already been severely damaged by unfettered tourist development, untreated sewage, pollution from sea tankers and iron ore mining, poor local land management, and eyesore chemical plants. Though clean, clear areas still exist – for now – many once beautiful spots are today tragedies of wasted opportunity.

Wildlife

Despite Goa's diminutive size, the state is home to an amazing array of fauna, though some of the most impressive mammalian species, such as wild elephants and leopards, occur only in small numbers, are incredibly shy, and are thus very hard to spot.

Bird enthusiasts, however, will likely find Goa a twitchers' heaven. With iridescent avian life flitting casually past even your beach-hut balcony, pack your binoculars and prepare for a spectacular feathery show.

Animals

Mammals

The wild animals you'll most likely encounter in Goa are the state's mischievous monkeys: most visible are smallish, scavenging bonnet macaques, and larger, black-faced, long-limbed Hanuman langurs.

Other inhabitants include common mongooses, often found near settlements, common otters, and smooth Indian otters. The Western Ghats are also home to Indian giant squirrels, which are double the size of their European counterparts and can leap distances of 20m. There are also occasional sightings of slender lorises and shaggy sloth bears, which grow up to 1.5m long; flying foxes, meanwhile, are easiest to spot, boasting wingspans of more than a metre.

In Goa's wildlife sanctuaries, you may come across gaur (Indian bison), porcupines, sambars (buff-coloured deer), chitals (spotted deer) and barking deer. One of the rarer animals inhabiting Goa's forests is the nocturnal pangolin, otherwise known as the scaly anteater. The 'mini-leopard' (known as the *vagati* in Konkani), a greyish fluffy-tailed creature about the size of a domestic cat, is also sometimes seen, along with the Indian civet, slightly larger and with a striped tail and long pointed snout. Jackals, striped hyenas and wild dogs are all occasionally sighted in the Goan hinterlands.

Common dolphins can often be found frolicking among the waves, while fruit bats and Malay fox vampire bats come out in force as the Goan sun goes down.

Reptiles, Snakes & Amphibians

The best place to find reptiles and amphibians – aside from the common house geckos you'll see roaming your hotel walls – is in the paddy fields of rural Goa.

Snakes are common, though reclusive, with 23 species of which eight are venomous. The Indian and King cobra and the krait comprise three of the latter, all of whose venom is lethal if not treated quickly. You're more likely, however, to see nonpoisonous green whip snakes, golden tree snakes, rat snakes, cat snakes, wolf snakes and Russel sand boas.

Kusadas (sea snakes) are common along the coastline, but are most often seen dead on the beach; they generally live in deep waters, far off the coast, and though they have lethal venom are also extremely timid, with fangs located so far back in their mouths that they rarely give a proper bite.

Goa is also home to chameleons, monitor lizards, turtles and two species of crocodile. Flap-shell turtles and black-pond turtles are freshwater species plentiful during the monsoon, while a third species, the olive ridley sea turtle, is in grave danger of extinction (see The Turtle Wind, p78).

Though crocs are also threatened with extinction, they're still pretty easy to spot, especially the saltwater variety (known locally as 'salties'), which inhabit stretches of the Mandovi and Zuari estuaries, and the Cambarjua Ca-

S Prater's *The Book of Indian Animals* and Romulus Whitaker's *Common Indian Snakes* are two reliable guides to the nonhuman residents of Goa.

nal near Old Goa. The second type, known as 'Mandovi Muggers', is less aggressive despite its title, and mostly inhabits Mandovi River waters around Divar and Chorao Islands. Several Goan day-tripping companies advertise 'crocodile-spotting' trips, to observe muggers and salties from a safe distance.

Birds

Keen birdwatchers will be in seventh heaven in Goa: see p29 for more.

OUT OF TOWN

In open spaces, a flash of colour may turn out to be an Indian roller, easily identified by its brilliant blue flight feathers. Drongos (shiny black birds with distinctive forked tails) are also quite common, while pipits and wagtails strut in large flocks among the harvest stubble.

Common hoopoes are often seen (or their distinctive 'hoo-po-po' bird call heard) in open country, while birds of prey such as harriers and buzzards soar overhead. Kites and vultures can wheel on thermals for hours; ospreys, another large hawk, patrol reservoirs and waterways for fish suppers.

WATERWAYS

Stalking long-legged at the shallow edges of ponds are various species of egret, graceful white tapers of birds with long necks and daggerlike bills. Cattle egrets wander among livestock, looking for large insects stirred up by their namesake.

Indian pond herons, also known as paddy birds, are small and well camouflaged in greys and browns.

Colourful kingfishers, Goa's unofficial mascot made famous by its cold, frothy namesake beverage, patiently await their prey on overhanging branches. You might see several species, including black-and-white pied kingfishers, colourful common kingfishers (also known as river kingfishers), and stork-billed kingfishers, sporting massive red bills. The water's edge is also home to plovers, water hens and coots that feed and nest among dense vegetation.

FORESTS

Patches of Goan forest support a rich variety of feathered species. Among those more often heard than seen are woodpeckers, whose characteristic drumming sound is made as they chisel grubs from the bark of trees. Their colourful relatives include barbets, and Indian koels, whose loud, piercing cry can be relentless in spring.

Fruiting trees are a magnet for many species, including green pigeons and imperial pigeons, noisy flocks of parrots and minivets, and various cuckoo-shrikes and mynahs. Hill mynahs are an all-black bird with a distinctive yellow 'wattle' about the face.

The jewels in Goa's avian crown must be its three magnificent species of hornbill, resembling South American toucans. At the other end of the size spectrum, the iridescent, nectar-feeding purple sunbird is equally brilliant. A host of smaller birds, such as flycatchers, warblers, babblers and little tailorbirds (so-called because they make a neat little 'purse' of woven grass as a nest), forage for insects in every layer of vegetation.

Plants

A bumper crop of flowering plants, grasses, brackens and ferns all play their part in Goa's ecology, and the Western Ghats comprise some of Asia's densest rainforest. On their lower slopes, thinner, drier soil supports semi-evergreen forest; in other places (such as Cotigao Wildlife Sanctuary) the arid landscape leads to savannah-like vegetation. In wetter patches of the lower slopes, timbers such as teak are grown.

Birds of Southern India by Richard Grimmet and Tim Inskipp is a comprehensive birdwatching field guide, considered by many as the 'must have' guide to the region. Also comprehensive is *A Field Guide to the Birds of the Indian Subcontinent* by Krys Kazmierczak and Ber van Perlo.

When's best for wildlife watching? As soon after the monsoon as possible. October is perfect, when tourist numbers and temperatures are low and animals are attracted to still-verdant watering holes.

WILDLIFE & THE ENVIRONMENT WILDLIFE

GOA'S WILDLIFE SANCTUARIES

Roughly 12%, or 455 sq km, of Goa's total area is given over to wildlife sanctuaries and reserves. Add to this the forestry-department-protected beaches and forest areas on the southern coast, and Goa remains (despite its environmental woes) a decidedly green place.

Its three main wildlife sanctuaries were created in the late 1960s: Bondla (p140), which also contains Molem National Park; Bhagwan Mahavir (p141); and Cotigao (p183). All are well worth exploring. There's also tiny Dr Salim Ali Bird Sanctuary on Chorao Island (p125), a haven for bird species. In 1999 two new wildlife reserves – Madei (208 sq km) in Satari *taluka* (district) and Netravali (211 sq km; p182) in Sanguem *taluka* – were declared protected areas; so far these fledgling reserves lack infrastructure, and consequently are seldom visited. However, their creation links the sanctuaries running along the Western Ghats, providing a crucial corridor for Goa's wildlife.

In the folds between hills, small valleys are often extremely fertile. Coconut palms are cultivated not only for the nuts and toddy, but also to give shade to less hardy trees. Beneath their canopy, slender areca nut palms can be grown. These, in turn, shelter a variety of trees and plants, including pineapples, bananas, pepper and cinnamon.

The coastal region has a wide range of flora, with saline conditions supporting mangrove swamps. In villages, banyan and peepul trees provide shade for Hindu and Buddhist shrines that are often beneath them.

Environmental Issues

Deforestation

Over-cutting of the forested Western Ghats began at the start of the 20th century, and environmental groups estimate that more than 500 hectares of Goa's forests continue to disappear every year.

The damage caused by deforestation is far-reaching. Animal habitats are diminishing, as are the homelands of the tribal Dhangar, Kunbi and Velip peoples. In an effort to curb the damage, the government has stepped up its efforts to protect Goa's forests: felling fees now apply, licences must be issued, and reforestation projects are underway. See the Goa Forestry Department website (www.goaforest.com) for more.

Mining

Nearly half the iron ore exported annually from India comes from Goa. For eight months a year, huge barges ferry the ore along the Zuari and Mandovi Rivers to waiting ships, representing around 10% of Goa's GDP.

But of the 80 million tonnes of rock and soil extracted annually, only 13 million tonnes are saleable ore. Surplus is dumped on spoil tips and is washed away come the monsoon, smothering both river and marine life. Other side-effects of mining include the disruption of local water tables and pollution of air and drinking water. Moreover, since no stipulation for environmental reconstruction was made when most mining concessions were issued, many have simply been abandoned once extraction was complete, leaving barren scars on otherwise lovely countryside.

Tourism

While bringing countless jobs and raising standards of living for many in Goa, unchecked hotel building, inadequate sewage facilities, water-guzzling swimming pools and landscaped golf courses have all taken their toll. Count up the plastic water bottles you might use during your visit, multiply this figure by two million, then refill your own with filtered water to do your bit towards saving Goa from an avalanche of non-biodegradable plastic.

Green Resources

» **World Wildlife Fund** (www.wwfindia.org)

» **Save Goa Campaign** (www.savegoa.com)

» **Green Cross** (www.greencrossgoa.org)

» **Goa Foundation** (www.goafoundation.org)

Conservation Organisations

» **Peaceful Society** (www.peacefulsociety.org)

» **Archaeological Survey of India** (asi.nic.in)

» **United Planet** (www.unitedplanet.org)

Survival
Guide

DIRECTORY A–Z 220

Accommodation 220

Business Hours 221

Climate 222

Customs Regulations . . . 222

Dangers & Annoyances . . 222

Electricity 224

Embassies &
Consulates 224

Food 224

Gay & Lesbian Travellers . . 224

Health 225

Internet Access 228

Legal Matters 228

Money 228

Post 229

Safe Travel 229

Telephone 229

Time 230

Tourist Information 230

Travellers with
Disabilities 230

Visas 230

Women Travellers 231

TRANSPORT 232

GETTING THERE
& AWAY 232

Air 232

Land 232

GETTING AROUND 234

Bicycle 234

Boat 235

Bus 235

Car 235

Hitching 235

Local Transport 235

Motorcycle 236

Train 237

LANGUAGE 238

GLOSSARY 243

Directory A–Z

Accommodation

Goa's accommodation ranges from basic beach huts to opulent five-star and boutique hotel havens. In this guide, we've listed reviews by author preference; standout options are indicated by [TOP CHOICE]. Always check out the checkout times, which vary enormously: Panaji's are often a harsh 9am, or sometimes (gulp) even earlier.

Budget

Budget accommodation covers the most basic guesthouses and beach huts, many with shared bathrooms and most without air conditioning (AC), which you only really need from March onwards, particularly if you're beside the sea, where you'll usually benefit from nice cooling breezes.

Beach huts will likely be simple, palm-thatched rooms; the best might have a porch and a hammock, and some will have a mosquito net. Basic guesthouse rooms are likely to be quite spartan (think bed, and not much else) and some may be devoid of even the simple luxury of a window.

Midrange

Midrange accommodation is usually in basic, serviceable hotels, simple but comfortable family-run guesthouses (usually with more atmosphere than midrange hotels), or more comfortable beach huts. Expect a private bathroom and, in the case of beach huts, sturdier walls, a porch or balcony with seats or a hammock, and closer proximity to the sea.

Top-end

Top-end options are generally swish five-star resorts or heritage boutique hotels.

Heritage properties will have bags of character; five-stars, bountiful amenities. You will also find the occasional luxury tent encampment or fabulously equipped private villa in this price range.

Costs

Unless otherwise stated, prices in this book are for high (November to February) but not peak (between Christmas and New Year) season.

Outside high season, count on discounts of between 25% and 60%; during the peak Christmas season, which runs between around Christmas Eve and New Year's Day, you can expect high-season prices to go up by at least 50%, or even (crazily) double.

Bear in mind there's a 'luxury' tax of 8% on rooms over ₹500, and up to 12% for those around ₹800 and above. For most budget places, the prices quoted include this tax, but at midrange and top-end hotels, expect tax to be added to the bill.

BEACH HUTS

The quintessential Goan accommodation experience is the bamboo beach hut, also sometimes known locally as 'coco-huts'. These were originally constructed on stilts, using surrounding coconut trees as support, but nowadays bamboo huts have moved far beyond their primitive genesis.

In terms of quality, there's an infinite array available, and it's not hard to tell a budget hut from a more expensive one: the better it looks, and the further away from the neighbours it's sited, the more it costs. Palolem offers a good example of the range of huts available; the beach is still predominantly lined with cheaper, flimsy, coconut-matting versions, but sandwiched between them are an increasing number of larger, pricier and infinitely more stylish options. Some are even double-decker affairs with spacious bathrooms, hot running water, and four-poster beds. The decor in these kit homes often accounts for price variations – a coat of paint and a few decorative pillows on a makeshift balcony can mean a price difference of several hundred rupees. There are also more linear, but often roughly slapped together, wooden huts constructed of plywood, not as pretty as their original, ecofriendly neighbours.

Though absolutely atmospheric (and, if you're lucky, with sea-front views), and far better value than a hotel or guesthouse in the same price range, the downside to the beach-hut experience can be the proximity to one's neighbours, whose nocturnal noises are often no more than a foot of air and a sheet of bamboo away. If you're bothered by noise, don't forget to pack earplugs, or plump for a slightly wider-spaced option. They're also not the most secure structures: keep valuables elsewhere, in the beach-hut operation's safe, if it has one.

Remember, too, that almost all beach huts are packed away (by law) during April and May, in preparation for the arrival of the monsoon, to be reassembled around mid-October when the tourists trickle back. Any exceptions to this rule are noted in individual listings.

Many midrange and top-end hotels add a further, hefty 10% 'service tax' and sometimes even more; this can be up to 20% in the fanciest five-stars. Clarify upon check-in whether taxes are included in your tariff or not, to avoid any nasty surprises at check-out.

Long-term Rental Accommodation

Renting houses by the month or longer is extremely common in Goa, particularly given the number of Westerners who live in Goa for six or so months of every year. Ask around, check noticeboards at foreigner hot spots, or pursue 'for rent' signs. Prices go from ₹10,000 per month for a simple local-style village house, to ₹50,000 or more per month for a well-equipped apartment, with wi-fi, TV and daily cleaning service.

Price Icons

The price indicators in this book refer to the cost of a double room, unless otherwise noted. Prices in Mumbai are significantly higher than in Goa, and therefore have separate price indicators. It's also crucial to note that, within the lifetime of this edition, prices may rise considerably; inflation in India stands at around 10% and accommodation prices, in many cases, are rising by as much as 30% per year.

Business Hours

Note that outside high season (November to March), many tourist-oriented shops, restaurants and services may be closed.

Business hours are fairly flexible in Goa, and some offices, shops and services may close for an hour or more at lunchtime, or take an hour or two's afternoon siesta (or even a day off), often on a whim.

Reduced opening hours for sights may also apply during the low season (May to September).

ACCOMMODATION PRICES

The following price ranges refer to a double room with bathroom in high (November to February) but not peak (Christmas and New Year) season.

CATEGORY	GOA	MUMBAI
$ Budget	<₹1000	<₹1000
$$ Midrange	₹1000–2500	₹1000–4000
$$$ Top end	>₹2500	>₹4000

STANDARD HOURS

We've only listed business hours where they differ from the following standards:

BUSINESS	OPENING HOURS
Banks	10am-2pm Mon-Fri, 10am-noon Sat
Offices	9.30am-5.30pm Mon-Fri
Post Offices	9am-6pm Mon-Fri, to noon Sat
Restaurants	8am-10pm daily (breakfast 8-11am, lunch 11am-4pm, dinner 4-11pm)
Drinking	noon-midnight daily
Sights	10am-5pm
Shopping	10am-6pm daily

Climate

Goa (Panaji)

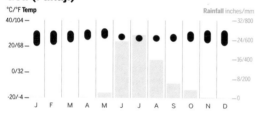

Mumbai (Bombay)

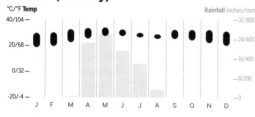

Customs Regulations

The usual duty-free regulations for India apply in Goa: 1L of spirits and 200 cigarettes (or 50 cigars, or 250g of tobacco) per person.

Antiques more than 100 years old are not permitted to be exported from India without an export clearance certificate. Many antique dealers are familiar with the formalities; if in doubt, check with the **Archaeological Survey of India** (http://asi.nic.in/) at the Archaeological Museum in Old Goa.

Dangers & Annoyances

Despite stories of violent crime, drug-related misdeeds and police corruption (some of them internationally high-profile and involving tourists) Goa remains essentially a safe destination for travellers. So long as you check the news before you travel, and adhere to a few very basic safety precautions, you should stay safe and secure in Goa.

Airport Taxis

To avoid paying an exorbitant amount for a taxi from Mumbai's Chhatrapati Shivaji Airport or Goa's Dabolim Airport, make for one of the prepaid taxi counters. This will ensure you a fair, fixed price to any destination in Goa. When you arrive, it's fine to tip your taxi driver, but don't stand for any nonsense regarding 'additional charges'.

Muggings & Druggings

From time to time there are reports of 'date rape' or theft-related druggings, usually in busy, trendy tourist bars. Be wary, though not terrified, of accepting food or drinks from strangers or even new friends.

There have also been incidents of attacks on women. Some measures have been introduced, such as limited street lighting and security patrols on some beaches, but it's still not a good idea for women – or men, for that matter – to wander alone at night.

Prices

Whether it's an autorickshaw ride, a bike rental, a daytrip with fishermen or something as simple as a haircut at the local barber, always, always, always clarify the cost upfront. There's no better way to kill an otherwise magical moment than a heated ar-

PRACTICALITIES

» **Newspapers** Goa has three English-language dailies: the *Herald*, the *Navhind Times* and the local version of the *Times of India*. Many foreign newspapers and magazines are available in bookshops and large hotels, though they're usually more expensive than back home.

» **Radio** All India Radio (AIR) transmits local and international news. There are plenty of private broadcasters in addition to this government-controlled station, many broadcasting in English.

» **TV** The government TV broadcaster is Doordarshan. Satellite TV, which has BBC World, CNN, Star World and Star Movies, MTV, VH1 and HBO, is more widely watched.

» **Weights & Measures** Although India officially uses the metric system, imperial weights and measures are still sometimes used. You may hear the term lakh (one lakh equals 100,000) and crore (one crore equals 10 million) referring to rupees, car costs or anything else.

gument when you find out the price is more than twice what you (perhaps rightly) expected it to be.

Scams

Incredibly, the age-old export scam is still doing the rounds in India. Even more incredibly, people are still falling for it. The scam involves being befriended and eventually offered the opportunity to export products (jewellery, precious stones or carpets are common) to sell elsewhere at enormous profit. Or, after you've been plied with meals and entertainment, you'll be given a sob story about your new friend's inability to obtain an export licence. Don't be fooled; these guys are smooth operators and even worldly travellers have been successfully buttered up by the initial hospitality and generosity.

Swimming

Though lifeguards are now present during daylight hours at most Goan beaches, the water remains deceptively treacherous. Heed local warnings, and don't swim near estuaries, where the currents can be particularly nasty.

Theft

If you're staying in a hotel, guesthouse, beach hut or family home where there is a safe or similar lockable facility, it's always worthwhile using it.

There have been isolated reports, over the years, of violent robberies of tourists in Goa, so exercise the same sort of caution you would when at home. Remember that, if you do have something stolen while in Goa, you must report it to the police if you want to make an insurance claim at home; being friendly, patient and persistent with the local police should get you your paperwork in the end. Many police officers are helpful, but if you continually have trouble reporting a crime, try enlisting the assistance of the Goa Tourism Development Corporation (GTDC) in Panaji.

Touts

When arriving by train or bus at any destination, visitors may be met by taxi drivers, autorickshaw drivers or other individuals who want to take you to a 'nice' hotel – usually the one that pays them a healthy commission. Touts do have a use, though – not all of their recommendations are bad ones, and they can be of definite use in finding you a place to stay during the sometimes jam-packed peak season.

TIPS FOR SAFE TRAVEL

While the majority of travellers in Goa will have no serious or life-threatening problems, tourists have occasionally been the target of theft or assault. There are some common-sense steps you can take to minimise the risk:

» Don't open the door to someone you don't know.

» Leave windows and doors locked when you're sleeping and when you're out; things have been stolen using hooks through windows.

» Avoid quiet, poorly lit streets or lanes – take the longer way if it's brighter and more populated, and walk with confidence and purpose.

» If you are being sexually harassed or assaulted on public transport, embarrass the culprit by loudly complaining, and report them to the conductor or driver.

» As tempting as it is to stare someone down, women should just ignore stares. Dark or reflective glasses can help.

Electricity

230V/50Hz

Embassies & Consulates

Australia Mumbai (Map p46; ☑022-66692000; 36 Maker Chambers VI, 3rd fl, 220 Nariman Point)

Canada Mumbai (Map p46; ☑022-67494444; 6th fl, Fort House, 221 Dr DN Rd)

France Mumbai (Map p46; ☑022-66694000; 7th fl, Hoechst House, Nariman Point)

Germany Mumbai (Map p46; ☑022-22832422; 10th fl, Hoechst House, Nariman Point)

Israel Mumbai (Map p46; ☑022-22822822/22819993; Earnest House, 16th fl, NCPA Marg, Nariman Point)

Italy Mumbai (Map p42; ☑022-23804071; Kanchanjunga, 1st fl, 72G Deshmukh Marg, Kemp's Corner)

Japan Mumbai (Map p42; ☑022-23517101; 1 ML Dahanukar Marg, Cumballa Hill)

Malaysia Mumbai (Map p54; ☑022-26455751/2; Notan Plaza, 4th fl, Turner Rd, Bandra West)

Maldives Mumbai (Map p46; ☑022-22078041; 212A Maker Bhawan No 3, New Marine Lines, Churchgate)

Netherlands Mumbai (Map p46; ☑022-22194200; Forbes Bldg, Home St, Fort)

New Zealand Mumbai (Map p54; ☑022-23520022; Aashiana, 1st fl, 5 Altamount Rd, Breach Candy)

Singapore Mumbai (Map p46; ☑022-22043205; Maker Chambers IV, 10th fl, 222 Jamnalal Bajaj Rd, Nariman Point)

South Africa Mumbai (Map p42; ☑022-23513725; Gandhi Mansion, 20 Altamount Rd, Cumballa Hill)

Sri Lanka Mumbai (Map p46; ☑022-22045861; Mulla House, 34 Homi Modi St, Fort)

Switzerland Mumbai (Map p46; ☑022-22884563-65; 102 Maker Chambers IV, 10th fl, 222 Jamnalal Bajaj Marg, Nariman Point)

Thailand Mumbai (Map p46; ☑022-22823535; Dalamal House, 1st fl, Jamnalal Bajaj Marg, Nariman Point)

UK Mumbai (Map p54; ☑022-66502222; Naman Chambers, C/32 G Block Bandra Kurla Complex, Bandra East)

USA Mumbai (Map p42; ☑022-23663611; Lincoln House, 78 Bhulabhai Desai Rd, Breach Candy)

Food

The price indicators in this book refer to the cost of a main course, unless otherwise noted. For more on Goan food, see p206.

Gay & Lesbian Travellers

In July 2009 Delhi's High Court overturned India's 148-year-old antihomosexuality law, making homosexuality legal in India.

Goa's liberal reputation draws a lot of gay men, and there's a discrete scene, mainly around the Calangute/Baga area. A couple of the beach shacks are also becoming a bit braver with respect to gay events, and you might find the occasional gay night on offer. However, India remains largely conservative and public displays of affection are generally frowned upon for all.

Publications & Websites

Time Out Mumbai
(www.timeoutmumbai.net)
Gay events in Mumbai.
Gay Bombay (www.gaybom
bay.org) Lists gay events and
offers support and advice.
Humsafar Trust
(www.humsafar.org) Gay and
transgender advocacy, support groups and events in
Mumbai.

Health

Few travellers to Goa will experience anything more than
upset stomachs. These days
many travellers to Goa also
travel with their children –
even tiny babies – and the
overwhelming majority of
small visitors contract nothing worse than an itchy dose
of heat rash.

Before You Go

Pack medications in their
original containers.
    Bring a letter from your
physician describing medical
conditions and medications
or syringes you may need
to carry.
    If you have a heart condi-
tion, bring a copy of your ECG.
    Bring extra medication in
case of loss or theft; it can be
difficult to find the latest anti-
depressants, blood-pressure
medications and contracep-
tive pills.

Vaccinations

Specialised travel-medicine
clinics are your best source
of information. They stock
all available vaccines and
will be able to give specific
recommendations for you
and your trip.
    Most vaccines don't give
immunity until at least two
weeks after they're taken,
so visit a doctor four to eight
weeks before departure.

RECOMMENDED VACCINATIONS

The World Health Organization (WHO) recommends

HOSPITALS IN GOA & MUMBAI

Mumbai

» Bombay Hospital (Map p46; ☎22067676, ambulance
☎22067309; www.bombayhospital.com; 12 New Marine
Lines)

» Breach Candy Hospital (Map p42; ☎23672888; www.
breachcandyhospital.org; 60 Bhulabhai Desai Rd, Breach
Candy) The very best in Mumbai.

North Goa

» Mapusa Clinic, Mapusa (☎2263343; ⊕consultations
10.30am-1.30pm Mon-Sat, 3.30-7pm Mon, Wed & Fri) A
good medical clinic, with 24-hour emergency services.
Be sure to go to the 'new' Mapusa Clinic, behind the
'old' one.

Central Goa

» Goa Medical College Hospital, near Panaji (☎2458700;
Bambolin) Situated 9km south of Panaji on NH17.

» Vintage Hospitals, near Panaji (☎6644401-05, ambulance ☎2232533; www.vintage3.com; Cacula Enclave,
St Inez) A good choice, located a couple of kilometres
southwest of Panaji.

South Goa

» Apollo Victor Hospital, Margao (Hospicio; ☎2705664;
Padre Miranda Rd) Has a casualty department and a
well-stocked 24-hour pharmacy. It's about 500m
northeast of the Municipal Gardens.

---

these vaccinations for
travellers to India (as well
as being up to date with
measles, mumps and rubella
vaccinations):
**Adult diphtheria and
tetanus** Single booster
recommended if none in the
previous 10 years.
Hepatitis A Provides
almost 100% protection for
up to a year; a booster after
12 months provides another
20 years' protection.
Hepatitis B Considered
routine for most travellers.
Given as three shots over
six months. A rapid schedule is also available, as is a
combined vaccination with
hepatitis A. In 95% of people
lifetime protection results.
Polio Polio is still present
in India. Only one booster is
required as an adult for life-

time protection. Inactivated
polio vaccine is safe during
pregnancy.
Typhoid Recommended
for all travellers to India,
even if you only visit urban
areas. The vaccine offers
around 70% protection,
lasts for two to three years
and comes as a single shot.
Tablets are also available but
the injection has fewer side
effects.
Varicella If you haven't had
chickenpox, discuss this
vaccination with your doctor.
    These immunisations are
recommended for long-term
travellers (more than one
month) or those at special
risk.
**Japanese B encephali-
tis** Three injections in all.
Booster recommended after
two years.

226

DIRECTORY A-Z HEALTH

Meningitis Single injection. There are two types of vaccination: quadrivalent vaccine gives two to three years' protection; meningitis group C vaccine gives around 10 years' protection. Recommended for long-term backpackers aged under 25.

Rabies Three injections in all. A booster after one year will then provide 10 years' protection.

Tuberculosis (TB) Adult long-term travellers are usually recommended to have a TB skin test before and after travel, rather than vaccination. Only one vaccine given in a lifetime.

Healthcare in Goa

Although there are reasonable facilities in Panaji (Panjim), Margao (Madgaon) and Vasco da Gama, Goa does not have the quality of medical care available in the West.

Goa's ambulance service (☑108) isn't always the quickest to respond; it may be quicker, in case of an emergency, to jump in a taxi.

For minor ailments and complaints, Goa has lots of GPs (general practitioners) and family doctors: just ask at your hotel or guest house, or check with locals for a good recommendation. Upmarket hotels also often have a reliable doctor on call.

Often, you just need to drop in to a GP's office during consultation hours (without an appointment) and a consultation costs in the region of ₹100.

Prescriptions rarely cost more than ₹50 when filled at pharmacies.

There are well-stocked pharmacies in all Goan towns selling drugs manufactured under licence to Western companies. You can buy far more over the counter here than you can in the West, often without prescription.

Infectious Diseases

Dengue Fever This mosquito-borne disease is becoming increasingly problematic in Goa. As there is no vaccine available, it can only be prevented by avoiding mosquito bites. Symptoms include high fever, severe headache and body ache; some people develop a rash and experience diarrhoea. There is no specific treatment – just rest and paracetamol. Don't take aspirin; it increases the likelihood of haemorrhaging. See a doctor so you can be diagnosed and monitored.

Hepatitis A This food- and water-borne virus infects the liver, causing jaundice (yellow skin and eyes), nausea and lethargy. There is no specific treatment for hepatitis A, other than time for the liver to heal. All travellers to India should be vaccinated.

Hepatitis B The only sexually transmitted disease that can be prevented by vaccination, hepatitis B is spread by body fluids. Long-term consequences can include liver cancer.

Hepatitis E Transmitted through contaminated food and water, hepatitis E has similar symptoms to hepatitis A, but is less common. It is a severe problem in pregnant women and can result in the death of both mother and baby. There is no vaccine; prevention is by following safe eating and drinking guidelines.

HIV India has one of the highest growth rates of HIV in the world. HIV is spread via contaminated body fluids. Avoid unsafe sex, unsterile needles (including in medical facilities) and procedures such as tattoos, unless you're certain the equipment is sterile.

Rabies Around 30,000 people die annually in India from rabies. This fatal disease is spread by the bite or lick of an infected animal – most commonly a dog or monkey. Pre-travel vaccination means post-bite treatment is greatly simplified. If you are bitten, gently wash the wound with soap and water, apply iodine-based antiseptic, and seek medical help immediately.

Typhoid Spread via food and water, this bacterial infection gives a high and slowly progressive fever, headache and maybe a dry cough and stomach pain. It is treated with antibiotics. Vaccination is recommended for travellers spending more than a week in India. Vaccination is not 100% effective; still be careful with what you eat and drink.

Traveller's Diarrhoea Defined as the passage of more than three watery bowel actions within 24 hours, plus at least one other symptom such as fever, cramps, nausea, vomiting or feeling generally unwell. This is by far the most common problem affecting travellers; in over 80% of cases it is caused by bacteria, and therefore responds promptly to antibiotics. Treatment consists of staying well hydrated; rehydration solutions such as Gastrolyte are best. Antibiotics such as Norfloxacin, Ciprofloxacin or Azithromycin kill the bacteria quickly. Loperamide is a 'stopper' and doesn't

TRADITIONAL MEDICINE

You've come to the right place if you're interested in traditional medicine. There is a strong culture of holistic healing in Goa, from ayurveda to reflexology to reiki. As with all medicine, some practitioners are better than others. Ask around for local recommendations before you commit to anything.

address the problem. It can be helpful for long bus rides, though. Don't take Loperamide if you have a fever or blood in your stools.

Amoebic Dysentery
Amoebic dysentery is rare in travellers but is often misdiagnosed. Symptoms are similar to bacterial diarrhoea: fever, bloody diarrhoea and generally feeling unwell. Always seek reliable medical care if you have blood in your diarrhoea. Treatment involves Tinidazole or Metronidazole to kill the parasite and a second drug to kill the cysts. If left untreated, complications such as liver or gut abscesses can result.

Giardiasis A relatively common parasite in travellers. Symptoms include nausea, bloating, excess gas, fatigue and intermittent diarrhoea. The parasite eventually goes away if left untreated, but can take months. The treatment of choice is Tinidazole with Metronidazole.

Environmental Hazards

DIVING & SURFING
Divers and surfers should seek specialised advice before they travel to ensure their medical kit contains treatment for coral cuts and tropical ear infections. Divers should also get specialised dive insurance through an organisation such as **Divers Alert Network** (DAN; www .danseap.org) and have a dive medical before they travel.

HEAT
Dehydration The main contributor to heat exhaustion. Symptoms include: weakness, headache, irritability, nausea, sweaty skin, a fast, weak pulse, and a normal or slightly elevated body temperature. Treatment involves getting out of the heat, fanning the sufferer and applying cool wet cloths to the skin, laying the sufferer flat with their legs raised

INTERNET RESOURCES

There is a wealth of travel health advice on the internet. Some good resources:

» **Centers for Disease Control and Prevention** (CDC; www.cdc.gov) Good general information.

» **MD Travel Health** (www.mdtravelhealth.com) Complete travel health recommendations for every country, updated daily.

» **World Health Organization** (WHO; www.who.int/ith/en/) Superb, annually revised book International Travel & Health is available online.

and rehydrating them with water and salt (¼ teaspoon per litre).

Heatstroke A serious medical emergency. Symptoms come on suddenly and include weakness, nausea, a hot dry body with a body temperature of over 41°C, dizziness, confusion, loss of coordination, fits and eventually collapse and loss of consciousness. Seek medical help and get the person out of the heat, removing their clothes, fanning them and applying cool wet cloths or ice to their body, especially the groin and armpits.

Prickly heat A common rash in the tropical regions, caused by sweat trapped under the skin. The result is an itchy rash of tiny lumps. Treat prickly heat by moving out of the heat and into an air-conditioned area for a few hours. Cool showers also help in treating the rash. Creams and ointments clog the skin and should be avoided. Locally purchased prickly heat powder can be helpful.

INSECT BITES & STINGS
Bedbugs don't carry disease but their bites are itchy. You can treat the itch with an antihistamine.

Ticks are contracted while walking in rural areas. Ticks are commonly found behind the ears, on the belly and in armpits. See a doctor if you get a rash at the site of the bite or elsewhere, fever or muscle aches. The antibiotic

Doxycycline prevents tick-borne diseases.

SKIN PROBLEMS
There are two common fungal rashes that affect travellers in humid climates. In either case, consult a doctor.

The first occurs in moist areas such as the groin, armpits and between toes. It starts as a red patch that slowly spreads and is usually itchy. Treatment involves keeping the skin dry, avoiding chafing and using antifungal cream such as Clotrimazole or Lamisil.

Tinea versicolour is the second common rash; this fungus causes small, light-coloured patches, mostly on the back, chest and shoulders.

SUNBURN
Even on a cloudy day sunburn can occur rapidly. Use strong sunscreen (at least SPF30), making sure you reapply after swimming, and wear a wide-brimmed hat and sunglasses.

Avoid lying in the sun during the hottest part of the day (10am to 2pm).

If you become sunburnt, apply cool compresses and take painkillers. One percent hydrocortisone cream applied twice daily is also helpful.

Health Insurance
A travel insurance policy to cover theft, loss and medical problems is highly recommended; if only because of

the cosmic law that if you have it you won't need it.

Some policies specifically exclude 'dangerous activities', which can mean diving or motorcycling. Check your fine-print carefully.

If your goods are stolen, be sure to file a police report at the nearest police station to claim insurance.

Worldwide travel insurance is available at www.lonelyplanet.com/travel_services. You can buy, extend and claim online anytime – even if you're already on the road.

Internet Access

Internet and email services in Goa are plentiful, reliable and relatively cheap.

In all major towns, beach resorts and even some small villages, you'll easily find somewhere to check email.

Many hotels and guesthouses also offer internet access, and free wi-fi is becoming more common in both hotels and cafes, and is now widespread among beach shacks.

In this book, hotels offering internet access are marked by @ and wi-fi establishments with 🛜.

Practicalities

Internet charges are around ₹40 per hour (though some places charge up to ₹60), usually with a minimum of 15 minutes (₹10 to ₹15).

If you're travelling with a laptop remember you'll need a universal adaptor. These are readily available in Goa, though finding a surge protector is more difficult: bring one from home.

Legal Matters

It's important to realise what your own embassy can and can't do to help you if you get into trouble. Generally it won't be much help if the

trouble you're in is your own fault. Remember that you are bound by the laws of the country you are in; your embassy will not be sympathetic if you end up in jail after committing a crime locally, even if such actions are legal in your own country.

Drugs

The drug laws in India are among the toughest in the world; possession of even a relatively small amount of *charas* or hashish (10g or so) can lead to a *minimum* 10 years in jail and a ₹100,000 fine. Fort Aguada jail, which is not a pleasant place, houses a number of prisoners, including Westerners, who are serving drug-related sentences. Be aware that you may be held in jail (without the possibility of bail) on drug-related charges before going to trial. These pre-trial stays can be lengthy.

Police

Police corruption can be a problem in Goa, with drug use among travellers giving some poorly paid police officers opportunities for extortion.

Probably the best way to deal with police extortion, should it happen to you, is through polite, respectful persuasion. If that fails, attempt to bargain down the 'fine' before paying up, and try to establish the identity (or at least a good mental image) of the police officer.

In practical terms, the most contact the average traveller is likely to have with the law will be on the street. You may be unlucky enough to be flagged down for not wearing a helmet on certain parts of the NH17, or checked for papers by an opportunistic police officer who is hoping to extract a 'fine'. If this happens, keep your cool and you may be able to negotiate the fine down to zero.

Smoking & Spitting

On 1 January 2000, a law came into force in Goa banning smoking, spitting and the chewing of tobacco in all public places. It was a welcome move, but has proven impossible to enforce except in government buildings and places such as railway stations, where transgressors face a ₹1000 fine. Smoking is banned in many, but not all, restaurants; open-air beach shacks are fine with (cigarette) smoking.

Money

The Indian rupee (₹) is divided into 100 paise (p) but paise coins are becoming increasingly rare, and you'll likely not see one at all. Notes come in denominations of ₹10, ₹20, ₹50, ₹100, ₹500 and ₹1000.

See p13 for exchange rates at the time of writing.

ATMs

There are ever-increasing numbers of 24-hour ATMs into Goa, particularly in the cities of Panaji, Margao and Mapusa, but nowadays even in smaller beach resorts such as Agonda. These largely take international cards using the Cirrus, Maestro, MasterCard and Visa networks.

The main banks with ATMs are ICICI, Centurion, HDFC and UTI. Often ATMs are attached to the bank, but not inside it, installed in an air-conditioned cubicle (which you may need your card to access) and sometimes guarded by 24-hour armed security.

See individual listings for more details: some beach destinations still don't have ATMs, and you'll need to bring cash along with you.

Cash

It can pay to have some US dollars, pounds sterling or

euros for times when you can't find an ATM.

The best exchange rates are usually at Thomas Cook and the State Bank of India, while next best are private moneychangers. Hotels offer the least attractive rates.

Credit Cards

Credit cards are accepted in upmarket hotels and restaurants, most travel agencies and higher-end stores.

MasterCard and Visa are most widely accepted credit cards.

Cash advances on credit cards can be made at branches of Thomas Cook and Bank of Baroda.

Encashment Certificates

With every exchange transaction, you are supposed to be provided with an encashment certificate.

Encashment certificates can be useful if you want to change excess rupees back to hard currency, buy a tourist-quota train ticket or if you need to show a tax clearance certificate.

ATM receipts serve the same purpose.

International Transfers

International money transfers can be arranged through Thomas Cook or Western Union; both have branches in Panaji and some of the larger towns in Goa.

Western Union transfers can also frequently be made at post offices.

Tipping

There's no official policy on tipping in India, though it's always appreciated; 10% of a bill is absolutely acceptable.

The exceptions to this rule are five-star international hotels, where tipping hotel porters is the norm, as elsewhere in the world.

Taxi drivers don't need to be tipped, but if you've hired the driver for the day, adding a little extra is fair.

Post

The Indian postal service, though behemoth, is generally good. Letters sent almost invariably reach their destination, although they can take up to three weeks.

It costs ₹10 to send a small postcard anywhere in the world from India, and ₹20 for a large postcard or a standard letter (up to 20g).

Sending Parcels Overseas

First, take the parcel to a wrapping service (there's usually one very close to the post office – look for signs reading 'parcel post'), and get it stitched up.

Book packages (up to 5kg) can be sent without a customs form and for ₹350. They will need to be wrapped in a manner that allows the contents to be seen by postal inspectors.

At the post office you'll get the necessary customs declaration forms, which will be attached to the parcel. To avoid excise duty at the delivery end, specify that the contents are a 'gift' with a value of less than ₹1000.

Safe Travel

The greatest danger in Goa is undoubtedly the sea. Many drownings occur each year, and even usually safe stretches of beach can turn

treacherous depending on the weather or the tide. Be vigilant when swimming, especially with children.

Telephone

Mobile Phones & Getting Connected

Your own mobile phone will likely work while in Goa, though call costs are, unsurprisingly, excessive.

Though cheap international calls can still be made at the many internet cafes, which also have an STD/ISD phone booth or two (costing ₹25 to ₹40 per minute, depending on the country you're calling), many visitors opt to purchase a local SIM card, with prepaid credit.

You can buy a local SIM card from many internet cafes and mobile phone shops; it costs around ₹700, plus the cost of 'unlocking' your phone if it's not already done.

If you want to buy a local phone, the most basic model of Nokia phone (usefully equipped with a flashlight to see you through all those late-night power cuts) costs around ₹1000. Bring along two passport photos of yourself, and a copy of your passport and visa. Note that local SIM cards won't work outside Goa, except for receiving calls and sending text messages.

GOVERNMENT TRAVEL ADVICE

The following government websites offer travel advisories and information on current hot spots.

» **Australian Department of Foreign Affairs** (☎1300 139 281; www.smarttraveller.gov.au)

» **British Foreign Office** (☎0845-850-2829; www.fco.gov.uk/countryadvice)

» **Canadian Department of Foreign Affairs** (☎800-267 6788; www.dfait-maeci.gc.ca)

» **US State Department** (☎888-407 4747; http://travel.state.gov)

Fax

Many STD/ISD offices have fax facilities, but these don't generally come cheap. Sending a fax internationally can cost between ₹40 and ₹100 per page, while faxes sent within India should only cost around ₹10 per page. You can receive faxes for around ₹10 per page. Private internet cafes also often offer this service, and many hotels have fax facilities.

Phone Codes

The area code for everywhere within the state of Goa is ☏0832, which you only need to dial when calling from outside the state or from a mobile phone.

To make an international call, you need to dial ☏00 (international access code from India), plus the country code (of the country you are calling), the area code and local number.

To make a call to Goa from outside the country, dial the international access code plus ☏91 (international country code for India), then ☏832 (Goa's area code omitting the initial 0) and then the local number.

Time

India is 5½ hours ahead of GMT/UTC, 4½ hours behind Australia (EST) and 10½ hours ahead of the USA (EST). It is officially known as IST – Indian Standard Time, although many Indians prefer to think it stands for Indian Stretchable Time. When it's noon in London, it's 5.30pm in Goa.

Tourist Information

Within Goa you'll find representatives of the national **Government of India Tourist Office** (www.incredible india.org), and the state gov-

ernment's own tourism body, the **Goa Tourism Development Corporation** (GTDC; www.goa-tourism.com), both with head offices in Panaji (p123).

The GTDC is the most active of the two in Goa, running a number of decent (though not exciting) hotels and a range of whirlwind day trips. These are bookable at the Panaji office or at any GTDC hotel, and many depart daily. If you're on a very tight time schedule, they can prove a good way of seeing a number of sights at a breakneck pace.

Travellers with Disabilities

There are few provisions for disabled travellers in Goa outside of the most top-end hotels, and thus the mobility-impaired traveller will face a number of challenges. Few older buildings have wheelchair access; toilets have certainly not been designed to accommodate wheelchairs; and footpaths are generally riddled with potholes and crevices, littered with obstacles and packed with throngs of people. Nevertheless, the difficulties are far from insurmountable and if you want to visit Goa, don't be put off. If your mobility is restricted you will need an able-bodied companion to accompany you, and you'd be well-advised to hire a private vehicle with a driver.

Resources

Royal Association for Disability and Rehabilitation (RADAR; ☏+44 (0)20-72503222; www.radar.org.uk; 12 City Forum, 250 City Rd, London EC1V 8AF, UK)

Mobility International USA (MIUSA; ☏541-3431284; www.miusa.org; PO Box 10767, Eugene, OR 97440, USA).

Disability Goa (www.disabilitygoa.com)

Timeless Excursions (www.timelessexcursions.com)

Visas

Almost everyone, except nationals of Nepal and Bhutan, needs a visa before arriving in India. Note that your passport should be valid for at least six months beyond your intended stay, and have two blank pages.

A pilot scheme is currently in place to provide 30-day tourist visas on arrival to nationals of Japan, New Zealand, Singapore, Luxembourg and Finland at Mumbai, Chennai, Kolkata and New Delhi airports. In theory, this is fantastic; in practice, it's bureaucratic and time-consuming (think four-hour waits at the airport after arrival). You need to bring passport photos, proof (on paper) of outward travel, and proof (also on paper) of a hotel booking in India. Check the status of this scheme before you fly, but if you have time, arrange a visa the old-fashioned way, in advance, instead.

Visa Extensions

Officially, you can only get another six-month tourist visa by leaving the country and coming back in on a new visa, and many travellers head off on a quick 'visa run' to Sri Lanka, Nepal or home, to replenish their tourist visa. You may hear stories of people obtaining visa extensions through 'unofficial' channels; ask someone who's done this successfully, and expect to pay dearly for the rather shady service.

Visa Registration

People travelling on tourist visas are not required to register with the Foreigners' Regional Registration Office (FRRO); the form that you fill out each time you check into a hotel, beach hut or guest house takes the place of this. Only foreigners with visas valid for longer than 180 days are officially required to register, as are nationals of Pakistan and Afghanistan. FRRO can be located in Mumbai as follows:

FRRO Mumbai (☎022-22620446; Annex Bldg No 2, CID, Badaruddin Tyabji Rd, near Special Branch)

Women Travellers

Most solo female travellers to Goa experience few problems during a stay in the state, aside from the occasional lewd comment or beachside ogling.

If you find yourself the target of unwanted attention or advances, raise your voice to embarrass the offender, preferably referring to him as 'brother'; this association, in general, is enough to rob the culprit of a substantial degree of his passion.

It pays to keep your wits about you and avoid situations that make you more vulnerable, including walking alone at night along unlit stretches of road or beach.

WOMEN'S HEALTH

» In most places in Goa, sanitary products (pads, and sometimes tampons) are readily available. Birth control options may be limited, so bring adequate supplies of your own form of contraception.

» Heat, humidity and antibiotics can contribute to thrush. Treatment is with antifungal creams and pessaries such as Clotrimazole. A practical alternative is a single tablet of Fluconazole (Diflucan). Urinary tract infections can be precipitated by dehydration or long bus journeys without toilet stops; bring suitable antibiotics.

» Pregnant women should receive specialised advice before travelling. The ideal time to travel is in the second trimester (between 16 and 28 weeks), when the risk of pregnancy-related problems is at its lowest. Ensure that your travel insurance policy covers all pregnancy-related possibilities, including premature labour.

» Traveller's diarrhoea in pregnant women can quickly lead to dehydration and result in inadequate blood flow to the placenta. Many drugs used to treat various diarrhoea bugs are not recommended in pregnancy. Azithromycin is considered safe.

Diminished mental alertness, through use of drugs and alcohol, might make you more of a target and less able to defend yourself, should the worst come to the worst.

In all, it's best to stay vigilant, though not fearful, throughout your stay.

Transport

GETTING THERE & AWAY

Air

Airports & Airlines

INTERNATIONAL FLIGHTS
From **Mumbai Airport** (www.csia.in) many travellers take onward domestic connections into Goa. See p66 for details.

Goa's only airport is **Dabolim Airport** (DABOLIM; Dabolim International Airport; ☑0832-2540806), around 30km from Goa's capital, Panaji.

Only a handful of charter companies operate international flights into Dabolim Airport, most from the UK, Germany and Russia. Be aware that in principle, at least, it's illegal to enter India on a scheduled flight and leave on a chartered flight, or vice versa. However, chances are this won't be checked.

DOMESTIC FLIGHTS
Numerous domestic airlines fly daily in and out of Goa, most flights taking off and landing throughout the morning and early afternoon.

Dabolim Airport's arrivals hall is equipped with a money-exchange office, GTDC tourist office, Airtel office for purchasing mobile-phone credit, and charter airline offices. There are two prepaid taxi booths (one in the arrivals hall and the other just outside), for heading by taxi elsewhere in the state.

A return flight from Mumbai to Goa can cost around US$150, sometimes even less. The flight takes around 45 minutes.

It's cheapest and easiest to book online direct with the airline as far in advance of your travel as possible.

Of those listed below, Kingfisher and Jet Airways

CHARTER FLIGHTS TO GOA

Reliable charter flights into Goa from the UK or Germany:

» **Thomson Airlines** (www. thomson.co.uk)

» **Monarch Airlines** (www.monarch.co.uk)

» **Condor Airlines** (www.condor.com)

---

are the most comfortable (and most expensive) options.

» **Indigo** (☑1800 1803838 toll free; http://book.goindigo.in)

» **GoAir** (☑1800 222111 toll free; www.goair.in)

» **Spicejet** (☑1800 1803333 toll free; www.spicejet.com)

» **Kingfisher** (☑1800 200 9000 toll free; www.flyking fisher.com)

» **Jet Airways** (www.jetairways.com)

Land

Car

Hiring a self-drive car in any major Indian city and driving to Goa is possible, but given the dangers of the roads (and consequently how tiring this makes driving here) and the high cost, this sort of a rental isn't really recommended unless you've absolutely got your heart set on it. It's important to note that not all rental cars can be taken out of the state in which they were rented.

An alternative is to make your way to the nearest taxi rank and start bargaining. The 600km trip from Mumbai to Goa takes about 14 hours; many drivers will happily do this in one stretch. You'll have to pay for the taxi's return trip, so the cost will be at least ₹8000. Unless you're part of a group, it's likely to be cheaper to fly.

Bus

From neighbouring states you'll find frequent bus services into Goa – it's just a matter of turning up at the bus station and checking timetables or jumping on the next available bus.

Buses vary wildly in terms of comfort. Both long-distance state-run and private companies offer 'ordinary' and 'deluxe' services, but definitions are flexible. Find out when you book exactly what your bus has to offer.

CLIMATE CHANGE & TRAVEL

Every form of transport that relies on carbon-based fuel generates CO_2, the main cause of human-induced climate change. Modern travel is dependent on aeroplanes, which might use less fuel per kilometre per person than most cars but travel much greater distances. The altitude at which aircraft emit gases (including CO_2) and particles also contributes to their climate change impact. Many websites offer 'carbon calculators' that allow people to estimate the carbon emissions generated by their journey and, for those who wish to do so, to offset the impact of the greenhouse gases emitted with contributions to portfolios of climate-friendly initiatives throughout the world. Lonely Planet offsets the carbon footprint of all staff and author travel.

They range from less decrepit versions of ordinary buses to flashy Volvo buses with AC, reclining two-by-two seating, and even lie-flat berths.

One of the most popular options for booking bus travel to and from Goa is **Paulo Travels** (www.paulotravels .com). Consult its website for up-to-date prices, route information and bookings.

BUSES TO AND FROM MUMBAI

For details of bus services from Mumbai, see p66

Buses for Mumbai depart from Panaji (p123) and Margao (p157) daily; see individual chapters for details and prices.

Train

The 760km-long **Konkan Railway** (www.konkanrailway. com), the main train line running through Goa, connects Goa with Mumbai to the north, and Mangalore to the south.

Services and prices change seasonally; check the Konkan Railway website, **Indian Railways** (www. indianrail.gov.in) or **Cleartrip** (www.cleartrip.com/trains) for up-to-date information.

Children under the age of five travel for free; those between five and 12 are charged half price.

You can reliably book and pay online for train tickets at **Cleartrip** (www.cleartrip. com/trains) and **Makemytrip** (www.makemytrip.com/rail ways), but you can't book tourist quota tickets through them (tourist quota tickets being especially useful when all other tickets have already

been sold). For these, go to the railway station in person.

Main train stations in Goa (at which most long-distance trains stop) are Madgaon station in Margao (p157), and Karmali station (p123) in Old Goa, 12km from Panaji.

In-person train bookings are best made at Margao's Madgaon station (p157), at the train reservation office at Panaji's Kadamba bus stand (p123) or at any travel agent selling train tickets.

Make sure you book as far in advance as possible for sleepers, since they fill up quickly. Reservations fees generally range from ₹40 to ₹60, or slightly more if booking through a travel agent.

Other smaller, useful Goan railway stations (which not all interstate trains stop at) include Pernem for Arambol, Thivim for Mapusa, and Canacona for Palolem.

For more details on travelling by train from, and within, Mumbai, see p66 and p68.

TRAIN CLASSES

There are a host of different classes, making for various comfort levels. Not all are available on all trains.

AC First Class (1A) The most expensive class of train travel. Air-conditioned accommodation in simple two-berth or four-berth lockable compartments, whose seats convert into beds for night. Bedclothes and meals are provided.

AC 2 Tier (2A) Two-tier berths arranged in groups of two and four-berth cubicles in an air-conditioned open-

plan carriage that sleeps 46 people in total. The bunks are converted to seats by day, and there are curtains for some semblance of privacy. Bedclothes are provided and drinks and meals are offered, for extra cost, regularly.

AC 3 Tier (3A) Three-tier berths arranged in groups of six in an open-plan carriage; there are usually no curtains though you might get bedclothes.

First Class (FC) A non-AC version of AC First Class (1A).

AC Chair Car (CC) Air-conditioned carriage with reclining seats.

Sleeper (SL) Similar to AC 3 Tier (3A) but without air-conditioning.

Second Sitting (2S) Unreserved second-class seating on plastic chairs or wooden benches. Crowded, but cheap.

TOURIST QUOTA

At most major stations there's a separate section in the booking hall dealing with the tourist quota, a small number of tickets set aside for foreigners and non-resident Indians, which are sometimes still available long after all other tickets are sold out. You must show your passport and visa, and pay in foreign currency (US dollars, euros or pounds sterling in cash or travellers cheques) or with rupees backed up by exchange certificates or ATM receipts. When booking any ticket at a train station, fill out a reservation form *before* queuing.

Around Goa

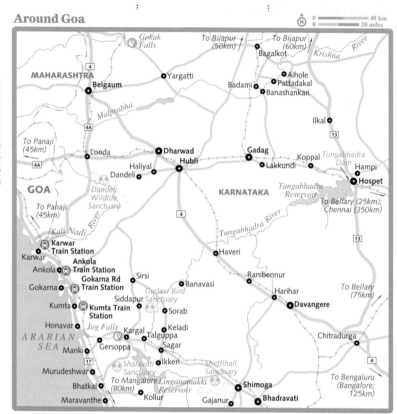

WAITLIST (WL)

Trains are frequently over-booked, but many passengers cancel and there are regular no-shows. So if you buy a ticket on the waiting list, you're still quite likely to get a seat, even if there are a number of people in front of you. A refund is available if you don't: ask at the ticket office about your chances.

RESERVATION AGAINST CANCELLATION (RAC)

Even when a train is fully booked, Indian Railways sells a handful of seats in each class as 'Reservation Against Cancellation' (RAC). This entitles you to board the train and at least get a simple seat. Once the train is

moving, the Travelling Ticket Examiner (TTE) will find you a berth – which he usually, quite miraculously, does.

GETTING AROUND

Bicycle

Goa offers plenty of variety for cycling, with relatively smooth-surfaced highways, rocky dirt tracks, coastal routes through coconut palms and winding country roads through spice plantations, rural villages and ancient temples. A bicycle can also simply be a convenient

way of getting around beach towns.

If you want a quality machine for serious touring, it's worth bringing your own. Check with your airline for travel regulations.

The downside is that your bike is likely to be a curiosity and more vulnerable to theft. Bring spare tyres, tubes, patch kits, chassis, cables, freewheels, a pump with the necessary connection and spokes, tools and a repair manual.

Hire

Hiring a bicycle is not difficult in Goa, but hiring a *good* bicycle is not so easy. Every beach in Goa has a multitude of people who are prepared to rent out bicycles – just ask around and someone will rent you *their* bicycle, more often than not an Indian-made single-gear rattler.

Away from main tourist areas, you won't find bicycle-hire places.

Expect to pay around ₹5 an hour or ₹30 per day (less to hire for a week or more). If you just want to hire a bike for a day in the high season, you may have to pay up to ₹80.

Purchase

For a long stay of three months or more in Goa, it's worth considering buying a bicycle locally.

Every town has at least a couple of shops selling various brands of basic Indian bikes including Hero, Atlas, BSA and Raleigh, almost always painted jet black. You should be able to pick up a second-hand bike for ₹1000 to ₹1500.

Boat

One of the joys of travelling around Goa is joining locals on flat-bottomed passenger-vehicle ferries that cross the state's many rivers. See p173 for more details.

Bus

Goa boasts an extensive network of buses, shuttling to and from almost every tiny town and village.

There are no timetables, bus numbers, or, it seems, fixed fares, though it would be hard to spend more than ₹20 on any one single journey (and fares are usually far less).

Buses range from serviceable to spluttering, and most pack passengers to bursting point, but are a fun and colourful way to experience local life.

Head to the nearest bus stand (often called the Kadamba bus stand, after

the state's biggest bus company) and scan the signs posted on the buses' windscreens to find the service you're after, or ask a driver who'll point you in the right direction.

Check individual destination listings for more detailed information on services.

Car

It's easy, in most destinations, to organise a private car with a driver if you're planning on taking some long-distance day trips. Prices vary, but you should bank on paying around ₹1500 to ₹2000 for a full day out on the road.

It's also possible, if you've the nerves and the skills, to procure a self-drive car, giving you the (white-knuckle) freedom to explore Goa's highways and byways at your own pace.

A small Chevrolet or Maruti will cost around ₹600 to ₹900 per day and a jeep around ₹1000, excluding petrol; there are few organised car-hire outlets, so ask around for a man with a car he's willing to rent to you.

Note the slightly mystifying signs posted on Goa's major NH17 national highway, which advise of different speed limits (on the largely single-carriageway road) for different types of vehicle.

Hitching

Hitching is never entirely safe in any country in the world, and we don't recommend it. On the other hand, many travellers argue that it offers an interesting insight into a country. If you decide to try it, be mindful of the fact that people travelling in pairs will be safer than those going it alone. Solo women in particular are unwise to hitchhike.

Local Transport

Autorickshaw

An autorickshaw is a yellow-and-black three-wheeled contraption powered by a noisy two-stroke motorcycle engine. It has a canopy, a driver up front and seats for two (though we've managed two with four small children) passengers behind.

This typically Indian mode of transport is cheaper than a taxi and generally a better option for short trips – count on ₹50 for a very short journey and ₹100 for a slightly longer one.

Flag down an autorickshaw and negotiate the fare before you jump in (don't even try asking the driver to turn on the meter); if he's charging too much, let him go – there'll be another along soon.

Motorcycle Taxi

Goa is the only state in India where motorcycles are a licensed form of taxi.

You can tell the motorcycle taxis (or pilots as they are sometimes called) by the yellow front mudguard. They gather, along with taxis and autorickshaws, at strategic points in towns and beach resorts.

As with autorickshaws, negotiate a good rate before jumping on.

Taxi

Taxis, ranging from black and yellow Ford Ambassadors to white air-conditioned Maruti vans, are widely available for hopping town-to-town.

A full day's sightseeing, depending on the distance, is likely to be around ₹1500 to ₹2000.

You'll rarely find a taxi with a functioning meter, so agree on a price before you agree to be a passenger. The exception to this rule is in Mumbai, where newer taxis are all equipped with good meters. Insist this is turned on before you go anywhere.

ROAD DISTANCES (KM)

	Bicholim	Calangute	Hampi	Mapusa	Margao	Molem	Old Goa	Palolem	Panaji	Pernem	Ponda
Calangute	35										
Hampi	390	396									
Mapusa	25	10	392								
Margao	53	50	370	46							
Molem	70	76	320	72	50						
Old Goa	23	26	370	22	37	50					
Palolem	93	90	403	86	40	83	75				
Panaji	19	16	380	12	34	60	10	74			
Pernem	43	28	410	18	64	90	40	104	30		
Ponda	38	43	350	39	25	30	19	53	29	47	
Vasco da Gama	49	46	390	42	30	70	35	70	30	60	34

Motorcycle

Getting around Goa by scooter or motorcycle is probably the most popular form of transport, both for locals and tourists.

Driving Licence

An international driving permit is not technically mandatory, but it's wise to bring one. The first thing a policeman will want to see if he stops you is your licence, and an international permit is incontrovertible. Permits are available from your home automobile association.

Fuel & Spare Parts

At the time of research petrol cost ₹65 per litre.

Distances are generally short and small bikes (such as the Honda Kinetic or Activa) are very economical.

There are increasing numbers of petrol stations in all main towns including Panaji, Margao, Mapusa, Ponda and Vasco da Gama, a 24-hour service station in Margao and another on the NH17 highway near Cuncolim. There's also a busy pump in Vagator.

Where there are no petrol pumps, general stores sell petrol by the litre; they don't advertise the fact, so you'll have to ask around. Beware that sometimes petrol in plastic bottles has been diluted.

A Honda Kinetic holds 7L of fuel, and should go 40km on 1L. A 100cc Yamaha takes 10L to 11L and also does 40km per litre. Enfields hold about 18L; new models will do about 35km per litre, while older ones do considerably less.

Hire

Hiring a motorcycle in Goa is easy. Hirers will probably find you, and are more often than not decent guys who are just looking to make a bit of cash on the side.

Private bike owners are not technically allowed to rent out a machine. This means that if you are stopped by the police for any reason, your hirer would prefer that you say you have borrowed it from a 'friend'.

It's a good idea to keep registration papers in the bike – it gives the police one less argument against you, and if you don't have a valid licence, or you're not wearing a helmet on NH17 (the national highway), you'll need all the help you can get.

WHICH MOTORBIKE?

At the bottom end of the scale are the most popular rental bikes – gearless scooters such as the 100cc Honda Kinetics or Bajaj scooters. They are extremely practical and easy to ride. You only need a car driving licence to ride these bikes.

Next up are the 100cc and 135cc bikes – Yamaha being the most common. Fuel economy is good, they go faster than a Kinetic, and are more comfortable over long distances. Although they're easy to ride, you'll need to have had some experience on a motorcycle.

At the top of the pile are the real bikes – classic Enfield Bullets, made in India since the 1950s. They are far less fuel-friendly, require more maintenance than the others, and take a little getting used to. Most Enfields available for hire are 350cc, but there are also some 500cc models around.

COSTS & PRACTICALITIES
Outside of the high season you can get a scooter for as little as ₹100 per day. During high season (December to February) the standard rate is ₹250 to ₹350.

Expect to pay ₹400 for a 100cc bike and up to ₹700 for an Enfield.

The longer you hire a bike (and the older it is), the cheaper it becomes.

Make absolutely sure that you agree with the owner about the price. Clarify whether one day is 24 hours, and that you won't be asked to pay extra for keeping it overnight.

You may be asked to pay cash up front; get a written receipt or something to that effect.

Take down the phone number of the owner, or his mechanic, in case something goes wrong with the bike.

On the Road
HELMETS
Helmets became mandatory in Goa in 2004.

The Motorcycle Action Group (MAG) strongly opposes the law. It argues that casualties would be decreased through less reckless, negligent and drink driving, rather than through compulsory use of helmets.

Many people choose to ride without helmets, though in theory (rarely in practice) you could be pulled over and fined.

ROAD CONDITIONS & SAFETY
Bear in mind that Goan roads are treacherous, filled with human, bovine, canine, feline, mechanical and avian obstacles, as well as a good sprinkling of potholes and hairpin bends.

Be on the lookout for 'speed breakers'. Speed humps are stand-alone back breakers or come in triplets. The extra nasty ones are lined up in groups of fives, and none of them are particularly well signed.

Take it slowly, try not to drive at night (and if you do, watch out for sleeping black cows – a serious obstacle on an unlit road), and don't attempt a north–south day trip on a 50cc bike.

Bear in mind that Goa's NH17 is a highway in name only: in no other way does it resemble the highways – or even byways – you'll be used to back home.

ROAD RULES
Road rules in India are applied mainly in theory. Driving is on the left, vehicles give way to the right and road signs are universal pictorial signs.

At busy intersections, traffic police are often on hand to reduce the chaos. Otherwise, make good use of your horn.

Also, never forget that the highway code in India can be reduced to one essential truth – 'Might is Right' – meaning the bigger the vehicle, the more priority you're accorded.

Organised Tours
Classic Bike Adventure (☑0832-2268467; www.classic-bike-india.com; Casa Tres Amigos, Assagao) is a long-established company that organises motorbike tours on Enfields through the Himalayas, Nepal, South India and Goa.

Purchase
There are plenty of second-hand machines around – check advertisements in the daily papers or head to the Anjuna flea market on Wednesday.

Train
Goa's rail services, though great for getting to and from the state itself, aren't actually very useful for getting around. You're far better off travelling by bus, taxi or under your own steam, since intercity train services aren't particularly fast, frequent or reliable.

There are two railways in Goa, the first of which is the South Central Railway, which has its terminus in Mormugao (past Vasco da Gama) and runs east, through Margao and into Karnataka. This line is most useful for day-tripping to Dudhsagar Falls; see p142 for details.

The interstate Konkan Railway train line also passes through Goa. Konkan Railway stations in Goa, from north to south, are: Pernem (for Arambol), Thivim (for Mapusa), Karmali (for Old Goa and Panaji), Verna, Margao (for Colva and Benaulim), Bali, Barcem and Canacona (for Palolem).

Book tickets through travel agents or at the stations themselves; the main booking offices are at Panaji's Kadamba bus station, and at Margao's Madgaon train station. See p233 for more details.

Language

WANT MORE?

For in-depth language information and handy phrases, check out Lonely Planet's *India Phrasebook*. You'll find it at **shop .lonelyplanet.com**, or you can buy Lonely Planet's iPhone phrasebooks at the Apple App Store.

Thanks to its unusual colonial history, Goa has inherited a mixture of languages. Portuguese is still spoken as a second language by a few Goans, although it is gradually dying out. Konkani is the official language of Goa, whereas Marathi is taught as a standard subject in the state, as well as being the main language of Mumbai. Children in Goa are obliged to learn Hindi in school, and the primary language used in many schools is actually English, since both Hindi and English have official status in India. English is widely spoken in tourist areas in Goa and Mumbai.

HINDI

Hindi has about 600 million speakers worldwide, of which 180 million are in India. It developed from Classical Sanskrit, and is written in the Devanagari script. In 1947 it was granted official status along with English.

Most Hindi sounds are similar to their English counterparts. The main difference is that Hindi has both 'aspirated' consonants (pronounced with a puff of air, like saying 'h' after the sound) and unaspirated ones, as well as 'retroflex' (pronounced with the tongue bent backwards) and nonretroflex consonants. Our simplified pronunciation guides don't include these distinctions – if you read them as if they were English, you'll be understood just fine.

The pronunciation of vowels is important, especially their length (eg a and aa). The consonant combination ng after a vowel indicates nasalisation (ie the vowel is pronounced 'through the nose'). Note also that au is pronounced as the 'ow' in 'how'.

Word stress in Hindi is very light; we've indicated the stressed syllables with italics.

Basics

Hindi verbs change form depending on the gender of the speaker (or the subject of the sentence in general) – meaning it's the verbs, not the pronouns 'he' or 'she', which show whether the subject of the sentence is masculine or feminine. In these phrases we include the options for male and female speakers, marked 'm' and 'f' respectively.

Hello./Goodbye.	नमस्ते ।	na·ma·*ste*
Yes.	जी हाँ ।	jee haang
No.	जी नहीं ।	jee na·*heeng*
Excuse me.	सुनिये ।	su·ni·ye
Sorry.	माफ़ कीजिये ।	maaf *kee*·ji·ye
Please ...	कृपया ...	kri·pa·*yaa* ...
Thank you.	थैंक्यू ।	*thayn*·kyoo
You're welcome.	कोई बात नहीं ।	*ko*·ee baat na·*heeng*

How are you?

आप कैसे/कैसी हैं?
aap *kay*·se/*kay*·see hayng (m/f)

Fine. And you?

मैं ठीक हूँ ।
mayng teek hoong
आप सुनाइये ।
aap su·*naa*·i·ye

What's your name?

आप का नाम क्या है?
aap kaa naam kyaa hay

My name is ...

मेरा नाम ... है ।
me·raa naam ... hay

Do you speak English?

क्या आपको अंग्रेज़ी   kyaa aap ko an·*gre*·zee
आती है?   *aa*·tee hay

I don't understand.

मैं नहीं समझा/   mayng na·*heeng* sam·*jaa*/
समझी।   sam·jee (m/f)

Accommodation

Where's a ...?	... कहाँ है?	... ka·*haang* hay
guesthouse	गेस्ट हाउस	gest *haa*·us
hotel	होटल	*ho*·tal
youth hostel	यूथ हास्टल	yoot *haas*·tal

Do you have a ... room?	क्या ... कमरा है?	kyaa ... *kam*·raa hay
single	सिंगल	*sin*·gal
double	डबल	da·*bal*

How much is it per ...?	... के लिये कितने पैसे लगते हैं?	... ke li·*ye* kit·ne *pay*·se *lag*·te hayng
night	एक रात	ek raat
person	हर व्यक्ति	har *vyak*·ti

Numbers – Hindi			
1	१	एक	ek
2	२	दो	do
3	३	तीन	teen
4	४	चार	chaar
5	५	पाँच	paanch
6	६	छह	chay
7	७	सात	saat
8	८	आठ	aat
9	९	नौ	nau
10	१०	दस	das
20	२०	बीस	bees
30	३०	तीस	tees
40	४०	चालीस	*chaa*·lees
50	५०	पचास	pa·*chaas*
60	६०	साठ	saat
70	७०	सत्तर	*sat*·tar
80	८०	अस्सी	*as*·see
90	९०	नब्बे	*nab*·be
100	१००	सौ	sau
1000	१०००	एक हज़ार	ek ha·*zaar*

Eating & Drinking

What would you recommend?

आपके ख़्याल में   aap ke kyaal meng
क्या अच्छा होगा?   kyaa *ach*·chaa ho·gaa

Do you have vegetarian food?

क्या आप का खाना   kyaa aap kaa *kaa*·naa
शाकाहारी है?   shaa·kaa·*haa*·ree hay

I don't eat (meat).

मैं (गोश्त) नहीं   mayng (gosht) na·*heeng*
खाता/खाती।   *kaa*·taa/*kaa*·tee (m/f)

I'll have ...

मुझे ... दीजिये।   mu·*je* ... *dee*·ji·ye

That was delicious.

बहुत मज़ेदार हुआ।   ba·*hut* ma·ze·*daar* hu·aa

Please bring the menu/bill.

मेन्यू/बिल लाइये।   *men*·yoo/bil *laa*·i·ye

Emergencies

Help!

मदद कीजिये!   ma·*dad* kee·ji·ye

Go away!

जाओ!   *jaa*·o

I'm lost.

मैं रास्ता भूल   mayng *raas*·taa bool
गया/गयी हूँ।   ga·*yaa*/ga·*yee* hoong (m/f)

Call a doctor!

डॉक्टर को बुलाओ!   *daak*·tar ko bu·*laa*·o

Call the police!

पुलिस को बुलाओ!   pu·*lis* ko bu·*laa*·o

I'm ill.

मैं बीमार हूँ।   mayng *bee*·maar hoong

I'm allergic to (antibiotics).

मुझे (एंटीबायोटिकिस)   mu·*je* (en·tee·baa·*yo*·tiks)
की एलरजी है।   kee e·*lar*·jee hay

Where's the toilet?

टॉइलेट कहाँ है?   *taa*·i·let ka·*haang* hay

Shopping & Services

I'd like to buy ...

मुझे ... चाहिये।   mu·*je* ... *chaa*·hi·ye

I'm just looking.

सिर्फ़ देखने आया/   sirf *dek*·ne aa·yaa/
आयी हूँ।   aa·yee hoong (m/f)

Can I look at it?

दिखाइये।   di·*kaa*·i·ye

Do you have any others?

दूसरा है?   *doos*·raa hay

How much is it?
कितने का है? *kit*·ne kaa hay

It's too expensive.
यह बहुत महंगा/ yeh ba·*hut* ma·han·gaa/
महंगी है । ma·*han*·gee hay (m/f)

Can you lower the price?
क्या आप दाम kyaa aap daam
कम करेंगे? kam ka·*reng*·ge

There's a mistake in the bill.
बिल में गलती है। bil meng *gal*·tee hay

Transport & Directions

When's the ... (bus)?	... (बस) कब जाती है?	... (bas) kab *jaa*·tee hay
first	पहली	*peh*·lee
next	अगली	*ag*·lee
last	आखिरी	*aa*·ki·ree
bicycle	साइकिल	*saa*·i·kil
rickshaw	रिक्शा	*rik*·shaa
boat	जहाज़	ja·*haaz*
bus	बस	bas
plane	हवाई जहाज़	ha·*vaa*·ee ja·*haaz*
train	ट्रेन	tren

a ... ticket	के लिये ... टिकट दीजिये।	ke li·*ye* ... ti·*kat* dee·ji·ye
1st-class	फ़र्स्ट क्लास	farst klaas
2nd-class	सेकंड क्लास	se·*kand* klaas
one-way	एक तरफ़ा	ek ta·ra·*faa*
return	आने जाने का	*aa*·ne *jaa*·ne kaa

I'd like to hire a ...	मुझे ... किराये पर लेना है।	mu·*je* ... ki·*raa*·ye par le·*naa* hay
4WD	फ़ोर व्हील ड्राइव	for vheel *draa*·iv
bicycle	साइकिल	*saa*·i·kil
car	कार	kaar
motorbike	मोटर साइकिल	*mo*·tar *saa*·i·kil

Where's ...?
... कहाँ है? ... ka·*haang* hay

How far is it?
वह कितनी दूर है? voh *kit*·nee door hay

What's the address?
पता क्या है? pa·*taa* kyaa hay

Can you write it down, please?
कृपया यह लिखिये। kri·pa·*yaa* yeh li·*ki*·ye

Can you show me (on the map)?
(नक्शे में) दिखा (*nak*·she meng) di·*kaa*
सकते है? *sak*·te hayng

KONKANI

After a long and hard-fought battle, Konkani was recognised as the official language of Goa in 1987, becoming a national language in 1992. Before that, argument had raged that Konkani was actually no more than a dialect of Marathi, the official language of the much larger Maharashtra. Konkani is an Indo-Aryan language and has 2.5 million speakers. The Devanagari script (also used to write Hindi and Marathi) is the official writing system for Konkani in Goa. However, Konkani speakers also use the Kannada script, as given here.

A few pronunciation tips: ai is pronounced as in 'aisle', eu as the 'u' in 'nurse' (a short sound), oh as the 'o' in 'note' and ts as in 'hats'. The symbol ng (as in 'sing') indicates the nasalisation of the preceding consonant, meaning that the consonant sound is pronounced 'through the nose'.

Basics

Hello.	ಹಲ್ಲೋ.	*hal*·lo
Goodbye.	ಮೆಳ್ಯಾಂ.	*mel*·yaang
How are you?	ಕಸೊ/ಕಶಿ ಆಸಾಯ್?	*keu*·so/*keu*·shi aa·saay (m/f)
Fine, thanks.	ಹಾಂವ್ಂ ಬರೆಂ ಆಸಾಂ.	*haang*·ung *beu*·rong aa·saang
Yes.	ವ್ಹಯ್.	*weu*·i
No.	ನಾಂ.	naang
Please.	ಉಪ್ಕಾರ್ ಕರ್ನ್.	*up*·kaar keurn
Thank you.	ದೇವ್ ಬರೆಂ ಕರುಂ.	*day*·u bo·*reng* ko·roong
Excuse me.	ಉಪ್ಕಾರ್ ಕರ್ನ್.	*up*·kaar keurn
Sorry.	ಚೂಕ್ ಝಾಲಿ, ಮಾಫ್ ಕರ್.	tsook *zaa*·li, maaf keur

What's your name?
ತುಜೆಂ ನಾಂವ್ಂ ಕಿತೆಂ? *tu*·jeng *naang*·ung *ki*·teng

My name is ...
ಮ್ಹಜೆಂ ನಾಂವ್ಂ ... *meu*·jeng *naang*·ung ...

Do you speak English?
ಇಂಗ್ಲಿಶ್ ಉಲೈತಾಯ್ಗೀ? *ing*·leesh *u*·leuy·taay·gee

I don't understand.
ನಾಂ, ಸಮ್ಜೊಂಕ್–ನಾಂ. naang *som*·zonk·naang

Accommodation

Do you have a single/double room?
ಸಿಂಗಲ್/ಡಬಲ್ ರೂಮ್   *sin*·gal/*da*·bal room
ಮೆಳಾತ್ಗೀ?   me·laat·gee

How much is it per night?
ಏಕಾ ರಾತೀಚೆಂ   e·kaa *raa*·ti·cheng
ಭಾಡೆಂ ಕಿತ್ಲೆಂ?   baa·deng kit·leng

How much is it per person?
ಏಕ್ಲ್ಯಾಕ್ ಭಾಡೆಂ ಕಿತ್ಲೆಂ?   ek·lyaak *baa*·deng *kit*·leng

Eating & Drinking

Can you recommend a dish?
ಬರೆಂ ಏಕ್ ನಿಸ್ತೆಂ   *beu*·reng ayk *nis*·teng
ಝಾಲ್ಯಾರ್ ಖ್ಯೆಚೆಂ?   *zaa*·lyaar *keu*·ing·cheng

I'd like the menu, please.
ಮೆನೂ ಝಾಯ್ ಆಸ್−ಲ್ಲೊ.   *me*·noo zaay *aa*·sul·lo

I'd like the bill, please.
ಬಿಲ್ಲ್ ಝಾಯ್ ಆಸ್−ಲ್ಲಿಂ.   bil zaay *aa*·sul·leng

Emergencies

Help!   ಮ್ಯಾ ಕಾ   *maa*·kaa
   ಕುಮೆಕ್ ಕರ್!   *ku*·meuk keur
Go away!   ವಸ್!   weuts

Numbers – Konkani

1	ಏಕ್	ayk
2	ದೋನ್	dohn
3	ತೀನ್	teen
4	ಚಾರ್	chaar
5	ಪಾಂಚ್	paants
6	ಸೊ	so
7	ಸಾತ್	saat
8	ಆಟ್	aat
9	ನೋವ್	nohw
10	ಧಾ	daa
20	ವೀಸ್	wees
30	ತೀಸ್	tees
40	ಚಾಳೀಸ್	*tsaa*·lees
50	ಪನ್ನಾಸ್	*pon*·naas
60	ಸಾಟ್	saat
70	ಸತ್ತರ್	*seut*·teur
80	ಐಂಶಿಂ	*euyng*·shing
90	ನೊವ್ವೋದ್	*no*·wod
100	ಶೆಂಭರ್	*shem*·bor
1000	ಹಜ್ಜಾರ್	*ha*·zaar

Call ...!   ... ಆಪೈ!   ...*aa*·pai
   a doctor   ದಾಕ್ತೆರಾಕ್   *daak*·te·raak
   the police   ಪೊಲಿಸಾಂಕ್   *po*·li·saank

I'm lost.
ಮ್ಹಜೀ ವಾಟ್ ಚುಕ್ಲ್ಯಾ.   *meu*·ji waat *tsuk*·lyaa
Where are the toilets?
ಟೊಯ್ಲೆಟ್ ಖ್ಯೆಂಚರ್   *toy*·let *keu*·ing·tseur
ಆಸಾತ್?   *aa*·saat

Shopping

Can I look at it?
ಪಳಯೆತ್ಗೀ?   *peu*·leu·yet·gee
How much is it?
ತಾಕಾ ಕಿತ್ಲೆ ಪೈಶೆ?   *taa*·kaa *kit*·le *peuy*·she
That's too expensive.
ತೆಂ ಏಕ್ಧಮ್ ಮ್ಹಾರಗ್.   teng *ayk*·dam *maa*·reug

Transport & Directions

Where's the ...?
... ಖ್ಯೆಂ ಆಸಾ?   ... *keuyng aa*·saa
Can you show me (on the map)?
(ಮೇಪಾಚೆರ್)   (*mae*·paa·cher)
ದಾಕ್ಯೆಶಿಗೀ?   daa·*keuy*·shi·gee
What time's the first/last bus?
ಪಯ್ಲೆಂ/ಆಖ್ರೇಚೆಂ   *peuy*·leng/ak·*ray*·cheng
ಬಸ್ ಕಿತ್ಲ್ಯಾಕ್ ವೆಳಾರ್   bas *kit*·lyaa *we*·laar
ಯೆತಾ?   *ye*·taa

One ... ticket   (ಪೆರ್ಮುದೆ) ...   (*per*·mu·de) ...
to (Permude),   ಮ್ಯಾ ಕಾ ಏಕ್   *maa*·kaa ayk
please.   ಟಿಕೇಟ್ ಝಾಯ್.   *ti*·kayt zaay
   one-way   ವಚೊಂಕ್   *wo*·tsonk
   ಮಾತ್ರ್   maatr
   return   ವಚೊಂಕ್   *wo*·tsonk
   ಆನಿಂ ಪಾಟೀಂ   *aan*·ing *paa*·ting
   ಯೆಂವ್ಕ್,   *ayng*·wuk

MARATHI

Marathi is the official language of the state of Maharashtra and is widely spoken in Mumbai. It belongs to the Indo-Aryan language family and is spoken by an estimated 71 million people. It's written in the Devanagari script. You may notice considerable dialectal variation in Marathi as you move around the region, and in Mumbai you may hear 'Mumbai slang', which mixes Marathi with Hindi, Gujarati, Konkani and English.

Basics

Hello.   नमस्कार.   na·mas·*kaar*
Goodbye.   बाय.   bai
Yes./No.   होय./नाही.   hoy/naa·*hee*

Please.	कृपया.	kri·pa·yaa
Thank you.	धन्यवाद.	dan·ya·vaad
Excuse me.	क्षमस्व.	ksha·mas·va
Sorry.	खेद आहे.	ked aa·he

How are you?
आपण कसे आहात ? — aa·pan ka·se aa·haat

Fine, thanks.
छान आहे, आभार. — chaan aa·he aa·baar

What's your name?
आपले नांव ? — aa·pa·le naa·nav

My name is ...
माझे नांव ... — maa·je naa·nav ...

Do you speak English?
आपण इंग्रजी बोलता का ? — aa·pan ing·re·jee bol·taa kaa

I don't understand.
मला समजत नाही. — ma·laa sam·jat naa·hee

Accommodation

Do you have a single/double room?
तुमच्या कडे सिंगल/ — tu·ma·chyaa ka·de sin·gal/
डबल खोली आहे ? — da·bal ko·lee aa·he

How much is it per night/person?
दर रात्रीसाठी/ — dar raa·tree·saa·tee/
माणशी किती भाडे — maa·na·shee ki·tee baa·de
आहे ? — aa·he

Eating & Drinking

Can you recommend a dish?
आपण एखादे पदार्थ — aa·pan e·kaa·de pa·daart
सुचवाल का ? — su·cha·vaal kaa

I'd like the ..., please.	मला ... पाहिजे आहे.	ma·laa ... paa·hi·je aa·he
bill	बिल	bil
menu	पदार्थांची सूची	pa·daar·taan· chee soo·chee

Emergencies

Help!	मदत !	ma·dat
Go away!	दूर जा !	door jaa
Call ...!	कॉल करा ... !	kaal ka·raa ...
a doctor	डॉक्टरांना	dok·ta·raan·naa
the police	पोलिसांना	po·li·saa·naa

I'm lost.
मी हरवले आहे. — mee ha·ra·va·le aa·he

Where are the toilets?
शौचालय कुठे आहे ? — shoh·chaa·lai ku·te aa·he

Numbers – Marathi

1	एक	ek
2	दोन	don
3	तीन	teen
4	चार	chaar
5	पाच	paach
6	सहा	sa·haa
7	सात	saat
8	आठ	aat
9	नऊ	na·oo
10	दहा	da·haa
20	वीस	vees
30	तीस	tees
40	चाळीस	chaa·lees
50	पन्नास	pan·naas
60	साठ	saat'
70	सत्तर	sat·tar
80	ऐंशी	ain·shee
90	नव्वद	nav·vad
100	शंभर	sham·bar
1000	एक हजार	ek ha·jaar

Shopping & Services

Can I look at it?
मी ते पाहू शकतो का ? — mee te paa·hoo sha·ka·to kaa

How much is it?
याची काय किंमत आहे ? — yaa·chee kaay ki·mat aa·he

That's too expensive.
हे खूप महाग आहे. — he koop ma·haag aa·he

Transport & Directions

Where's the ...?
... कुठे आहे ? — ... u·te aa·he

Can you show me (on the map)?
मला (नकाशात) — ma·laa (na·kaa·shaat)
दाखवू शकता ? — daa·ka·voo sha·ka·taa

What time's the first/last bus?
पहिली/पुढची — pa·hi·lee/pu·da·chee
बस कधी आहे ? — bas ka·dee aa·he

One ... ticket (to Pune), please.	कृपया एक (पुण्याचे) ... तिकीट.	kri·pa·yaa ek (pu·ne) ... ti·keet
one-way	एकेरी	e·ke·ree
return	जाण्यायेण्याचे	jaa·nyaa· yen·yaa·che

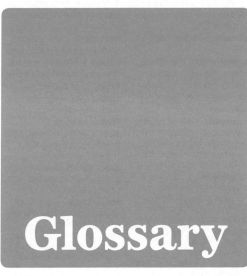

Glossary

The following are terms you may come across during your Goan travels. For some definitions of Goan foods, see p206.

auto-da-fé – trial of faith

autorickshaw – small, noisy, three-wheeled, motorised contraption used for transporting passengers short distances

ayurveda – ancient study of healing arts and herbal medicine

baksheesh – tip, bribe or donation

balcão – shady porch at front of traditional Goan house, usually with benches built into the walls

betel – nut of the areca palm; the nut is mildly intoxicating and is chewed with *paan* as a stimulant and digestive

Bhagavad Gita – Hindu song of the Divine One; *Krishna*'s lessons to Arjuna, emphasising the philosophy of *bhakti* (faith); part of the *Mahabharata*

Brahma – the source of all existence and also worshipped as the creator in the Hindu Trimurti (triple form) of Vishnu, Brahma and Shiva; depicted as having four heads (a fifth head was burnt by Shiva's 'central eye' when Brahma spoke disrespectfully)

Brahmin – member of the priest *caste*, the highest Hindu *caste*

caste – four classes into which Hindu society is divided; one's hereditary station in life

charas – resin of the cannabis plant; also referred to as hashish

crore – 10 million

Dalit – preferred term for India's casteless class; see *Untouchable*

deepastambha – lamp tower; a prominent and distinctive feature of many temples

dhaba – basic restaurant or snack bar

Dhangars – tribe of Goa's indigenous people

dharma – Hindu and Buddhist moral code of behaviour; natural law

Dravidian – general term for the cultures and languages of the south of India, including Tamil, Malayalam, Telugu and Kannada

Durga – the Inaccessible; a form of Shiva's wife Devi; a beautiful but fierce woman riding a tiger; major goddess of the Sakti cult

fado – melancholy song of longing, popular in Portuguese colonial era

Ganesh – Hindu god of good fortune; elephant-headed son of Shiva and Parvati; also known as Ganpati

garbhagriha – inner sanctum of a Hindu temple

ghat – steps or landing on a river; range of hills, or road up hills; the Western Ghats are the range of mountains that run along India's west coast, effectively forming the eastern border of Goa

GTDC – Goa Tourism Development Corporation

Hanuman – Hindu monkey god and follower of Rama; prominent in the *Ramayana*

Harijan – name given by Gandhi to India's *Untouchables;* the term is no longer considered acceptable; see also *Dalit* and *Untouchable*

Jainism – religion and philosophy founded by Mahavira in the 6th century BC in India; its fundamental tenet is nonviolence

karma – principle of retributive justice for past deeds

khadi – homespun cloth

Krishna – *Vishnu*'s eighth incarnation, often coloured blue; he revealed the *Bhagavad Gita* to Anjuna

Kshatriya – Hindu *caste* of warriors and administrators

KTC – Kadamba Transport Corporation; Goa's state bus company

Kunbis – Descendants of Goa's first inhabitants; among the state's poorest groups

lakh – 100,000

lingam – phallic symbol representing the god *Shiva*

Mahabharata – Great Vedic (see *Vedas*) epic poem of the Bharata dynasty

Mahadeva – Great God; *Shiva*

Mahadevi – Great Goddess; Devi

mahatma – literally 'great soul'

maidan – open grassed area in a city

mandapa – pillared pavilion of a temple

mando – famous song and dance form, introduced originally by the Goan Catholic community

Manguesh – an incarnation of *Shiva*, worshipped particularly in Goa

Manueline – style of architecture typical of that built by the Portuguese during the reign of Manuel I (r 1495-1521)

Maratha – warlike central Indian people who controlled much of India at various times; fought the *Mughals*

marg – major road

masjid – mosque

monsoon – rainy season between June and October

Mughal – Muslim dynasty of Indian emperors from Babur to Aurangzeb, which lasted from 1526 to 1707

Nandi – bull, vehicle of *Shiva;* his images are usually found at *Shiva* temples

paan – mixture of betel nut and various spices, chewed for its mildly intoxicating effect, and as a digestive after meals

panchayat – local government; a panchayat area typically consists of two to three villages, from which volunteers are elected to represent the interests of the local people (the elected representative is called the panch; the elected leader is the sarpanch)

Parasurama – sixth incarnation of *Vishnu*, and the 'founder' of Goa

Parvati – the Mountaineer; a form of Devi

pousada – Portuguese for hostel

prasad – food offering

puja – offerings or prayers; literally 'respect'

raj – rule or sovereignty

raja, rana – king

Ramayana – story of Rama and *Sita;* one of India's most well-known legends, retold in various forms throughout almost all of southeast Asia

ramponkar – traditional Goan fisherman; fishes the coastal waters from a wooden boat, using a hand-hauled net (rampon)

reredos – ornamental screen behind the altar in Goan churches

saquão – central courtyard in traditional Goan houses

Sati – wife of *Shiva;* became a *sati* (honourable woman) by immolating herself; although banned more than a century ago, the act of *sati* is occasionally performed, though not in Goa

satyagraha – literally 'insistence on truth'; nonviolent protest involving a fast, popularised by Gandhi; protesters are *satyagrahis*

Shiva – the Hindu Destroyer god; also the Creator, in which form he is worshipped as a *lingam;* also spelt Siva

shri – honorific; these days the Indian equivalent of Mr or Mrs; also spelt sri, sree, shree

Sita – the goddess of agriculture in the *Vedas;* commonly associated with the *Ramayana,* in which she is abducted by Ravana and carted off to Lanka

sitar – Indian stringed instrument

sossegado – see susegad

Sudra – caste of labourers

susegad – Goan expression meaning relaxed or laid-back

tabla – pair of drums

taluka – administrative district or region

tank – reservoir

tiatr – locally written and produced drama in the Konkani language

tikka – mark devout Hindus put on their foreheads with *tikka* powder

toddy tapper – one who extracts toddy (palm sap) from palm trees

Untouchable – lowest *caste* or 'casteless' for whom the most menial tasks are reserved; name derives from the belief that higher castes risk defilement if they touch one (formerly known as *Harijan,* now *Dalit* or *Scheduled Castes*)

varna – concept of *caste*

veda – knowledge

Vedas – Hindu sacred books; a collection of hymns composed in preclassical Sanskrit during the second millennium BC and divided into four books: *Rig-Veda, Yajur-Veda, Sama-Veda* and *Atharva-Veda*

Vishnu – the Preserver and Restorer; part of the Trimurti (triple form) with *Brahma* and *Shiva*

waddo – section or ward of a village; also known as a vaddo

wallah – man or person; can be added onto almost anything to denote an occupation, thus dhobi-wallah, taxi-wallah, chai-wallah

behind the scenes

SEND US YOUR FEEDBACK

We love to hear from travellers – your comments keep us on our toes and help make our books better. Our well-travelled team reads every word on what you loved or loathed about this book. Although we cannot reply individually to postal submissions, we always guarantee that your feedback goes straight to the appropriate authors, in time for the next edition. Each person who sends us information is thanked in the next edition – the most useful submissions are rewarded with a selection of digital PDF chapters.

Visit **lonelyplanet.com/contact** to submit your updates and suggestions or to ask for help. Our award-winning website also features inspirational travel stories, news and discussions.

Note: We may edit, reproduce and incorporate your comments in Lonely Planet products such as guidebooks, websites and digital products, so let us know if you don't want your comments reproduced or your name acknowledged. For a copy of our privacy policy visit lonelyplanet.com/privacy.

OUR READERS

Many thanks to the travellers who used the last edition and wrote to us with helpful hints, useful advice and interesting anecdotes:

Tom Bacon, Karsten Bischoff, Janelle Bracken, Laura Dambrosio, Gareth Daniel, Stuart & Pamela Davis, Sandra Grune, Kevin Kelly, Ian Morley, Gordon Revell, Jo Sampson, Aman Sharma, Lawrence Shepherd, Gay Watton, Nicole Welt

AUTHOR THANKS

Amelia Thomas

Many thanks, as ever, to the wonderful Pinky, and to Tanya, Elisa and the staff at the magical Vrindhavan. Thanks, too, to Dani, for sharing white-knuckle rush hour adventures, and to Nich and Cheryl for evenings of *aloo gobi*. Thanks to Suki Gear and Alison Ridgway at Lonely Planet for making this title such a pleasure to work on, and to Cassidy, Tyger, Cairo, Zeyah and Gal for being the very best travelling companions a girl could wish for.

ACKNOWLEDGMENTS

Climate map data adapted from Peel MC, Finlayson BL & McMahon TA (2007) 'Updated World Map of the Köppen-Geiger Climate Classification', *Hydrology and Earth System Sciences*, 11, 163344.

Cover photograph: Sunset river crossing, Goa, Alan Compton/Corbis

Many of the images in this guide are available for licensing from Lonely Planet Images: www.lonelyplanetimages.com.

THIS BOOK

This 6th edition of Lonely Planet's *Goa & Mumbai* was researched and written by Amelia Thomas. Kevin Raub contributed much of the Mumbai chapter. The previous edition was written by Amelia Thomas and Amy Karafin. This guidebook was commissioned in Lonely Planet's Oakland office, and produced by the following:

Commissioning Editors Suki Gear, Kate Morgan, Suzannah Schwer

Coordinating Editor Alison Ridgway

Coordinating Cartographer Jacqueline Nguyen

Coordinating Layout Designer Jessica Rose

Managing Editors Barbara Delissen, Brigitte Ellemor, Annelies Mertens

Managing Cartographer Adrian Persoglia

Managing Layout Designer Chris Girdler

Assisting Editors Laura Gibb, Kate Kiely, Saralinda Turner

Cover Research Naomi Parker

Language Content Branislava Vladisavljevic

Thanks to Sasha Baskett, Melanie Dankel, Bruce Evans, Ryan Evans, Larissa Frost, Yvonne Kirk, Eddie Lopez, Lynn Lopez, Trent Paton, Kirsten Rawlings, Gerard Walker

NOTES

index

A

accommodation 220-1, *see also individual locations*
child-friendly 32
activities 27-31, *see also individual activities & individual locations*
Agonda 176-7
air travel 232
Aldona 108
amoebic dysentery 227
Anegundi 148-9, **144**
animals 216-17, *see also individual species*
Anjuna 35, 87-91, **88**, 2
accommodation 89-90
activities 88-9
dangers 87
drinking 90-1
food 90-1
information 91
travel to/from 91
antiques 213
Arambol (Harmal) 71-4, 11
architecture 15, 204
Candolim 103
forts 175
Mumbai (Bombay) 6, 39
Old Goa 128
temples 139
area codes 13, 230
Arossim 164
Arpora 99
art galleries, *see* museums & galleries
arts 203-5
Assagao 84
Assolna 174
Aswem 76-7
ATMs 228
autorickshaws 235
ayurveda 28
Agonda 176

000 Map pages
000 Photo pages

Anjuna 88
Arambol (Harmal) 71
Assagao 84
Benaulim 170
Calangute 93, 95
Cavelossim 173
Chapora 81
Gokarna 185
Majorda 165
Mandrem 75
Molem 141
Palolem 178
Vagator 81

B

Backwoods Camp 142
Baga 92-9, **95**
accommodation 96-7
activities 94
drinking 98
entertainment 98
food 97-8
information 99
shopping 99
tours 94
travel to/from 99
travel within 99
Bahmanis, the 191
Banganga Festival 16
bars, *see* drinking
beach huts 221
beaches 24-6
for children 32
bears 216
Dandeli 186
Daroji Sloth Bear Sanctuary 147
bedbugs 227
Benaulim 169-71, **170**
Betalbatim 166
Betim 107
Betul 174-5
Bhagwan Mahavir Wildlife Sanctuary 141
bicycle travel, *see* cycling
birds 217
birdwatching 217
Backwoods Camp 142
Bondla Wildlife Sanctuary 140-1
Cavelossim 172
Cotigao Wildlife Sanctuary 183
Dandeli 186
Dr Salim Ali Bird Sanctuary 125-6
Mumbai (Bombay) 51
boat travel
to/from Goa 173
within Goa 235
Bogmalo 163-4
Bollywood 50

Bonderam 18
Bondla Wildlife Sanctuary 140-1
books 188, 204
bookstores 212
Britona 108
budgeting 12
bus travel
to/from Goa 232-3
within Goa 235
business hours 221, 222

C

Cabo da Rama 175
Calangute 92-9, **92**
accommodation 95-7
activities 93-4
drinking 98
entertainment 98
food 97
information 99
shopping 98
tours 94
travel to/from 99
travel within 99
Camões, Luís Vaz de 117
Candolim 99-106, **100**
accommodation 103-4
activities 101-3
drinking 105
entertainment 105
food 104-5
information 106
shopping 106
sights 101-3
travel to/from 106
travel within 106
Carnival 16
car travel 13, *see also* motorcycle travel
driving licences 236
road distance chart 236
road rules 237
to/from Goa 232
within Goa 235
carpets 213
cathedrals, *see* churches & cathedrals
Cavelossim 172-4
caves
Elephanta Island 68
Khandepar 140
Rivona Buddhist caves 160
Sanjay Gandhi National Park 69
cell phones 13, 229
Central Goa 35, 110-49, **112**
accommodation 110
food 110
Chandor 159

Chapora 79-84, **80**
  activities 80-1
  drinking 83
  entertainment 83-4
  food 83
  information 84
  shopping 84
  sights 80-1
  travel to/from 84
Chapora Fort 80
Chaudi 177
Chhatrapati Shivaji Maharaj Vastu
  Sangrahalaya
  (Prince of Wales Museum) 45
Chhatrapati Shivaji Terminus
  (Victoria Terminus) 47, **6**
children, travel with 32-3
Chorao Island 125-6
Christianity 201
Christmas 19
churches & cathedrals
  Basilica of Bom Jesus 129-30
  Chapel of St Anthony 132
  Chapel of St Catherine 129
  Chapel of St Sebastian 113
  Church & Convent of St Cajetan
    130-1, **9**
  Church & Convent of St Monica
    131-2
  Church of Nossa Senhora Mae de
    Deus 108
  Church of Our Lady of Compassion
    134
  Church of Our Lady of Miracles
    85
  Church of Our Lady of Pilar 135
  Church of Our Lady of the
    Immaculate Conception 113
  Church of Our Lady of the Mount
    132
  Church of Our Lady of the Rosary
    132
  Church of St Andrew 134
  Church of St Anne 135
  Church of St Augustine 131
  Church of St Francis of Assisi
    129
  Church of St Lawrence
    (Agassim) 135
  Church of St Lawrence
    (Fort Aguada) 102
  Church of St Thomas 108
  Church of the Holy Spirit 151
  Nossa Senhora de Penha de
    Franca 108
  Nossa Senhora de Saude 162
  Our Lady of Mercy Church 168
  Rachol Seminary & Church 158
  Reis Magos Church 106
  Sé Cathedral 128-9

cinema 205
  Bollywood 50
  International Film Festival of
    India 19
climate 12, 16-19, 222
coconuts 207
Colomb 181
Colva 166-9, **167**
Colvale 85
consulates 224
Corjuem Fort 108-9
Corjuem Island 108
costs 12
  accommodation 221
  food 224
Cotigao Wildlife Sanctuary 183
courses
  cooking 117, 208
  diving 29
  meditation 51, 76
  spiritual 74
  yoga 27-8
credit cards 229
cricket 202
crocodiles 216-17, **10**
culture 188-9, 197-202
currency 12
Curtorim 160
customs regulations 222
cycling 234-5

D
da Gama, Vasco 191
dabba-wallahs 57
dance 203-4
dance parties 82, 179
Dandeli 186
dangers 222-3, *see also* safety
death 199
deforestation 218
Dengue Fever 226
Dhangars, the 143
Dharavi 52
diarrhoea 226
disabilities, travellers with 230
Divar Island 133-4
diving 28-9
  Baga 94
  Bogmalo 163
  safety 227
Diwali 18
DJ Pramz 62
dolphin-watching
  Baga 93
  Benaulim 170
  Cavelossim 172
  Colva 167
  Fort Aguada 102

  Morjim 78
  Palolem 178
  Panaji 118
  Utorda 165
Dona Paula 124-5
Dr Salim Ali Bird Sanctuary
  125-6
drinking 15, *see also individual
  locations*
drinks 208-9
driving licences 236
driving, *see* car travel
drugs 228
Dudhsagar Falls 142
Dusshera 18

E
Easter 17
economy 189
Eid al-Fitr 18
electricity 224
Elephanta Festival 16
Elephanta Island 68-9
embassies 224
emergencies 13
environment 215-18
  environmental hazards
    227
  environmental issues 189, 218
etiquette 189
events, *see* festivals & events
exchange rates 13

F
fado 203
Faria, Abbé 111
fax services 230
Feast of our Lady of Livrament
  19
Feast of Our Lady of Miracles 17
Feast of Our Lady of the Immaculate
  Conception 19
Feast of St Anthony 17
Feast of St Francis Xavier
  19, 130
Feast of the Chapel 18
Feast of the Menino Jesus 18
feni 208
Fernandes, Remo 203
ferry travel, *see* boat travel
Festa das Bandeiras 16
festivals & events 16-19
  food 209
  Mumbai (Bombay) 39
film 205
  Bollywood 50
  International Film Festival of
    India 19

fishing industry 162
food 14, 206-11, 224, *see also individual locations*
  for children 33
  glossary 210-11
football 202
Fort Aguada 99-106, **100**
  activities 101-3
  sights 101-3
Fort Tiracol (Terekhol) 75
forts 175
  Chapora Fort 80
  Corjuem Fort 108-9
  Fort Aguada 101
  Fort Tiracol (Terekhol) 75
  Reis Magos 106

G
Galgibag 183-4
Ganesh Chaturthi 18
Gateway of India 44
gay travellers 224-5
geography 215
geology 215
giardiasis 227
Goa Velha 134
Gokarna 184-6

H
haggling 213
Hampi 143-8, **144**, **22**
  accommodation 146-7
  food 147-8
  history 144-5
  information 148
  safety 146
  sights 145-6
  travel to/from 148
  travel within 148
Hanuman Festival 17
health 225-8
  children's 33
  women travellers 231
heat exhaustion 227
heatstroke 227
hepatitis A 226
hepatitis B 226
hepatitis E 226
Hinduism 201
history 190-6
hitching 235
HIV 226
holidays 16-19

000 Map pages
000 Photo pages

Hospet 149
hospitals 225

I
Igitun Chalne 17
immigration 222, 224, 230
Independence 194
Independence Day 18
Inquisition, the 192, 193
insect bites 227
insurance
  diving 227
  health 227-8
  pregnant women 231
  travel 228
International Film Festival of India 19
internet access 228
internet resources 13
  environmental 189, 218
  gay travellers 225
  health 227
  lesbian travellers 225
  planning 13
  travel advice 229
Islam 201
itineraries 20-3

J
Jog Falls 186

K
Kadambas, the 140, 191
Kala Ghoda Festival 16
Khandepar 140
kindergartens 33
Kishkinda Trust 148, 149
Kotachiwadi 56

L
languages 12
leatherwork 213
legal matters 228
lesbian travellers 224-5
Liberation Day 19
literature 188, 204
Loutolim 158-9

M
magazines 223
mando 203
Mandrem 74-6
Mapusa 84-7
Margao 151-7, **154**
  accommodation 155-6
  activities 151-5
  food 156

  information 156
  shopping 156
  sights 151-5
  travel to/from 157
  travel within 157
markets 8, 14, 212-13
  Anjuna 87
  Arpora 99
  Baga 99
  Mapusa 86, **9**
  Panaji 122
marriage 198
massage 28
  Calangute 93
  Majorda 165
  Mandrem 74, 75
  Patnem 182
Mauryan empire 191
Mayem Lake 109
measures 223
medical services 226
meditation courses 51, 76
mining 218
Miramar 124
mobile phones 13, 229
Mobor 174
Molem 141
money 13, 228-9
Morjim 78
mosques
  Haji Ali's Mosque 50
  Jama Masjid 116
  Safa Shahouri Masjid 136
motorcycle taxis 235
motorcycle travel 157, 236-7
Mumbai (Bombay) 34, 38-69, **41**, **42-3**, **44**, **46-7**, **54**
  accommodation 38, 51-6
  climate 38
  drinking 60-1
  entertainment 61-3
  festivals 39
  food 38, 39, 56-9
  history 40
  information 65-6
  internet access 65
  medical services 65
  money 65
  postal services 65
  shopping 63-9
  sights 40-51
  tourist information 66
  tours 51
  travel to/from 66
  travel within 66-8
museums & galleries
  Archaeological Museum (Hampi) 146

Archaeological Museum (Old Goa) 129
Chhatrapati Shivaji Maharaj Vastu Sangrahalaya (Prince of Wales Museum) 45
Goa Chitra Museum 169
Goa State Museum 116
Houses of Goa Museum 108
Jehangir Art Gallery 47
Mario Gallery 108
Museum of Christian Art 132
National Gallery of Modern Art 47
Naval Aviation Museum 163
music 188, 203-4

N
Nariyal Poornima 18
Naroa 109
National Gallery of Modern Art 47
national parks, *see* sanctuaries & protected areas
Nehru, Jawaharlal 194
Nerul (Coco) Beach 106
Netravali Bubble Lake 182
newspapers 223
North Goa 35, 70-109, **72**, **107**
    accommodation 70
    food 70

O
Old Goa 126-33, **127**, *194*
    accommodation 133
    architecture 128
    food 133
    history 126-7
    information 133
    sights 128-33
    travel to/from 133
olive ridley marine turtles 78
opening hours 221, 222

P
painting 205
Palolem 35, 177-81, **152-3**, **178**, *10*, *25*
    accommodation 179-80
    activities 178
    food 180-1
    shopping 181
    tours 178-9
Panaji 35, 111-24, **112**, **114**, *7*
    accommodation 110, 118-20
    courses 117
    drinking 121
    entertainment 121-2
    food 110, 120-1
    information 122-3
    internet access 122

medical services 122
money 123
postal services 123
shopping 122
sights 113-17
tourist information 123
tours 117-18
travel to/from 123
travel within 124
papier-mâché 213-14
passports 230
Patnem 182-3
Pilar 135
Pinto revolt 102
Piró, Caterina a 131
planning 12-13
    beaches 24-6
    budgeting 12
    calendar of events 16-19
    children, travel with 32-3
    Goa basics 12-13
    Goa's regions 34-5
    internet resources 13
    itineraries 20-3
    Mumbai 34
    travel seasons 12
plants 217-18
Polem 184
police 228
politics 196
Pomburpa 108
Ponda 135-7, **136**
population 188
Portuguese rule 191-4
postal services 229
prehistoric Goa 190
prickly heat 227
Procession of All Saints 17

Q
Quepem 160
Querim 75, *22*

R
rabies 226
radio 223
Rajbag 183
Ramadan 18
Reis Magos 106-7
Reis Magos Festival 16
religion 189, 197, 200-1
reptiles 216
Republic Day 16
Ribandar 125
Rivona Buddhist caves 160
road distances 236
road rules 237

S
safety 222-3, 229
    car travel 237
    hitching 235
    road 237
    swimming 24, 223
Sá, Garcia de 131
Sancoale 162
sanctuaries & protected areas 218
    Backwoods Camp 142
    Bhagwan Mahavir Wildlife Sanctuary 141
    Bondla Wildlife Sanctuary 140-1
    Cotigao Wildlife Sanctuary 183
    Dandeli 186
    Daroji Sloth Bear Sanctuary 147
    Dr Salim Ali Bird Sanctuary 125-6
    Netravali Protected Area 182
    Sanjay Gandhi National Park 69
Sangodd 17
Sanjay Gandhi National Park 69
Sanjuan 17
Sao Antonio Islet 162
Sao Jacinto 162
scams 223
Shantadurga 16
Shigmotsav (Shigmo) 16
Shivratri 17
shopping 14, 212-14, *see also* markets, *individual locations*
Shri Saptakoteshwara Temple 109
silent dance parties 179
Sinquerim 99-106, **100**
    accommodation 103-4
    activities 101-3
    sights 101-3
Siolim 78-9
Siolim Zagor 19
Sippy, Pramod 62
skin problems 227
smoking 228
snakes 216
soccer 202
South Goa 35, 150-86, **152-3**
    accommodation 150
    food 150
spas 14
    Dudhsagar Spa Resort 141
spice farms 8, 137, *8*
spiritual courses 74
spitting 228
sports 202
St Francis Xavier 130, 193, 195
sunburn 227
Sunburn Festival 19
susegad 197
swimming safety 24, 223

T

Taj Mahal Palace, Mumbai 44, 51
Talaulim 135
Tambdi Surla 142-3
taxis 222, 235
telephone services 13, 229-30
temples 139
  Achyutaraya Temple 146
  Ganapati Temple 184
  Hanuman Temple 148
  Koorti Teertha 184
  Mahabaleshwara Temple 184
  Mahalaxmi Temple 116
  Maruti Temple 116
  Shri Chandreshwar (Bhutnath)
    Temple 161
  Shri Damodar Temple 160
  Shri Laxmi Narasimha Temple
    138-9
  Shri Mahadeva Temple 142-3
  Shri Mahalaxmi Temple 139
  Shri Mahalsa Templ 138
  Shri Manguesh Temple 137-8
  Shri Naguesh Temple 139
  Shri Ramnath temple 140
  Shri Shantadurga Temple
    140
  Venkataraman Temple 184
  Virupaksha Temple 145
  Vittala Temple 145
textiles 214
theatre 205
theft 223
ticks 227
tiffins 57
time 230
tipping 229
tourism 188, 189, 218
tourist information 230
tours, see individual locations
touts 223

train travel
  to/from Goa 233-4, 11
  within Goa 237
trance parties 82
transport 232-7
  local transport 235-6
travel seasons 12
travel to/from Goa 232-4
travel within Goa 234-7
turtles 78
TV 223
typhoid 226

U

Usgalimal Rock Carvings 160-1,
  190
Utorda 165

V

vacations 16-19
vaccinations 225-6
Vagator 79-84, **80**, 25
  accommodation 81-2
  activities 80-1
  drinking 83
  entertainment 83-4
  food 83
  information 84
  shopping 84
  sights 80-1
  travel to/from 84
Varca 171-2
Vasco da Gama 161-2
vegetarian travellers 210
Velsao 164
Verem 106
Vipassana 76
visas 13, 230-1
volleyball 202
volunteering 30-1

W

waterfalls
  Dudhsagar Falls 142
  Jog Falls 186
water sports 29
weather 12, 16-19, 222
weights 223
wildlife 216-18
wildlife watching 29-30
  Backwoods Camp 142
  Bhagwan Mahavir Wildlife
    Sanctuary 141
  Bondla Wildlife Sanctuary 140-1
  Cotigao Wildlife Sanctuary 183
  Dandeli 186
  Daroji Sloth Bear Sanctuary 147
  Dr Salim Ali Bird Sanctuary 125-6
  Netravali Protected Area 182
  Sanjay Gandhi National Park 69
women in Goa 199-200
women travellers 231
women's health 231

Y

yoga 27-8
  Agonda 176
  Anjuna 88, 89
  Arambol (Harmal) 71
  Assagao 84
  Aswem 77
  Baga 93
  Calangute 93
  Chapora 81
  Mandrem 74, 75, 9
  Palolem 178
  Patnem 182
  Vagator 81

Z

Zagor Festival 79